Learning from Success

Worcester Polytechnic Institute
Studies in Science, Technology and Culture

Lance Schachterle and Francis C. Lutz
Co-Editors

Vol. 15

PETER LANG
New York • Washington, D.C./Baltimore
Bern • Frankfurt am Main • Berlin • Vienna • Paris

Ann Kelleher

Learning from Success

Campus Case Studies in International Program Development

PETER LANG
New York • Washington, D.C./Baltimore
Bern • Frankfurt am Main • Berlin • Vienna • Paris

Library of Congress Cataloging-in-Publication Data

Kelleher, Ann.
Learning from success: campus case studies in
international program development / Ann Kelleher.
p. cm. — (Worcester Polytechnic Institute studies in science,
technology and culture; vol. 15)
Includes bibliographical references.
1. International education—United States—Case studies. 2. Student exchange
programs—United States—Case studies. I. Title. II. Series.
LC1090.K38 370.11'5—dc20 95-16663
ISBN 0-8204-2407-2
ISSN 0897-926X

Die Deutsche Bibliothek-CIP-Einheitsaufnahme

Kelleher, Ann:
Learning from success: campus case studies in
international program development /Ann Kelleher. – New York; Washington,
D.C./Baltimore; Bern; Frankfurt am Main; Berlin; Vienna; Paris: Lang.
(Worcester Polytechnic Institute studies in science,
technology and culture; Vol. 15)
ISBN 0-8204-2407-2
NE: Worcester Polytechnic Institute: Worcester Polytechnic Institute ...

The paper in this book meets the guidelines for permanence and durability
of the Committee on Production Guidelines for Book Longevity
of the Council of Library Resources.

© 1996 Peter Lang Publishing, Inc., New York

Printed in the United States of America.

Contents

Introduction

International education programs declare notable and far-reaching objectives. Most reflect the contemporary world in its complexity; for example, international education aims to prepare students to analyze events, work effectively, and live ethically in a world of increasing cultural, ecological, economic, and political diversity as well as interdependence. For students to make sense of such enigmatic and ambiguous intricacy requires them to have acquired considerable knowledge, critical thinking ability, and an awareness of consequences.

Claiming such a pressing purpose, international educators seek to initiate new endeavors and to improve on the effectiveness of existing ones. Examples of exemplary, enduring programs can provide guidance. Yet educators can look further for help and inspiration. In many ways, the program development process has parallels with successful, sustained development in a variety of social contexts around the world.

International educators can learn from village people in the developing world. They share a common challenge, i.e., to mobilize available resources in order to change human behavior and achieve sustainable development. While it may seem a conceptual stretch to compare what it means to do a better job feeding people with doing a better job teaching North American students, juxtaposing the two can prove instructive. The principles of human-centered development may be applied to international education programs as well as to village-level projects.

Both start with real needs. In effective developing world projects, participants make decisions based on their own knowledge and willingness to work. Outside assistance plays a supporting, not a leading, role. New activities are legitimized by the group's existing cultural values. Respected, stable, local leadership takes responsibility for carrying out the changes. Projects do not draw more resources from the environment than can be sustained over time. This book demonstrates that these general factors, appropriately rephrased, also account for successful international education program development.

As the case studies will show, most often a faculty member or administrator emerging from the institution's own ranks initiates a successful program and continues directing it for years. Each program fits comfortably with its campus' culture—the institution's ethos, to use the word often found in international education articles. Outside grant assistance may or may not play a vital role initially, but sooner or later the programs become institutionalized and rely on the college or university's own resources. Senior administrators make clear, affirming decisions and continue to provide active, not passive, support. Taken together, these factors account for program sustainability.

Identifying general parallels between success in developing countries and on campus implies commonalities in human behavior across country, cultural, and institutional boundaries. Whatever the social context, positive human traits surface as a result of successful change strategies. They produce supportive interpersonal relations, creativity and adaptability, practicality, and a confidence that builds as problems are overcome.

The Study's Motive and Method

Considered either an administrative unit or an academic field, international education is actually both. Perhaps because it is a crossbreed, programs have proliferated with little systematic study of the reasons why some succeed and some fail. The renewed interest in international programs would benefit from comparative data on their development and an analysis of factors leading to their success.

As with the introduction of any new species, adding programs often disturbs the environmental equilibrium on campus. Strengthened institutions can emerge from the discussions and decisions such change engenders. This does not always happen, however. International initiatives can remain stunted and infertile, their administrative structures fragmented, their growth nonexistent, and spin-offs only a forlorn hope. To avoid this contingency, an overt commitment is needed which grows out of a campuswide consensus. Information about the change process on other campuses could help ease the transition and produce flourishing programs.

Research on successful programs can prove useful at this time because examples of long-term, quality programs exist. Institutions beginning an internationalization process can learn from many models. This study's comparative analysis of exemplary international education programs at the least produces a record of proven innovations and effective strategies. At most, systematic analysis reveals specific program development guidelines.

A convergence of circumstances in the mid-1990s creates the need for a study of successful undergraduate international education programs. Not only do many such programs exist with proven track records while hundreds of colleges and universities are planning new initiatives, but all this activity is taking place amid an increasing international awareness on the part of the general public. World events have produced a strengthened global interdependence. This trend, predictable in the 1970s, has become a part of conventional wisdom.

In the past, undergraduate international education received intermittent attention. Stimulated by events in the 1970s, the Vietnam War and the oil embargo among others, a flurry of activity culminated in the 1979 Report of President Carter's Commission on Foreign Language and International Studies. This report, "Strength Through Wisdom: A Critique of U.S. Capability," established a broad national agenda with recommendations for kindergarten through twelfth grade and general citizen education as well as those relevant to university undergraduates and advanced, specialized graduate degrees. In the 1980s this larger agenda languished. It became reformulated and narrowed into readying U.S. students for overseas economic competition.

Now, in the early 1990s, international education has taken on its former inclusive connotation. Yet what seems to distinguish the present process from its 1970s counterpart is more discussion of methods to involve the whole campus. In this context, specific programs should serve as foci for broader, multidimensional efforts.

The present focus on a holistic approach promises to continue based on twenty-first century realities. Although the national agenda is still preoccupied with economic issues, these have taken on an irrevocably global dimension.

The fact that international education has become an important priority in U.S. higher education is recognized by one of internationalization's key advocates, Sven Groennings. In 1990 he noted,

> Within the last five years, nearly half the nation's colleges and universities have been considering ways to increase the international aspects of their curricula. It is now generally assumed that international education is an essential component of general education, that a true liberal arts education must be international in scope, and that students not in the liberal arts should be exposed to international perspectives.[1]

The descriptions of individual programs provided in the following chapters offer data on successful undergraduate international education innovations in a wide variety of categories; curriculum, co-curriculum, study abroad, community outreach, faculty development, and international students. Successful, distinctive programs thrive on campuses of all sizes and in all institutional classifications. Even at the descriptive level, information about specific programs can prove useful in the whole range of higher education environments.

Yet this study also has the objective of comparing these examples of successful programs to determine general reasons for their development. Colleges and universities undertaking an internationalization process can learn from each other.

Reference to grass-roots development in communities worldwide can prove instructive. Common questions arise in studying both campus and community change processes: What factors account for the initiation of successful, ongoing change? How do they continue to sustain the process? Is permanent development more effectively initiated with a "top-down" or a "bottom-up" process? Do similar patterns of causation and continuation exist in varying settings? What is the appropriate role of outside financing? How important are campus cultural values in sanctioning the changes? What program and organizational choices have proven the most effective? Taken together, the answers to these questions will explain why specific programs developed at a particular time and place.

Effectively answering these questions requires comparative information about solid, sustaining, high-impact programs. Thus, defining what are successful programs was crucial in this study's research design process. Careful program selection was also needed to ensure that each one studied would have characteristics worthy of emulation.

Five criteria were established: Programs designated as successful and selected for study

1. Possess a distinctive, perhaps unique, characteristic which sets them apart from similar programs, and this fact is recognized by directors of like programs at other institutions.
2. Attract significant numbers of participants relative to similar programs elsewhere.
3. Have continued for at least five years.
4. Are institutionalized, that is, administered by a unit of the college or university as one of its ongoing, non-grant supported programs.
5. Have achieved "takeoff" by producing a spinoff that succeeded. Program takeoff means the density of activity has reached the point where refinements and new initiatives occur as a matter of course.

These criteria will ensure that readers applying information from this book to their own programs will draw lessons from success. The twenty-five program descriptions include sufficient detail to assist program developers on other campuses.

Because of their exemplary and replicable characteristics, a few of the case studies do not conform to the five criteria. The first such exception, the University of Southern California's South Africa theme semester, occurred once. Yet it has several useful elements to commend it, i.e., its scope of campus involvement, detailed attention to cultural authenticity, overt focus on the methodology of instruction as well as content, and volume of spin-offs.

A second exception to the five criteria, the University of Hartford's summer program for business students from France, had existed for only three years when studied. Yet it clearly illustrates what can evolve from personal contacts with overseas institutions and commonly perceived mutual benefits. In addition, the program has served as a precedent for several others and has undergone extensive evaluation.

Another exception has not yet been packaged into a specific program. It involves the participation of Pacific University's Spanish majors in service programs both in their local area and in Ecuador. Yet this curriculum deserves attention as a creative way to teach languages and their cultural contexts as part of an ethical approach to education.

Some of the programs selected provide detailed examples of how program takeoff can work. Whitworth College's Center for International and Multicultural Education, for example, is one of many such centers across the country. Yet its long, evolutionary development, variety of activities in all categories of international education programming, and acknowledged leadership role on campus all make its experience instructive.

Two other factors affected program selection. First, the case studies include at least one example in all categories of undergraduate international education programs. Second, an effort proved successful to find programs at institutions within each category of the Carnegie Classification System; i.e., research universities, doctorate-granting universities, comprehensive universities and colleges, liberal arts colleges, and two-year colleges. In addition, the case studies include one women's college, a Canadian two-year college, an HBU, Historically Black University, and a college emphasizing engineering and science.

This study describes specific programs and the campus environments in which they thrive. It also provides comparative data answering the questions raised previously concerning program initiation and continuation. In addition, based upon the collective experiences of successful programs, the final chapter offers guidelines for developing sustainable undergraduate international education programs.

Models and Measures

The analysis in this book builds on previous publications in international education. It tests several propositions derived from prior work in the field.

Several conceptualizations developed by international educators serve as originating premises for this study. The first defines an internationalized campus. The second offers useful concepts for analysis. The last summarizes a list of factors needed for successful program development.

Clarifying the definition of internationalization implies its goal. It makes explicit the field's general parameters. An article by Humphrey Tonkins and Jane Edwards provides a particularly helpful analysis. In "Internationalizing the University, the Arduous Road to Euphoria," the authors distinguish between two paradigms on campuses which claim to be heavily internationalized.

"Ardua," a hypothetical university, has a range of programs, an international studies major, international students, study abroad with increasing student participation, and a restored foreign language requirement. Unfortunately, however, it "has a tendency to do things piecemeal and reactively instead of building on existing strengths and maximizing existing resources."[2] Such scattered programming creates the problem of keeping international education a priority in the battle for scarce resources.

Contrast this situation with another the authors call "Euphoria," a "Truly International University." Here the usual array of programs exist, but with a difference. New ideas are welcomed. Dedication to diversity among students and hiring practices for faculty and staff have resulted in extraordinary human resources. Also, the place has become a grant trap. International content has become so embedded across the curriculum that "No student graduates who has never been asked to think about the rights and responsibilities of this country in the world community, or who has never been brought to empathize with people of a different culture."[3]

As Tonkin and Edwards point out, the former hypothetical example rather than the latter reflects the experience of most institutions. The article goes on to explain the purposeful, dynamic, steady change process occurring at Euphoria in all areas of international education. Not all departments and disciplines may exude enthusiasm, and not all administrators act supportively, but at least tacit agreement exists that international education is necessary for a quality general education.

This description of Euphoria proposes a high standard of achievement. By its measure, a few colleges and universities may have accomplished their internationalization goal, but most have not. Lest international educators become unduly dispirited, they could choose to think of internationalization not as a condition, the end goal described as Euphoria, but as a process. All institutions having set international education as a priority may be visualized as moving, wandering, or purposefully striding down a similar path, road, thoroughfare, highway, or interstate, whichever metaphor proves useful. With this imagery, side trips are allowed and the pace can be set by each college or university.

Still, differentiating institutions well along in the internationalizing process from those just setting out has a planning function. The Tonkins and Edwards article moves the field forward. It implies measures of campus internationalization are possible. This contrasts with many writers on the subject who make safe comments designed not to awaken any latent opposition to international programs. Unfortunately this approach avoids the kind of debate needed for a field to progress. Saying what everyone already agrees with does not clarify definitions and boundaries. Constructive disagreements cause a field to mature.

International education practitioners must engage in research and analysis to move the field forward. The work of Tonkins and Edwards has contributed by presenting what can be an uncomfortable dichotomy. Most international educators recognize "Euphoria" as their objective. Its ongoing, campuswide internationalization process best characterizes their definition and objectives. Yet many self proclaimed advocates of international education actually seem to have "Ardua" in mind. They understand internationalization as a checklist of program categories, i.e. international students with an advisor and English as a Second Language instruction, study abroad programs, at least one international curriculum specialization and a foreign language graduation requirement, perhaps an ongoing outreach effort. If programs exist in these areas, then the campus has been internationalized, or so some proponents assume. Unfortunately, the segmentation this approach implies can preclude further initiatives.

In their beginning stages, the two paradigms presented by Tonkins and Edwards may look similar, i.e. some initial programs in international education's major categories. Also, the Ardua-Euphoria distinction becomes blurred when applied to the internationalization process on actual campuses. As the case studies in this book illustrate, the two paradigms blend to the point where systematically using them for making direct comparisons may not be constructive. It could also lead to a debilitating debate on which institution is more international than another. Providing mutual assistance should be the goal, not mutual antagonism.

Each campus has its own identity. This produces many sub-variations in each international education category. For instance, study abroad programs can include classroom instruction in overseas settings, internships, service placements, language emphasis to the point where students integrate into overseas universities, individual research projects, and probably other examples limited only by the imagination of their founders. No useful way exists to compare directly the learning each program produces. Each situation itself has a utility. Each university and college can formulate its own variations based on its campus culture, overseas contacts, and the expertise of its faculty.

Detailed comparisons of study abroad programs from campus to campus with the goal of concluding which is best can produce distorting conclusions. Such an exercise channels international education into destructive comparisons. The issue is not what is the best kind of study abroad program but which programs will thrive on which campuses. Yet cross-fertilization can produce a healthier offspring if it takes root in a favorable campus environment.

Obviously campuses vary as to the depth and breadth of their international education programs, and the Euphoria-Ardua conceptualization can help highlight this difference. Yet a careful analyst quickly discovers that no precise comparative measure is possible. Programs producing valued pedagogy in one campus context may well not attract support in another.

Thus the Ardua-Euphoria dichotomy cannot be taken too far. The two paradigms should not be conceptualized as points along a continuum with few international courses and programs visualized on one end, Euphoria on the other, and Ardua placed in the middle. Such a mental image distorts more than it illumines when used to review an internationalization process at specific colleges and universities. It traps the observer into making direct comparisons. In international education, one size does not fit all. Internationalization is too complex to be thought of as a linear process. Not only is it multidimensional as defined by its various program categories, but each category in itself is multidimensional as illustrated by the example of study abroad programs described above.

Yet how to move along in the internationalization process remains an issue. Here, Maurice Harari provides some answers. He has written extensively and travelled this country visiting many colleges and universities in his effort to articulate useful concepts.

In his work, Harari has identified what he has called the campus "ethos" as an important consideration in the internationalization process. He points out the need to "create an international ethos on campus,"[4] and in so doing has drawn attention to an often overlooked but valuable consideration for international educators. Ethos does not lend itself to quantifiable measurement like other categories of international education, such as collecting data on the numbers and countries of origin of international students. Yet, as Harari emphasizes, a systematic internationalization plan should build in ways to create a favorable campus culture.

While Harari does not directly advocate merging international education's mission and objectives with the existing campus ethos, this is a logical extension of his position. As many of the studies in this book will illustrate, successful, sustainable international programs are identified with the existing values already in the minds of faculty and administrators. The direct link between a campus' culture and its international programs is often not articulated in this way by program administrators. It surfaces in the words and underlying values they use to describe their programs.

Maurice Harari also has explained the need for a strong center or office capable of functioning as a locus of leadership. As a result of advocating it for years, Harari has come to symbolize this key administrative concept. He uses the phrase "a stable and permanent structure" and points out that, regardless of the institution's mission, size, environment, or history, sporadic and disconnected efforts are not viable in the long run. "To internationalize successfully, a single, prominent individual or office must be made responsible for providing direction and mobilizing support for the internationalization process."[5]

Harari offers guidance as to the preferred location of this central office:

> Because internationalization requires a multidisciplinary and institution-wide approach, the focal point of leadership must lie outside narrow territorial boundaries. The designated individual should report directly to the president, provost, or chief academic officer and enjoy the necessary status and resources to lead in establishing objectives and priorities, deploying resources, and monitoring and evaluating progress.[6]

The importance of merging the rationale for international programs with the campus ethos, and establishing a central locus of leadership, have become incorporated into the work of others in the field of international education. They are included in one of the more recent, thoughtful, empirically-based, and inclusive lists of guidelines on how to develop successful programs. The concluding chapter of *Beyond Borders* by Joseph Johnston and Richard Edelstein[7] reviews several recommendations which summarize in one place the points often made in conference presentations and articles on international education. Johnston and Edelstein draw "Lessons From Campus Practice" as follows:

—   There is no one best approach
—   Know your institution
—   Attend to the challenge of pedagogy, integrating material
    from different disciplines presents complex demands
—   Leadership makes a difference; this refers to both the pro-
    gram's creator as well as supportive senior administrators
—   Create an international ethos on campus
—   Engage faculty colleagues
—   Funding is necessary but not sufficient; most successful
    programs do not depend exclusively on external support
—   Select an appropriate campus home, a wide range is men-
    tioned, such as a center, separate colleges, existing cur-
    riculum, student life programs

This list includes one valuable addition to the usual set of guidelines, i.e., the vital importance of an able, creative, energetic
individual.

These factors listed in *Beyond Borders* will be compared with
those identified by the directors of the successful programs
described in this book. Thus the factors will be systematically
tested with evidence from in-depth case studies.

Information in each of the twenty-five case studies is organized according to a common format. Four headings are used.
The first, "Campus Context," provides an overview of each
campus' undergraduate international education programs. The
second section of each case study provides a detailed description of the program selected for study, including its administration and budget. The third, "Issues and Answers," introduces
readers to problems that accompanied the program's development and how they were handled effectively. The last section,
on "Lessons Learned," lists guidelines suggested by the program's director. The directors were asked, "If you were to make
a formal presentation to international educators interested in
initiating a program like yours, what recommendations would
you make?"

The "Campus Context" section of each chapter needed a set
of subcategories to summarize clearly what seems to be a bewil-
dering array of curriculum and other international education
programs. Information is presented according to categories

generally accepted as measures of campus internationalization. These categories may be listed as:

1. Incorporation of international education into the college or university's mission statement
2. Curriculum programs in three areas: core graduation requirements, such as in languages and multicultural diversity; specialized programs, such as majors, minors, or concentrations; and infusion of international courses throughout the general curriculum
3. International students, including English as a Second Language instruction
4. Student off-campus programs, usually study abroad but increasingly including domestic multicultural experiences as well
5. Faculty and staff development
6. Community outreach
7. A central administrative office

Co-curriculum programs are not listed as a separate category. They merge easily with curriculum activities in their broadest sense. A film or speakers series, for example, is common on many campuses and usually is organized by faculty as a part of their teaching responsibilities. Yet some campuses included in this book consider cocurricular enhancements as a separate program. In these cases, they are duly described as such in the "Campus Context" narrative.

Faculty and staff development does appear on the list. This includes the hiring of international faculty or faculty with international expertise as well as incentives for re-educating existing faculty. It is treated as an independent category because the importance of faculty and staff expertise is often overlooked. Few campuses, even those overtly dedicated to providing an international education, have a systematic, ongoing process for increasing the international expertise of the key people needed to carry out its stated goal. For students to develop their international knowledge, skills, and attitudes, the faculty have to do it first.

Programmatic and not content classifications comprise the three designations within the curriculum category; i.e., core requirements, specialized programs, and infusion throughout the whole curriculum. This study is not designed to engage in a content debate over what international knowledge, skills, and perspectives are essential for a general education. The list changes often including multicultural knowledge and cross-cultural skills, knowledge of environmental issues, analysis of the international political system, knowledge of international economic institutions and processes, and foreign language facility. Each campus makes different decisions as to what to include in its general education requirements.

However, information in this book may prove useful as part of the ongoing discussion. Its final chapter will note patterns which emerge from the summaries of international curriculum on the twenty five campuses.

In each case study information under the seventh category, "A central administrative office," highlights the campus' structure for carrying out international programs. Only some colleges and universities have a central coordinating office. Most divide international education programs among various units; for example, international student advising is often located in student services while study abroad programs may be part of a faculty member's responsibility. However, the issue of centrally coordinating international education programs has been explicitly raised by Harari among many others. Therefore, each of this book's twenty-five case studies discusses the college or university's administrative organization for its undergraduate international education programs.

Means

Research on all case studies followed the same process. After an initial screening by telephone, every campus was visited and interviews conducted with directors and others knowledgeable about the program selected for study. Often those responsible for activities in other international education categories were also interviewed. Typically, document review and more lengthy telephone conversations followed the campus visit. A second interview in person of the key informant on a campus occurred in four cases.

All interviews occurred from the spring of 1993 through the spring of 1994. Changes since the campus visit are not incorporated into program descriptions. All informants gave of their time generously and answered questions openly, limited only by their sense of campus propriety. Some program directors, for example, did not feel free to divulge budget information. This produces some of the variation among the case studies. Also, based on areas of personal investment, some key interviewees provided more information on specific points; for instance, in the case of study abroad programs, some directors emphasized the orientation process while others elaborated on the selection of faculty leaders.

Campus directors received a draft of each study for review. In some cases, other interviewees were sent a copy and invited to comment. Once their revisions were incorporated into the text, the process was repeated. In some cases third and fourth drafts were necessary. This procedure was designed to eliminate mistakes of fact as well as of interpretation. Yet any errors remain the responsibility of the author.

Notes

1 Groennings, Sven ed, *Group Portrait: Internationalizing The Disciplines*, New York: The American Forum, 1990, 25.

2 Tonkin, Humphrey and Jane Edwards, "Internationalizing the University: The Arduous Road to Euphoria," *Educational Record*, Spring 1990, 15.

3 Ibid., 15.

4 Maurice Harari discusses campus ethos in his monograph *Internationalization of Higher Education: Effecting Institutional Change in the Curriculum and Campus Ethos*, California State University at Long Beach, 1989.

5 Harari, Maurice and Richard Reiff, "Halfway There: A View From the Bridge," *International Educator*, Spring 1993, 19.

6 Ibid., 19.

7 Johnston, Joseph S., Jr. and Richard J. Edelstein, *Beyond Borders: Profiles in International Education*, Washington D.C.: Association of American Colleges, 1993.

Augsburg College

Educating for a More Just World

Within several blocks of downtown Minneapolis, and even closer to the Mississippi River, a high-rise dormitory announces Augsburg College in large white letters to passersby on Interstate-94. The campus triangle is enclosed on the interstate side by a sound barrier. On its second side, the college pushes against an array of multi-story professional buildings. On the third side, houses converted to Augsburg offices merge with blocks of others privately owned until they reach Minneapolis' downtown skyscrapers.

The campus seems pleasantly compact, yet open. The central "quad" offers a small landscaped urban oasis with grass, flowers, and seven trees. As a reminder of Minnesota's winters, a series of skyways and tunnels connect the core campus' ten buildings. Walking to the sports fields and outlying buildings means crossing a city park, complete with grass, trees, swings, and benches.

Founded as a Lutheran seminary in 1869, Augsburg began as a liberal arts college when it first offered undergraduate classes in 1874. Its late-nineteenth-century presidents emphasized the practicality of a good education and a commitment to community. The college's "non-elitist" tradition is noted with pride in its catalog. This past is reflected in Augsburg's current emphasis on the experiential components of a good education, service learning, cooperative education, and academic internships, as described in the college viewbook "Opening Doors to Opportunity."

During the 1960s, Augsburg's president established the policy of reaching out to "non-traditional student populations." The college enrolls over 1,500 undergraduates and another 1,300 in graduate programs and weekend college. In 1992, 313 of its undergraduates were U.S. people of color, about 20 percent.

Augsburg radiates an urban energy, the kind that flows from compactness and an interaction by humans of many varieties. Secure in its Scandinavian heritage, the college devotes resources to people of varying backgrounds as reflected in its curriculum and co-curriculum support programs. These offer services and advocacy to students of color; i.e., the American Indian Support Program, Black Student Support Program, Asian-American Support Program, and Hispanic/Latino Support Program. Similar services are provided for the learning and physically disabled by the Center for Learning and Adaptive Student Services, CLASS.

Fostering multi-ethnicity creates a comfortable home for the Center for Global Education. This Augsburg program aims to educate campus and community alike about global social justice issues. It began in 1982 as an effort to "help North Americans to think more critically about global issues so that they might work toward a more just and sustainable world." By 1994, the Center was organizing twenty to thirty short term travel seminars a year for community groups, four semester programs for undergraduates in Mexico, one summer study program in Europe, and two semester programs in Southern Africa. Through its programs, the Center actively synthesizes Augsburg's experiential and multicultural traditions.

Campus Context

Its catalog statement incorporates international education into Augsburg's identity. The first sentences read:

> Augsburg College is grounded in traditions—the traditions of its founders, of the church and of higher education in the liberal arts. From this framework springs a dynamic, challenging and evolving institution that rises to the challenges of today's—and tomorrow's — changing world.

Several phrases dear to the hearts of international educators follow this statement, i.e., "respecting diversity," "Think globally, act locally," and "Students who graduate from Augsburg are well prepared to make a difference in the world."

These commitments form a preamble to the Augsburg Mission Statement: "To develop future leaders of service to the world by providing high quality educational opportunities which are based in the liberal arts and shaped by the faith and values of the Christian Church, by the context of a vital metropolitan setting, and by an intentionally diverse campus community."

Multiple support centers for various U.S. ethnicities help implement this goal, as noted previously. This effort to attract diversity was augmented by the presence of 40 international students in 1992. Their advising became the responsibility of the admissions office in 1993.

Previously, one person had served as both international student and study abroad advisor with reporting lines to two deans. In the fall of 1993 she moved to the Center for Global Education to work full-time with Augsburg students going overseas. About thirty to thirty-five per year participate, mostly on programs sponsored by a multi-college consortium.

In various ways, Augsburg's curriculum reflects both its Western and Scandinavian heritage as well as its decades-old commitment to diversity; for instance, languages offered include two courses in Ojibwe (Chippewa) as well as a major in Norwegian. The other language majors in French, German, and Spanish are joined by two years of Russian offerings. Chinese and Japanese are available at the University of Minnesota through a local consortium. The two English as a Second Language courses can be taken for credit.

Two minors illustrate the college's orientation: the American Indian Studies Minor and the Woman's Studies Minor, which has several international courses. These join several area studies and other international majors, i.e., East Asian Studies, Russian Area Studies, Scandinavian Area Studies, International Relations, and an International Business Concentration in the Business Major.

The General Education Curriculum Requirements include two related to international education. The "Intercultural Awareness Perspective" requires three courses, two in a foreign language and one covering a culture "other than European or mainstream North American." Two courses are required under the "Western Heritage" heading.

Several courses rarely available at institutions the size of Augsburg are infused throughout the curriculum. The Education Department offers a course in International Education for both elementary and secondary majors. Other departments also contribute to the college's international and multicultural curriculum; these include Environmental Psychology in the Psychology Department, the Religion Department contributes American Indian Spirituality and Philosophical Thought, the Art and Music departments list Tribal Arts and Culture and Ethnic Music, and Sociology teaches Family Systems: A Cross-Cultural Perspective and Culture: Ethnicity, Gender and Race.

The 1991-93 catalog also lists courses in the three Center for Global Education semester programs existing at that time in Mexico: Program in Global Community, Social Policy and Human Services in Latin America, and Women and Development: Latin American Perspectives. In 1993 a fourth program was added, Contemporary Issues in Mexico and Central America.

Center for Global Education
The Center's purpose appears in Augsburg's catalog:

> The Center for Global Education, a program of Augsburg College, facilitates cross-cultural learning experiences which prepare people to think more critically about global issues and to work toward a more just and sustainable world. The Center's Programs explore a diversity of viewpoints and are grounded in the perspectives of the poor and of others struggling for justice and human dignity.

The Center has an expansive vision of what education is both by market and methodology. It offers travel seminars for community organizations as well as semester programs for undergraduates. The Center's pedagogical approach highlights observation and reflection as well as including formal presentations. Every program, whether short-term travel seminars or semester-long with academic courses, ensures that participants experience multiple encounters with ordinary people in the host country.

Program planners intend to teach global issues not as abstractions. World-wide issues exist because they directly impact all socioeconomic classes, especially the poor. The Center for Global Education's programs point out that global economic interdependence has negatively impacted the poor in many societies. This negative implication of a concept basic to international education is often overlooked. The Center contends that this knowledge gap is filled best through interaction with local people. Such a learning-through-experience strategy is fostered by Augsburg itself, as noted previously.

Center programs have grown exponentially in numbers of both programs and participants. This success provides evidence that they have synthesized several felt needs by both younger and older people in this country. The Center's community programs, for example, have appealed to people in many occupations and in various parts of the United States. These "reality tours" offer about two weeks of alternative, educational travel tailored to the interests of specific groups, lawyers, medical professionals, musicians, as well as church groups. Often these seminars are co-sponsored; for example, with the Philadelphia Interfaith Delegation, an alliance of thirty-four Protestant, Roman Catholic and Jewish congregations in northwest Philadelphia.

The first Center programs for undergraduate students were organized at the house it purchased in Cuernavaca, Mexico. Later another house was added given the rapid increase in demand for Center programs. They all share several elements which teach via action and reflection as well as classroom instruction. The goal is to create a living/learning community. Each student group is responsible for household maintenance. After formal lectures, discussion, and field work, the group divides to spend several weeks living with a working class Mexican family.

The formal sessions are careful to include talks by government and business leaders as well as community organizers and ordinary people. Thus different perspectives become an integral part of the instructional design. Day trips give students a sense of time and tradition by including archaeological and historical sites. Near the end of the program, the group travels to two of the Center for Global Education's three Central American centers in El Salvador, Guatemala, or Nicaragua.

Although specific courses are tailored to each of the four programs, Spanish is always included. In fact, one semester of

Spanish or its equivalent is a prerequisite for acceptance into the Mexican programs. The Contemporary Issues in Mexico and Central America Program, for example, offers The Development Process (for credit in Interdisciplinary Studies), Cultural Issues Seminar (General Studies), MesoAmerica: The Legacy of the Conquest (History), The Church and Social Change in Latin America (Religion), and Intensive Individualized Spanish (Spanish). A Maximum of 25 students from any college and university may participate. In 1993-94, a one-semester program cost $8,200.

In 1993 two new programs were inaugurated in Southern Africa, i.e., Women and Development: A Southern Africa Perspective, and Southern African Societies in Transition: The View from Namibia. They use the same model as developed in Mexico, i.e., community living, formal instruction, interaction with individuals from many subgroups of society, field trips, and a two week homestay. The center in Namibia provides the living and instructional base. Then the group travels to South Africa to learn first hand of that country's struggle. The Center's other new program is offered during the summer: Global Issues and World Churches in Europe has no living center but all other parts of the model are in place, including a family stay in Eastern Germany.

To administer its international centers and multiple programs, the Center for Global Education employs about thirty to forty people, including drivers and other in-country staff, many on a part-time basis. The central office at Augsburg has a staff of sixteen of which about one-half are full-time. Others vary from half-time to 80 percent. The director, Joel Mugge, reports to Augsburg's Vice President for Academic Affairs and Dean of the College.

When the Center was formally established it had five staff, two at Augsburg and three in Mexico. Then the guest house in Nicaragua was added to the two houses in Cuernavaca, Mexico. This increased host country staff as did the Center's expansion of its activities to El Salvador and Guatemala. In these two countries sites are rented as needed and vehicles were purchased at three locations. The number of personnel grew rapidly including support staff as well as office directors. In 1993 the center in Namibia was added.

At its headquarters, the Center has always paid its own operating expenses. Augsburg College has provided overhead, such as office space. The cost for the far-flung operation was approaching two million dollars per year in 1993. Fees covered the great majority of this but about $200,000 came from grants and donations. The latter provided about $60,000 in 1992-93, which marked an increase because of growing support from previous participants.

The Center's History

The story of Joel Mugge tells the Center's history. Created from his vision and with his energy, it evolved from 1970 when he led the first group to Mexico. At that time he was Youth Director in a Lutheran church in Albert Lea, Minnesota. He organized a group of high school students to learn through observation about global justice issues.

When asked to reflect on the reasons why he began global education initiatives, Mugge thinks back to his own learning. Two transforming experiences taught the young college student about a world very different from his own. His first such awakening occurred far away, not geographically but in lifestyle. During his junior year at Valparaiso University, Mugge took part in an internship program in inner-city Detroit. This was a requirement of his Youth Leadership Training Program major. One month later, the 1968 riot engulfed the city. Mugge realized poverty not only has causes but also consequences.

To this consciousness raising was added a multicultural experience. The second semester of his senior year, Mugge went to Germany on a study abroad program. He returned not only with a cross-cultural awareness but a new sense of personal confidence. Together, the Detroit and Germany programs dramatically demonstrated that first-hand experience was the most effective way to learn about this multicultural world in need of social justice.

Having reached this realization, Joel Mugge organized travel-reflection trips to Mexico during his first employment at the church in Albert Lea. A Lutheran pastor provided the original contact in Mexico, the Benedictine monastery in Cuernavaca.

In 1972 Mugge joined the Student Affairs Division of Augsburg College. In 1975 he proposed a January interim program in Mexico. For four years this continued with excellent student evaluations. In addition, participating students showed significant attitudinal changes. These were measured by using the World Mindedness Scale as a pre- and posttest. The degree of change was surprising for a short-term experience. This showed the effectiveness of the program's community involvement and action-reflection methodology.

The analysis of these results was the subject of Mugge's Master's Thesis at the University of Minnesota. Upon completion of his degree in speech communication, with a specialization in intercultural communication, Mugge became an Augsburg faculty member in 1976.

In 1979 the semester Program in Global Community began. Mugge bought a van to transport students to and from Mexico, leasing it to the college for the purpose. The college bought it the next year. Mugge also organized travel seminars for local congregations, usually lasting for about 10 days. In January 1982 this expanded when the Lutheran Hunger Program wanted a two-week program for their congregation coordinators. This group went to Mexico and Nicaragua. Other community programs followed lasting around two weeks. These set the pattern of always going to Mexico and then to one of two sites in Guatemala and Nicaragua.

In the fall of 1981, while on sabbatical, Mugge worked on his idea of a Center for Global Education. This was initiated in 1982 with American Lutheran Church funding.

By the late 1980s, Center programs were attracting people nationwide. A variety of occupational groups were requesting the Center to organize travel seminars. The undergraduate semesters in Mexico drew participants from over a hundred colleges including some of the nation's most prestigious private and large state universities.

New programs became a matter of course. Their initiation followed a pattern of partnership with a U.S. organization in the case of travel seminars, or a university for new undergraduate semester programs. The Women in Development semester in Mexico evolved from a contract with Colgate University. The recent Namibia program was produced in cooperation with Valparaiso University and the Global Issues and World Churches summer program in Europe had been administered by Wittenberg University since 1981. Cosponsorships ensure the existence of an established market.

The second element in new program initiation is trust through an entree into the part of the world of interest to a specific U.S. group. Church connections often prove the most effective although the Center works with secular contacts as well, such as the university in Namibia. The key is to develop partnerships with organizations as well as individuals. This helps ensure program stability. To illustrate, Middle East seminars have been organized through the auspices of the Middle East Council of Churches.

Compatibility is a third issue the Center considers in developing new programs. All partners, within the U.S. and the host country, share the Center's specific content focus and endorse its methodology.

In the early 1990s the Center began faculty development programs for colleges and seminaries. By 1994, workshops for faculty had been held at two colleges providing training in education for critical consciousness.

Issues and Answers

As with any transnational organization, the Center for Global Education faces the need to keep clear lines of communication between the central office and overseas staff. Part of the Center's response is to emphasize its educational mission, i.e., educating for a more just world. The Director perceives that this common sense of purpose has proven essential in retaining both the vitality and tenure stability of far-flung program personnel. To reinforce shared perception, and deal with any administrative issues needing attention, in-country coordinators attend an annual retreat at the Augsburg headquarters.

As with any entrepreneurial effort, finances present an ongoing issue. Given the Center's constant programmatic growth, any financial constrictions become manifested as pressures on personnel. Designing new programs and making new contacts requires high intensity staff work. Even maintaining existing programs, which gather people from all parts of the United States and send them to various places in the world, means diplomatically dealing with a myriad of details. Often program opportunities run ahead of available staff time. This becomes, at least in part, a budget issue.

In many cases, Center overhead is not covered by money raised from each program. Market realities, and the Center's mission, mean it attempts to charge each participant a reasonable price. Since there is such a high staff-participant ratio, the Center cannot charge what the programs really cost in staff time.

For most semester programs, the budget is based on twenty participants while for travel seminars the number is fifteen. If fewer apply, a hard decision has to be made and often the Center absorbs a loss. Fortunately, sometimes the number is higher than twenty so this program can, in effect, subsidize others.

In response to the need to develop programs before they begin to pay for themselves, the Center applies for grant funding through Lutheran agencies and private foundations. Also, in recent years, the Center has campaigned to raise donations from past participants, as noted previously, which is proving more and more effective.

The complexity of the central office's administrative structure also has become a concern. The Center's activities produce a three dimensional logic for administrative organization: First, the geographical spread of programs means personnel are divided according to Mexico, Central America, and Developing Areas. Second, the Center organizes two general types of programs, seminars and semesters, which correspond to various clientele, i.e., students, professional groups, church members. All want a different content emphasis, a medical seminar, for instance, or one focussing on human rights in general. Third, personnel are assigned on a functional basis covering marketing and fund raising activities.

Whatever their specific position description, Center staff have to function with crisscross lines of communication and authority. The situation was in some ways helped and in some hindered by the director-founder's strong personality. Referring administrative as well as policy decisions to him resolved issues, yet sometimes it forestalled the development of effective interpersonal relations. The growth in the Center's activities necessitated an alternative to centralized decision-making.

Moving to a cooperative decision-making process made sense. Center staff realized that the action-reflection model could apply to learning to work together as well as it could to learning about global issues. Not only did intensive staff discussions take place, but they were directly applicable to office administration because the director took a ten-month leave of absence in 1992. The need for the collaborative process continued since he returned in 1993 on a 75 percent basis.

Another oft-discussed issue concerned the low level of participation by Augsburg students in the Center's semester programs. In response, the college's Study Abroad Advisor became part of the Center in the summer of 1993. By the spring of 1994, the number of students applying for Center programs had doubled, jumping from four or five a year to nine or ten.

Greater faculty awareness could lead to increased student participation as well. In the 1980s, when the Center initiated its Mexican program on Social Policy in the Latin American Context, Augsburg social work faculty travelled with students and taught courses at the Cuernavaca guest house. Since then, virtually all instruction for all semester programs is provided by local specialists. It should be noted, however, that Augsburg faculty have accepted and provide credit for all the Center's undergraduate programs.

Sensitive to the criticism that it has "gone its own way," the Center initiated a new kind of program. By 1994, three faculty-student groups had participated in ten-day programs in Cuernavaca. The success of these short programs has encouraged planning for their continuation.

Lessons Learned

The following points reflect the fact that the Center maintains its own personnel, financing, and distinctive approach to global issues.

1. *Maintain the vitality of local community links both in the United States and at the program sites.* Given the nature of the Center's programs, its personnel must have a working knowledge of both the U.S. markets and the host countries' communities.

2. *Ensure detailed attention to logistical arrangements by assigning adequate staff time.*

3. *Realize that fostering academic quality through face-to-face encounters with local people of many perspectives requires much time and preparation.* An interactive methodology is sometimes thought of as less rigorous. Yet course preparation by host country academics and the Center's on-site staff must be thorough.

Their exponential growth testifies to the Center's program quality. By 1994, around 5,500 people had attended over 325 seminars and forty semester programs. This success is attributable to the creativity as well as the workability of Joel Mugge's original design. Another factor is the quality of the Center's personnel over successive generations. Acceptance by Augsburg administration and faculty must be cited as an important factor. The social justice content theme and experiential methodology fit comfortably with the college's traditional identity.

Brookdale Community College

Establishing an Overseas Learning Center for Local Students

In 1986, Brookdale's Center in Guayaquil began operation offering courses for qualified Ecuadorean students. Its growth and continuation through successive Brookdale administrations provide ample evidence of its success. The center's creativity, both in conceptualization and administration, derives from its purpose. It was not established to internationally educate U.S. students; it brings a U.S. education to Ecuadoreans.

The Guayaquil Center presents a useful case study, not because it is directly replicable by many colleges, but because it expands the boundaries of program possibilities. It substantially widens the consideration of what is feasible. The Center resulted from a unique convergence of creative, able, top college administrators combined with a competent, resourceful, hardworking representative in Ecuador, who formerly taught Spanish at the college.

The extraordinary program in Ecuador was not a predictable result of Brookdale's particular characteristics. Yet the Center is compatible with the college's sense of mission, i.e., to provide an education for anyone wanting one. Unlike many community colleges, Brookdale has an open admissions policy. With another interpretation of "openness," the college also sustains an effective International Center on campus.

Brookdale was founded in 1967 with classes starting in 1969. Located in central-eastern New Jersey, the campus forms part of the Monmouth County town of Lincroft. As with other New Jersey community colleges, financial support comes mainly from county funding. About fifty-six percent of its 12,000 full- and part-time students transfer to four-year institutions. Consistent with the educational role of a community college, Brookdale also offers a variety of vocational and career programs.

The campus' external appearance fits well with its location in an area of New Jersey moving from a rural to a suburban lifestyle. The weathered wood, fieldstone, and brick main buildings center a large wooded area. All are located on the site of a century-old thoroughbred horse farm. One barn and a corn crib remain on the donated land. These give the campus a traditional feel, a sense of having evolved even if the property's previous enterprise is remote from its present purpose.

Brookdale's appearance reflects both the architectural and educational ideas of the 1960s. The top floors of its main interconnected buildings have few rooms and very high ceilings. The lack of closed-in space was designed to convey a sense of openness and flexibility. These reflect the theme of accessibility which provided the raison d'etre for the community college movement in the 1960s. These two-year institutions filled a perceived gap in U.S. higher education. They allowed an alternative route to a college education as well as technical training for those who otherwise would not qualify or be able to afford it.

Brookdale still functions on an open admission basis accepting anyone over eighteen years of age. Thus the college emphasizes pedagogical flexibility, small classes, and practical instructional methodologies. In part, this approach finds expression in the objective-based, individualized instruction available for some courses. Brookdale's Testing Center allows individual students to learn at their own pace using alternative curriculum materials.

This flexibility in curriculum design finds an echo in the original architectural conception of the campus buildings. Their lack of walls allows an interior space capable of multiple uses. The perceived efficiency of this has diminished over the years and dividers have been added to stake out office space. Yet the sense of openness persists given the vastness of the area overhead.

In this environment, international education programs have steadily grown. Brookdale Community College is known for its student overseas and outreach programs. This internationalization of the accessibility theme has become particularly innovative through the success of the Guayaquil Center.

Campus Context

Brookdale Community College carries out activities in each of international education's major categories. Two international curriculum specializations are offered, the International Business Option in the Business Administration Program, and the International Studies Option in the Social Sciences Program. More modern languages are taught than at many community colleges with courses through the intermediate level available in German, Russian, French, Japanese, Italian, and Spanish. Also, Chinese can be taken through the elementary level. The Modern Language Department offers a full program of English as a Second Language courses. All are taken for Brookdale credit but only the more advanced count toward graduation.

A variety of international courses are infused throughout the liberal arts curriculum. Within the Social Sciences, students can choose a Holocaust course in the Interdisciplinary Studies Program, several Anthropology courses including Puerto Rican Culture, many history courses which provide a mainstay for the International Studies Option and cover Africa, Latin America, Asia, Russia, and the Middle East. In addition, the Natural Sciences includes Environmental Science courses, and Humanities is represented by a Comparative Religions course and one on Contemporary Latin American Literature.

Brookdale now has its third president since President Robert Barringer actively supported international education in the early 1980s. Among other actions, he led the negotiations which established the Guayaquil Center.

Commitment to one of international education's main themes is implied by the new President in his personal message at the beginning of the 1991-93 catalog. Its wording shows his English teacher background and commitment to diversity. The President noted that nontraditional students, as defined by age and ethnicity, are "to form a social mosaic of bright and diverse colors and shapes, backgrounds and experiences—a montage that, in itself, helps educate the educators." In a real way the Guayaquil Center has contributed to this mosaic by supplying several students a year to the Brookdale campus.

During the 1992-93 academic year, 120 international students attended Brookdale. Between fifteen and twenty of these were from the Guayaquil Center. A semester on the New Jersey campus is required for their associate's degree. The Registrar's Office handles international student admissions and any needed support services. If non-U.S. citizens other than those on an F-1 or tourist visa are added, then the international student total goes up by a few hundred.

Study abroad and outreach programs are administered by the International Center on campus. It sponsors five overseas programs which also are offered to other colleges via two consortial networks. The service learning programs in Ecuador and France are open to members of the Partnership for Service Learning. The Cyprus, Canada, and Colombia programs, as well as the one in Ecuador, send students from the College Consortium for International Studies. Non-Brookdale students numbered eighty-two during the 1992-93 academic year. In the same year, thirty-five Brookdale students went to ten countries in consortial programs as well as on the college's own. All Brookdale study abroad students are required to take a Sociology course in Intercultural Communication before departure.

The International Center also has faculty development responsibilities, for international visitors as well as Brookdale professors. Faculty have come from Laica University in Guayaquil for both semester-long and short-term visits. They have made presentations and taught Psychology, Spanish, and History courses. The Center also has organized the visits of two groups from a Canadian community college to study the U.S. criminal justice system. They attended classes and went on field trips, one group for a week and the other for ten days.

For forty to fifty Brookdale faculty, the Guayaquil Center has provided a very effective professional growth experience since they comprise part of the Center's teaching staff on a rotating basis. Also, a Brookdale business faculty member has gone to Cyprus and professors of French have lectured at the college's program in France.

At a community college, community outreach remains important. The International Center organizes several activities throughout the year. Language instruction for primary and middle-school children is provided by two summer programs.

For two weeks, International Adventures attracts between seventy and one-hundred first through eighth graders. They come to learn one of five languages: French, Spanish, Italian, Russian, or Chinese. This has continued for thirteen years. A spin-off, a one-week Language Sampler, is offered for children four through six years of age. This program presents a variety of languages using games and other inventive introductory teaching techniques.

A third language program is administered with Brookdale's Community Services Division. It too offers non-credit language "courses" using individualized instructional technologies and techniques. Tapes and mentors provide instruction in many languages formatted over 15 hours. This time can be scheduled in any way the student decides. Thus students can personalize their instruction. Small group sessions are also arranged upon demand.

Ethnic festivals are organized by the Community Services Division with assistance from the International Center. A mega festival, International Week, occurs annually and brings thousands of people to campus. A craft and food fair comprise the heart of this major event, augmented by continuous ethnic entertainment and special events, such as fashions from around the world and international talks by faculty.

In 1993, the fair was combined with a children's peace fair. Originally organized for five years by a local peace and disarmament group, the children's activities followed those of International Week. In 1994, both will be called a "Kaleidoscope of Kith and Kin."

The International Center's two full-time staff are led by a dynamic coordinator of International Education, Elaine Baran. She is formally released from teaching for the 80 percent-time coordinator's position. Baran has taught Spanish for Brookdale and now teaches Italian. The normal course load at Brookdale is five courses per semester. In actuality, she teaches three courses per semester instead of her contracted one, given the need for language instruction. She also teaches the Intercultural Communication course required for all students going on an overseas program.

Besides the coordinator, the International Center has two full-time staff, an administrative assistant and a secretary. A half-time student worker is always an international student.

The International Center has an Advisory Committee made up of community people. Businesses, churches, and schools are represented. The committee reflects the country's ethnic diversity both by its individual and organizational membership, the latter consisting of the Association of Indians in America and the Jersey Shore Chinese School.

Until the early 1990s, the campus International Center also administered the Guayaquil Center. In 1992 this responsibility was transferred to Paul Zigo, the director of Extension Services, who administers the college's other four off-campus learning centers in Monmouth County. Yet the Guayaquil Center's Director, Al Eyde, still reports to the International Center concerning the programs he organizes for U.S. students, such as the Service Learning Program. Both the International Center's coordinator and the director of Extension Services report to the Vice President for Education Services, the college's highest academic oficer.

Before Brookdale's International Center was established in the late 1980s, Al Eyde in Guayaquil reported to the Vice President for Education Services. Thus, since the Center in Ecuador has existed, its director has had three different contact points on campus overseeing his work.

Quayaquil Learning Center
The legal entity under Ecuadorean law is called the Brookdale in Ecuador Development Foundation. The Center was originally organized and developed by President Robert Barringer, his academic Vice President Margaret Gwynne, and Al Eyde, formerly a Spanish teacher at Brookdale.

In the early 1980s, Eyde moved to Guayaquil to become director of one of Ecuador's leading English-language high schools. He also organized an overseas Spanish language program for Brookdale students. This evolved into a service learning program open to students from members of a U.S. consortium called the Partnership for Service Learning. In 1986, the

Guayaquil Center began teaching students and its subsequent growth enabled Eyde to become the full-time Director.

By 1993, a cap of thirty-five to forty had to be placed on the number of sections per semester offered at the Center. Its seven-week courses are scheduled primarily in the evening. Each one has classes two times a week, either Monday and Wednesday or Tuesday and Thursday. Thus students can take two per term. All are taught in English by qualified, Brookdale-approved faculty. During the summer as many as ten Brookdale faculty may be teaching in Ecuador. Several also teach in the spring. The Center operates year-round with six seven-week terms. In 1993, an average of 352 students attended classes at any one time; this was up from 1992's figure of 280. This increasing demand reflects the Center's established reputation.

For an associate's degree, three semesters of course credit can be taken in Ecuador, leaving one semester to be completed at Brookdale. This conforms to the guidelines for the college's two other Extension Learning Centers. Thus students can earn up to forty-five credits in Ecuador. Like Brookdale's U.S. students, those at the Guayaquil Center take a New Jersey Basic Skills Test before they begin classes. If necessary, they must complete developmental courses. These students can take more than the forty-five-hour cap because developmental courses do not count toward a degree. In May of 1992, twelve students from Ecuador took part in Brookdale's graduation.

The Guayaquil Center operates like Brookdale's other Learning Centers, not only for reasons of administrative efficiency. The college's administrators perceive this policy as useful because it helps New Jersey state officials understand the Guayaquil Center as a normal part of Brookdale's operation. Extension centers require state government approval and must conform to its regulations; for example, upper level courses must be taught on campus.

Registration and grade records are kept on the Jersey campus as well as in Ecuador. The Guayaquil Center can provide grade reports, but official ones can only be issued from New Jersey. Some long-range academic supervision occurred when the division chairs of Humanities and Social Sciences travelled to Guayaquil to evaluate its instruction. In addition, the Center was visited by staff of the Middle States Association of Colleges and Schools which included Brookdale's Ecuador site in its general accreditation report. Several college administrators also have reviewed the Ecuador operation first hand; for instance, Brookdale's lawyer and the head of its accounting office. A member of the Board of Trustees has visited as well.

The following courses were offered during the two fall terms in 1993: Principles of Accounting, Introduction to Marketing, Recent American History, Modern Latin American History, Statistics, General Physics, Introduction to Psychology, Microeconomics, Macroeconomics, Calculus I, Personal Finance, Principles of Management, and seven English as a Second Language courses from Elementary to Advanced.

A total of six Brookdale faculty taught in the Guayaquil Center during the spring and summer of 1993, four full-timers and two adjuncts. The college covers the cost of their airfare while they pay for meals, local transportation, and $200 per month for host family accommodations. Generally each faculty member stays for one seven-week term.

Faculty can choose to teach a seven-week term in Ecuador as part of their normal course load if they teach the rest of the Brookdale semester at the Fort Monmouth Center. This extension center shares Guayaquil's seven week calendar. Receiving adjunct pay provides the other alternative for faculty who choose to teach in Guayaquil. No one familiar with the Center's operation reports major problems in getting faculty to teach in Ecuador.

The Guayaquil Center has affiliations with the University of South Carolina and Edison State College in New Jersey. This provides Ecuadorean students with several options which vary in the amount of credits that can be taken at the Guayaquil Center and those required at the U.S. institutions. All articulation programs with these four-year institutions are in subfields of business, such as Finance and Marketing/Retailing.

The Center also offers programs which can transfer to U.S. universities in general or lead to an associate of arts degree from Brookdale. Business programs comprise half this list: Business Finance, Business Administration, International Business Administration, Accounting, Marketing, Personnel Man-

agement, Psychology, Liberal Studies, Mathematics, English/
Literature, International Studies, Economics. The Center allows
students to take courses on a non-degree basis up to eleven
credits.

Ten full-time staff work at the Center. Only the Director is on
Brookdale's payroll and receives his salary directly from the college. The rest are paid on a contract basis given the lower pay
levels in Ecuador. The Center has a library, computerized systems, and a computer lab which needs updating. The 1992-93
operating budget of $302,000 had specific line items, such as
travel, supplies, etc., but no discretionary funds. Thus it conforms to the other Learning Center budgets.

The Center makes a U.S. education available to those who
otherwise may not be able to afford it. Although requiring
English and tuition payments in U.S. dollars precludes the vast
majority of Ecuadoreans, a wider cross-section of local people
than before are provided with the U.S. education and English
training necessary for scarce jobs. Prior to the Center's existence, the only way to acquire any U.S. academic qualification
was in the United States at a cost prohibitive to all but the
wealthiest.

Issues and Answers
The Center did not experience instant success. Its development
took much energy, patience, knowledge of Ecuadorean society,
plus administrative creativity on the part of Brookdale's administration. When the Center began, the Director was not full-
time because there was not enough income to support his
salary plus other costs. This presented a chicken-egg situation.
Without the Director full-time tending to organization and
publicity the Center drew fewer students than needed, and
without more students funding was not sufficient to pay the
Director full-time.

At this point, Director Eyde and Vice President Gwynne took
a risk. The Director became full-time and five years was set for
the Center to become self-sustaining. This proposal passed the
Board of Trustees. The decision was vindicated when the numbers of Center students began increasing rapidly. The Center
not only became self-sustaining; it began to produce a surplus.

Yet the Center was to face another time of crisis. Judging from information pieced together from interviews, it seems 1991-92 proved to be another period of decision. President Barringer's departure precipitated months of concern over whether to retain the Guayaquil Center. Its second mainstay, Vice President Gwynne, left within months of President Barringer. The new President turned the issue over to his interim vice president who went to Guayaquil. He came back enthused and supportive. Center oversight was turned over to Extension Services in July 1992.

All this took place after the president of Brookdale and the executive director of the Middle States Association of Colleges and Schools visited the Guayaquil Center as part of the organization's periodic accreditation of Brookdale. The Association's report included a favorable review of the Guayaquil Center.

It appears the new Brookdale administration perceived the Guayaquil operation as too autonomous. It noted "communication lapses" and the Center's budget flexibility. Yet the director was thousands of miles away, knew about and had to respond to Ecuadorean contingencies, and was using funds earned from the tuition payments of Center students. Bringing the Center into conformance with the college's other Extension Centers testifies as to the director's dedication, flexibility, and administrative ability.

In the years since, the Center has weathered yet a third turnover in Brookdale's two top administrators. Now there can be no question as to the success in Guayaquil given exponential increases in Center student numbers and the hundreds of thousands of dollars it raises for the college. A cultivation process by Al Eyde is having a positive effect; for example, he met informally with Brookdale Community College's Board of Trustees in the Spring of 1993.

This provides part of an answer to the need to continually update campus administrators on the Guayaquil Center's benefits. To successive generations of new presidents and vice presidents, the far away operation presents too many unknowns. This matters even more because they do not share both the knowledge of and commitment to international education possessed by the Center's initiating president and vice president.

They have to go through a learning process and be presented with economic rationales. The director of Extension Services sees his policy of integrating the Center with campus policies and procedures as helpful in this education process. The fact that the Center has earned strong faculty support creates a favorable environment, yet decisions are made at the top. New high level Brookdale administrators see the Center as less of an anomaly because it applies home campus practices.

Another issue concerns how much tuition Ecuadorean students are charged. Presently they pay in U.S. dollars at the same rate as Monmouth County students. They are not charged out-of-state tuition. This has been a Center policy since it was established. A rationale then and now is the fact that the Center has its own support personnel and covers its own expenses. It makes minimal use of Brookdale's support services. Also, in recent years, the Center pays its own way even if Brookdale's overhead is included in the calculation.

Lessons Learned and Future Plans
The following are from the point of view of on-campus administration of the overseas center.

1. *Know the country, the society, legal system, and physical setting.* Without the director's thorough knowledge of and connections with Ecuadorean people, the Center would not exist.
2. *To earn the support of successive generations of college administrators, apply the home institution's policies.*
3. *Have the program evaluated externally.* The fact that the Middle States Association's accrediting report had only positive comments on the Guayaquil Center has proven vital in gaining the support of new Brookdale administrators.

According to a five-year plan drawn up by the Center's director and the director of Extension Services, a permanent facility will be built in Guayaquil. After its mortgage is paid, Brookdale will lease the building free of charge from the Brookdale in Ecuador Development Foundation, the Center's legal Ecuadorean designation. Student demand has overtaken the Center's present facility, a leased house in one of Guayaquil's suburbs. As an interim measure, the Center plans to move. It will lease space in a local English-language high school.

In summarizing the reasons for the Center's success, those factors that account for its initiation must be differentiated from those contributing to its continuation through two successive college administrations. The Center was established and sustained through its difficult early years by the dedication and abilities of the man in Ecuador, Al Eyde, and because of overt decisions by the two top college administrators, President Barringer and Vice President Gwynne. These two not only expressed a commitment to international education, they actively supported a creative and risky program.

With changes in Brookdale's administration, the director and his flexibility proved crucial to the Center's continuation. Faculty and the coordinator of the campus International Center provided an essential support network. The teaching effectiveness of the Guayaquil extension must be noted since a favorable review by the Middle States accreditation team became a major factor. It helped convince a new Brookdale administration the Center deserved to continue. Also, the fact that it was making money cannot be overlooked.

Unlike most of the other programs described in this book, Brookdale's Guayaquil extension illustrates that successful programs can outlive major disagreements. The Center experienced a dynamic tension between two contrasting administrative perceptions. The Center's director had exercised some decision-making independence through budgetary discretion until a new campus administration demanded standardization with other extension centers, including budgetary centralization. In the long run, it seems making the Ecuador Center conform to home campus administrative procedures has made it intelligible to a third group of top administrators. Disputes, and their resolution, can strengthen a program in the context of an overall commitment to its goals and when contested by competent people.

Capilano College

Producing International Managers

In the 1980s, this two-year college in North Vancouver, Canada undertook an outreach program remarkable for its vision, long-term impact, depth of learning, and multicountry scope. The Asia Pacific Management Cooperative Program offers Canadians who have completed their undergraduate degrees nine months of course work and a full one-year internship in an Asian country.

Another outreach initiative links Canada and ASEAN, the common market Association of South East Asian Nations. Called CANASEAN, this program brings younger managers from the ASEAN countries, plus Vietnam and China, to Capilano for a four-month business orientation and internship program. Both CANASEAN and the Management Cooperative Program will be described in this case study. The latter, however, will receive a full analysis because its training is both intensive and extensive.

When the Asia Pacific Management Cooperative Program was initiated in 1987 its success was not guaranteed. Yet Capilano's senior administrators, faculty-administrative planning committee, and the governments of Canada and British Columbia who were financing the program thought it was a risk worth taking. Capilano College's location augured well for the success of this international management program, unique in Canada.

On a clear day, which happens now and then in North America's Pacific Northwest, the Port of Vancouver is visible from Capilano's campus. As Canada's opening to Asia, Vancouver experienced rapid economic growth in the 1980s and 1990s. The population of Greater Vancouver also grew, increasing by 15.4 percent from 1986 to 1991. Multiethnicity characterizes the area's population with 37 percent identifying languages other than English or French as their "mother tongue."

Capilano opened its doors in 1968, educating its 700 students in portables. In 1973, the college moved to its present location and, in the early 1990s, provides instruction to approximately 6,000 students with another 6,000 taking non-credit courses. The full-time teaching faculty number approximately 150 with another 150 working part-time.

The campus has mostly three and four-floor buildings arranged close together and enclosed by a mini-northwest forest. The manmade structures are dwarfed by cedar and fir trees which tower above a dense undergrowth of holly, philodendron, and other typical examples of the region's flora. The competition of trees and buildings for space imparts a sense of intimacy and intensity, a feeling that much is happening in a confined area.

Immediately beyond the campus and its forest, suburban North Vancouver spills out over its mountainside overlooking an inlet and the city of Vancouver. North and West Vancouver have the highest level of education and the highest per capita income of any municipal region in British Columbia. Their population, and that of the city of Vancouver, generate a demand for Capilano's university preparatory and career curriculum programs.

As well as degree programs offered in conjunction with The Open University of British Columbia and postbaccalaureate programs like the Asia Pacific Management Coop Program, Capilano College also offers associate of arts and associate of science degrees and other diplomas in a wide variety of academic and career fields. Some of these include Business Administration, Music, Applied Information Technology, Jazz Studies, and Textile Arts. In addition, students can earn certificates for shorter programs in some career fields. Some students take Capilano's preparatory courses which upgrade their academic skills and enable them to qualify for the other programs. Also, as with most community colleges in the United States, extension programs and services, such as short courses, seminars, and workshops, are offered to the local community on a non-credit basis.

Campus Context

International education is incorporated into the mission of Capilano College. The second sentence of the "Mission and Values" statement in the college calendar, its catalog, reads, "Our dedication to excellence and commitment to a set of values will prepare students to contribute effectively as responsible citizens in a rapidly changing global community." Adopted by the College Board in 1990, the statement goes on to define the Capilano community in the broadest sense: "The College considers itself an important resource in the economic and cultural life of its immediate region and beyond: to the rest of the province, the nation, and internationally."

Courses listed under Academic Studies/University Transfer cover a wide range of first- and second-year university courses, all of which transfer to Canadian universities. The college offers seven languages: French, German, Spanish, Japanese, Mandarin Chinese, Thai, and Bahasa Indonesian. There are many offerings in Anthropology. The History courses cover not only Europe but the U.S. as well. The Labour Studies program, the only college program in Canada devoted to the educational needs of union members, includes a Race and Ethnic Relations course. Sociology offers Sociology of the Third World and Current Social Issues, which actually is a global issues course. Biology has two ecology courses and Philosophy includes Environmental Ethics which covers global issues as well as Canadian. Two non-Western art courses are offered as are many in Geography. Political Studies courses include Comparative Government, International Relations and International Organizations. Women's Studies is heavily internationalized including a course on Contemporary American Women Writers.

Capilano offers a certificate in Ethnic and Cross-Cultural Relations with its two-term focus on the Canadian "mosaic." The Tourism Management diploma program includes courses on The Japanese Tourism Market and Cross-cultural Tourism. International Business is listed as an elective for a diploma in Business Administration and Cross-cultural Perspectives is a course required for an Advanced Business diploma. This latter diploma is a rung in the curriculum ladder between a one-year certificate in Business Administration and the four-year degree with the Open University. Yet another business program offers the Accelerated Marketing Management diploma. This ten-month program for mature students already in the workforce includes an International Marketing course.

Capilano's two postbaccalaureate diploma programs are international. In addition to the Asia Pacific Management Cooperative Program described in detail below, Capilano's Environmental Science program is for students who already have a four-year baccalaureate in science or engineering. The program is twelve months in duration and prepares graduates to work on environmental issues in Canada and other Pacific Rim nations. A maximum of twenty-five students take twelve courses and a practicum.

The college had 157 international students in the spring of 1994, and two international student advisors work in the Advising Centre. Six faculty teach English as a Second Language which operates as a separate unit with its own coordinator. The program includes a course on the Introduction to Canadian Culture.

The manager of the Asia Pacific Management Cooperative Program also teaches German and advises study abroad students. In the spring of 1994, three students were in Japan on an exchange with Aichi Gakusen College. The agreement between Capilano and Aichi Gakusen also authorizes a faculty exchange. In addition, students may participate in a summer multicountry cooperative program organized by a regional consortium of U.S. and Canadian colleges and universities.

Senior administrators as well as faculty view the college mission statement as a significant guide for actual activities. Therefore, international education outreach is taken seriously since it implements Capilano's commitment to be an "important resource" to the "rest of the province, the nation, and internationally." In addition to the two programs described in detail below, the Asia Pacific Management Cooperative Program and CANASEAN, Capilano's outreach emphasizes technical assistance on an ongoing basis.

Members of the Capilano faculty and administration consult overseas on nonteaching projects with higher educational institutions, other organizations, and governments. The latest provides four years of Capilano support for curriculum development with the University of Ho Chi Minh City. It involves 10 faculty and administrators in three areas particularly, i.e. business, distance education, and women's studies.

Previous projects included a dean on leave to assist a two-year college in Abu Dhabi and a psychologist working with a ministry in Thailand on public policy toward AIDS. Capilano faculty from business, tourism, media arts, and studio arts have been working with the Rajamangala Institute of Technology in Bangkok for eight years. Faculty and administrators from the Institute have been visiting the Capilano campus as well as Capilano counterparts serving as consultants in Thailand. Such exchanges are also a mainstay of Capilano's technical assistance with the China Management Training Center for Chengdu, China. This college trains teachers of business management and, since 1985, twenty of its personnel have exchanged visits with their Capilano counterparts.

There is always a project in operation. To Capilano's president, these projects "are what move the institution as a whole towards a realization of how global our village has become. For administrators who want to internationalize their institutions, this approach of getting administrators and faculty 'into the field' is a strategic imperative."

Asia Pacific Management Cooperative Program
For students who have already completed an undergraduate degree, the Asia Pacific Management Cooperative Program offers a post baccalaureate diploma. The course of study covers the language, culture, history, and current economic-political system of a country in Asia. The program also requires courses in Economics and International Business. After an intensive nine-month academic program at Capilano, students spend a minimum of one year gaining work experience as professional management trainees in the Asian country they have selected as their country of focus. Each year the program accepts a maximum of thirty-two students from about 500-600 applications on average.

The program originated in the deliberations of a committee convened in the early 1980s by the then dean of Student and

Instructional Services Douglas Jardine. He is now Capilano's president. The five to six person faculty-administrator committee was charged with designing an international education plan. The current program manager of the Asia Pacific Management Cooperative Program, Barbara Hankin, was on this committee. She was chair of the Humanities Division at the time and taught German. She had extensive travel-study experience and in her career had worked with international students.

The committee had to plan at a time of diminishing resources. The 1982 recession in Canada prompted Capilano to systematically search for a new educational niche capable of bringing outside financing into the institution. Both the governments of British Columbia and Canada were interested in developing programs which would enhance their competitive positions in the rapidly growing international economy. The international cooperative program would accomplish this goal both educationally and through overseas networking. It also fit into the two-year college's emphasis on practical and applied education. The program's curriculum would be designed in consultation with businesspersons in Canada and Asia.

As described in the Capilano College Calendar, the Asia Pacific Management Cooperative Program (APMCP) is full-time and "offers an intensive curriculum designed to serve the student in future international work." Each student takes Asia Pacific Perspectives for both semesters of coursework. Also, International Finance covers the whole academic year. Three other courses emphasize the business environment of Pacific Rim countries and are listed as International Business and Trade, International Marketing, and Business Strategies. Students take an Introduction to Economic Thought course during their first semester.

Thus far, the program's curriculum reflects a generalist approach. This initial decision by program planners has proven its worth by how well the students have done while on their postings in Asia during year two. Yet the rest of the coursework shows the need for in-depth training as well.

Three other courses required of all students are Directed Studies, Business Plans, and Management Seminars. The first of these allows students to choose a topic for independent study. It was designed specifically to accommodate those students who come to the program with greater knowledge and experience than others. The Management Seminars also were added to satisfy the demands of the same student group. The Business Plan credit enables students to gain practical experience by working on a supervised team project. Each team develops a marketing plan for a Vancouver-based company to do business in an Asian location.

Courses in an Asian language are required during the whole academic year. Students study the language of the country in which they will be applying for their placement during the program's second year. Language offerings cover Japanese, Mandarin Chinese, Bahasa Indonesian, and Thai. Students also must take a Cross Culture course and choose ten workshops out of many offered during the academic year.

After the formal course work at Capilano, students travel to their chosen country in Asia. Before their internship postings, they are required to take one to two months of intensive language study. This Intensive InCountry Language Immersion part of the program is funded separately by the Canadian government. Students receive their tuition, room, and board at a language training center costing approximately $25,000-30,000 a year for the whole group.

The intensive on-site language studies portion of the program began in 1990. It illustrates the fact that the program is continually being refined. Every year adjustments are made. As a result, several specialized components have been developed. The Business Plan, Directed Studies, and Workshop components for course credit demonstrate this flexibility.

As the program element allowing the greatest choice, students attend the workshops they think will provide the information and hands-on practice sessions most useful for them as individuals. Throughout the nine months of formal training, a variety of workshops are offered on team building, presentation skills, time management, and how to deal with the media, to list just a few. In the case of computer skills, an assessment of each student's capability is made at the beginning of the program with workshops planned as needed.

For two weeks in May, before leaving Canada, all students take the noncredit Career Planning Workshop. Each year this program component has been strengthened and expanded. It demonstrates again how much fine tuning the Asia Pacific Management Cooperative Program receives. Activities during the two weeks include INTERNET training and other practical instruction about the international information highway. Students also refine their business writing skills. The 1994 edition of the career workshop introduced a "how to run a business" simulation. Student response to this latest activity was overwhelmingly positive according to the program's administrators.

The addition of a final comprehensive examination is illustrative of the ongoing adjustments made in the program each year. The team's managers and instructors know that students will be faced with the rigors of working effectively in a completely different society. Therefore the examination is integrative; it requires the students to respond to a case study situation. They have three hours to write, incorporating both business and cultural information into their answer. They are told the issue in advance but not the specific country. Two of the program's instructors assign the grade with a third called in to resolve any differences. This is the same process used for grading the individual research papers.

Preparing for reentry into Canada is as important as preparing for and working through the work placement in Asia. The annual week-long midterm conference held in a Southeast Asian country is an important opportunity for the students to reassess their career and personal plans. The presence of employers, program alumni, Canadian and foreign government officials, and Capilano faculty and administrators, operating with a preset agenda, make the conference an effective think-tank experience. Each student gives an in-depth oral presentation on her/his work placement; guests provide lectures and panel sessions; and there is specific attention directed towards having the students visualize their careers and their personal development. An often overlooked yet important matter which is specifically addressed is the cultural shock upon returning to Canada.

From the program's beginning in 1987 until 1990, both the academic and cooperative components were coordinated by one person, Robert Bagshaw. He had been a counsellor at the college and had an undergraduate degree in business. In recognition that this was entirely too much work for one person, in 1990 the two responsibilities were divided. Bagshaw retained internship responsibilities, and Barbara Hankin became the academic manager.

Hankin has a half-time release from teaching which means she teaches four courses during the academic year. Her relevant professional experience includes a semester of travel in Asia in the late 1980s. Since the program's initiation, its administrators have reported to Jon Jessiman, the dean of Student and Instructional Services and head of the International Office. He has a law degree and twenty years experience in this field as well as a doctorate from the University of London.

In 1993 Bagshaw took a well earned sabbatical and Laurie Grant from outside the college was hired as coop manager. Her prior experience includes three years with a Canadian manufacturer in Japan. Then she moved back to Canada and was the Asian trade advisor for the Canadian Manufacturing Association before taking the position at Capilano.

As coop manager, Grant makes a two-month trip to Asia twice a year. Keeping in touch with both employers and students in their postings has proven a necessary part of program administration. Part of her discussions with potential and participating employers asks for their input. She wants to know how the program can prove more useful to the company or government agency. Yet the four months away from the campus means the coop manager can provide less support for the first year students as they prepare their job search plans.

While overseas, the coop manager has an evaluative personal interview with interning students. In addition, both students and their supervisors send written evaluations back to Capilano.

In 1994, students were working in twenty-two cities located in eleven countries including Vietnam, Korea, and Malaysia. There are a variety of placements with governments, small- to medium-sized companies, and multinationals. The smaller firms are preferred since students potentially can learn more about the whole operation. Yet presently multinational employers predominate. All trainees earn a salary. Since the program has gone on for several years, there are many repeating internships. Coop Manager Grant is using her Asian connections in trying to secure new posting possibilities. She is emphasizing private sector placements.

Lining up new positions is not an easy task. The program asks a great deal of employers. They must provide salaries plus the time it takes to train the new employee. Program alumni with jobs in Asia are becoming helpful in finding new placements. Systematically developing an alumni network has become the responsibility of the coop manager. By 1994, the program has over 200 graduates with about 65 percent still working in Asia.

Language training is an important element in the success of the cooperative part of the program. While a few employers want the students to begin work right away, most want them to take the intensive two months of language instruction upon arriving in Asia. This follows the eight hours a week of course work the students have taken during their nine months at Capilano. The program aims to prepare students through the intermediate level before they leave Canada.

The identification of postings and application process are treated as a job search. Each student develops a professional job search file including a resume, information on leads, cover letters, writing samples, and letters of recommendation. Grant teaches a course on coop preparation. Part of her material originates with discussions she has had with employers in Asia. Also, many speakers are invited to class sessions.

To strengthen the perception that the job search process is real, the element of competition is introduced. Four or five students apply for each posting. Grant sends a letter on behalf of each student. In most cases, the applicants are interviewed in Canada by a representative of the company or an official of the consulate of the relevant country. It is rare that students find their own postings but this does happen upon occasion.

The Asia Pacific Management Cooperative Program costs about one million Canadian dollars annually. The Canadian International Development Agency provides around one quarter of this sum. This federal government funding is supplemented by another Canadian government agency, the Asia Pacific Foundation, which grants the $40,000-50,000 it takes to pay for the two months of intensive language training in Asia. Student fees generate substantial financing. They have been increased from about $1,000 originally to $3,700 in 1994. The second year's tuition is lower, at $900. The rest of the budget, about $260,000, comes from the British Columbian provincial government. Capilano College contributes the program overhead, i.e., space, student services, and other logistical support.

Close to 95 percent of the program's graduates find relevant employment. As noted previously, about 60 percent are working in Asia. Most of the rest are with companies in Canada engaged in international business. Some have careers in the public sector with a few in CIDA itself, the Canadian International Development Agency.

Since the program operates at the graduate level, some of its faculty are hired on a part-time basis from outside the college. The International Finance course, for example, is taught by a banker. He uses the *Far Eastern Economic Review* as one source of information to introduce a sense of authenticity. Yet Capilano full-time faculty are important to the program. They provide all the instruction on Asian Perspectives, culture, and languages.

The CANASEAN program mentioned in the first paragraphs of this case study is not a spin-off of the Asia Pacific Management Cooperative Program. In fact CANASEAN predates the international cooperative program by several years. It has a separate history since it originated in Capilano's Department of Business Administration and not from the deliberations of the campuswide committee which developed the cooperative program. Yet the form CANASEAN had taken by the early 1990s reflects an educational approach similar to that used successfully by the Asia Pacific Management Cooperative Program. CANASEAN deserves description because it offers a replicable model for training young managers from overseas.

CANASEAN—International Entrepreneurial Program
The first activity using CANASEAN as the program title was initiated by Capilano's Business faculty in 1984. It consisted of a six-week series of visitations to Canadian companies by relatively high-level managers from Asian countries. The idea was to foster trade relations between firms in Canada and businesses or governments in Asia. Activities included lectures, seminars, field trips, and on-the-job observation as well as pairing ASEAN entrepreneurs with Canadian counterparts.

In 1989 the Manager Program was added. It marked a substantial change in emphasis from senior business and government managers to younger ones. The program objective shifted as well. Fostering trade yielded to training managers who were chosen because of their future promise. By 1993, this Manager Program had become the only CANASEAN activity Capilano carried out because the Canadian government had suspended funding for the senior executive program.

In 1989 Capilano hired Ed Wong from the business community to direct the CANASEAN Program. After some discussion weighing the relative merits of a four- or six-month program, the four-month option was selected in 1990 because it fit with Capilano's semester schedule. Training the young Asian managers takes from mid-August to mid-December.

Wong selects applicants from the ASEAN countries plus Vietnam and China based on personal interviews. He travels through Asia promoting the program and interviewing potential participants about four weeks a year. Ten or so mid-level managers are selected by the college from a group of candidates who must meet the following general criteria: They must speak English well, be twenty-five to thirty-five years of age, been employed by their sponsoring organization for at least five years, and, in most cases, receive full pay from their employers while in the program.

In the interview, Wong looks for desirable personal traits, such as openness to new learning. In accepting people he also creates a balanced group. Not only must various countries be represented, with command as well as market economies. But gender and employer characteristics are taken into consideration. Participants come from corporations big and small as well as government agencies and sometimes private organizations. Over the years groups have reflected about a sixty—forty private to government split. Approximately 50 percent each year are women.

The program's first month is divided into three sections. The first takes two weeks and invites speakers to discuss Canada and its business culture. Also participants are oriented into living in Canada. They engage in banking, shopping, learning to cook for themselves, taking public transportation, doing their own laundry. In some cases this is the first time in their lives they have been responsible for life's logistics. Participants live near the college in a motel with cooking facilities.

The third week Ed Wong leads more intensive sessions on Canadian business practices. The third section occurs during the fourth week when several Capilano faculty explain Canada's political system, history, society, and business management practices.

During CANSEAN's next six weeks, participants go through a rigorous program with several educational objectives, i.e., improving verbal English skills as well as deepening their knowledge of Canadian culture and business. The day begins with intensive morning briefings from Canadian government officials and private businesspersons. Many of the presenters are senior executives who focus on economic and business issues facing Canada.

Every afternoon Wong and others facilitate discussions of what the morning's speakers had to say. Participants are asked at random to summarize the points made. This process provides a "true test" not only of content information but of developing English language skills and cultural understanding. Also during these sessions, participants are asked how the morning's topics relate to issues in their own countries. This enables the young managers to discuss in English subjects they know well. The process trains them to think comparatively, a useful trait for people whose professional careers will be spent in some way dealing with people from many societies. Also, during the discussions information is shared about the business environment in each other's countries. If the morning speaker were from fisheries, for example, the afternoon's comparative discussion of this sector would appraise participants of its economic potential in each country represented as well as of its production and marketing in Canada.

During this six week training period, each participant must give the first of two public lectures to Vancouver's business community. Called ASEAN Week One, the trainees must choose a business topic, preferably one they know well. This enables them to extol their companies or agencies as well as to enlighten their audience as to economic realities in their countries. Such a requirement develops formal presentation skills using English, something they most likely will have to do in their future careers. Since the Canadian government provides most of the funding for the CANASEAN program, the lecture series gives at least something back to the Canadian taxpayer.

A field trip to Victoria culminates the six weeks of training. The participants visit British Columbia's government departments to discuss economic issues. The ombudsman's office and provincial legislature prove particularly instructive since often they, or their actual function, are new in the participants' experience.

A four week internship follows the Victoria visit. Participants are hosted by a private business, government agency, or other organization where the work is comparable to the trainee's occupation back home.

A succession of activities, each lasting for a few days, completes the four month program. After the internship, participants are back on campus for debriefing discussions and to give their second public lecture. This time they choose more general "soft topics," such as daily life in their country. These sessions are called ASEAN Week Two.

Then a second field trip is organized, this time to a small lumber town in rural British Columbia. Here participants learn about another aspect of Canadian life. They also visit with native Canadians. During this part of the program, subsistence and primary commodity development issues are discussed instead of growth and Canada's industrialized economy, which had been the focus thus far. Some of the grassroots development issues presented during these few days prove particularly relevant to problems in the participants' countries.

The program moves back to campus for more debriefing discussions and a grand finale. Held in a hotel ballroom in downtown Vancouver, about eighty people come to a formal luncheon which ends the program's activities. Decorations include flags from each country and help create a gala event environment. Senior political and business personalities attend and speeches are made. In the past the British Columbia's Premier and the head of the Canadian International Development Agency have figured prominently in the proceedings.

The Canadian International Development Agency provides a majority of CANASEAN's funding, upwards from $200,000 a year, but the Provincial Education Ministry also provides an annual grant. This includes the director's salary and that of his 80-percent-time assistant. The director's administrative reporting line is the same as that for the Asia Pacific Management Cooperative Program, to the dean of Student and Instructional Services and head of the International Office, Jon Jessiman. The dean also has responsibilities for eighteen other international programs and projects conducted by the college.

Issues and Answers

The discussion now returns to the Asia Pacific Management Cooperative Program. The need to "upgrade" course content has presented the major ongoing issue. In its eight years of operation, the program has attracted very qualified students, many with baccalaureate degrees in business. This created a student demand for some advanced business courses, for example in management. Yet this perceived need to upgrade instruction had to be balanced with the fact that most students reported learning from the "back to basics" approach used during the first semester, especially in the Introduction to Economic Thought course.

The upgrade issue arises also because of the preference given to people with prior work experience. Students with more experience are favored by Asian employers who want older manager trainees. This practice is good from Canada's point of view as well since more mature workers can put their new learning into effect quicker upon their return. This preference has been adopted in participant selection since the applicant pool for this program is large.

Additions have been made to the curriculum in response to the student demand for more in-depth content. The Management Seminars, Directed Studies, and Business Plan have been added. In extreme cases, exceptionally well prepared students are advised not to come during the program's first few weeks. As of 1994, the need to upgrade continues, this time in the area of International Finance. Discussions are ongoing whether or not to offer two levels of this course.

In more recent years students have had greater overseas travel experience. Thus the Asian courses are being upgraded as well. Also contributing to this need is the fact that colleges and universities are offering more Asian courses at the undergraduate level. Therefore some of the students in the program have prior knowledge about this part of the world. This situation exists in the area of computer training as well. In response, a variety of computer skills workshops have been added.

Another issue arises from the fact that about one-quarter of the program's faculty must be hired from outside Capilano. Since the international cooperative program is designed to prepare students for real work experiences, it engages specialists from Vancouver's international business community as part-time faculty. Yet the use of such faculty has created two difficulties. In the first place, part-time faculty have some protection from being fired since Capilano faculty enjoy substantial job security, requiring repeated unsatisfactory evaluations before they can be "released." In one case this presented a problem and, instead of going through the extensive evaluation process, the program managers waited until the part-time instructor decided to move on voluntarily. In another case, persuasion by the dean expedited the departure of a less-than-satisfactory instructor.

The second difficulty arising from the use of part-time faculty involves the need for coordinating the material in various courses in such an intensive program. Employing various instructors who have other occupations makes it difficult for them to meet and compare their course content. In answer to this situation, program planning meetings have been emphasized in recent years. Also, most of the instructors have been with the program over time and have come to know the topics covered in other courses. In an additional attempt to strengthen the program's curriculum, a new business faculty member was hired in 1993. His background includes service as the Vice President of the Canadian Manufacturers' Association as well as teaching experience. One-half of his course load is devoted to the international cooperative program.

Another issue is less precise but may prove important to Canadian competiveness in the long run. A majority of the work placement postings are with Asian companies. Against this, some sentiment exists among college faculty and administration that the program should be closer to the Canadian business community. Unfortunately, the Canadian business community often does not recognize that cultural and language proficiency is part of gaining a competitive edge in the global marketplace. If the college could entice more Canadian companies to be involved with the program, perhaps it would lead them to focus more attention on their business possibilities in Asia.

Student demand for placements more specific to their career plans has created an issue. This occurs in spite of the fact that they are reminded that getting experience from a particular kind of posting is not the point of the program. The coop manager does not run a placement agency. Experience in Asia is the educational objective and students must keep this in mind when they do not land the job they wanted initially.

Yet the felt need of students to begin building their careers as well as having a cultural business experience is a reality. The job search files are part of the answer to this situation. Such professionalism also assists in responding to pressure from employers who want their interns to be useful from the beginning of their posting.

As originally envisioned, the program was to attract applicants sponsored by their present Canadian employers who would pay the program's fees. Over the years, less than 1 percent of the students have such support. Most come directly from a university or employment without corporate financial assistance. Program managers need time to market their product with Canadian companies.

This lack of time for significant program-related tasks is an issue for both the managers. In the case of the coop manager, having to travel overseas for three months presents a problem since it removes one major source of student information and support for long periods of time. One suggestion floated recently is to hire another person to provide either ongoing advice for students or the networking with companies and students in Asia. This is the subject of an experiment to take place during the 1994-95 academic year. The manager of the program's formal courses also has to divide her time since she must continue to teach German as well.

One issue is raised by students each year. They protest the amount of time spent on language instruction. Yet this is actually a pseudoissue since after they arrive at their postings they always express gratitude for the demanding language course work. This pattern of questioning followed by acceptance after experiencing an actual work setting also characterizes student reaction to the team aspect of the Business Plan course.

Lessons Learned

The following guidelines reflect the thinking of various administrators involved in the international cooperative program.

1. *Establish a functional administrative structure in the first place.* The Asia Pacific Management Cooperative Program was understaffed in the beginning. Leaving all academic and placement administration to one person meant several important tasks were not accomplished, such as data collection and evaluation.

2. *Develop general policies and procedural rules, write them down, and implement them.* Without clearly established, written processes set before issues arise, many students will insistently press their need for exceptions; for example, every year a few students want to defer their internships in Asia. They experience financial or other problems and so decide they cannot accept their postings immediately after their nine months of training at Capilano. This situation required the program's managers to develop policies and procedures to deal with such contingencies. The resulting administrative ruling allowed students to take time out of

the program but priority in the next year would be given to that year's group of students in locating placements. The students deferring their postings would have to apply for the positions that remained.

3. *Plan ahead.* Even though no plan can anticipate all issues, take the time before a program is initiated to establish structures, roles, and processes. Establishing clear lines of authority and procedures provides the structure needed to solve problems as they arise.

4. *Invest the time and expense in developing relationships with employers well before the program begins.* This will result in smoother handling of the inevitable problems arising when students experience the stress of having to learn a new job in a new culture using a new language.

5. *Accept only the highest caliber students.* The international management cooperative program makes extraordinary demands of its students.

6. *Realistically portray the cooperative experience to students.* Provide them with as much first-hand information as possible in explaining what they will encounter in their internships.

7. *Involve the private sector as partners not only in developing the program but in its administration.* The program's success depends on its practical preparation of students for the workforce. The academic courses, language training, and cooperative experiences must relate directly to what managers actually do.

8. *Hire full-time administrators and faculty.* Such an intensive program requires undivided attention and systematic instructional coordination.

The success of the Asia Pacific Management Cooperative Program may be attributed to the dynamic nature and competence of key faculty and administrators. Also, judging from the number of applications, the program's objectives and methodologies provide a response to a real educational need. Substantial financial support from the British Columbian and Canadian governments must be noted as well. Lastly, the quality of the students should be included in this list of factors contributing to the program's viability.

Davidson College

Sponsoring Individual Student International Projects

Founded in 1837, Davidson nourishes its image as a quality liberal arts college with a long history and noteworthy graduates. The college, and the small town in which it is located, were named after a Revolutionary War general who died in battle. His son donated the land.

Since 1985, Davidson has sponsored the Dean Rusk Program, named after one of the college's more famous graduates, class of 1931, the secretary of state under both Presidents Kennedy and Johnson. The program was established to "give each student, first, an informed awareness of our whole planet, and second, direct knowledge of at least one foreign area," according to the Davidson catalog.

Among several international education activities, the program has provided grants to students each summer and fall to fund their own research projects or other international activities. On average, about thirty grants are awarded annually in amounts ranging from a few hundred to over two thousand dollars. Students have studied topics of their own interest in virtually every part of the world; for example, a biology major surveyed insects and spiders in Kakamega, a district in western Kenya. An economics major from Ethiopia experienced firsthand economic dislocations in the Soviet Union, while another student went to Egypt to observe and report on Islamic resurgence and Western ideas as reflected in contemporary Egyptian art. Students also engage in other worthwhile learning activities, such as an internship at the U.S. Mission to NATO in Brussels.

Some other colleges and universities provide support for individual student overseas projects, generally after previous study abroad experience. Yet at Davidson this focus was established as central to the Dean Rusk Program from its beginning.

This distinctive, individualized, undergraduate international education program fits the Davidson emphasis on a selective student body with a high percentage of graduates going on to professional or graduate school. The college reports this figure at 70 percent or more. Most departments have honors programs and, for many, a thesis is required. Students can use the Dean Rusk Program to help fund their research for this study.

The Davidson campus lies in one of North Carolina's richest and fastest growing counties. Within a half-hour drive on the interstate west of Charlotte, Davidson's large, many columned, neoclassical brick buildings mix with its nineteenth-century houses to project a traditional assurance. The main hall has the college seal and motto sculptured in stone over three stories high above the entrance. The motto, inscribed in Latin and evoking Davidson's roots in the American Revolution, means, "Let Learning Be Cherished Where Liberty Has Arisen."

Until 1972, Davidson operated as an undergraduate college for men. It became coeducational in that year and since then student numbers have grown steadily. Current plans call for a leveling off at 1,600 by the late 1990s, although in 1994 the number was already 1,550. Full-time faculty number 128. The college has retained an affiliation with the Presbyterian Church.

Campus Context
Davidson's curriculum reflects a choice of depth over breadth. International courses remain in the traditional disciplines since there are no interdisciplinary majors, except through the Center for Interdisciplinary Studies, and the college offers no minors. Music Department courses include World Music and Philosophy offers Chinese Philosophy. These join Asian Art and the Economics of South Asia in the relevant departments. Anthropology courses cover Africa and Asia, and the Religion Department lists five courses on Asia. History and Political Science carry many of Davidson's international offerings with history having at least one course on all of the major world regions. Many of these courses are listed also in the South Asian Studies Program. This is not a major, a minor, or a concentration.

The college does have an International Studies Concentration. Students must apply, take six international courses, demonstrate language proficiency "at a level significantly above that required for graduation," participate in a summer, semester, or year-long overseas program, and submit a "reflective and substantial paper based on the experience abroad to the chair of the International Education Committee." Participation is high; for example, in 1991, thirty students graduated with an International Studies Concentration.

One noteworthy characteristic of the Davidson curriculum may be designated by some as "international" in a broad historical sense. The college has a strong Classical Studies Department offering Latin, Greek, Sanskrit and many courses on the ancient world in Europe and Asia.

As another sidenote, the catalog lists nine Military Studies courses which together constitute the Army ROTC program. Three of these carry Davidson credit.

Davidson offers majors in French, German, and Spanish with more than the usual number of courses in each department. Several courses in Russian are also available including one at the 400 level. Yet Russian is not a freestanding major. Students wanting a Russian major can apply at the Center for Interdisciplinary Studies.

This Center also provides the means for students to create multidisciplinary majors. The areas listed as examples in a Davidson brochure are all international: Comparative Literature, International Relations, Third World/Developing Countries Studies, International Political Economy, Global Issues.

Davidson also offers at least fourteen languages using a self-instructional methodology. Subject to the availability of tutors, credit through the intermediate level is available for such a variety of languages as Dutch, Chinese, Arabic, Japanese, Italian, and Urdu, among many others.

These self-instructional courses cannot fulfill Davidson's foreign language graduation requirement. Students must take or test out of one of the college's four main languages through the first course at the Intermediate level. In addition, a Cultural Diversity course is required dealing with "societies or cultures which differ from that of the United States or Europe."

Around 40 to 50 percent of Davidson graduates have had an overseas experience. Of the 367 graduates in 1993, 177, or 48 percent, had participated in a summer, semester, or year-long program. About 30 to 40 percent of those going overseas choose a non-Davidson program. The Office for Study Abroad has a faculty coordinator who teaches for one third of his time in the French Department. He has a half-time assistant, the associate coordinator.

The college has several of its own programs. Students may choose to spend a semester in India, Spain, or travelling in the lands of classical antiquity, namely Turkey, Greece, Italy, and southern France. Also they can study art history in France or Italy. Summer programs in Guadalajara, Mexico, and in Cambridge, United Kingdom, are also available. As a member of the American Collegiate Consortium for East-West Cultural and Academic Exchange, Davidson hosts two students from Russia and sends its own there for a full year. Also, the college has supported full year programs in Wurzburg, Germany and Montpelier, France since 1964. Some of Davidson's programs are administered by a faculty director in the relevant department. Others are organized by the Study Abroad Program's personnel.

This major involvement by the academic departments extends also to partnerships with U.S. brokering organizations; for instance, the Biology Department has a affiliation with the School for Field Studies in Massachusetts and sent fourteen students on their programs during the 1992-93 academic year.

In 1994, sixty-five international students attended Davidson, about 3.5 percent of the student body. They are advised by the assistant dean for international students and Bonner scholars, who reports to the vice president for student life and dean of students. Parenthetically, Bonner scholars are U.S. students who receive financial aid from the Corella and Bertram F. Bonner Foundation in Princeton, New Jersey, in exchange for ten hours of service per week. Overseas service projects can be included.

Most international students are recipients of Davidson financial aid. They come from several countries with none predominating. The most represented world regions are Europe, both West and East, Northeast Asia, and South Asia.

In the 1991-92 annual report of the Dean Rusk Program an international student speakers project is mentioned. It states that over seventy-five students, including many U.S. students with study abroad experience, spoke to local schools, churches, and community groups on international topics during the academic year.

The Dean Rusk Program funds a share of the college's international co-curricular, faculty development, and outreach activities. During the 1991-92 academic year, for example, the Rusk Program sponsored campus visits of over sixty speakers. This level of activity is maintained annually. Ambassadors, academics, novelists, journalists, performing artists, political leaders from many countries, in short, every category of international specialist has been represented over the years.

As for faculty development in international education, the Dean Rusk Program funds around three or four faculty projects each year. This financing of research or paper presentations at international conferences augments the available discipline-specific funds. It thus provides an incentive for faculty to emphasize the international dimensions of their fields.

The Dean Rusk Program also has engaged in outreach activities. In 1992, thirty five high school teachers from eight states in the U.S. southeast attended a Summer Institute at Davidson. Organized by the Dean Rusk Program, the week long conference provided information and pedagogical materials about the areas where Russian, Japanese, Chinese and Arabic are spoken. In 1993 the program, in cooperation with the Education and French Departments, sponsored a Summer Institute for high school teachers of French. The State Department of Public Instruction offered North Carolina teacher certificate renewal credits for the one week of intensive training. Another institute for high school language teachers is planned for 1994, funded by the Knight Foundation.

An additional activity of the Dean Rusk Program combines its co-curricular and outreach functions. The Program sponsors conferences bringing to campus distinguished speakers on major international topics. Funded by a quarter of a million dollar endowment donated by the NationsBank of Charlotte, formerly the NCNB Corporation, the series of annual conferences began in 1988 and provided information on "World Hunger: Responsibility and Resolution," "Gorbachev's Soviet Union: Reform or Revolution?" "Toward a Healthy Environment: Preservation, Development, Restoration," "America's Place in the New International Order," and "Conscience and Foreign Policy." Usually from fifty to over 200 people attend each session. Substantial books summarizing the proceedings of some conferences have been published.

Origin of the Dean Rusk Program
During the late 1970s, Davidson's President and a group of alumni in Atlanta, Georgia began conversations about starting a development fund to pay for some tribute in the name of Dean Rusk at the college. He had voiced the opinion that he "didn't need another tombstone." This focussed planning discussions on an ongoing, living program. It was understood that whatever was created should model a major international education initiative.

An endowment of over one million dollars was raised for a comprehensive, multidimensional program. This initial financing has served to attract additional donations. For visibility, credibility, and useful contacts, the decision was made to hire a director with experience as a high-level diplomat who also possessed solid academic credentials.

Dr. Jack Perry met these qualifications. He had earned a doctorate in Soviet Studies from Columbia University while continuing a long Foreign Service career. This culminated in his appointment as ambassador to Bulgaria from 1979 to 1981. Upon his retirement, he became the John C. West Professor of Government and International Studies at The Citadel. Thus, he added teaching and publishing to his distinguished public service experience. In the summer of 1985 he began his newest career as full-time director of Davidson's Dean Rusk Program.

Dean Rusk Program—Student Grants
This program's potential for producing a life-changing experience is reflected in the following statement by a senior history

major. He received a Rusk grant to spend three weeks during the summer of 1991 working with the Black Lawyers Association of South Africa, and is now at the New York University School of Law.

> I worked at the Black Lawyers Association for two and a half weeks before the trial workshops began. Spending the early part of each day editing reports or articles for the next *African Law Review* gave me insight into the political questions of the time and the reactions of the black professional class.
>
> When we traveled teaching trial advocacy workshops, I discovered an element of the legal profession that I had never known before. It occurred to me that with the right combination of skill, tenacity, and integrity, that profession can made people's lives better. I want to do that.

This, and numerous other testimonials taken from student reports, reveal several noteworthy aspects to the Student Grants part of the Dean Rusk Program. First, they emphasize direct interaction between the students and local people. Second, all reflect a major impact on the lives of the student participants. Third, the program has funded great diversity both in activities and locations.

Program staff estimate that about one-third of the grants are awarded for individual projects, such as the one alluded to in the above quote. That student had accompanied a civil rights attorney, the father of a good friend, who had gone to South African for five previous summers to conduct workshops on trial skills for black lawyers and law students. Such personal networking and individual project design comprises the first category of student grant recipients. Students often use their experience as the basis for academic work carrying Independent Study credit.

A second variety of student grants are awarded to students who need funding to participate in Davidson's study abroad programs, or those sponsored by other organizations; for example, one student used her grant to participate in a Middle East Student Study Tour organized by the University of Iowa. A third kind of grant recipient is a student who wants to attend institutions overseas, like studying Italian language and culture at the Centro Linguistico Italiano in Florence.

Students can apply for Rusk funding to engage in independent research for their senior thesis required by their major; for example, the student whose project in Mexico consisted of gathering information about and personally viewing the work of four of Mexico's most prominent painters in the modern era: Orozco, Rivera, Siqueiros, and Tamayo.

These examples illustrate one of the more significant characteristics of this Davidson program, i.e., it reinforces the college's emphasis on individual academic achievement. The Dean Rusk Program also fits neatly into the college calendar. Along with several Study Abroad options, the program assists in providing academically valid summer experiences since Davidson offers no courses on campus during this season.

The program has a Faculty Advisory Committee which makes the award decisions based on student applications. Six faculty are appointed by the individual who is both dean of the faculty and vice president for academic affairs, currently Robert C. Williams. Students submit one page essays and a budget. Since most students are known by various faculty, the application process does not require recommendations or personal interviews.

In 1987, the first summer student grants were awarded, only about eleven were made on a pilot basis to assess the program's feasibility. Since then, the numbers have been substantial, ranging from nineteen in 1990 to forty-four in 1991 to eighty-four in 1994. This last figure represents a doubling in the number of awards granted in 1993. From the first year, more students submitted proposals than were funded and, in 1993, the ratio of applicants to awards was two to one. In 1994 many more were funded than turned down because the available financing was spread thinner.

Independent projects are favored although the Faculty Advisory Committee balances this with other criteria. Academic substance counts; also, whether the student has sufficient previous overseas experience to carry out the proposed study. On the other hand, the Committee also attempts to select students who have little or no prior experience. They generally choose to participate in travel-study programs or attend institutions overseas. Funding students who need this first overseas experience is balanced with the goal of providing other students with the means to carry out projects on their own. All students must write reports about their experience upon returning to campus.

Three full-time positions staff the Dean Rusk Program with three work-study students assisting on a part-time basis. The director reports to the dean of the faculty and the vice president for academic affairs and supervises the work of a program coordinator and an intern given the title assistant to the director. This third position goes to a newly graduated student who works full time for one or two years after graduation. This is seen as a good preparation for other employment or graduate school. The Director teaches one course a year in the Political Science Department.

The vice president's budget pays Dean Rusk Program salaries while the Development and Alumni Programming offices finance its activities and handle the bookkeeping. Several special funds are used; for instance, the White Family Fund provides much of the financing for the Student Grants program. Each year the amount changes given other budgetary priorities in relation to how many projects are selected. Some years cuts are made in other Rusk Program budget lines, such as travel, to ensure funding for good student proposals. Annual reports show a substantial level of activity: In 1990, nineteen students participated requiring $26,650 in expenditures while in 1991, forty-four projects cost $37,000. The number dropped to twenty-nine plus eight Medical Internships in 1992, with the level of funding left unstated.

The 1992 data reflect one of the Student Grant program's significant spin-offs, Medical Volunteers in Developing Countries. The Dean Rusk office's 1990-91 Annual Report announces this new variation on individual student overseas projects. The Medical Volunteers Program places primarily premed students in medical facilities in a variety of locations in the Developing World. Two alumni, one a physician, initiated the idea and the special fund which finances it. A letter to all Davidson medical alumni produced a substantial list of possible sites.

Student interest has been high with nine students participating in the summer of 1992. Two went to Guatemala, four to Pakistan, and one each to Bolivia, India and Honduras. In 1993 eight students ventured overseas as medical volunteers, three to India, two to Cameroon, and one each to Jamaica, Haiti, and Thailand. According to the 1991-92 Annual Report, The Medical Volunteers Program "seeks to instill students with a concern for and commitment to the improvement of health care in developing countries."

Another of the Rusk Program's distinctive innovations has resulted in an extraordinarily high level of student involvement. The Student Advisory Committee meets twice a month and thinks of new activities, which is just one of its tasks. From its voluntary membership, the program's staff chooses an Executive Committee which plans and carries out ongoing functions as well as new ones.

Initially, the student committee informally discussed current international issues and built friendships as its primary objective. Soon, however, the students began to initiate programmatic ideas. Now it helps administer past student innovations, such as a photography contest for pictures taken while overseas, a game of International Jeopardy, and a monthly information sheet summarizing an international issue in the news. This digest of facts and perspectives on a specific topic is called the "Toilet Paper" because of where the brightly colored fliers are hung. These, and other activities, are coordinated by the Rusk Program's full-time intern.

The Student Advisory Committee also has planned and organized major academic events. Several times over the years it has sponsored several days of speakers and events on a certain theme; for example, in the spring of 1990 a Central America Week was held, timed to coincide with the Nicaraguan elections. The students invited speakers with varying points of view, including a Guatemalan refugee, a Panamanian publisher in exile, a former Sandinista turned contra, and a Johns Hopkins professor. As with other conferences organized and financed through the Dean Rusk Program, Davidson professors served prominently as presenters.

As one of the Committee's newest and most popular ideas, international study breaks have attracted significant participation. They are offered throughout the semester and the Rusk Program provides refreshments, ice cream for example. Also some activity is planned, an international slide show or presentation by a study abroad student.

Each year a Rusk Award is presented to one student who personifies the program's spirit and goals. At the Spring Convocation and Awards Ceremony a gift is presented, usually a very good atlas.

Issues and Answers

Over the years, no major problem has surfaced concerning the Student Grant Program. Two issues, however, have required an administrative response. The first involves parental concerns about security. If they worry that their daughter or son plans to spend the summer in a country perceived to have a potential for violence, the Rusk Program Director calls or writes a letter. His attitude is summed up by the comment, "I cannot do too much to reassure parents."

To respond with specificity to parents, the director talks to personnel in the relevant embassy as well as friends he has made over his career in the State Department. Specific quotes from these authoritative sources have proven effective.

The second issue emerged when international students began applying for grants to return to their own countries. A policy was established that their applications would be considered if they proposed a project in a location other than their homeland.

The Rusk Program has noteworthy experience administering additional international education activities. One of these involves bringing many visiting speakers to campus. This co-curriculum program has created issues of its own and the response may prove instructive. Since as many as eight or nine notable visitors may arrive in a month, many donating their time, adequately hosting them can become a burden.

Students have proven the key to providing hospitality for large numbers of guests. Each year, Rusk Program personnel update a list of student volunteers, their academic backgrounds, personal interests, and relevant logistical information, such as whether they have a car. They provide airport transportation and have proven eager to accompany visiting dignitaries during meals and on campus tours. Students often organize discussion groups and help with other special arrangements, such as formal dinners.

Another issue involves insuring adequate attendance at the presentations of visiting guests. Again, students have proven particularly enthusiastic and imaginative in publicizing these events. The most effective strategies have used brightly colored fliers with clever announcements. These are hung not only in general traffic areas, such as the Student Union, but in campus locations where students with a particular interest tend to congregate. Also, the Rusk Program Director sends personal notes to faculty when a speaker will be addressing a topic relevant to their field and interest.

Lessons Learned
The following recommendations for administering a multidimensional center such as the Dean Rusk Program are listed in order of their priority. Most noteworthy is the fact that the first and third suggestions involve the important role students can play. They not only provide a constant flow of vitality and willing workers; they are a renewable source of creative, new ideas.

1. *Organize a student committee.* The Dean Rusk Program's Student Advisory Committee, SAC, is open to anyone wanting to attend its bimonthly meetings regularly. This group has provided enthusiastic administrative assistance for the Program's office staff. The Student Committee's own innovations have created an exponential expansion in its work, some of which has been described previously. Thus an Executive Committee organizes SAC's activities, and subcommittees have been established; for example, one has the responsibility for hosting visiting speakers.
2. *Develop faculty support.* In various ways the Rusk Program interacts with faculty; for example, it includes Davidson faculty as speakers at the conferences it sponsors. Also the

Program funds the research each year of selected faculty. The Faculty Advisory Committee, with new members appointed each year by the vice president, provides the formal vehicle for faculty involvement. This Committee selects Student Grant recipients and designates the student who will receive the annual Rusk Award. In addition, the Rusk Program Director has an individual touch. His small account to host visiting speakers often provides a meal for guests of individual faculty. These scholars also serve as classroom resources.

3. *Engage students with programs specifically for them.* The Student Grants themselves illustrate the Rusk Program's key premise that international education activities should focus on students. Of all he does, the director is proudest of the Student Grant Program. Also, given the role of the Student Advisory Committee, he spends a great deal of time working with students. He often assists them in developing their individual career goals; for example, in using his Foreign Service contacts to set up internships. He also writes many letters of recommendation.

4. *Hire a recently graduated student as a full-time intern.* This position has worked extremely well for the Rusk Program in helping the Student Advisory Committee develop its activities as well as in general program administration.

5. *Nurture local businesses.* Many Charlotte area firms have a formal relationship as Corporate Affiliates of the Dean Rusk Program. As such, their key administrators are invited to Davidson events as special guests. The Director of the Rusk program meets with this group every month for breakfast in Charlotte. These events host a visiting speaker. Davidson's international activities have benefited from the fact that most of these corporations have a fund for community assistance.

6. *Invite diplomats to campus.* These people do not charge an honorarium yet can present an up-to-date summary of their country's positions. Too often overlooked, they love to get out of Washington D.C. for a few days, especially with their families. Cultivating embassy contacts also can

prove helpful on those rare occasions when visa problems arise.

7. *Employ former practioners in directing international education programs.* In the case of Davidson, the director has firmly established the Dean Rusk Program as a center of practical expertise. In addition, his academic credentials have allowed him to contribute by teaching. His personability and willingness to work with students has enabled the program to develop an extraordinarily high level of student involvement.

The Dean Rusk Program was initiated by Davidson's then president and a group of alumni. During the years since, it has provided international education with several distinct innovations. The director must be highlighted as a key factor in their success, as well as the willingness of alumni and other friends of Davidson to fund Rusk Program activities.

Earlham College

Enabling Cultural Learning with Ethnographic Projects

Earlham is one of a growing number of colleges and universities to have achieved both depth and breadth in its globalization process. This enviable situation has resulted from many years of symbiotic curriculum and overseas program development. As one illustration of the scale and scope of Earlham's commitment, the college is one of few where a substantial majority of its graduates have participated in off-campus programs, most in another cultural environment; this figure averages 65 percent of each graduating class. Global program development has evolved to the point where it is self-generating. This takeoff has been characterized by several refinements, among these a focus on improving learning in overseas programs and strengthening the articulation of on and off-campus education.

Earlham's study abroad programming began in the late 1950s and through the 1970s programs continued to expand, while following a traditional content and pedagogy. In the late 1970s, however, Earlham began to experiment with a new paradigm in program design, and in the 1980s and early 1990s this pedagogy was redefined and institutionalized. This key transition in programming began when a group of faculty from various disciplines who had led student programs overseas asked and answered several basic, interrelated questions: What do overseas programs have in common? What should be learned? How is it learned and what learning strategies would be effective? The short answer to these questions may be summarized by the phrase "the nature of cultural identity." Cultural content and skill ascription provide the common denominator of Earlham's overseas student programs. After making this decision, the faculty group engaged in long discussions about what pedagogical approach would best assure cultural learning as well as make it apparent and measurable. The faculty then adopted an ethnographic methodology.

Earlham College describes itself as an "independent Quaker institution" offering "an education program conducted under the care of the Society of Friends." Founded in 1847 to provide teachers for Quaker schools in Indiana, the college has "preserved and interpreted the best of Quaker traditions to serve contemporary students. Because Quakerism is egalitarian and open-minded, it works in harmony with an intellectual pursuit of truth." A liberal arts college, Earlham is attended by 1,150 students taught by about 102 full-time faculty.

Earlham College owns 800 acres at the edge of Richmond, Indiana, a town of approximately 40,000 people. The 200 acre main campus invites a stroll with its seemingly unending, well tended lawns, graced by trees of many varieties, and laced with walkways. These connect three story buildings of red brick and white trim. The oldest, the focus of a tree-lined central road, establishes the campus center. It has been refurbished into a dormitory, with administrative buildings set off to the side.

Past the main campus and from the crest of slight hill, the other 600 acres unfold. Woodlands as far as the eye can see to the right balance a view of suburban Richmond to the left. Athletic fields take up the foreground, including a horse jumping and showing ring, with an open field in the background dotted with horses whose grey, brown, and black shapes move slowly across the green landscape.

Earlham's peaceful, contemplative atmosphere echoes Quaker harmony, as noted in college brochures. The goal is to send students from this place into the world who "are well prepared for the future. They know how to evaluate situations and take action. The future will demand people who can face the unknown, make long-range assumptions, and adapt to constantly changing conditions with confidence and grace." As part of this objective, Earlham's statement of purpose highlights global studies and foreign languages. It is within this context that a group of faculty used their academic expertise and program experience to integrate an innovative, experiential teaching-learning strategy into their international off-campus programs.

Campus Context

The first two pages of Earlham's 1993-94 Curriculum Guide, called "Envisioning the Future," places global education at the core of the college mission. Providing "a great liberal arts education results from the interplay of several characteristics." These characteristics present a balanced approach to defining a liberal arts education: the college is dedicated to "strong traditional disciplinary offerings, which lead students to the best graduate and professional schools and to meaningful careers," as well as to using "classical texts of our own and other civilizations." At the same time, Earlham promises "opportunities to encounter interdisciplinary issues, so disciplines are seen as complementary tools for addressing real-world questions," and an "emphasis on global studies and foreign languages."

Its long history of international education is intertwined with Earlham's strong connection to Japan. The college initiated Japanese language classes in 1962 and an interdisciplinary Japanese Studies degree in 1972. Given the depth of faculty expertise, and the growing national focus on Japan, the Institute for Education on Japan was established in 1986. Along with its on-campus curriculum and three student programs in Japan, the Institute organizes several outreach programs for business, K-12 educators, and non-profit institutions.

Earlham takes pride in its long history of positive interactions with people from Japan and Japanese-Americans. In 1993, the college observed the 100th anniversary of the graduation of its first Japanese student. This is one illustration of the continuing exchange of people between Earlham and Japan which began in the late nineteenth century. Information and material about the college cites other noteworthy events: the college president from 1946 to 1957 had authored an ethnographic study of Japanese life; during World War II, an Earlham graduate serving as chaplain at Stanford University organized the sending of some Japanese-Americans to Earlham rather than to relocation camps.

The commitment to international education in general, and Japan Studies in particular, is reflected in Earlham's curriculum. Several relevant interdisciplinary majors complement departmental majors, i.e., African/African-American Studies, International Studies, Japanese Studies, and Peace and Global Studies.

The requirements for the International Studies major show the extent of campus capabilities in global/international education. Majors must complete at least two advanced courses in a language appropriate to their chosen geographic area of concentration. They also must study for at least a semester in another country and successfully pass not only a comprehensive examination, also required by several other majors, but a foreign language examination as well. Under exceptional circumstances, students may be invited to write a thesis instead of all or part of the comprehensive examination.

Earlham's program and major in Peace and Global Studies reflects the college's Quaker identity and commitment to peace education. A four-course introduction sequence demonstrates the dynamics of an interconnected world, focusing on specific issues such as world hunger, the global distribution of resources, human rights, and state terrorism. These courses, which also serve as introductory courses to the International Studies major, are Culture and Conflict (Sociology/Anthropology), Politics of Global Problems (Politics), Capitalism and Socialism (Economics), and Introduction to Philosophy: Ethics and World Food Policy (Philosophy). Off-campus programs in Northern Ireland and Jerusalem focus specifically on issues of peace and conflict.

The Department of Languages and Literatures provides full programs in French, German, Spanish, and Japanese, and all Earlham students are required to complete at least one year of a second language. Formal courses in Chinese are offered through the first year, with others available as Independent Studies. The culture and literature curriculum in Japanese is supplemented by such practical courses as Newspaper Reading and Readings in Japanese Culture. The department's listings also include several specialized courses, i.e., Linguistics, Sociolinguistics, Comparative Literature: Themes in Twentieth-Century World Literature, Theory and Practice of Translation, and Teaching English to Speakers of Other Languages. Earlham's program in Foreign Languages in the Curriculum provides students with opportunities to use and to apply foreign language skills in courses beyond the language classroom.

To begin their language study at Earlham, students may take what Earlham calls Super Language courses which have been offered since 1975. Available in the four main languages, these courses provide small groups of students intensive instruction for three hours a day, five days a week, which is two thirds of a term's credit load. Advanced students, usually following an international study experience, are able to apply their linguistic and cultural skills and earn a small salary as student instructors in Super Language classes and in the language laboratory. International language assistants—native speakers from the Japanese-, French-, German-, and Spanish-speaking worlds— enrich the Super classes as well.

International courses throughout the curriculum often reflect distinctive specializations; for example, Chemistry in Societal Context is taught as well as the usual Environmental Chemistry. Fine Art's Introduction to Art History is inherently multi-cultural, Biology has a Population and Community Ecology course which focuses primarily on Africa, Religion offers several courses on Eastern religions, and the Sociology/Anthropology Department has courses which cover Latin America and Africa-America as well as Japan. The college's long affiliation with Japan is reflected in several departmental offerings such as the Geography of Japan in Geology, Japanese Philosophical Thought in Philosophy, Families East and West in Psychology, and Japanese Culture and Society in Anthropology.

The English, History, Politics, and Economics Departments cover their usual range of international curriculum specializations, such as International Economics and International Relations, as well as distinctive individual courses not ordinarily offered at a small college. Comparative Literature in the English Department is not one course but several on Russia, the Middle East, and Africa. English also offers a War and Literature course. Courses in the History and Politics Departments reflect distinct specializations; for example, History lists four courses on Africa which differentiate East Africa and West Africa. The Politics Department's course depth includes Political Cultures as well as the Economic and Political

Development of the Pacific Rim. The Economics Department international curriculum contribution includes Introduction to Global Economy, and Introduction to Japanese Economy and Society.

The themes linking courses in several departments are also reflected in Earlham's study abroad programs list. Usually about 175 students a year venture overseas, virtually all as participants in one of Earlham's own fifteen programs. These last for a minimum of one term, or three months, while most also take a summer and a winter term adding up to six months. Two programs are almost a year long. Virtually all have homestays for at least part of the time and, except for the course taught by the Earlham faculty leader, host academics provide all instruction.

Earlham student groups go to Colombia, England, France, Germany/Austria, Jerusalem, Kenya, Northern Ireland, Spain and Vienna, which is designed specifically for students in the Concert Choir. Mexico hosts two programs, one for students with little or no prior knowledge of Spanish and one for students with more advanced language skills. Three separate programs travel to Japan: One emphasizes language and culture; a second provides opportunities for students to serve as English tutors and workers on a reforestation project; and a third for 11 months is administered by Earlham on behalf of the Great Lakes College Association (GLCA) and the Associated Colleges of the Midwest. Through the GLCA, Earlham students also have the opportunity to study in India, the Czech Republic, China, Scotland, Senegal, and Poland.

Two-thirds of Earlham's full-time faculty have led student groups overseas. This includes most of the college's natural scientists. The programs they led were not necessarily focused on natural science content nor on environmental studies, yet the courses they taught sought to relate the cultural context to areas of scientific interest. This illustrates campus-wide support for international education and the willingness of faculty to engage in global and multicultural education both on-campus and abroad.

Earlham's International Programs Office administers off-campus programs, including orientation and re-entry programs, international education grant projects, visiting international faculty activities, international student responsibilities, and several other specialized programs, i.e., the Wilderness and Southwest Field Studies Programs as well as the Institute for Education on Japan. Faculty with reduced teaching loads serve as directors of these program activities while International Programs Office personnel handle overall responsibilities.

Three full-time positions staff the office, i.e., a director, who reports to the provost and academic dean, an assistant director, and a secretary. Director Patty O'Maley holds a doctorate in Applied Linguistics, and two Master's degrees, one in English as a Second Language and a second in Latin American Studies. She speaks Spanish and her work experience includes an extended period overseas. In 1994 she had been at Earlham for 14 years, as Director since 1986. Assistant Director Kelley Lawson-Khalidi, an Earlham graduate, speaks French, has studied overseas, and has served as leader of the Peace Studies Program in Jerusalem. Both exude the high level of energy and enthusiasm as that evidenced by the faculty leaders in Earlham's global education process. All involved come alive when explaining how students grow personally as well as intellectually while participating in overseas programs.

The Assistant Director of the International Programs Office is responsible for advising international students and organizing the activities of international scholars. About fifty international students attend Earlham each year, some on scholarship. Four endowed funds are earmarked specifically to provide financial aid for international students.

From 1989 through 1995 Earlham hosted twenty-two visiting scholars. Virtually all teach in departments and interdisciplinary programs. Their other activities demonstrate how mutually reinforcing well developed international programs can be when administered through a central office. Almost all scholars have participated in an ongoing seminar with Earlham faculty on global issues and challenges. In addition to the usual campus-wide and in-class presentations, some international scholars have helped design orientations for off-campus student programs while others have helped organize the programs themselves. Another was featured in Earlham's major exhibit of Japanese Art. These examples reflect the fact that most scholars are drawn from Earlham's overseas program locations. Yet international faculty from other areas of the world have come as well, such as visiting professors from Catholic University in Lima, Peru and the University of Sarajevo in Bosnia-Hercegovina. Financing for specific scholars is provided by the Fulbright Program, institutional exchange agreements, and private foundation grants.

The yearly integration of several international scholars into Earlham's curriculum, the high percentage of faculty who have led study abroad programs, and the depth of the international curriculum itself, provide overwhelming evidence of the faculty's high level of expertise and the college's strong commitment to international education. This combination has generated a next stage in international curriculum refinement.

Two major grants in the late 1970s and 1980s helped Earlham begin the process of educational revitalization to develop a more integrated, globally focused curriculum. A third major grant from 1991-93 allowed the college to fine-tune its international education programming. With a grant funded by the National Endowment for the Humanities in 1979, the college began to modify and extend global issues into the existing language curriculum as well as to reinforce the continuation and development of language skills among faculty in the humanities in the social sciences. A second two-year grant from the U.S. Department of Education in 1980 had a dual, yet related purpose: to globalize the peace studies program into Peace and Global Studies, and to develop a new framework for off-campus study. This grant also produced an extensive credit bearing orientation for each off-campus program, an ethnographic project incorporated into all programs, and various ways to deal with the transition period following students' returning to campus.

The third major grant, funded from 1991-1993 by the U.S. Department of Education, allowed a group of Earlham faculty to study intensive Spanish on campus and in the off-campus study site in Mexico. In addition to language study, each faculty member carried out an ethnographic project from which course components were developed and incorporated across disciplines such as Biology, History, Religion, Physics, Philosophy, and English. This grant has given the college the opportunity to make further refinements in the ethnographic project, and the articulation of on- and off-campus education.

Ethnographic Projects

Every one of Earlham's overseas programs requires students to observe a lifestyle setting in another society, reflect on its cultural meaning with the assistance of a host informant, and incorporate the observations and analysis into a written report. An explanation of how Earlham faculty define "ethnographic" will clarify what the innovative projects require of students. The learning strategies summarized as ethnographic were chosen after long discussions by a group of Earlham faculty who had led groups of students overseas. Yet, several years later, there is still some unease in referring to them as "ethnographies;" for example, an Earlham anthropologist calls the student projects "field study components," or "studies in culture." Also, the director of the International Programs Office has used the phrase "cultural interaction projects" in speeches.

Ethnography has a precise meaning to an anthropologist. It refers to in-depth cultural studies resulting from long-term research, often taking years. The field work requires taking painstakingly detailed notes about the life of one village or cultural group. Therefore, some scholars have difficulty using the word "ethnographic" to refer to the fifteen-plus-page projects produced by Earlham undergraduates after a few weeks of part-time observation and participation.

Yet, in spite of their reservations, Earlham faculty decided to adopt and adapt ethnographic methods in their overseas programs. There are compelling reasons for selecting this instructional approach. First, ethnography has an academically sound conceptual basis as well as a well-defined, effective methodology. Even beginners can apply participant-observation techniques and produce some substantive, informative insights. Also, students learn skills to last a lifetime. Getting past superficial observations and facile comments to explanations with conceptual applicability can lead to successful and satisfying social interactions in one's own society as well others.

Systematic discussions by the faculty group, and its design of the ethnographic curriculum, were part of the Study Abroad Articulation Project, or SAAP as it came to be known. Funding for this project was provided by the U.S. Department of Education's Undergraduate International Studies and Foreign Language Program. Richard Jurasek, a professor of German and one of the SAAP faculty, provides a clear articulation of the cultural learning potential in study abroad programs:

> As a result of this work we now systematically teach about the nature of cultural identity and interaction and bring students to reflect on their cultural assumptions, values, and behavior. It is our basic working assumption that all monocultural people initially apprehend the world with a view that is bound and limited. No matter how globally oriented and cosmopolitan we all might think we are, each of us can make real progress in further refining what can be called perspective consciousness and empathetic understanding.[1]

Once cultural learning was recognized as the common denominator of overseas programs, the faculty group systematically compared what happens to students overseas with on-campus instruction. This analysis produced a long list of connections and parallels between the content and skills taught on campus with those learned in another country. A brief example is cited below, this one defining the relationship between Humanities instruction and learning about other cultures.

Culture learning off-campus	Humanities learning on-campus
To learn about other cultures is to learn about perceptual processes and one's own place in a cultural/perceptual system.	Reading requires cultivating the imagination so that one can explore other cultures from within. Reading also requires an honest awareness of one's own cultural context and ethnocentricity.[2]

In this way, SAAP's systematic analysis identified specific teaching objectives. It is evident that this pedagogical clarification process proved helpful because the specific concepts and skills it identified were applied directly to the ethnographic assignment. To illustrate, the phrase quoted above, "explore other cultures from within," is echoed in written explanations of the ethnography assignment given students; for example, students are told to keep in mind, "How do they (the observed) view their work within their society?" Also, "the more questions asked, the more likely the researcher will come to understand things from the point of view of the insiders."

The previous quotations are drawn from an extensive, detailed, highly useful manual prepared for faculty. It includes a well developed definition of ethnography as well as examples of its application in the form of a collection of materials prepared by faculty leaders of Earlham student groups. The materials explain the observing, interviewing, thinking and analysis skills needed to research and write ethnographic projects. They are replete with useful phrases, such as reminding students they will be, "not studying people but learning from people," "finding meaning in the patterns of behavior," the meaning that a "people's own culture gives to the action." Students should ask "not what do I see these people doing but what do these people see themselves doing." As an integral part of the observation process, students are told always to check and correct for their own reactions.

The following sample list of guidelines is compiled from instructions Earlham faculty give to their students as they work on their ethnographic projects:

— use people's own words
— detail is vital, so take notes with as many specifics as possible
— draw a diagram of the physical setting
— carefully note interaction patterns
— find out what people's own words mean culturally
— return to the same setting chosen for study several times and, the most important
— choose an informant from the society being studied, someone you feel comfortable with and can ask culturally sensitive questions getting candid answers in response

This last guideline for students is considered vital to carrying out a successful ethnographic project, so much so that one handout suggests selecting a project based on the informant's lifestyle.

Another equally well-designed and substantial manual has been prepared for faculty to use during the predeparture orientation. Exercises interpreting cultural events comprise the "Critical Incidents" section of the manual. Here are many handouts written by Earlham faculty, each briefly summarizing an actual situation that can arise while living in another society. Information of equal practicality is contained in the manual's other sections; namely, Intercultural Awareness, Expectations, Sample Schedules, Working with Groups, Journal (writing), and Culture Shock/Return.

Orientation meetings are held for ten weeks. Students meet once a week in their program groups under the direction of the faculty member who will serve as faculty leader. This person is assisted by either the director or assistant director of the International Programs Office. Students receive .2 academic credit based on the Earlham system of one credit per course. Faculty teach the orientation without compensation since it is considered part of their responsibilities as the program leader. The overseas program itself counts as one-third of the usual six courses taught annually by Earlham faculty.

The orientation introduces the skills needed to carry out ethnographic projects. During this predeparture phase, students do a mini-ethnographic study in the Richmond community to observe and culturally analyze a lifestyle situation. They visit school classrooms, churches, barber shops, laundromats, a mental hospital, a shoemaker, fire and police stations, among many other locations. Generally they are well received. This activity allows students to practice thinking through the cultural complexity of real life situations in this country before attempting such an analysis in another culture.

Each overseas program produces ethnographic projects as varied as daily life. The topics also exemplify the students' expertise, interests, and personalities, as demonstrated by the following partial list of projects completed in Mexico during 1993:

— indigenous musical instruments
— Mexican cooking
— herbs and a healer

— U.S. football in Mexico
— work in a government-sponsored daycare center
— base communities and liberation theology

Another sample project list is taken from the 1992 Kenya program:

— women's sales activities on village market days
— girl's training in the household (informal education)
— stories about monkeys
— a funeral in Kaimosi
— cows: care, beliefs, costs, functions
— dance traditions and practices
— effects of Earlham students on prices and availability of foods
— storytelling in host family
— agricultural practices
— young woman's death from abortion attempt

For each program, the ethnographic projects are part of the course taught by the Earlham faculty member. Therefore, individual faculty decide the amount of course time allotted to the projects and their percentage of the final grade. Five examples show how specific off-campus programs have incorporated the ethnographic assignment: Mexico, Kenya, Germany/Austria, Japan, and Northern Ireland.

The ethnographic project has been particularly successful in the program in Mexico. In addition to a series of lectures and readings on Mexican culture, the ethnographic project is approximately 50 percent of the work done for the Mexican Culture course, one of three academic courses given during the term program. The students build on the participant-observation skills introduced during the on-campus orientation. An important first step is for students to locate a contact person who will facilitate their participation in and study of a particular setting. This person will become an important teacher about his or her cultural world.

Students observe and begin being part of daily interactions in stores, schools, or families. After about five weeks preparation, they begin their own field work for ten to fifteen hours a week for four weeks. The faculty leader emphasizes that project research involves not just watching, but also participating and interacting in Spanish while working side by side with people in their setting. The final project report is written in Spanish. Other, in-class, academic work continues at the same time.

After four weeks of participant observation, another week is devoted to writing an ethnographic description of the setting. As a final step in the process, students make half-hour oral presentations to the entire group, in Spanish of course. As a frequent leader of student groups, Howard Lamson reports that, "having come to know their setting in a very personal way, these presentations reflect a kind of excitement and pride rarely seen in normal class presentations." He adds that students often reflect a real respect "for the people with whom they have shared many moments."

Briefer descriptions of how ethnographic projects are integrated into other Earlham programs demonstrate the assignment's pedagogical flexibility. In Kenya, a fifteen-week program, the ethnographic project is part of a course on People and Cultures of Kenya. The ethnographic portion of the program is a primary focus of the three-week homestay in rural western Kenya. During this time, students read an ethnography about Kenya and choose an aspect of daily life for their own ethnographies. The group meets for feedback sessions two evenings a week. The final projects are written and then presented to the group at the end of the program. An introduction to Swahili is part of the overall program, but instruction and the project are in English.

In one of the programs in Japan, students participate in local school life by serving as assistant English teachers in junior high schools three days a week for three months. The student ethnographies in this program revolve around an aspect of a student's experience in the schools. The formal presentation of the ethnographic work is a major part of the Multicultural Education Perspectives course. In the Germany/Austria program, a six-month experience, the ethnographic project is approximately 20 percent of the Culture Course. Students carry out their projects during the second half of the program when they are in Vienna and their language skills are more advanced. Projects have included investigating child care organizations, volunteering in a refugee service organization, participating in a bilingual preschool for immigrant children, and working with a local chapter of Greenpeace.

In other Earlham programs the ethnographic projects are part of a course on internship/field studies. One example of the way the ethnographic projects are incorporated into a field study is in Northern Ireland, where students participate in extensive work situations with agencies that do cross-community programming. At the same time, students are enrolled in a course called Conflict and Identity, which gives them the opportunity to reflect in a structured way and write about their work experiences.

The years of Earlham's experience in applying an ethnographic pedagogy has produced solid evidence of its benefits. In the first place, the student response has been overwhelmingly positive, especially upon completion of the assignment and returning to campus. In most cases, students exhibit the exhilaration resulting from having foregone the safety of passive classroom instruction and overcoming anxieties about interacting with new people in an unknown social environment. Each student becomes a bonafide expert on one aspect of the host society and produces an original work on her/his own. Projects can be very rewarding because the student probably knows more than practically anyone else what it is to be a milkman in Mexico, for example. In the words of one program administrator, "They design it; they own it."

Students enjoy being more than just casual visitors. They thrive on human contact and gain "an insight into people's lives." As expressed by an Earlham faculty member, students experience the "validation and acknowledgment that comes from an unblueprinted learning experience."

The project assignment enables students to meet the goal of learning cultural content. Not only does community experience focus students' attention, it moves them past superficial observations more quickly than programs without the ethnographic assignment. As expressed by Howard Lamson, an Earlham Spanish professor, "These projects have gradually become one of the main components of study abroad and have, in most cases, accomplished the objective of deepening students' insights into how people in their host culture experience their world."[3]

Lamson also points out another benefit of the projects. Interactions with host informants often lead to strong personal friendships.

> The relationships are mutually rewarding in so far as representatives of both cultures get to know each other on a very human, sharing level. When I returned to visit one site in July of 1990, the people there expressed to me how much they enjoyed having one of our students take a real interest in their lives and would warmly welcome others who would like to participate in their setting.[4]

It should be said that because of the campus orientation's practice projects, community-based learning reveals linkages between Richmond, Indiana and other places in the world.

Language learning also benefits from the ethnographic projects. They necessitate using language for more thoughtful communication with host country people than that needed for everyday interactions, such as purchasing items in the market. More meaningful conversation is satisfying and reflective of the way humans relate to each other. Learning languages through social interaction eliminates their abstractness. Languages are no longer "disembodied knowledge," in the phrase of an Earlham faculty member. Learning from cultural authenticity augments the authority of teacher and text. Multicultural education becomes holistic with human experience as the teacher and language as the technique.

One caveat worth noting: the projects generally are not examples of quality, polished writing. For practical reasons students must finish them before returning to the United States, as well as completing other academic work at the same time. While the projects virtually always reflect substantial cultural learning, their command of written language is not of the same constancy. Faculty leaders consider the process more important than the written product.

Issues and Answers

The decision to require ethnographic projects raised primarily process issues. Yet one content implication necessitated a conscious adjustment. In the case of the European programs especially, adopting an ethnographic approach caused a broadening redefinition of "culture;" for example, using ethnographic projects as a learning tool means students had to move from museums and classrooms into more varied social settings. Also, in the London program students now spend approximately six hours a week working in multiethnic social service agencies as well as taking three academic courses. The ethnographic project is based on experiences in the social service agencies and incorporated into the course taught by the faculty leader.

The ethnographic projects were not incorporated into faculty leaders' courses when they first were introduced. The half credit was earned separately from the program's other academic work. Therefore, students perceived the projects as added on, disconnected from the rest of the program. More debilitating, the faculty leaders were removed from direct responsibility since the Director of the International Programs Office was to grade the projects. Thus faculty, under the usual pressures created by U.S. student groups overseas, did not allot the time the projects needed.

After only one trial round, the projects became part of the courses taught by Earlham faculty. This mandated systematic faculty development because "I am not an anthropologist" summed up the faculty response. Grant financing paid for faculty development activities while the Director of the International Programs Office organized workshops and kept the process on track. She fulfilled a role distinct from that of the faculty, i.e. compiling relevant information, ensuring completion of curriculum handouts, producing the manuals.

Incorporating the ethnographic assignment into all Earlham's overseas programs created the issue of what amount of course time should be devoted to the projects and what percentage of the grade they should earn. Of course the prevailing faculty attitude was, "I can't fit another thing in." Complicating the discussion was the fact that faculty leading the programs changed from year to year.

The group responsible for developing the ethnographic curriculum responded by not mandating the amount of time and percentage of grade. Program leaders decide how to adapt the projects into their courses. This has produced much variation. A pattern has evolved, however, that when a faculty member is new to the ethnographic approach, the projects are assigned less time and grade weight. After seeing students come alive, and becoming more comfortable with the methodology, faculty have tended to allot more course time to the projects.

Over the years of shared program planning, faculty leading the same program have settled on a common pattern for assigning the ethnographic projects. Faculty leading the program in France, for example, used to assign the projects during the first half while in Nantes. The second half occurs in Paris. As a smaller city, Nantes was deemed to be less intimidating for students as they initiated community encounters. Soon the projects were assigned in Paris during the program's second half as faculty learned that students needed better language facility.

The issue of risk in all its dimensions was discussed during the curriculum planning process. Physically, students would be wandering about on their own in a location new to them. Psychologically, they risked failure because in order to research a successful project, they would have to find entry into a new culture, often using a new language. It was thought that some students could experience a debilitating level of anxiety. However, in practice, risk quickly became a nonissue. All students, even the shy ones, developed the contacts needed to complete their projects.

Not only students have benefited from the ethnographic projects. Many faculty have learned by researching the conceptual basis for ethnographic analysis. Some feel that adding variety to course assignments has made them better teachers. They have improved by developing helpful handouts and being better able to explain the ethnographic assignment. One faculty member emphasized that this attention to pedagogical strategies should not be taken for granted by faculty at other institutions perhaps thinking of applying an ethnographic approach. Students need thoughtful and clear preparation given the "elusive character" of writing "thick descriptions."

Lessons Learned

Earlham has become a laboratory, a place where faculty and administrators have experimented with new approaches in international education. Regarding the ethnographic projects, a consensus has developed at Earlham as to the importance of the following:

1. *Faculty initiation and ongoing support is essential.* Participating faculty members must make their own curriculum decisions, i.e., the design of the student training and debriefing process, and how much course time to allot to the projects. Faculty decision-making is the key to successful adaptation of an ethnographic teaching-learning strategy.

2. *Faculty must design their own development process.* Operating on a consensus basis, a group of Earlham faculty held a succession of meetings, not thinking of them as workshops. The process proved its worth by producing a curriculum applied in all overseas programs.

3. *The central international programs office plays a crucial leadership role.* The International Programs Office developed a plan, organized meetings, set their agendas, and compiled materials. The office also coordinates and oversees the orientations and re-entry for all programs as well as provides materials and guidance to faculty leaders.

4. *Apply an ethnographic approach to already established programs.* A high level of trust must exist in the host community since ethnographic methods depend on student interaction with local people.

5. *Understand global education as an integrated process.* As a college internationalizes, the components of scholarship, curriculum, overseas student programs, faculty development, and visiting scholars reinforce each other.

6. *Realize planning never ends.* Do not expect to finalize a program. Change will continue as faculty keep "tinkering."

These guidelines reflect the factors enabling Earlham to redesign its overseas courses with success. Key faculty initiated and continue to sustain the innovations. A central office which provides on-going faculty training and support, and outside grant financing proved vital elements. All this occurred in a context of senior administration support for international and global education.

Perhaps the most noteworthy element, often overlooked in planning new initiatives, is the fact that Earlham built on a solid foundation of existing programs. For decades Earlham faculty had led student groups overseas. They had the confidence to attempt an innovation previously untried on an institutionwide basis.

Notes

1 Jurasek, Richard, "Earlham College: Connecting Off-Campus and On-Campus Learning," in *Integrating Study Abroad into the Undergraduate Liberal Arts Curriculum*, ed. Barbara Burn (Greenwood Press, 1991), 7-8.

2 Ibid., 13.

3 Lamson, Howard, "Learning Culture Through Participation: The Use of Ethnographic Projects on Foreign Study," 4.

4 Ibid.

Eastern Michigan University

Linking Languages with Business

Language faculty at Eastern Michigan University use phrases like "kept us alive" and "turned this department around" when discussing the effect of their Language and International Trade (L&IT) Program. This pioneering program, since emulated by other universities, was conceived in crisis, born and developed during threats from the Michigan legislature and a Governor's special commission, and lived on to refute predictions of the language department's demise.

In the mid-1970s, language department enrollments at Eastern Michigan dropped precipitously. In two years the number of majors decreased by 90 percent until there were only four or five total among all three languages. In 1978, the Language and International Trade Program began and by its second year the department's enrollments and number of majors had doubled. They took off from there peaking at well over 200 majors in the 1984-85 academic year. By the early 1990s the number of majors had levelled off to around 120 to 150, with the decrease roughly corresponding to the majors in a 1988 spin-off, the Language and World Business Program.

Even with Language and International Trade's decrease, it and its parallel master's degree program place Eastern Michigan in a national leadership position. Because of the master's in Language and International Trade, the university was ranked eleventh in the list of the top twenty graduate schools for international business compiled in the June, 1990 edition of *North American International Business*.

As a large regional university, Eastern Michigan enrolled about 26,000 students in 1992, 19,270 as undergraduates. The university is located in Ypsilanti, Michigan, thirty miles west of Detroit and ten miles east of Ann Arbor, home of the University of Michigan. Established in 1849 as Michigan State Normal

School, EMU was Michigan's first institution to educate public school teachers. The legislature made it a university in 1959 with three colleges, Education, Arts and Sciences, and the Graduate School. The College of Business was added in 1964, the College of Health and Human Services in 1975, and the College of Technology in 1988. University representatives report that Education remains central since EMU graduates and certifies annually more students in education than virtually any other U.S. university. In the early 1990s EMU initiated a doctorate in Educational Leadership.

The inner campus has a functional appearance with mainly three and four story red brick buildings relatively close together and neatly laid out. A small green belt separates part of the campus from the town, yet small businesses and houses directly border the central campus, all within a few blocks of Ypsilanti's downtown. In that area, EMU opened its new business building in 1990. Several other campus buildings are not much older, which shows the Michigan government had reversed its 1970s posture overtly and invested in Eastern Michigan.

Like the university, Ypsilanti, Michigan finds itself between the different influences of Detroit and Ann Arbor. Also like the university, Ypsilanti has a proud history and identity of its own. Near the campus, early nineteenth-century houses have been renovated and a block of shops and pubs have emerged from their previous life as abandoned warehouses.

Perhaps practicality best characterizes Eastern Michigan's physical appearance and major programs. Utility is symbolized by the campus' distinguishing feature, an historic three-story, round, stone water tower near EMU's main entrance. Thus the Language and International Trade Program, with its required internship and emphasis on applied language competence, developed naturally within its institutional setting.

Campus Context
Eastern Michigan University's long mission statement contains international education phraseology in its first sentence: "Eastern Michigan University is committed to distinguishing itself as a comprehensive educational institution that prepares people and organizations to adapt readily to a changing world."

This assertion is followed by four ways in which the university will accomplish its mission, with the fourth committing it to "continually interpreting and responding to a changing regional, national, and global society." Other relevant phrases are laced throughout the following paragraphs, such as an "appreciation of human diversity" and dedication to assist "organizations to function effectively in a global economic environment."

In carrying out its mission, EMU revised its Basic Studies Program in January 1988. It requires all Eastern Michigan graduates to take at least one course in cross-cultural or international studies. Other references to such courses and to foreign languages appear as options among three of the four Basic Studies Program areas; i.e, Symbolics and Communication (five courses), Social Science (four courses), and Arts and Humanities (four courses).

The catalog describes many international majors offered by the foreign languages and bilingual studies department, the history and philosophy department, and one by the College of Business, which co-sponsors Language and World Business with foreign languages. There is one U.S. intercultural major, the African American Studies major, which is housed in a separate department. The specializations listed in the history and philosophy department are multidisciplinary area studies majors on Africa, Asia-Far East, Latin America, the Middle East and North Africa, and the Soviet Union. All require Economics I and II and Geography's World Regions course. Area studies majors must minor in one of the following disciplines; Anthropology, Economics, Geography, History, Political Science, or Sociology.

The strength of the Department of Foreign Languages and Bilingual Studies is shown by its long list of majors. Many reflect Eastern Michigan's emphasis on educating future teachers. As well as the Language and International Trade, and Language and World Business programs, there are majors offered in French/German/Spanish for Business, French/German/Spanish for Secondary Education, French/German Language and Literature, French/German Language and Literature for Elementary education, Spanish for Elementary Education, Japanese Language and Culture Teaching for Elementary Education, Japanese Language and Culture Teaching for K-12 Education. As well as minors parallel to these majors, the department also offers minors in Bilingual Bicultural Teacher Education (Spanish-English) for Elementary Education, Bilingual Bicultural Teacher Education (Spanish-English) for Secondary, K-12, and Special Education-Secondary, English as a Second Language for Non-native Speakers of English, and Teaching English to Speakers of Other Languages. One other multidisciplinary program at Eastern Michigan rounds out the list. Called Language, Journalism, Telecommunications and Film, it is cosponsored with several other departments.

Curriculum internationalization at the university has taken several other forms as well. The biology department lists a multidisciplinary minor in conservation and resource use. In addition, several majors require an international course or list choices of core courses which include international courses. The wording for Political Science's required courses means students must take either Introduction to Comparative Government or Introduction to International Politics, or both. The sociology major requires Introduction to Cultural Anthropology, and the finance major in the College of Business lists International Business Finance as a choice in two out of three required courses.

Several departments have international concentrations students can choose for their major. Economics has Comparative Economic Systems. It joins Biology's Ecosystem Biology, Political Science's Comparative Politics and International Relations, and the International Business concentration of the College of Business's Marketing major.

Various departments and colleges have individual courses not included in the previous list of majors and minors. The English language and literature department has a Language and Culture Course, for example. Communication has Intercultural Communication, and Interracial/Interethnic Communication. Geography offers World Food Systems, Cultural Geography, and The Geopolitics of World Geography, among several others. Besides the usual International Economics courses, Economics listings include two focusing on the development issue. French/German/Spanish for International Affairs are offered by the Foreign Language Department, Chinese and Japanese Art History by the Art Department, and Psychology of Contemporary Issues by Psychology, which discusses world problems. The Management Department in the College of Business lists Managing World Business Communication as well as the usual International Management course. In the College of Health and Human Services, the Social Work Department offers Practice Issues with People of Color. Finally, the following departments each have courses covering all the world's major cultural regions: Geography, Political Science, History and Philosophy, and the Sociology, Anthropology and Criminology Department.

Figures on human diversity at Eastern Michigan include faculty as well as students. Of 689 full-time faculty in 1993, there were forty-four African-Americans, thirty-three Asians, four American Indians, and eleven Hispanics, totalling ninety-two. Within the undergraduate population in 1992, African-Americans totalled 9.75 percent, Asians 1.42 percent, Hispanics 1.71 percent, and American Indians .44 percent. Also in 1992, 556 undergraduates were international students—2.92 percent of the student body, mainly from Taiwan, Japan, and Indonesia. The university employs one international student advisor working in student services.

Student overseas programs are organized and administered by the Office of Academic Programs Abroad. The office reports that, during the 1993-94 academic year, 130 EMU undergraduates participated in overseas programs, 120 of these going on those sponsored by the university. Most students choose the short-term summer programs but some take part in one of Eastern Michigan's semester-long cultural history tours. Many more participants on the tours come from other colleges and universities around the United States.

Begun as a summer program in the 1970s by an EMU History professor, The European Cultural History Tour takes from thirty-five to forty students each fall to about forty-seven cities. Three EMU faculty travel with the students offering fifteen semester hours credit in History, Art, Literature, and Political Science. The tour begins in London and travels as far east as Moscow, then moves through Germany and Italy to Greece, Turkey, and Egypt and ends in Jerusalem. A shorter summer version costs less and does not visit Scandinavia, Russia, or Poland. In 1994, the program cost $7,975, not including airfare to London and return from Jerusalem.

In the winter semester of 1993, the new Asian Cultural History Tour visited at least twenty-nine cities. It began in Hong Kong and, after moving through China and across Russia to Moscow, went to Greece, Turkey, Egypt, and Jerusalem. India was next, then Nepal, and last Thailand before ending at Honolulu. The fifteen hours of credit covered history, art, comparative religion, and political science. As with the European program, three faculty travelled with the student group. The cost of $7,595 did not include trans-Pacific airfare.

Two administrators from the Office of Academic Programs Abroad also accompany the student groups: the tour director, a Ph. D., and the tour manager, usually a recent graduate with overseas experience. These are two of the office's six full-time staff which include the director, program coordinator, secretary, and Study Abroad advisor.

The Office administers EMU's exchange with a university in the Netherlands and processes students who go to the Japan Center, sponsored by a consortium of Michigan's fifteen public universities. Office staff also assist in organizing the short-term summer programs. In 1994, for example, there were eight for undergraduates. Intensive language programs were offered in Mexico, Austria, and Quebec, while several other departments also sent faculty and students overseas; i.e., Art, Marketing, Health and Human Services, and the Labor Studies Program in Economics. In addition, a masters' level Multicultural Education program took place in Jamaica. Language faculty encourage students in Language and International Trade to go overseas on a summer program as preparation for their internship.

Language and International Trade Program

As a pioneer in what has become a growing national trend to link languages with business, Eastern Michigan's program set several precedents. It balanced three fields, business, languages, and social science. It also required an internship as the capstone experience.

According to the program flier,

The major in Language and International Trade is designed to integrate the study of modern foreign languages and cultures with preparation in the field of international trade and business. The major objective of the program is to provide students with skills, knowledge, and understanding needed to function in a foreign environment. Students completing this group major have met the major and minor requirements for graduation.

Students must take sixty semester-hours for the language and international trade major. Of these, fifty-seven consist of thirty hours of business and economics and twenty-seven hours of language and area studies; the remaining three hours are earned by completing a semester-long internship. Two specific courses must be taken in International Business, and either Comparative Economic Systems or International Economics. Students must complete a minor in an area of business they choose.

A minimum of eighteen hours of a language must be completed including the advanced 300-level French/German/Japanese/Spanish for International Trade and the 400-level Business French/German/Japanese/Spanish. Students are required to take one political science course from a list of international relations and comparative courses, and two relevant Geography or History courses, one of which must be the 300 level Geography/History of either Modern Europe, Spanish America, or Modern Asia. When, as part of an evaluation process, students were asked to note the strengths of the program, they cited the internship and the new Geography/History courses.

Eastern Michigan uses several terms for Language and International Trade's full-time, one semester, capstone internship. In one sense it forms part of the university's International Cooperative Education Exchange (ICEE) Program. Yet the Language and International Trade handouts outlining the language program call it a Field Experience. A large majority of majors have an internship. For various reasons (e.g., recession, unavailability of placements) other students have to settle for an additional business course instead. Approval for an overseas internship depends on meeting two conditions, a 3.25 minimum GPA, and a rating of at least Intermediate High on an oral proficiency examination. This is based on the rating system developed by the American Council on Teaching Foreign Languages. To increase their language facility and cultural learning, the Language and International Trade adviser suggests students take an intensive language summer study abroad program between their junior and senior years.

Domestic internships are available for students not meeting these criteria or who have other compelling reasons to remain in Michigan. Having chosen Japanese is one of these reasons. Since conversing in Japanese requires more language training, students in this language usually have a relevant domestic field experience. Exceptions occur if they have had prior experience in Japan or have become conversant in Japanese.

Students have reported that the Field Experience provides professional level, real jobs. Some are with major multinational corporations, such as Ford, Bechtel, and Siemens in the United States as well as in Germany, General Motors, Renault, and Kiwi in France, Pepsico and the Foreign Trade Bank in Spain. Overseas placements are made through partner Business and Technical schools in Europe and Latin America. The partner institution's placement directors attempt to visit each student at least once while they are on assignment abroad. An average of twenty-five U.S. and foreign students a year participate in the ICEE program.

Placements follow several guidelines. They should provide a progression of assignments, although students spend a larger amount of work time in their business specialty. Program planners want students to experience as much as possible about the company's full operation. Assignments may be project-based or research-based depending on the student's abilities. Formal job descriptions are required to complete the placement process. Since placement parity is the goal, all this applies as well to U.S. placements.

All internships pay salaries, at least enough to cover living expenses. Students are charged no tuition for the semester they spend interning, but they do pay a $500 administrative fee as well as their own airfare.

If the application process results in a student's being turned down, reasons are given and a reapplication allowed. If language capability is the problem, students may be interviewed by a group of language faculty a second time. They must pass on this second try, however. Program administrators note that usually the self-selection process works very well and few students are rejected. The overall effectiveness of the ICEE selection process is reflected in the program's low failure rate. Of the approximately 400 participants who have been placed since the program began in 1979, only two have returned home without completing their assignments.

The foreign language department administers the Language and International Trade Program. John Hubbard, a professor of German and one of the group that designed the program originally, receives one course release from the usual four courses per semester to advise the program. A Spanish professor, Ronald Cere, also with a one-course release, organizes and oversees domestic internships. The director and associate director of the World College, Ray Schaub and Geoffrey Voght, coordinate International Cooperative Education placements. Prior to creating the World College, about which more will be said later, both Schaub and Voght were foreign language department faculty and served as director and assistant director, respectively, of the Language and International Trade Program. The Language and International Trade Program has a separate budget line, providing one half-time secretary and some supply money to its support.

A majority of L&IT graduates take positions with international companies. Not surprisingly, some are hired by the companies where they had worked as interns. A few go on to graduate school.

In summarizing the results of the program, Ray Schaub writes that

> L&IT has been a truly remarkable success at EMU. It has had a broad impact on program development and administrative realignment at the university, and has provided a model for innovation at other institutions. On the basis of our experience with L&IT, we strongly advocate that other universities comparable in structure and mission to ours consider taking similar interdisciplinary approaches to the development of international business programs. (quoted in "Language and International Trade at Eastern Michigan University," *Internationalizing Business Education: Meeting the Challenge*, S. Tamer Cavusgil (ed.), Michigan State University Press, East Lansing, Michigan, 1993, p. 196.)

As one L&IT spin-off, Eastern Michigan has become a regional center in the United States for taking rigorous, internationally normed Business French, German, or Spanish examinations. These International Diplomas are considered resume builders and the fact that the language ability of some students is strong enough for them to pass speaks well for EMU's foreign language department.

Administration of this internationally recognized examination in business French was brought to EMU by a since retired professor of French, Brigitte Muller. Eastern Michigan was the first university in the United States to be granted the right to administer the examinations, which are sanctioned by the Chamber of Commerce and Industry of Paris (CCIP), the organization of the same name in Madrid, and the National Chamber of Commerce and Industry, the Goethe Institute and the Carl Duisberg Centers in Germany. As will be explained below, Muller was one of the farsighted, hardworking group of Language Department colleagues who stayed with their idea of linking languages with business throughout its discouraging formative years, and saw it develop into a resounding success.

The Struggle to Initiate L&IT

The saga of the creation of the Language and International Trade Program provides a lesson in persistence, perhaps produced by necessity and desperation. The crisis faced by EMU's Foreign Language Department in the 1970s dramatically shows the truth of a main message of international educators, that is, international events can have devastating local effects. The 1973 oil boycott directly affected the sale of cars and, therefore, the state of Michigan's budget. Severe reductions were passed on to school districts and they stopped hiring language teachers, among other measures. One result, the dramatic drop in enrollments and numbers of majors in EMU's Foreign Language Department, the largest provider of the state's language teachers.

Yet the foreign language department's students suggested that a new curriculum to train them for a different occupation would turn the situation around. They wanted Business Spanish, French, and German. Brigitte Muller responded first, and offered a one-semester Business French course. This worked well enough that it grew to two semesters. She then went to Paris on her own time and money, and gained permission to administer the CCIP test to her students. Most passed and added the International Diploma to their credentials.

This provided convincing evidence for the feasibility of a Business French curriculum, and by implication one for German and Spanish as well. One current foreign language department faculty member notes Muller's contribution to the program as, "otherwise we wouldn't have been able to do it." While she was working with her students, she and several others in the department were engaged in planning for a larger effort. Thus student demand laid the foundation for the future Language and International Trade Program.

Reversing the language department's dire situation was achieved as a result of a group effort, although involving by no means a majority of the department's members. Three of the original key people still are active in the program: John Hubbard, Ray Schaub, and Geoffrey Voght. Hubbard also served as the Foreign Language Department head from 1980 to 1985.

To launch the program took several years of work by a solid core of at least five colleagues, and an ally or two among the university's senior administration. Hubbard and Schaub in German were joined by Brigitte Muller in French and Geoffrey Voght in Spanish, all led by Jean Bidwell, French professor and department head from 1975 to 1980. As new ideas were being discussed by these department members they became painfully aware that the university could provide no resources. Then Rose Hayden, a national spokesperson for international education, came to Michigan to make a presentation. She spoke personally with Jean Bidwell explaining that a grant program administered by the federal government was designed specifically to help institutions like Eastern Michigan; namely the U.S. Department of Education's Undergraduate International Studies and Foreign Language Program.

To provide vital assistance and real-world advice, Brigitte Muller's husband George helped organize the business community advisory group. Some members were at the vice presidential level. Muller's husband is described by program planners as essential in providing ideas and credibility. He was a French-speaking Swiss, an automotive engineer working for Ford, and had prior experience with a German machine tool company. At this stage in the program development process, during the mid-1970s, all the program's development work, the planning, some new course development, grant writing, and organizing initial placements in Germany, occurred without any financial support, except for sabbaticals, while the organizers taught full time.

Another difficulty became evident as grant preparation proceeded. Some senior administrators at the time resisted the idea of a new program linking foreign languages with business. Fortunately, however, others were more farsighted.

When the grant was funded the next academic year, the new dean of the College of Business had a very positive attitude toward the Language and International Trade Program. Another significant supportive action was taken by the dean of the College of Arts and Sciences, Donald Drummond. He established the policy of recognizing work on grants and program development as contributing to professional growth and, therefore, as equivalent to traditional definitions of scholarship and service.

There were, however, still some hurdles to be surmounted. The first two grant proposals were rejected. Readers' comments explained that more business courses were needed. Program organizers look back on this as providing useful advice. Also, the first proposal applied only to German. The rejections served to strengthen the program in the long run. When the third grant proposal was funded in 1978 it produced a respectable and marketable program with professional credibility.

One potential source of either overt or latent opposition was muted. Given the crisis nature of the situation, the foreign language faculty who felt reticent about retraining themselves offered no real resistance. Also, the groundwork for approval of the future program by the university wide faculty committee was laid through the multidisciplinary Language and International Trade Advisory Council. Input from these faculty became part of the program.

With outside financial support the program took shape quickly. Curriculum development took the form of several new courses in business languages, international business, and social sciences, namely the History and Geography of Modern Europe, and a parallel course on Spanish America. Faculty were granted teaching releases to design the courses and to organize internships. Also, John Hubbard received course releases for recruitment purposes. He organized a process and, accompanied by an admissions staff member, spent much time visiting area high schools. He not only made presentations but met with counselors and students. The report by foreign language faculty that Hubbard was very effective is valid, judging by the immediate and rapid growth of the L&IT program. Formal approval came by the fall of 1980 when, after favorable action by the university's curriculum committee, the Board of Regents also voted its assent.

The years of struggle paid off quickly. In two years the foreign language department had from ten to fifteen majors, up from four or five, and in four years the number was 125. The increase continued until the mid-1980s when L&IT alone attracted well over 200 majors. This caused an increase in the number of foreign language faculty. From eleven in the early 1980s, the department grew to twenty-one full-time, tenure track positions by the 1990s. This increase resulted from another supportive decision by senior administrators; i.e., increases in enrollments would be matched with new faculty positions.

Since the L&IT program was designed to produce graduates with enough business and language expertise to quickly contribute to a company's international business unit, its semester-long internship is vital as a capstone experience. At the time, it was an innovative educational methodology. Serendipity played a role as Ray Schaub, a EMU German professor, initiated the L&IT internship component.

While on sabbatical in Germany in 1977-78 researching a topic in early German Romantic literature, the conversations between Schaub and a German friend began taking a programmatic turn. The friend was teaching Business English to

German business students. Discussions revealed their students' mutual need for practical experience. This related to the objective of the proposed L&IT program, and the idea for a reciprocal internship exchange evolved. The discussions also resulted in making L&IT's Field Experience a required capstone course. Returning from sabbatical, Schaub organized the International Cooperative Education Exchange (ICEE) Program.

For years after the first grant was finally funded, a series of grants followed in succession. A 1980 seed-money grant of over $5,000 from the German Foreign Office supported the ICEE Program and helped to attract major funding. From 1981-84 the U.S. Department of Education's Fund for the Improvement of Postsecondary Education provided $120,000 for the coordination of ICEE and L&IT. The Exxon Foundation funded two proposals from 1983 to 1985 to support further development of ICEE, L&IT, and the annual Eastern Michigan University conference on languages for world business. In 1985, the growing variety of interrelated activities attracted a small corporate grant from the Ford Motor Company.

Student input continued to be important and several surveys were conducted over the years. Time and again they showed the effectiveness of high school recruiting visits. When L&IT graduates were asked in a 1987 survey how to improve the program, they recommended strengthening the business component. This provided support for one of the program's most significant spin-offs, the Language and World Business Program.

The new program, this time cosponsored by the College of Business and the foreign languages department, upgraded the international business component to a major. In the L&IT program a business minor is required. A number of new international business courses needed development, and funding was provided by another successful grant proposal to the U.S. Department of Education's Undergraduate International Studies and Foreign Language Program.

Another spin-off, the World College, was established in 1987 with Ray Schaub as director, Geoffrey Voght as associate director, and a full-time secretary. This new administrative unit has a multifaceted mandate. It was created to develop and promote international programs and initiatives across the entire campus including expansion of the ICEE program to include other departments in the university. In addition, the World College organizes the annual conference on language and communication for World Business and the professions, subsidizes faculty travel to international meetings, prepares grant proposals, and offers workshops. It also administers scholar exchanges.

The decision to create the World College was made by Eastern Michigan's President, John Porter. He had served as Michigan State's Secretary of Education and became an advocate of international education. Porter wanted international cooperative education for all disciplines. He liked the idea of expanding EMU's close working relationship with the business community.

Initially, World College financing came from special state funding and a budget line which had provided matching money for an AID-financed project. With the project finished, the matching budget was held over by the provost. Thus the World College did not draw funding away from another unit of the university. The director reports to the provost and academic vice president as well as to the executive vice president.

The latest spin-off was approved in 1993. The Language and International Relations Program links languages, political science, history, and sociology, and it has a practical training component.

Issues and Answers

In spite of years of planning, trial and error often plays a role. Business languages were first offered at the 100 level. By the mid-1980s, it was clear from comments by students and overseas placement supervisors that interns needed greater language competence. The Business Language Committee, formed to review the program and recommend changes, suggested offering business language courses at the 400 level after students had taken the 300 level composition course. The committee also decided that only upperdivision language credits would count toward the L&IT program's required eighteen hours of language credits. These changes have provided an effective response to the problem.

The Business-Language Committee was composed of one representative from each of the four languages and ESL. The

ESL faculty member was included because of the number of international students in the undergraduate, and especially in the graduate L&IT program. By the early 1990s, a majority of students in the graduate L&IT program were international students.

The committee had to deal with another issue which produced "furious" debates, to use one faculty member's description. The question concerned whether or not to allow native speakers into business language courses. Finally it was decided they could take these courses and fully participate in the program. This has worked out well because the language skills and cultural knowledge of international students represent a resource in their courses. Also some local firms appreciate having international student interns.

A third major issue surfaced by the late 1980s when faculty were discussing the appropriate response to another set of student comments. These emerged from the 1987 alumni survey, noted in the previous section. Besides concurring with the recommendation that the number of higher level language courses be increased, L&IT graduates also advocated strengthening the business component. The now employed graduates pointed out the fact that the actual work setting required better preparation. The Business-Language Committee's deliberations arising from this issue produced the Language and World Business (L&WB) Program. By the early 1990s, over 100 students were attracted to this L&WB program, with a roughly corresponding decrease in the number of L&IT majors.

The committee also took on the necessary task of writing down the program's policies and procedures; for example, deadlines for student applications. It redesigned forms and made other administrative refinements. A student handbook was prepared including information on preparing for, applying, and successfully completing the overseas internship.

During the mid- to late 1980s, Jean Bidwell returned as department chair. She was considered best able to lead the department through another time of planning and significant change. Many faculty report that this second period of major discussions and program development has resulted in fatigue.

After its labors, the faculty committee took on a monitoring role.

The decline in enrollments is presently the key topic at Business-Language Committee meetings. All involved in L&IT recognize the need for another round of high school recruiting visits. To do this adequately, a faculty member must receive release time from teaching. This, in turn, relates directly to the even larger issue which all in the Foreign Language Department agree is the most basic. It restricts action on other issues, such as the need to maintain appropriate course offerings and equitable teaching loads.

The core issue is understaffing. Faculty at Eastern Michigan have eight-month contracts which cover two semesters. They teach four courses each semester. Graduate offerings are normally colisted with advanced undergraduate courses since, in most cases, enrollments at the graduate level are too small to support freestanding graduate classes. Clearly, the most experienced faculty should teach these "piggybacked" courses. Lecturers must be hired to replace these faculty in teaching lower-level courses. Given this situation, released time creates an additional financial burden on the department.

This explanation for the lack of aggressive recruitment and other program building efforts is countered by the view that the department has been victimized by success. Some say its faculty have been coasting on past accomplishments. Multidisciplinary programs require special attention because they need continual explanation. The student grapevine alone cannot maintain large numbers.

Another disagreement occurs over the issue of whether or not the L&IT program would be managed more effectively by a director and assistant director. It had one director for most of the 1980s when Ray Schaub and Geoffrey Voght had grant-funded, full-time releases from teaching. From 1978 to 1980 Hubbard was director; then he became department head. As explained previously, in the 1990s Hubbard advises undergraduate students, Bill Cline the graduates, Cere oversees domestic placements, and Schaub and Voght handle international placements through World College. Many involved find this arrangement not only acceptable but efficient. It certainly is cost effective. There is no end in sight to this debate.

Lessons Learned

Recommendations offered by the current department head, Steven Kirby, faculty, and administrators currently involved in the Language and International Trade Program reflect their attention to each of its component constituencies.

1. *Ensure internal and external support.* Program planners heeded the recommendations of advisory committees. The contributions of both the business community and faculty support network were incorporated into the final product.
2. *Create a specialized base in languages.* The Foreign Language Department's first concrete acts, the Business French courses, demonstrated the faculty's capability as well as L&IT's feasibility and potential.
3. *Heed student input.* Success means attracting students. They can contribute useful comments both before and after graduation. Not only did student suggestions provide an initial impetus for the L&IT Program, but periodic surveys of their views helped determine revisions.
4. *Allow faculty to administer the program.* Currently L&IT is administered on a collegial basis. Initially a single director had responsibility for advising students, coordinating course offerings, and overseeing domestic and international internship placements. Both administrative models have their advocates at Eastern Michigan University. Yet all agree that, whichever model is used, faculty should direct day-to-day program administration. Effective interaction involving students, colleagues, and the business community requires the authority that comes with content expertise and classroom experience.
5. *Design an interdisciplinary and multidisciplinary program.* In its formative stage, social scientists, business specialists, and foreign language faculty participated not only in the planning but in course development when L&IT went into effect. Therefore, several departments benefitted from increased enrollments. Also, a successful program creates

converts. Consequently, more faculty in the College of Business began to identify with international business, which explains why that college now cosponsors the Language and World Business Program. Faculty in both the Foreign Language Department and the College of Business note that a good working relationship between the two units has developed over the years.

6. *Promote the program in high schools on an ongoing basis.* Incentives to carry out marketing activities should be built into the program. A planned process is needed for publicizing the program to new generations of high school students.

7. *Continue pointing out the benefits to students.* Guard against complacency by making it a habit to promote the program to new and prospective majors.

8. *Work with experienced host country counterparts.* Placement administrators must have experience in dealing with U.S. undergraduates in the complex context of a cooperative program.

9. *Remain vigilant to changing trends.* Anticipating potential downturns means they can be minimized and managed. The Language and World Business Program is having an adverse effect on L&IT numbers. An aggressive marketing campaign could have meant increased numbers for both programs.

The history of the Language and International Trade Program can prove instructive. It has evolved, thrived, and endured long enough to illustrate how a curriculum program reacts to changes both in institutional context and in program administration. It has weathered being weaned from years of substantial grant support as well as the development of a competitive new spin-off. A new generation of faculty are now merging with some of those from the early years to maintain a viable program. Its institutionalization in the form of a collegial administration provides evidence this model can work. Yet without a greater institutional commitment in the form of resources for more release time, L&IT may continue maintaining its status quo, no growth situation.

Whatever the next chapter in the L&IT saga, its past shows what a persevering group of faculty can achieve. Farsighted senior administrators and outside funding were also crucial. The fact that the program took shape in the 1970s provides a useful lesson in timing and the influence of the larger social context. The decade of the 1970s was a time when the United States was discovering the adverse effects of international economic interdependence. Internationalism can produce vulnerability as well as venture opportunity. This contradiction was faced directly by EMU's Foreign Language Department and it responded by taking full advantage of an opportunity.

Goshen College

Requiring an Overseas Study-Service Experience

Few other undergraduate institutions have taken international education as seriously as has Goshen College. Beginning in the 1967-68 academic year, an international education graduation requirement went into effect. For about 80 percent of its students since then, this has meant going overseas for a Study-Service Term (SST). International students, approximately 8 percent of the student body, automatically meet the requirement. A small number of students go overseas on other foreign study programs approved by the International Education Committee. The rest take the on-campus alternative, twelve hours of approved courses with an international focus. In addition, virtually all students take a foreign language.

With hindsight's clear and perhaps oversimplified vision, Goshen's achievement appears almost natural. To a visitor, hearing the campus chimes announce every quarter hour, the college's self contained physical setting appears to reflect a common commitment. The compact campus at the edge of Goshen Indiana, has about 1,000 full-time students. Its modest brick buildings and new construction reflect an understated confidence. This liberal arts college's strong sense of identity includes service as one of its vital elements. Over 90 percent of Goshen's faculty and staff and about 65 percent of its students are Mennonite. This religious tradition values education for service and practical living as well as for academic achievement.

Campus Context

From the vantage point of the 1990s, the internationalization of the college motto "Culture for Service" looks like a logical step. It makes sense for a college with Goshen's ethos to require students to complete "a journey from apathy and incomprehension to empathy and insight," as stated in Goshen's international education brochure. Mennonites are a separate cultural group. They know the world as a mosaic where people live according to different social values and behavior. Consequently, the college's mission statement links service and international education: "We view education as a moral activity that produces servant-leaders for the church and the world."

Yet for Goshen to have over 80 percent of its students graduate with an overseas experience, and an experiential one at that, remains an extraordinary accomplishment. It is a tribute to all those who have been involved over the years when a program as pioneering as SST seems predictable. The Study-Service Term incorporates international education into the college's very identity.

Yet the observer suspects the program's impact has been as substantial, in important though subtle ways, on Goshen College itself as it has been on students who have participated. One small indication of this occurred in 1987 when ten objectives were added to the college's mission statement. Number two reads, "Intercultural openness with the ability to function effectively with people of other world views." Few other U.S. colleges and universities have incorporated international education as clearly into the very essence of the institution's *raison d'etre.*

Goshen's experience also is distinctive in that the graduation requirement and overseas programs stimulated an expansion in curriculum internationalization. Usually campuses experience the reverse; a graduation requirement is adopted following campuswide international curriculum development.

Courses infused throughout the college's curriculum reflect the fact that over 50 percent of the faculty have led SST student groups to sites in the developing world; for example, Economics' Introduction to Economic Development, Religion's Third World Theologies and War, Peace and Nonresistance, Biology's Environmental Ethics which includes "Third World concerns" as a major component, Sociology's Rural Development, Humanities' World Arts (non-Western societies), Political Science's Latin American Politics, and History's First/Third World History. These join multicultural courses in literature, education, communications, and nursing among other disciplines.

Goshen offers majors in Hispanic Ministries, German, and Spanish. These join minors in environmental studies, intercultural studies, peace studies, French, and Teaching English to Speakers of Other Languages. Two other modern language offerings are included in the catalog, i.e., the first year of Chinese and a course for credit in English as a Second Language.

International students and scholars also contribute to creating a global campus environment. During the 1990-91 academic year, eighty-five students from twenty-eight countries attended Goshen. Twenty-six were from Canada with the rest coming from a wide range of countries. In addition, Goshen hosted nine exchange lecturers and one visiting professor, all from China. The half-time international student advisor and admissions officer, a faculty member who also teaches astronomy, is located in the admissions office.

In addition to SST, Goshen faculty have organized several overseas programs: Irish Literature in Ireland, Theater in Great Britain, Art in Italy, and Teaching English in Poland. Two other courses are held mostly on campus yet include up to two weeks in Israel: Archaeology in Israel and Middle East Bible Seminar. A few students each year go overseas on programs sponsored by organizations Goshen College has joined, such as the Indiana Consortium for International Programs, The Council on International Educational Exchange, and Brethren Colleges Abroad.

All language majors are required to spend an academic year overseas. Some participate in non-Goshen study abroad programs in addition to an SST in a Spanish-speaking country.

The director of international education, Ruth Gunden, an international education advisor, an administrative assistant, and a secretary handle the administration of SST and other student overseas programs. The director reports to the academic dean and, enhancing her academic role, the coordinator of the intercultural studies minor reports to her.

Study-Service Term

Every academic year from eight to fourteen "units," groups of about twenty students each with a faculty leader, spend one trimester in a culture "significantly different from that of the

United States," as stated in the college catalog. Formal learning comprises the first half of the Study-Service Term, sometimes in cooperation with a local university. This always includes language training.

After initial instruction, the last six weeks are spent in a field service learning assignment, usually in a rural area. Typical placements include working in refugee camps, government-run nutrition centers, rural health clinics, a school for the deaf, or an English-language school. Sometimes the service experience involves more physical work such as construction or agricultural labor. Students live with families during both parts of their experience.

This division enables students, most of whom previously have never left the United States, to have the cushioning effect of a group "classroom" learning situation when they first experience another culture. After seven weeks, they leave this relative security and, in small groups, venture out to interact with local people.

Campus foreign language faculty do the final evaluating of language upon the students' return. Superior achievement nets an extra credit. The student chooses the grading plan for the four hours of language; the other nine hours, three each in Social Science and Intercultural Communication, two in Humanities, and one in Natural Science, are taken Pass/Fail.

Except for the languages, specific course content may vary with the disciplines of faculty leaders. They prepare syllabi which include a variety of assignments and measurements of learning, like examinations. All include journal writing. Faculty leaders serve as the unit coordinators in-country. Working with local agencies, they oversee family placements and service assignments, as well as lectures and field trips.

Units each year go to one of usually five countries in Asia, Latin America, Europe, and Africa. In 1992-93 these were China, Costa Rica, the Dominican Republic, Germany (formerly East Germany), and Côte d'Ivoire. Most sites have hosted Goshen students for several years with only the Costa Rican location receiving units every year since the program began in 1968. Past countries include Poland, Haiti, Nicaragua, Jamaica, Honduras, Guadeloupe, Belize, and South Korea. Contacts for the newest location, Côte d'Ivoire, were made through the Mennonite Mission Board and involved Goshen alumni.

The application and orientation process begins with students registering for a specific unit. Often these unit lists are initiated several trimesters or even years in advance; for example, the 1996 unit list for Germany began in 1993. Then the director of international education interviews each student. A few have been refused or channelled into other SST units based on medical problems, either physical or psychological.

In the trimester before departure readings are encouraged and two evening orientation sessions are held. These allow past faculty leaders and student participants to describe the program and their reactions, as well as to answer questions. This formal orientation process conveys very basic cultural and logistical information both orally and via a packet for each student. Prior preparation also includes language courses which are geared toward SST participation.

Each fall the director of international education requests faculty to express their interest in being SST leaders in future years. Potential faculty leaders then apply to the International Education Committee, which functions like a department for the faculty who are overseas at any one time. This policy committee reviews and approves the design of each overseas unit and deals with issues that arise once the group leaves the United States. Faculty leaders receive manuals and are expected to research and review academic as well as practical information about their future destinations.

In 1987 Ruth Gunden became Goshen's second director of international education. This quietly effective administrator is a Goshen graduate and served as a faculty member in physical education. She led an SST unit to Jamaica and then carried out research in Poland and Great Britain. Thus she embodies Goshen's emphasis on faculty development as an important component of the Study Service Term.

Goshen's policy keeps all program costs, including transportation, at a level no greater than the college's regular trimester billing. The current "added cost" units are in Germany, China, Côte d'Ivoire, and, in 1994, Indonesia.

A History of SST
When asked about SST's beginnings, Goshen faculty and administrators first mention Henry Weaver. As assistant to the president (1965-68), acting academic dean (1970-72), and Provost (1972-79), he was pivotal at every stage in the process. Yet the author of a May 1988 interview with President Emeritus Mininger assessed his contribution to SST with the following words: "It was the persistence and prodding of GC president, Paul Mininger, more than anyone else that focused the vision and kept it alive." Probably both Weaver and Mininger proved vital to the major changes Goshen experienced at the time. Yet it seems from current available information that Weaver led, listened, cajoled, and compromised in almost daily discussions as SST took shape.

The overseas program formed part of a larger plan for the Future of the College, to use the committee's name that originated the proposal. The plan's relevant section had five parts, presented and agreed to in principle by the faculty in 1966: A trimester calendar, study-service trimester, new concept in courses, new general education and graduation requirements, and schedule and plan for implementation. This amounted to a virtual redesign of the college structure, its graduation requirements, and its calendar, much of which has been retained. The final vote in May 1967 accepting the five-part proposal was unanimous with only one abstention; yet this individual served as an SST faculty leader the next year.

The first international education director, Arlin Hunsberger, was crucial to SST's early effectiveness. With experience as country director in Haiti for the Mennonite Central Committee and Church World Service, and several years as a high school teacher in Pennsylvania, Hunsberger was asked by Weaver in 1968 to give form and substance to the Study-Service idea. The fact that he served as director until 1987 testifies to his competence. The program has benefitted from administrative consistency since it has only had two directors in twenty-three years of operation.

Those currently involved in the program's administration attribute Goshen's visionary international education focus, in part, to the fact that a large number of faculty in the 1960s had done relief work following World War II and the Korean War. They were genuinely committed to the new program, as it represented their own experiential learning. They felt Goshen's responsibility was to ensure that most students, not just the highly motivated or the elite, learned that education included service in a multicultural world. The existence of a large percentage of faculty, put at 50 percent, with international expertise was pointed out by the North Central Association of Schools and Colleges report when Goshen's accreditation was renewed. Campus leaders, in advocating substantial change, cited this report as an impetus for their ideas.

One additional factor deserves mention. In the summer of 1967, three trial study-service units went to Haiti, Colombia, and Barbados. Reports from all three became part of the process for the program's full implementation in 1968. The use of a carefully designed and scrutinized pilot program shows idealism was well served by clear-headed planning. Another source of prior experience came from language faculty who had taken groups of students to Mexico and other countries.

It may be impossible to state definitively which factor or individual contributed most significantly to the Study-Service Term's initiation and development. Probably such a determination is unimportant anyway. A fortunate congruence of people, perspectives, and past experiences made such a far-reaching, campuswide commitment not only imaginable but realistic. It has withstood over two decades of testing by 4,800+ students. SST is a tribute to what a key, high level administrator with energy, vision, patience, and persuasive presence can accomplish, when combined with the able support of a president, a group of committed faculty, and overwhelmingly favorable student reactions.

Succeeding administrative leaders have continued the tradition. An article by President Victor Stoltzfus in the March 1985 *Goshen College Bulletin* offers "A Case for Global Education." His comments reflect a general rationale with the particular international education emphasis his college exemplifies.

A recent report stresses the need for students to be vitally involved in their own learning. Cross-cultural learning presses GC students to their adaptive limits. They learn language with the reinforcement of native teachers, host families, street signs and the experiences of bazaar bargaining and public transportation. They also learn about the connectedness of things. . . . Travel, study and service also stimulate learning of the traditional variety. . . . The connectedness of the global economy presents another reason for including an international component in higher education. Some 70 percent of the products manufactured in the United States compete with world market forces, including cheaper overseas labor costs.

A faculty committee has drafted a statement . . . "Goshen College gives opportunity for educational experiences in settings where students may experience and be a catalyst for reconciliation, restoration to wholeness and mediation."

This reasoning includes Mennonite convictions and practicality. President Mininger reflected the same balance when he included at the end of his rationale, "As a practical matter we also saw SST as a way to reduce costs by making the college facilities serve more people. Finally, we thought that the entire plan would give a distinctive character to the college that would attract students." [*Goshen College Bulletin,* July 1988]

This mixture of principle and practicality was reflected in Goshen's very early attention to evaluating its SST program. After the first year, a four-person commission from outside the college visited SST sites, interviewed students and faculty, reviewed data from a values inventory, and issued a report. Such an open process and full disclosure validated the program, since the summary statement noted that "most students derived great value from the SST experience." Yet much in the report was critical. A main critique reiterated what is said about experiential programs in general: they have problems "reconciling the academic and experiential components."

Goshen's constructive response included the development of sophisticated orientation materials so that students are trained to learn from living situations as well as from books. The latest publication designed to fill this need was written in 1990 by J. Daniel Hess, *Intercultural Study and Service, Guides for Learning About and Communicating with Strangers.* A revision of this practical guide will be published by Intercultural Press.

Four other evaluations have been conducted; an internal ten-year review, plus a second internal review in 1987, a doctoral study in 1981-82 assessing student attitudinal change, and a National Endowment of the Humanities-financed review of SST's impact on host countries (1982-83). Program adaptations followed each report. Thus evaluation data of every SST component not only exists, but has been used in program development. This is not surprising given Goshen's administrative style. Yet it deserves mention since such thorough, systematic, public appraisals seem rare in international education programs. Taken together, the evaluations validate the vision of SST's early founders.

Issues and Answers

As with experiential programs generally, at Goshen the burden of proof as to SST's academic validity rests with its faculty and administrators. The academic rigor of nontraditional, action-reflection-response learning remains a constant, albeit often unspoken, issue. This concern may be even greater since SST is a required general education program. Students from any background and discipline must be accommodated.

Goshen has developed several responses to this issue. Establishing a systematically applied, basic curriculum provides a standard framework for faculty leaders as they design their own discipline-specific content and learning objectives. Also, when organizing placements, faculty unit leaders look for ways to build on a student's major or prior learning.

Academic oversight is provided by the International Education Committee. Here, faculty seriously review syllabi of proposed SST units as to their content and measures of learning. Students must produce substantial products. As explained on the Participation Contract each student receives, expectations include (besides the standard journal) exams, reports, and other traditional academic work as well as a "culminating and integrative" project. In addition to general academic expectations, the contract establishes behavioral guidelines.

Student preparedness, a second issue, also relates to academic quality and is discussed on an ongoing basis at Goshen. As with the first concern, this issue has been tackled head-on. Various kinds of orientation processes have been tried, with the most useful described in this case study's previous section. Practical orientation sessions have proven effective with handouts and ample time to talk over what to expect with students and faculty who previously have been to the same overseas location.

The J. Daniel Hess book mentioned previously, *International Study and Service*, provides Goshen students with a full 260 pages of valuable information. It examines in detail how to learn from observing and participating in a society. Hess includes lists of questions to ask on many cultural topics, several case studies, ways to "move into cultural scenes" such as identifying nonverbal cues, an explanation of how to keep an academic journal, and much practical advice. The book was prepared in consultation with over 150 people in the countries hosting SST units.

Formal predeparture course requirements have proven their worth, such as language training. Also, some faculty leaders assign skill development activities during the SST's first seven week formal learning phase before students begin their placements; for example, early in SST's history a Sociology faculty member designed a village study which challenged students to go out into nearby villages in groups of three or four and carry out several tasks in an ethnographic exercise. Such an activity is designed to enhance the ability of students to observe human interaction patterns and determine what is appropriate cultural behavior. This strengthens the SST's academic component as well as increasing the students' comfort level when they move into their placement experience.

The prevailing campus culture also helps prepare students for the SST. Such a large percentage of the students on campus have completed their trimester overseas that its benefits as well as its pitfalls are part of the prevailing campus environment. Both the formal and informal preparation processes must work because, over the years, very few students have been denied credit or sent home.

The third issue sometimes relates to the second but more often arises from separate considerations, i.e., individual students experience problems while in the host country. Anxieties and personality variations do not always surface while on campus. Therefore faculty leaders must be able to recognize and deal with students' idiosyncratic reactions to completely new and unsettling situations.

The director of international education attempts to screen and prepare both faculty and students. Faculty are chosen, at least in part, because they are able to help students work through difficult emotional and interpersonal concerns. Also the director interviews each student, and faculty leaders get to know their prospective students before leaving campus.

Host families are carefully selected and often understand the reactions of young U.S. citizens under stress. Also, the Participation Contract given each student makes expectations clear as well as the consequences of inappropriate behavior. A statement to Costa Rican Host Families shows support for them in matters as sensitive as dating, an individual student's potential travel plans, and the use of the phone.

A fourth issue arises from Goshen's Mennonite peace and justice tradition. The impact of SST on local people at its overseas locations concerns SST faculty and staff as well as the larger Goshen campus community. The first SST evaluation recommended "a thorough study" of SST's effect in host countries. Funded by a National Endowment of the Humanities grant, such a study of Costa Rican units was conducted during the 1982-83 academic year by the Stutzmans, an associate professor of anthropology and his wife, a social worker. Both had previous service and research experience in Latin America.

The Stutzman report reached several conclusions after extensive data collection through firsthand participation and observation, as well as in-depth interviews with students, host families, and host educators. The Stutzmans determined that a major strength was the fact that SST fulfilled the program's service objectives to some extent. Many students in their placements did contribute to the local communities. Yet because such students were in a minority, the report also criticized the service assignment aspect of SST. Another major conclusion dealt with SST's learning objectives. Evidence showed that the placements did help students meet personal learning and growth objectives.

Host families generally were very positive about SST. Often students were not seen as paying boarders or house guests;

rather, they were treated as members of the family. Some members of families did note their minimal involvement in program decisions. The strongest criticisms came from host educators. They wanted to provide faculty leaders with local advice. Also, they pointed out the fact that Goshen students often left with only a shallow understanding of the link between U.S. affluence and Developing World poverty. In other words, the content of North-South global issues needed emphasizing.

In response to this study, and other feedback, Goshen has stressed the need for faculty to employ an inclusive process as they organize SST activities and deal with various problems. They attempt to treat families as partners in the education process. Also, a fuller explanation of the relationship between the United States and developing countries has received more emphasis. Subsequent conversations with local educators generally supported the position that the SST program "is having a positive impact in the study-service settings," according to an article in the March 1989 *Goshen College Bulletin* by John D. Yoder.

Financial matters raised by the Study-Service Term create the fifth general set of concerns faced by Goshen faculty, staff, and students. Most Goshen students must work to finance their education and time away creates some difficulty. The fact that SST is required makes this a major concern from the program's inception.

The response is Goshen's policy of keeping the cost of most SST trimesters the same as on-campus trimesters, including travel expenses. To accomplish this takes constant vigilance and flexible budgeting; for instance, allowing faculty leaders to shift money between categories and make substitutions where possible, like using public transportation instead of a hired bus for field trips.

Yet budget crunches occur even after years of experience and conservative budget preparation. A procedural policy has been implemented to help in the planning process. Students are required to make advance deposits for the extra cost units. Also penalties for late dropouts help, although this, as well as the advance deposit policy, has proven difficult to enforce.

The funding and academic standards issues are both being addressed by the development of an alternative to SST currently in the planning stage. Short-term, three-week overseas options are being developed directly related to specific fields of study. Under discussion is a major concern with this option, i.e., the need to insure an adequate cultural experience. The possibility of a shorter, more discipline-focused experience arises, in part, from the fact that over the years many students have had difficulty incorporating a full SST trimester into their schedules. This results from the fact that some curriculum programs require a sequencing of courses. Also, more and more older students attend Goshen. Often their family and work responsibilities mean they cannot leave the country for a whole trimester. This timing issue joins with the academic and expense issues to stimulate a new approach.

Lessons Learned and Spin-off
The following practical guidelines are derived from years of successful administration of SST, a program with complexities truly global in scope.

1. *Keep the program an integral part of the campus ethos.* As a general education program, SST's design grew out of the character and goals of Goshen College. Given the Mennonite tradition, this also meant adjustments had to be made to accommodate host country perceptions.

2. *Devise institutions and processes to ensure sustained faculty involvement and ownership.* In a narrow sense, some administrative efficiency must give way to the need for strong faculty leadership via the International Education Committee. This actually results in long-term efficiencies because it draws on a wide range of knowledge and the practical expertise of past unit leaders. Program administrators must be able to respond positively to many sources of advice.

3. *Recognize the students' changing agendas.* Both individual interviews and formal orientation sessions must accommodate changes in student concerns, and even fears. There have been some years when personal safety surfaces

as an issue. Other times, students seem preoccupied with course scheduling to complete professional training. Program planners must be aware of the student campus culture and lifestyle. Effective orientation and reentry consultations must deal directly with students' real concerns.

4. *Design a variety of instructional activities because learning through experience is not automatic.* Learning through observation must be taught. Preservice academic training should include practical ethnographic exercises.

5. *Remember the faculty and host families are crucial when engaging in daily program administration.* Respect for people in the host countries is vital in long-term program development. Families especially need to know they are part of the learning process. Formal get-together events help, but faculty leaders must incorporate the perspectives of local people.

6. *Occasionally initiate new locations.* This creates a necessary variety, added enthusiasm, and a programmatic response to changing world issues; however, it adds costs in time, energy, and financing.

7. *Have safety and health contingency plans.* Involve the campus health service as well as securing competent medical personnel on location. Actively seek out competent cultural informants to advise on personal safety and medical issues. Know the blood types of all students and make arrangements in advance in case students need transporting back to the United States.

One spin-off of Goshen's commitment to intercultural learning for every student is the Multicultural Affairs Office established in 1992. Funded for its initial three years with a major grant from the Lilly Endowment, the office works mainly with "traditionally underrepresented" U.S. cultural groups. The college has set a goal of having 8 percent of the student population from such groups and 10 percent from outside the United States and Canada. In 1993 this was achieved since twenty-four African-Americans, thirty-five Hispanic-Americans, five Native-Americans, and seventeen Asian-Pacific Islanders attended Goshen, for a total of eighty-one.

The director of the office, Zenebe Abebe, carries the title Associate Dean of Students for Multicultural Affairs. As a Goshen alumnus and former Psychology faculty member, Abebe coordinates the activities of an associate director, an office manager, and several student assistants. The director teaches part-time as well.

The office carries out three categories of activities, social, academic, and recruitment and retention. One relevant program uses a strategy common to most international education programs; for example, multicultural curriculum development is supported by faculty stipends for new courses or revisions of existing courses. The office pays particular attention to student recruitment and retention. In addition, the office has initiated a new faculty and staff development program with the annual presidential workshops comprising one aspect. Their goal is to celebrate diversity and reduce prejudice. Also, each year, minority alumni scholars are invited back to campus to share their experiences with both faculty and students. They are highlighted for two days in a campuswide forum, classroom presentations, a formal lunch, and other events.

To summarize the factors leading to the Study-Service Term's success, the president and his assistant initiated what proved to be a major restructuring of Goshen's calendar and general education graduation requirements in the 1960s. As one of the specific changes, the SST has proven its viability in spite of the fact that, at the time, it seemed ambitious and risky. A sizeable cross-section of the faculty supported the package of initiatives and, after months of discussion, the rest voted affirmatively as well. The SST gave focus to Goshen's traditional service mission. Also, the competence of its directors deserves noting as a factor in its success.

The Study-Service Term accepts as commonplace a goal many international educators can only contemplate. Goshen's purpose is to provide not only an in-depth multicultural academic experience, but to link this to service. The college wants to shape the future attitudes of participants as well as to provide assistance in host countries. The fact that this has been carried out is a tribute to Goshen's commitment to and understanding of the global human community.

Grambling State University

Achieving a Universitywide Current Issues Graduation Requirement

Located in Grambling, a small town in rural north central Louisiana, Grambling State University requires its second semester seniors, in professional schools as well as the College of Liberal Arts, to take GES 402: General Education Seminar in Current National and International Problems and Issues. The course is designed to insure that graduates have some knowledge of the major international issues of our time. This step was taken in the mid-1980s when the university was restructuring its general education requirements.

The decision to include international issues was built on the solid foundation of another general education approach to international curriculum development. Over some years, three survey level, multidisciplinary humanities courses have become part of the curriculum in the College of Liberal Arts. All majors in the College must take two of the three. The first course, Western Culture, was developed in the early 1970s, followed by the African Cultures course added a few years later, and joined in the mid-1980s by Non-Western Culture.

These two requirements show that twice in its history, Grambling State assumed a leadership role in mandating international curriculum for as large a percentage of its students as feasible. Adoption of the universitywide requirement coincided with Grambling's achieving a sense of assurance and security. The Louisiana legislature had appropriated money to improve the university's facilities and new programs were being added. These changes paralleled Coach Robinson's national recognition for establishing a tradition of winning football. There was reason to hope that Grambling was beginning a new history, distinct from its past of struggle and financial worry.

Grambling's history presents a lesson in perseverance. It also demonstrates the value of leaders capable of making hard decisions when institutional survival is at stake. The university's official history, written by Grambling State history professor Mildred Gallot, appears in its catalog. The facts imply a heroic struggle against heavy odds.

The idea for a school originated with a group of farmers who wanted an education for their children at the turn of the last century. They formed the North Louisiana Colored Agricultural Relief Association. This organization, of about 1,500 members, adopted as one of its objectives the operation of an "industrial" school. They purchased land and began a building. Since they could not raise enough money to finish the project, a store was leased in the meantime. Two teachers taught for three months each year in 1900 and 1901.

The farmers realized they needed educated expertise to establish and operate a full-time school. They wrote to Booker T. Washington for assistance and the answer came in the form of Charles Adams, destined to become known as Grambling's first president. He traveled all over northern Louisiana collecting financial support for the school. In taking over the construction project, he contributed money from the sale of a farm in his family. In November 1901, the Colored Industrial and Agricultural School opened with three teachers and 125 students. Most students paid the $5 a month fee in peas, potatoes and other commodities.

This hard beginning was echoed at other times in Grambling's history. In 1919, the local parish school board accepted the school and paid its teachers' salaries. The emphasis became training for elementary school teachers. In 1928, the Board said it could no longer afford to finance the school and President Adams appealed to Governor-elect Huey Long. Soon after the Governor took office, the Louisiana legislature passed a law making the school a state junior college called the Louisiana Negro Normal and Industrial Institute.

Subsequent history marked the institution's development as the state's leading black educational institution. In 1939 a third year of college work was added, quickly followed by a four-year program in 1940. This led, in 1946, to the legislature's voting to change the name to Grambling College. In 1953, the State Board of Education authorized Grambling to provide pre-medicine, law, and dentistry training. A Liberal Arts curriculum followed in 1957. The next major addition was a graduate program in Early Childhood and Elementary Education in 1973, followed by another name change in 1974 to Grambling State University.

Yet throughout all this apparent progress, financial constraints remained a major problem. Also, the university did not have a separate legal status. Then, says historian Gallot, "perhaps the single most significant event in the future of Grambling State University" occurred in 1981 when the now famous Consent Decree was signed implementing a decision by the U.S. Supreme Court. Grambling State University became a legal entity owning its own buildings. The legislature also voted money for major improvements under court order. Between 1986 and 1991, fifty million dollars was authorized. The College of Science and Technology and Nursing School were added in 1983, and in 1984 they were joined by the School of Social Work. As a result of all this expansion, the Spring 1993 graduating class was the largest ever with 500 degrees awarded.

Grambling State University has five colleges and two schools. The Colleges of Basic Studies, Business, Education, Liberal Arts, Science and Technology, are joined by the Schools of Nursing and Social Work. The university offers associate degrees in specific fields, such as office administration, criminal justice, and child development. Most of its graduates earn bachelor degrees while many masters are available as well. The highest degree awarded is the Ed.D. in developmental education.

The campus presents a neat, functional, and businesslike appearance with its mostly brick two- and three-story buildings. It features shrubbery-bordered walkways and grass dotted with southern pines. Grambling's lawn at its campus center is lined with hardwoods. A nature trail and fish ponds are maintained on part of the 300+-acre campus. The university's administration and faculty are proud of their heritage and enlivened by their university's expansion.

In this context, the institution's internationalization process proceeded, supported by outside grant funding, and highlighted by the current issues graduation requirement. Progress was substantial so that the new provost and vice president for academic affairs, joining the university in 1993, commented that its reputation for international studies was "one of the things that interested me in Grambling."

Campus Context

Grambling State University offers several international curriculum specializations. It has majors in French, Spanish, and German, as well as in French education and Spanish education. The biology major lists a speciality in Wildlife Biology. The geography major is, in effect, an international studies major with over half the courses in the department related to cultural geography; Geography of South America, for example, and two survey courses, Introduction to Global Development: Developed Nations, and Introduction to Global Development: Underdeveloped Nations. Over half the courses in the African-American studies major cover Africa. The catalog also lists a minor in Latin American studies and a certificate program in Asian studies.

The College of Business offers a masters in international business and trade. Business faculty say they proposed this degree as early as 1979 but it was not approved by both Grambling's board of trustees and the state board of regents until 1987. In the early 1990s, Grambling was the only state institution with such a degree. College of Business administrators report that about 40 percent of their faculty members were born overseas as Chinese, Arabs, Indians, and Africans. This list includes five Eritrians. International students comprise the majority of international masters degree recipients. The College of Business plans to expand its undergraduate international courses. At present, the management department offers International Business.

Besides its language programs offering majors, Grambling provides the first year of training in Arabic, Japanese and Italian. Students may take Chinese through the 300 level with the 400 level available as independent study. Linguistics courses include Applied Linguistics: French, and Great World Language Systems. Courses in the Honors Program list Cultural Diversity as one of three at the 300 level.

International and intercultural courses are infused throughout the curriculum of various departments. At Grambling, the departments usually offering relevant courses cover the world regions indicated by the multidisciplinary curriculum programs. Anthropology lists several on Latin America, Asia and Africa as well as cultural anthropology. History courses cover these regions plus Russian History, and a 100 level offering on The Modern World. Students taking political science can choose from several courses on international relations, including International Law, and comparative politics courses on Latin America and Africa. The department also has a course on Comparative Public Administration.

A degree in sociology requires nine hours in a foreign language. Departmental listings include several both international and intercultural courses; for example, one on the population issue, another called Social Adjustment of Black Americans, as well as a seminar on Third World Development, and Women in Cross-Cultural Perspective.

Other departments have developed relevant courses. Chemistry's Environmental Chemistry is at the introductory level and Biology has several ecology courses, e.g., Marine Ecology. The art department contributes Ethnic Art, and Economics offers Environmental Economics and Economic Development as well as the usual international and comparative courses. English has World Literature at both the 200 and 300 levels, and Comparative Literature and Afro-American Literature. Mass Communication offers International Communication and Blacks and the Media, Philosophy has African-American Philosophy, and Religion contributes a course on Comparative Religion. A social science course at the 400 level is called Workshop in Intercultural Education. Social Work lists Ethnic Sensitive Social Work while the speech and theatre department lists Theatre of Black Americans.

In other categories of international and intercultural education Grambling is also well represented. The university has a respectable record on campus diversity as measured by the figures at many U.S. colleges and universities. It has a minority student population of about 8 percent. These European-Americans are joined by about 100 to 120 undergraduate international students, predominantly from Mexico. The International Student Advisor works for the Student Life office.

Grambling's study abroad program in Mexico began in 1957. This establishes the university as one of the earliest to provide its students with an international program offered on a continuous basis. Administered by the foreign language department, the program sends groups two times a year, one in January during Christmas break, and the second extending through the summer session. From thirty to forty students participate each time.

The current chair of the Language Department and professor of Spanish, Charles Brooks, expanded the program in the early 1970s to include social science students. The host university in Mexico provides instruction for criminal justice and sociology students as well as Spanish majors. To add this component, Brooks drew on his contacts made while working on his doctorate at the Inter-American University. He also added an exchange to the program, thus bringing Mexican students to Grambling. In addition, about thirty Mexican students come to the Grambling campus each summer for intensive English instruction.

The language department also sponsors a summer study course at the University of Quebec at Trois Rivieres offering intensive language and culture training. About fifteen students participate. In addition, Grambling students can take part in exchange agreements with universities in Brazil, Mexico, China, India, Malaysia, and Kenya. These agreements include faculty exchanges as well. The agreement with a university in China will enable four students to study there during the fall of 1994. The most recent, a three year exchange project with the University of Malaya, was funded by the U.S. Information Agency. In 1985, this same agency funded an exchange between Grambling and Gandhigram Rural University in India.

The fee schedule for study abroad programs, set in the mid-1980s, provides a major incentive. Students can earn six credits for $50, nine for $75, and twelve or more for $100. Senior administrators want to encourage as many students as possible to participate. Students must pay their own maintenance and travel costs.

Another aspect of Grambling's international education programs is the series of visiting professors the institution has hosted. Funded either by the Foreign Curriculum Consultant Program in the U.S. Department of Education, or by the Council for International Exchange of Scholars, four resident scholars each have spent a year teaching and working on curriculum development at Grambling.

In the 1980s, the Department of Languages initiated a major outreach program as a result of its connections in Mexico. Kiddie College is open to children and young people from seven to fifteen years of age in both the United States and Mexico. The program begins the end of June and lasts for four weeks. During the first three weeks, the Mexican youth come to the United States while the U.S. young people go to Mexico. Both live with families, study the host country's language, and take part in planned social activities. For the last eight days or so, both groups join for a trip using Grambling's bus. The 1993 destination was San Antonio with thirty-eight Mexicans and seventeen U.S. nationals participating. Several of Grambling State's exchange students from Mexico teach in each summer's Kiddie College. This illustrates how the university has made its various international programs mutually supporting.

Grambling's international educators speak with pride about their resource center, the McIntosh International Center. It was established in 1988 with donated funding. Named after the dean who in the 1950s initiated the long running study abroad program in Mexico, the resource room houses films, study abroad program information, periodicals, and other reference materials.

As part of a balanced international education program, Grambling State has encouraged a major faculty development effort. The National Science Foundation has funded one faculty development project. It began in 1984 and enabled Grambling faculty to research "Science in Developing Countries." In addition, several travel-study seminars to various countries have been organized and funded by a succession of U.S. government grants. The person responsible for all this activity is Francis Abraham, professor of sociology and director of international studies. He has written successful proposals to the Fulbright-Hayes Group Projects Abroad Program in the U.S. Department of Education. About forty Grambling faculty have studied first-hand in India twice, in 1974 and 1978, Colombia in 1984, China in 1985, the Soviet Union in 1989, Brazil in 1991, and Egypt in 1992. Most of the participants have been social scientists and humanities faculty, but some have come from education and business as well.

Many of the participants in the Group Projects Abroad seminars have been faculty in other historically black colleges and universities. Abraham has put together a consortium named the Southwestern International Studies Consortium (SISCO). It has stressed faculty development and, in addition, sponsors an annual International Studies Conference. By the mid 1990s, the consortium, headquartered at Grambling, had twenty-three members in seven states, many in rural areas.

As the person responsible for faculty development, the annual conference, exchange agreements, a speaker's program, and the SISCO consortium, Abraham has effectively expanded international education not only at Grambling but at other institutions. Originally from India, his extraordinary energy keeps him always moving. The impression of quickness and having much to accomplish is tempered by a pleasant, gracious manner. A faculty member at Grambling for twenty-one years, Abraham has written seven books and over twenty successful grant proposals. Abraham has no teaching duties and, as director of international studies, reports to the Provost and vice president. He is assisted by a full-time secretary and a graduate assistant.

Abraham has assisted SISCO colleges and universities in several ways. Groups of SISCO institutions combine to participate not only in Group Projects Abroad seminars, but also in curriculum development projects. Five member colleges were funded by the U.S. Department of Education's Undergraduate International Studies and Foreign Language Program from 1987 to 1990. Abraham wrote the proposal, as he did the latest, funded in 1990, to develop international curriculum on another

10 SISCO campuses. The second project focuses on the developing world and on producing an international issues general education requirement modelled after Grambling's.

The Humanities and General Education Requirements
The 200 level Humanities culture courses were the first international curriculum to be required by a unit of Grambling State University. Most majors in the departments of the College of Liberal Arts must choose two of the following three: African Cultures, Western Culture, or Non-Western Culture. A few departments list which two its majors should take; for example, Political Science requires the Western and African courses.

All three are team-taught in the sense that two or three professors are responsible separately for the syllabus, lectures, student assignments, and grading for their sections. The specific content depends on who will be teaching in a given semester, yet humanities faculty report remarkable staffing stability over time.

A comparison of two syllabi for the Non-Western Culture course, one from the fall of 1993 and the other from the spring of 1994, illustrates the dominant pattern of content continuity as well as a provision for some flexibility. The stated purpose of the Non-Western Culture course is, "To introduce the student to the major cultural traditions of Asia, with particular attention to India, China, and Japan." The next sentence has a one word change which is noted parenthetically. "The student will become acquainted with the dominant religions, philosophies (literature, art) and social structures of the Eastern world." Taught every semester, the fall 1993 section was taught by two professors while in the spring they were joined by a third.

The African Cultures course, taught every spring semester, has three distinct syllabi. In 1993, for example, an historian and professors of music and art each taught a section on their own discipline. All report using various methodologies to insure authenticity and enliven class sessions. This approach is important to the effectiveness of the culture courses because they are taken by large numbers of students, generally over 200.

As explained by the music professor who teaches a section of the African Cultures course, the large student numbers seem to generate a positively charged atmosphere. She augments her lively course material by bringing in musicians, such as a sitar player. She uses films and presents artifacts such as musical instruments, cloth, and carvings. Faculty report that in another section of the same course, students were captivated by a speaker from Uganda who talked of his arranged marriage.

Generally students like the team-taught courses. The African course instructors sit in on each other's class sessions and sometimes get involved in discussions. Whatever confusion this may produce in student minds is offset by the vitality of such discussions. Student demand for the African Cultures course is reported as very high.

Each one of the Humanities culture courses has a separate origin. African Cultures, for example, is said to have originated with some Grambling faculty who, along with professors from other colleges and universities, participated in a group seminar to Africa in 1974. Financed by the Phelp Stokes Foundation in Washington D.C., the group toured Nigeria, Benin, Togo, and Ghana. Faculty on the program were to develop new curriculum upon their return from West Africa. At Grambling, this led to the African Cultures course. An historian, who was in the 1970s travel group to Africa, still teaches a section of the course.

Modelled on the previous Humanities culture courses, the Non-Western course was developed by a group of faculty as part of Grambling's 1982-84 curriculum development grant project. Third world studies was its theme, with funding from the U.S. Department of Education's Undergraduate International Studies and Foreign Language Program.

The GES 402 current issues course requirement for Grambling graduates was part of the new core adopted by 1985. Four-one credit General Education Seminars form the core, two at the 300 and two at the 400 level. It was decided to require the core during the junior and senior years because students by then would have achieved basic academic knowledge and skills.

One of the courses for juniors provides students with a background in the humanities, and the other covers social sciences. The first course for seniors applies the same multidisciplinary approach to the natural sciences. Breaking this pattern, the fourth course has a more specific focus as it introduces students to Current National and International Problems and Issues. All four have pre- and posttests and require passing the "Rising Junior Examination" as a prerequisite.

The Rising Junior Examination is designed to measure general knowledge and skills and is taken by all students who have earned between forty-five and sixty-one credits. According to Grambling's catalog, "Students who score at the 85th percentile are exempted from the GES 301, 302, 401 and 402." The university also requires the "Senior Comprehensive Competency Examination" of all graduating seniors. These examinations are in response to the mandate from Grambling's Board of Trustees for a system to certify the competencies of the university's graduates.

Although GES 402 is entitled "Current National and International Problems and Issues," all nine issues on a syllabus for the fall of 1993 are international; i.e., Continuing Unrest in the Persian Gulf Region, Population, Food and World Hunger, Decline of the Soviet Union, Creation of the Commonwealth of Independent States, Nuclear Nightmare, Human Rights, The Changing Economic Order.

The course states three objectives with the first, knowledge about events, supported by a second requiring students to locate countries in the world. Students will also have to demonstrate other geographical knowledge about the places where important world events have occurred. According to the third objective, the course is designed so that students completing it will be able to "Discuss major geopolitical issues which unite and divide the underdeveloped and industrially advanced countries." This issue, therefore, cuts across the current events topics and provides an underlying level of analysis.

GES 402 applies various classroom methodologies. *Time* magazine, its "News Highlights" and weekly quizzes are used in the course. Students also have to take geography quizzes which include the United States. Map exercises referencing each continent are a part of class activities. Many videos augment lectures and reading materials. The McIntosh Center has media on every third world country from Afghanistan to Zimbabwe. So a video can supply background information whatever current issue is being studied. Also, groups of students must choose one of the course's issues, review material provided by the professor, analyze it, and present the findings in a panel presentation to the rest of the class as well as in a paper. Members of the group receive the same grade for both the panel and the paper. The course's posttest is used as the final examination.

Several sections of GES 402 are offered each semester with forty to forty-five students in each. All are taught by social science faculty. In spite of the fact that each course carries one credit, it is counted as the equivalent of a regular three-credit course when determining a faculty member's teaching load. The administration made this decision in 1990 after computing fractions in faculty teaching assignments proved unwieldy. The normal course load at Grambling is five courses a semester.

The provost reports that the administration has "put teeth" in the GES 402 requirement. She illustrates with an example of a senior nursing student who, because of her need to complete clinical requirements for her major, wanted the current issues requirement waived. Student teachers also make this request periodically. The provost ruled that the nursing student could not graduate without taking and passing GES 402. Given the problem this example reveals, Grambling has instituted a special section of the course using an individual study format.

Issues and Answers
Grambling faculty who teach in the Humanities culture courses, recall an administrative issue as the most significant one to have surfaced over the years. When the Western Culture course was first offered, faculty teaching each section had it counted as one-third of a course toward their total teaching load since each professor was responsible for a separate section. This proved cumbersome and caused some resentment. It was changed in the 1970s, allowing faculty teaching the Humanities cultures courses to count their responsibility as the equivalent of a whole course. Part of the reasoning was that faculty teaching these courses were expected to spend time coordinating both content and instruction. In spite of this experience, the same

lesson had to be learned in determining faculty loads for the General Education Seminars.

In the case of GES 402, faculty report the decision to adopt this requirement produced much discussion. Yet once the International Education Subcommittee, part of the university's Committee on General Education, made its decision, there was no opposition. Perhaps one reason was that "everyone was involved" in the discussion, according to one professor who remembers the process. Also, the new course achieved a discipline balance. The humanities, already with the three College of Liberal Arts required courses, were satisfied with one GES course while the social sciences got two, in effect, counting the current issues course.

One issue needing attention arose from the fact that the first General Education current issues course was offered for no credit. Called Global Issues, students proved reticent to complete readings and other assignments faculty determined necessary. Soon the College of Liberal Arts decided to increase the number of class meetings and initiated the process to grant one credit for GES 402.

Lessons Learned

Faculty who have taught both types of Grambling's required courses offer the following guidelines.

1. *Apply a holistic approach to team-taught courses.* Even though, or perhaps because, Grambling's Humanities culture courses are organized into separate sections, faculty must consciously tie them together. For maximum learning, students need faculty to integrate what otherwise can seem isolated pieces of information. The African Cultures faculty sit in on each other's classes so they can make references to each other's concepts and content.

2. *Always offer required courses for credit.* Students did not take seriously the first attempt at a required current issues course.

3. *Coordinate instruction when several professors teach separate sections of a required general education course.* All faculty who

will be teaching the GES 402 course meet in the beginning of the semester. They decide which issues to include and prepare a common final examination for all sections.

4. *Use pre- and posttests.* This helps insure that students achieve commonly agreed upon competencies when a course has several sections each taught by a different faculty member. Such tests also make students aware of how much they have learned.

5. *Cultivate the support of senior administrators.* At key times throughout the development of international education at Grambling, crucial supportive decisions were made. One example, not mentioned in the previous narrative, occurred in 1989. Francis Abraham needed a subsidy when costs abruptly rose for a Group Projects Abroad seminar to the Soviet Union. Grambling's President provided the needed $10,000 from the academic enhancement fund.

6. *Integrate international education efforts.* In discussing the wide range of his activities, Abraham emphasizes that people met while carrying out one activity often lead to more contacts and another project. Spin-offs seem to happen as a matter of course; for example, his own research in India led to the first Group Projects Abroad seminar. As international activities at Gambling expanded, he met a person from China with contacts at Beijing University. The resulting Group Projects Abroad seminar set the stage for a guest scholar who initiated Grambling's Chinese language program. The program development by Charles Brooks in the Language Department also illustrates this point. He took the original program in Mexico and developed several creative spin-offs, such as Kiddie College.

Clearly a crucial factor in Grambling's internationalization process is the initiative of its individual faculty. Also, successive generations of senior administrators have made decisions in support of international programs, including funding commitments. They have agreed to cut tuition payments for students studying abroad, for example. Their actions are consistent with the Grambling tradition of strong leadership, the decisiveness that helped save the school in its earliest years. Lastly, grant support has proven essential in developing Grambling's extensive faculty and curriculum development, plus its related outreach programs.

Hollins College

Learning in Jamaica Through Mutual Human Development

In a valley deep within Southwestern Virginia's grandly rolling hills, the Hollins campus appears open and inviting. Its surrounding pastured slopes evoke a quiet contentment while just over the hills, lies the city of Roanoke. The campus reflects the confidence tradition imparts. Its quadrangle of trees is surrounded by three- to four-floor grandly columned brick buildings, many with porches.

The reassuring dignity of Tinker Mountain can be seen from anywhere on campus. It is the site of Tinker Day, the annual mountain climb in October when students, faculty, and administrators stride or scramble up its one-and-a-half to two mile trail to the top. There they are treated to student-led skits and a picnic lunch.

To a superficial observer it may seem surprising that, since 1988, Hollins has sustained a "Mini-Peace Corps" student program in Jamaica. Looking deeper, one discovers that this innovative short-cycle program flows logically from the college's educational commitment and practice.

As primarily a liberal arts women's college of 1,000 students, howbeit with a co-educational graduate program, Hollins has remained true to its long and respected tradition. Established in 1842 as Valley Union Seminary, the college became an institution for women in 1852. It acquired the name Hollins when a family of that name became its major benefactor. It provides an intellectual environment where women feel free to express themselves. They develop confidence both academically and personally. Not just clever phrases on slick brochures, small classes and individual attention best describe the behavior of faculty and administrators.

Detailed and individualized planning characterizes Hollins' service program in Jamaica. Each year approximately thirty-five students participate, a large proportion of the 100 or so students the college sends overseas per year. These figures indicate that the Jamaican program significantly contributes to the high rate of 50 percent of Hollins students who graduate with an overseas experience.

Campus Context

Hollins' mission statement implies support for the Jamaica service program. The college professes a "commitment to social justice" and "values diversity." In this context, the Hollins president, administrators, faculty, and students speak highly of the service program.

Campus decision-makers also view other international education activities as integral to the college's mission. In the category of curriculum, Hollins' offers several international specializations. Language majors are available in French, German, and Spanish. Courses in two other languages are listed in the catalog: Russian through the 300 level and Japanese at the 100 level.

The International Relations concentration also provides students with an international curriculum choice. In 1994 it attracted twenty students and included courses in economics, political science, and history, as well as requiring two years of a foreign language. Also in 1994, a new international studies major was approved by the faculty. It expands the number of participating disciplines to include art, music, philosophy, and religion. The decision on whether to continue the International Relations Concentration remains to be made.

The Departments of History, Political Science, and Economics provide the core of Hollins' international courses. The last mentioned has two International Economics courses as well as one each on Comparative Economics and Development. History courses cover the world regions of Europe, Latin America, and East Asia, as well as individual countries: Japan, Russia, France, and Germany. Courses on international issues and an historical approach to international relations are also offered, such as War and Society in the Twentieth Century, History of International Relations, Comparative Studies in Women's History, History of Socialism, Communism and Anarchism, and Revolution and War in Vietnam. Political Science offers an international relations and a comparative politics course, as well as Political Issues and Answers, which deals with international politics. Like the History Department, Political Science covers Latin America and Western Europe, and adds the Middle East. Specific courses deal with Canada and Britain, and seminars are available in International Relations, U.S. Foreign Policy, and National Security Policy.

Other departments also contribute to the college's international and intercultural catalog listings. Biology offers an Ecology course, Communication Studies an Intercultural/International Communication course, and English has Irish Literature and Afro-American Writers. Religion courses cover Introduction to Religions of the World and Judaism, Christianity, and Islam. The Sociology Department listings include three Anthropology courses and The Family, a Sociology course, which covers cross-cultural information. The Theatre Arts Department has Dance in a Selected Culture, Studies in World Cinema, and two courses on German Cinema. The Hollins World Geography course covers global issues.

Since it began with a semester Paris program in 1955, Hollins Abroad has been the college's flagship international education effort. It marks Hollins as one of the earliest colleges to recognize the value of an overseas experience in contributing to a liberal arts education. In 1974 a London site was added. Over the years, students from other colleges have taken courses and resided in both the Paris and London centers. Hollins students also participate in a consortium program in Kobe, Japan, and Vologda, Russia.

Its small number of international students, twenty-four in 1994, reflects Hollins' size. It also increases the college's reliance on its Jamaican program to implement its mission statement's diversity commitment. In addition, sixty-eight U.S. minority students attended Hollins in 1994.

In 1992, the International and Graduate Programs Office was established under the direction of an economics faculty member, Tom Edwards. He continues as the International Relations Concentration's advisor and teaches an International Economics course each year. The office also has two full-time staff, the assistant dean of international and special programs and the administrative assistant. The assistant dean had been the international student advisor. She continues working with these students in her new role while taking on the administration of Hollins' student overseas programs. Also in her previous position in student services she had initiated the service program in Jamaica.

Human Development in Jamaica Program
Twice a year in nine-day and two-week cycles, a maximum of twenty students live, work, and engage in structured learning activities in Lucea, Jamaica. The program aims to foster the visitors' human development through learning and service. At the same time, by providing ongoing support for Lucea's social services, the program aids human development projects in this town of about 12,000 people.

Both sides of the participant equation, those involved in Lucea as well as from Hollins, enthusiastically report positive results since the program began in 1988. Their reactions demonstrate that ongoing, carefully planned, sensitively administered activities can have a significant impact even if the in-country part of the program lasts a short time.

To ensure meaningful service for Lucea's residents, the Hollins program provides a steady stream of supplies and willing workers for the town's infirmary, primary and secondary schools, beautification plans, and a store selling products made by handicapped people. Over the years, the policy of concentrating on specified projects until they are completed has produced measurable results; for example, Hollins students have painted Lucea's high school library, bought it many books, including general reference materials such as encyclopedias, and catalogued the whole collection. This represents a real contribution because the library had been destroyed when hurricane Gilbert's eye moved through Lucea in September, 1988. The facility had remained closed until Hollins students rebuilt it.

The program in Lucea was initiated in 1979 by Richard Pyle, then a faculty member at Alma College in Michigan. He had served there as a Peace Corps volunteer. In 1988 while his daughter attended Hollins, he met the college's then director of special services and events, Jeri Suarez, and asked if she was interested in leading a group of students to Lucea. Other colleges, including the University of Texas-Austin, sent students as well but Hollins has continued this long-term commitment twice a year since 1988. As of 1994, William Jewell College is the only college other than Hollins to send students on an annual basis.

Now assistant dean of international and special programs, Jeri Suarez continues to administer the "mini-Peace Corps" program. She plans one major group work project each time students go to Jamaica; for instance, painting the infirmary and the town's bus sheds, or picking up trash and planting flowers downtown. This sort of activity generally takes half of every day. Students also carry out individual service projects, such as teaching recreational games in the park, reading or playing cards with infirmary patients, teaching a self-defense class for high school girls and first aid skills to the community. Home stays enhance the cultural learning through additional interpersonal interaction.

Past students have reported that their Jamaican experience proved useful later in their college careers. Therefore, to help retain accurate memories, a videotape is made of each group's experiences and a copy given to every participant after her return to campus.

The program also requires directed academic activities, including a reflective journal, not a diary, and evening seminars with community speakers. Tours of a sugar cane plantation and a factory manufacturing brassieres initiate discussions on the impact of international trade and United States' investment.

Specific assignments, such as asking market women questions about daily economic life, provide a focus for field research activities. The follow-up discussions comparing answers has become one of the tasks for each group. Initiating conversations with Lucea residents enables students to become more knowledgeable of and comfortable in their social environment. They also develop their communication, data gathering and processing skills.

Often individual students arrive in Jamaica with their own academic interests. Adjustments are made so there is time for a business major to interview a banker, and for an English major to write poetry, to cite two past examples.

The program ends with a tourist experience so participants can contrast the Jamaica they know with the country's tourist-driven economy and social behavior. Thus, what begins as learning about a political/economic topic leads to a consideration of its value-laden implications.

The January groups earn credit for one course because the program continues for four weeks, two weeks on campus separated by the two weeks in Jamaica. During the first on-campus week, students learn about the Jamaican contemporary political and economic situation as well as its history and society. They also prepare lesson plans for their individual project. The students gather either donated or purchased supplies they will need in Lucea, e.g., pens, paper, pencils, art supplies, recreation equipment, woodworking tools, paint and brushes, medical supplies, etc.

Organizing these, and general supplies for the town's needs, has proven one of the best instructional techniques to ensure an effective orientation. Inevitably the students ask why there is difficulty purchasing such "ordinary things" as marking pens, soap, aspirins, and paint brushes in Jamaica. The answers point out the economic realities in countries where most consumer goods must be imported from the United States with its much higher standard of living.

During the final week on campus, after their two weeks in Jamaica, students attend debriefing classes which allows the group to process the experience and to reflect on the lessons learned. At the end of the week, they turn in their research projects for a grade, along with their academic journal. These projects often include, but are not limited to, field research reports. Before leaving campus, students negotiate in detail their project's objectives and methodologies with faculty advisors in their majors. A sample of student work includes original literature, art, and business marketing projects.

The spring break service experience carries no credit but includes shorter versions of all the program components; i.e., evening lectures, a journal, field assignments, a group as well as individual service projects. In addition, students are required to attend orientation classes every Friday during the spring semester before they go to Lucea, as well as debriefing sessions upon their return.

The Lucea Rotary Club provides local sponsorship and the wife of one of its members, Beverly Lawrence, serves as the local contact for the program in Jamaica. After the death of her husband, her role has continued even though women cannot formally hold club membership. Beverly Lawrence was the principal of a primary school in one of the neighboring communities and presently teaches English in Lucea's high school.

Program costs remain low, a Hollins policy decision, so as many students as possible can afford to participate. The longer January experience costs about $900 while the spring break group pays about $800. This includes airfare, room and board, transportation, and a small stipend for the home stay family.

Even at this price, upon occasion some students cannot participate due to their inability to raise money. As an aside, Hollins' 4-1-4 academic calendar includes the one month January short term when all students concentrate on one course, internship or research project either on campus or off. The off campus programs always require additional travel costs.

Participating students often devise creative ways to raise the needed extra money. Some apply to their hometown Rotary Clubs or other groups for scholarships. Locally owned companies, like car dealerships, have proven one potential source of financial support. Churches also have provided aid funds. One aspiring program participant asked the students in the high school from which she had graduated to donate one dollar each. After her return from Jamaica, she gratefully presented a slide show at this high school.

The service program in Jamaica has provided a focus for faculty development. Virtually every student group has been accompanied by a faculty member, as well as the program's director. Some interested faculty have ventured to Jamaica twice, including professors in economics, chemistry, and mathematics. The college nurse has participated in four projects. All complete their own service projects, often tutoring Lucea's high school students. Their reaction has been so positive that many more faculty have expressed a desire to participate.

The last six years has produced evidence that the Jamaican service program led to an attitude change in many of its participants. Students continue volunteering upon their return to the United States. They discover service opportunities in Roanoke's soup kitchen, at its battered women's shelter, or in their home communities. This may mark the beginning of a commitment to a life of service.

Issues and Answers
Every problem needing attention over the years has concerned logistics. The cost to students remains the most significant and ongoing issue. One response has been implemented, and another is being discussed. The service program's director has prepared an information sheet and cover letter to help students in their quest for financial support. Yet a more systematic approach is needed.

The next issue may seem minor but actually is not since it threatens the effective transportation of supplies to Lucea. On occasion, Jamaican customs has questioned the quantity of a particular item and has wanted to charge a duty fee, e.g., for new shirts donated for the infirmary. A letter from the program's local sponsor explaining the use of the supplies avoided subsequent incidents. Otherwise customs would want a duty paid because the items could be sold for profit. This is especially true for large items; for example, an electric keyboard purchased for primary school music classes. Had there not been a letter stating that the school was expecting the item, a large duty would have been assessed.

Electronic hardware will be needed in Lucea for some contemplated projects. So far, the program director has handled the situation without paying customs duties, or any other fees. Yet in the future, the group would like to bring in a computer. One option under consideration is to establish a budget line for such contingencies. Yet this is not an easy decision given the need to assist students by keeping program costs low.

Another issue concerns continuation of some projects in the students' absence. Maintenance is an ongoing point of discussion with the program sponsors in Lucea. They have always taken part in deciding which projects to initiate, but have shown less enthusiasm for organizing project maintenance. The director is working with the local coordinator on these issues in hopes of organizing some youth groups to engage in community service on a regular basis.

There are hopeful signs of growing local ownership of the projects. Since the town leaders wanted beautification to induce tourists to stop, they realize trash pickups and plant care must continue throughout the year.

Lessons Learned and Future Ideas

The following list covers topics from the program's pedagogical justification to specific organizational guidelines. As such, it provides a useful summary of the factors needed for a successful experiential overseas student program.

1. *Keep the program's pedagogical rationale general allowing flexibility.* The service program provides experiences as varied as each individual student, yet within a context of common cultural, political, and economic content. Much group learning does occur, i.e. being a "racial" minority for the first time, valuing a "simple" way of life without television and convenience food, and on occasion, running water, and analyzing the local impact of international trade patterns. However, students also develop expertise within their individual majors and sort out their own psychological reactions.

   Flexibility also describes a shift in the campus community's perception of what service in Jamaica is designed to achieve. At first, "doing for others" rationales were given for the program but this has changed in response to the comments from students and faculty returning from Jamaica. The general understanding has shifted to viewing the program as a mutual exchange, primarily of human resources.

   The U.S. visitors and the Jamaicans learn from each other, often resulting in what may best be termed personal human development. As evidence, several secondary school students in Jamaica now see themselves as college bound. Also, every group of Hollins participants includes

some who shift their career plans to one of the service
professions.

2. *The program director must have dedication, organizational
   competence, the energy that comes from unending enthusiasm,
   and a love for both the facilities and foibles of individual human
   beings.* An experiential program never becomes pushbut-
   ton. In the case of the Hollins Jamaica program, individual
   student projects as well as group projects need organizing
   twice each year. Program administration seems constant,
   requiring patience and good interpersonal skills in two
   cultures.

3. *The in-country program administrator also needs these characteristics.* Since the U.S. and international organizers are
   equally important for successful program development,
   choosing the local coordinator is a vital decision. As with
   the campus program director, salary alone will not insure
   long-term, effective program administration at the overseas site. The local coordinator must be personally committed and steady in handling all sorts of human situations.

4. *Design programs for credit whenever possible.* In the case of
   the Hollins program, credit is offered for the January
   course but not during spring break. Offering a shortened
   spring program allows more students to participate and
   provides Lucea with more benefits. Yet, the spring students do not evidence the high level of academic work
   demanded when an academic project is required. This
   activity focuses learning, makes it overt, and more directly
   causes students to link their Jamaican experience to their
   on campus course work.

5. *Include faculty volunteers in all program components, especially
   in the service experience.* Hollins faculty participants have
   home stays, attend nightly presentations and field trips,
   and complete individual service projects. They have participated constructively in discussions, as one among many,
   and shown respect for student reactions. This flows naturally from their classroom role at Hollins given the college's goal of helping students develop as whole persons.

There is some evidence that faculty participants have made curriculum changes in reaction to their own Jamaican experiences; for example, one Economics professor who teaches about trade, has brought Jamaican newspapers back to use as class materials.

6. *Continue developing new service projects.* Creating new projects produces dual benefits. It gives Lucea residents a sense of momentum and progress. Also, the students register their own personal impact. Their accomplishments are distinct, not simply a repeat of their predecessors' efforts. If the service becomes routine, it loses some of its potency as a teaching-learning methodology.

7. *Institutionalization brings legitimacy.* In 1988, the first group of Hollins students came back from Jamaica effusively extolling the program's virtues. This not only produced visibility, and increased student demand and faculty support, it earned the attention of the college president, Paula Brownlee. She supported the program director's request to give it space in the college catalog for the January short term. Such institutionalization assured legitimacy and implied permanency. Moving quickly from one inspired person's "hip-pocket" operation to formal college sponsorship fostered the program's rapid expansion. This institutionalization has continued with the enthusiastic endorsement of the new president, Jane Margaret O'Brien. She recognized the program's contribution to a Hollins education.

The service program in Jamaica has surpassed even the expectations of its founder. It began tangentially, as a hopeful initiative by Jeri Suarez, director of special services and events in the Student Services Office. It seemed a risk to lead the first nine students and two staff members on an adventure in Jamaica. Now, more students and faculty enthusiastically await their turn as program participants.

Success stimulates new ideas. Thus far, they remain as dreams for the program director, but this was how the Jamaica service program itself began. Yet the current situation is different in at least one major respect. The original program was begun voluntarily, as an extra, self-assumed initiative of one administrator. Its very success means any spin-off would require the college to commit additional administrative resources.

Several of these new ideas involve a geographic expansion, both within Jamaica and in another country. The possibility exists of adding a new Jamaican site since leaders in other towns have indicated interest in hosting their own service program. Also, discussions have taken place with a Hollins Spanish faculty member. Under consideration are potential sites for a short cycle service program in a Latin American Spanish-speaking country.

In addition, the existing program could be expanded. A third group of students a year could go to Lucea during the summer.

The program director is contemplating yet another spin-off, establishing an exchange to enable young Jamaicans to engage in service projects in the Roanoke area. Also, leaders in the Lucea community could spend time at Hollins and in the Roanoke community as speakers, orientation leaders, classroom lecturers, or leaders of faculty development workshops.

A pilot of such an initiative occurred for a week in 1992 when Beverly Lawrence from Lucea visited the Hollins campus. She proved effective since her classroom presentations and meetings with faculty received high praise. Her visit produced a measurable increase in requests for information about the Jamaica program.

An additional program could establish support for the newly inspired college aspirations of some of Lucea's young women. An endowment fund could provide scholarships for these students to attend Hollins.

The Jamaican program fits the Hollins emphasis on small-scale, well-designed, supportive education with the individual student as its focus. In channeling the enthusiasm of successive generations of students, the program has earned the full support of two presidents, several faculty, and the people of Lucea. As the key factor in the program's success, the director has been creative and untiring in working with both students and townspeople to produce meaningful results.

Kalamazoo College

Making International Study Available for All Students

Established in 1833, Kalamazoo College is among the 100 oldest institutions of higher education in the United States. Its campus imparts a sense of dignity and scholarly purpose. Its large red brick buildings step up the campus hill with measured assurance. Older homes in a moderately well-to-do section of Kalamzaoo, Michigan immediately border the college, and a busy thoroughfare lies within easy access. This comfortable niche in a midsized American city provides a quality liberal arts environment for well over 1,200 undergraduates. As an indicator of Kalamazoo's distinctiveness, students back on campus for their first days of classes commonly use such greetings as, "How was Ecuador?" One returnee, in responding to the observation, "I haven't seen you in a while," stated matter-of-factly, "I was in Kenya." These observations validate the slogan on one of the college bookstore's T-shirts, "The World Is Our Campus."

During the past thirty years some 85 percent of Kalamazoo College's graduates have studied in another country. This results from the depth and breadth of the international curriculum and overseas study programs. Developed over the years, a carefully constructed, multifaceted incentive system stimulates demand. It includes several mutually reinforcing elements: The K-Plan for organizing the college calendar, subsidies from the S.R. Light Trust, senior staffing for the Foreign Study Program Office, plus curricular programs in seven modern languages, two classical languages, and five world regions. On the supply side, the college has established eighteen overseas centers and programs.

Campus Context

Its remarkably extensive interdependent network of curriculum and overseas study programs supports Kalamazoo's claim that international education lies at the heart of its *raison d'etre*. According to its mission statement,

> The mission of Kalamazoo College is to operate a nationally renowned, fiscally responsible, four-year liberal arts college which provides its graduates with an excellent learning experience that has a unique global perspective and that contributes to their ability to lead lives of significance. The college offers a coherent undergraduate experience through the interweaving of a traditional liberal arts curriculum, experiential education in both domestic and international settings, and an independent research quarter.

The college sees itself as having been founded with ideas giving rise over a century later to its particular international education focus:

> Kalamazoo College was founded in 1833 with a commitment to academic excellence, liberal learning, freedom of individual conscience, and an appreciation of difference . . . James and Lucinda Stone who led the college from 1842 to 1863 sustained their vision of a college that transcended barriers . . . between campus life and the larger life of American society and world events.

This statement embodies two themes linking the college's past and present, i.e., serious, open scholarly inquiry, and the direct relationship between college study and contemporary human issues.

These assumptions become reality in the college's current course offerings. "Over 30 percent of the curriculum deals significantly with Western Europe," according to a Kalamazoo brochure. The addition of courses on other world regions boosts the percentage of internationally related courses in the curriculum to about 40 percent. Most departments list at least one relevant course; for instance, THA 485, "Non-Western Film Directors," is offered by the Communication Arts Department.

Specialized programs and a three quarter foreign language graduation requirement highlight Kalamazoo's curriculum internationalization. Unlike many other U.S. colleges and universities, Kalamazoo never dropped its foreign language requirement. This reflects the area studies emphasis in the college curriculum.

The major in International and Area Studies includes five world regions: African, East Asian, Latin American, Russian

Eastern European Studies, and Western European Studies. The last is divided into Modern Europe, British, French, and German Studies. After completing two required international and comparative courses, students must choose a world area and take four of the courses listed. Students may select European countries other than those noted above and take relevant courses available through Kalamazoo's overseas programs. All the subfields of the International and Area Studies major are heavily interdisciplinary; for example, African Studies includes a Biology course on the "Ecology of Africa."

In addition, the college offers majors in three languages, German, French and Spanish, as well as a concentration in International Commerce. Also, students may opt for a concentration in International and Area Studies instead of a full major.

Several other international curriculum foci are listed in the college catalog as programs. This means students can select the program's courses but they do not carry a transcript designation. The area studies noted above can be emphasized in this way as can studies in the Environment, Chinese, Dutch, Italian, Russian, Japanese, and Neglected Languages. The named languages include courses at least through the intermediate level and some programs offer culture and/or conversation courses. The Neglected Languages category is a response to changing student demands. In the past, the college has offered Portuguese and Swahili, among others. Before Chinese and Japanese were added to Kalamazoo's regular curriculum, they were offered in this program and attracted more students than other non-traditional languages.

The depth of this curriculum, faculty scholarship, and library holdings, provided the basis for Kalamazoo's designation as a National Center for Western European Studies. In 1988, the college successfully applied to the U.S. Department of Education's National Resource Centers Program for funding and center status. The success of its initial application, and of the subsequent grant three years later, established Kalamazoo as the only liberal arts college to become a National Center.

Through the Center, Kalamazoo engages in outreach activities for local high school teachers. Once a year approximately

150 teachers attend a Foreign Language Day. During this event, the college hosts speakers and workshops on teaching languages. In addition, annual spring two-day conferences are held with twenty-five to thirty attendees. In 1991 the subject was the new Europe, while in 1992 Spanish language teachers were invited to hear updates on recent events in Spain.

Additional activities enhance Kalamazoo College's language specializations. Students may choose to live in one of four language houses where only French, Spanish, German, or Japanese is to be spoken in public areas. Three courses in the language is a prerequisite, and students are encouraged to live in a house before or after their Foreign Study. Each house has a Cultural Mentor who serves as a language and cultural informant. These mentors most often are international students recruited from Kalamazoo's various overseas centers.

These centers provide the college with many of its international students. In 1994, fifty-plus arrived on campus, thirty-four from the centers. The goal for most of them is not a Kalamazoo degree. On the whole, they want a U.S. experience coupled with some useful academic and practical work. Those who are teaching assistants receive full or partial tuition remission plus the U.S. minimum wage for the hours they tutor.

The makeup of Kalamazoo's faculty has changed since the early 1960s. When the Foreign Study Program was approved by the faculty, there were a few with international knowledge or experience. According to a professor present at the time, several had been overseas during wartime and six had been born in other countries, three in Latvia, one each in Germany, Algeria, and the United Kingdom.

By the early 1990s, twenty-five out of the approximately eighty full-time Kalamazoo faculty were involved in the Western European Center's activities. In addition, several science faculty were becoming professionally international. Two had engaged in research in Africa. A biology professor has been instrumental in the development of an environmental studies program in Quito, Ecuador. Hiring with international expertise as a secondary factor also had produced some change. At present, two mathematics faculty speak a language other than English. One recent hire in the philosophy department is fluent in German.

Increasing the faculty's international expertise was the purpose of a project which began in 1984. Stipends funded by a Mellon Foundation grant were provided for faculty to learn languages. Several took courses on campus and then overseas. The current provost had previously taught chemistry and, after taking four German courses at the college, went to a Goethe Institute program in Germany. He represents a campus consensus and commitment to increase both the number and quality of faculty international endeavors. This has resulted from the Foreign Study Program's success over the years and its incorporation into Kalamazoo's very identity.

History of the K-Plan

In 1961 Kalamazoo took a rare and relatively startling action. After much debate, the faculty adopted a new academic program and changed the college calendar. Academic activities would now cover a full twelve months divided into four equal quarters. This allowed three off-campus experiences to become a systematic part of student learning: a Career Development internship, Foreign Study, and a Senior Individualized Project. Students may deviate from this K-Plan, as it has come to be called, but they must receive approval in advance from the Committee on Academic Standards.

By reshaping its academic program, Kalamazoo also refined its mission. The college goal was clarified, i.e., preparing all students, if possible, to become self-reliant, mature individuals actively applying their learning in the increasingly interdependent world. The three elements of independence, applied learning, and international expertise were integrated with solid academic training.

Why did Kalamazoo, after considerable thought and debate, essentially redefine itself in the early 1960s? People knowledgeable about its formative years attribute the college's creative K-Plan to the farsightedness and financial support of one man, the chairman of the Board of Trustees from 1953 to 1974, Dr. Richard Upjohn Light. The story has become almost legendary: Richard Light, a medical doctor, took his children to Europe one summer. The experience so transformed them that he decided an overseas experience was essential to a quality education. To implement this decision, he provided Kalamazoo students with a scholarship program in the form of an endowment of approximately two-and-a-half million dollars. This endowment was named the S.R. Light Trust, after Richard Light's brother. As the special 1974 baccalaureate edition of the *Kalamazoo College Review* summed up Dr. Light's contribution, "It was Richard Light, more than any other man, who made the world a part of the campus of this college."

Beginning in 1958, the trust fund helped groups of students participate in noncredit summer academic programs at universities in Caen, Bonn, and Madrid. Light stayed involved by using his personal contacts to help establish these and other overseas centers added later. After the adoption of the K-Plan, the present credit-bearing Foreign Study Program began in the fall of 1962. Helping students achieve superior language facility was, and continues to be, an important focus, balanced with learning the host country's history, geography, art, and literature. All programs other than those in the United Kingdom include languages. Yet providing an "integrative cultural experience" also is the focus; for example, in Senegal, where the Wolof language is taught and where students are required to carry out mentored individual research. The emphasis on languages in their cultural context fits Kalamazoo's traditional concern for academic quality.

During the 1962-63 academic year, eighty out of the approximately 190-member junior class went overseas for two quarters and an additional twenty-four participated in a spring program. Meanwhile, arrangements were made to accommodate all qualified juniors who wanted to participate during the next year. About 86 percent of the next junior class attended Kalamazoo's overseas centers in 1963-64.

Since students do not always possess prerequisites enabling them to attain fluency, additional programs were added throughout the 1960s. These accommodate participants with varying levels of proficiency in French, German, and Spanish. Thus advanced students are provided with the best possible training. They take, along with native-speaking students, college level courses on a variety of subjects taught in their language of study. Also, students less prepared can take courses in programs set up for foreign students within universities overseas. A third kind of program involves courses designed specifically for Kalamazoo students.

Thus far, this program description has shown Kalamazoo's multiple overseas centers as the college's significant contribution to international education. These centers provide for participation by students with varying language capabilities. Another element of the college's Foreign Study Program proved a forerunner of what became a growing trend in U.S. undergraduate international education. During the 1960s, before third world studies attracted its current interest, Kalamazoo College established centers in Africa. The college's commitment to sending students to the developing world remains strong. In addition to three sites in Africa, Kalamazoo maintains programs in Ecuador, Mexico and China.

Early on, the Foreign Study Program's formulators consciously chose not to sponsor faculty-led groups but to establish programs at specific sites overseas. The traveling group strategy was tried but found wanting. The stability of a local staff at each center has proven its worth over three decades.

Establishing international education as central to Kalamazoo's mission, organizing its overseas programs, and rearranging the college calendar gave life and substance to Richard Light's vision, energy, and financial support. The K-Plan and the Foreign Study Program's ongoing success testify to the effectiveness of a dedicated group of faculty and high level administrators. Weimer Hicks, Kalamazoo's president from 1954 to 1971, added his active support to that of Provost Lawrence Barrett. Richard Stavig, a respected member of the English department, served as the Foreign Study Program's first director until 1974. He established its solid academic reputation during this period of rapid growth. This group, plus other active faculty, provided the critical mass needed to convince a majority of their colleagues to link Kalamazoo College's future with that of international education.

Joe Fugate, a member of the faculty and professor of German since 1961, was involved in the program almost from its inception. As assistant director, he traveled overseas to establish Kalamazoo's centers in Germany, France, and Spain. In 1974, he became the Foreign Study Program's second director. Since Fugate remained director until 1992, the already stable program benefitted from a continuity of leadership. His fluency in three languages, working knowledge of others, plus a personal attention to the overseas programs, provided Fugate with detailed knowledge of generations of students and overseas center staffing. Three decades of successful teaching and program administration is reflected in his forceful assurance. He exudes energy and competence. In both his comments and demeanor he emphasizes high academic standards.

These qualities are also present in the Foreign Study Office's third director. Michael Vande Berg continues the tradition of exemplary academic qualifications plus relevant program experience. His Ph.D. in Comparative Literature is supported by language specialities in French and Spanish. His administrative experience includes service as the director of the English Department at the Instituto Internacional in Madrid. This was followed by four years as assistant, then associate director, then director of Kalamazoo's Madrid center. Vande Berg spent the next four years as assistant director of the Foreign Study Office back on the Kalamazoo campus.

Kalamazoo's scholarly focus is balanced by its contribution to "the development of self-reliant, mature individuals," to use the catalog's phraseology. Foreign Study Program directors also have recognized the value of the institution's role in a student's personal development. In a February 1966 *Saturday Review* article, "Why Study Abroad Pays Off," Richard Stavig, the program's first director, explains at length the "personal dimension in foreign study." He concludes, "Any evaluation of foreign study is inadequate if it restricts itself only to what is academically creditable."

Foreign Study Program

Kalamazoo's Foreign Study Office administers all aspects of the overseas centers and programs. This includes screening students, hiring and overseeing the work of staff and faculty in the overseas programs, as well as recruiting teaching assistants and cultural mentors in the language houses and courses. Also, the director certifies each student's pass/fail credit based on a review of reports supplied by overseas faculty. These then go to the registrar for final processing.

Office personnel process visas for international students. Once they arrive on campus, however, advising services are provided by Academic Advising, a unit under the dean of students.

The office has a director, another Ph.D. as the associate director, an assistant director, an administrative assistant, a coordinator of office operations, an intern who is a recent Kalamazoo graduate, as well as work study students. The director reports to the provost.

Well over 200 students a year participate in Kalamazoo's various overseas programs with 70 percent or more staying for at least two quarters. The cost structure provides an incentive for staying long-term. The first quarter charges are the same as a quarter spent on campus, but the second term abroad costs less than the first. Students choosing to stay for a third quarter pay the same fees as they did for the first quarter. Differences between the actual and billed costs are made up from various sources with the S.R. Light Trust as the main one.

Program fees include roundtrip airfares from the point of embarkation, New York, Miami, or Los Angeles, tuition, room and board while classes abroad are in session, and some field trips. Independent travel is encouraged but not financed by the program.

Students make a nonrefundable deposit of $200, or $500 in the case of Africa and Ecuador. They must take a full course load on campus the quarter after their Foreign Study Term. No academic credit is awarded for their work overseas until this requirement is fulfilled. If they transfer to another institution prior to graduation, they must repay $400 to Kalamazoo. This system of regulations has evolved because so much support is provided each student by the Light Trust. The college must protect its investment in the education of its graduates.

In the early 1990s, the Foreign Study Office administers seventeen international programs, four in France, three in both Germany and Spain, two in Ecuador, one each in Mexico, China, Kenya, Senegal, and Sierra Leone. The college also sends students on programs collaboratively with other U.S.

institutions in the United Kingdom, Hungary, Denmark, Italy, Japan, Hong Kong, India, Nepal, and Russia. Homestays provide most accommodations for students except for students participating in affliated programs who are housed in dormitories.

Generally, the resident directors of Kalamazoo programs are respected academics with status in the local university hosting Kalamazoo's students. At some locations, all participating students have achieved sufficient language facility to be integrated into the university's courses. If this is the case, the program needs only a director. For most, however, students have various proficiency levels. A teaching and support staff is hired at these locations; for instance, the Madrid center has a resident director, a secretary, and about half a dozen professors.

Students apply for Foreign Study during the fall quarter of their sophomore year. They are placed according to individual qualifications and on a space available basis. In the term preceding departure, participants are required to attend several orientation meetings. These sessions provide opportunities to learn from faculty and former student participants, supplemented by reading material. Also, non-required sessions are available for students interested in learning about issues such as "culture shock and adaptation strategies," and "women on foreign study."

Orientation for the Africa programs is handled differently because non-Kalamazoo students participate. In September, right before departure, all students going to one of the three sites in Africa take part in a week-long orientation. This is followed by extensive and intensive orientations when they arrive at their various destinations. In Sierra Leone, for example, students spend two weeks in a different place from the program site. They study the Krio language and local culture. In other programs language and culture sessions are mixed with travel and homestays. The process takes six weeks in Kenya before students move into the Kalamazoo house in Nairobi.

Issues and Answers
The following issues arose from the tension between Kalamazoo's announced goal of making foreign study available to all

students and a second goal of providing in-depth programs
focusing on learning languages and having an "integrative cultural experience." Over time, a series of decisions by the program's directors attempted to achieve a synthesis of these
potentially conflicting goals.

The Foreign Study Program is designed to enable each participating student to gain some ability to function effectively in
a new culture. For the best prepared students this means full
integration into the classes of the host university. Thus several
operating guidelines were established. One of these was the
decision to limit the number of students at any one center.
Also, students would live wherever possible with host families. If
only dormitory housing were available, then the Kalamazoo
students would have roommates from the host country.

Integrating U.S. students into overseas institutions to the
fullest extent possible puts great responsibility on the overseas
resident directors. This makes it even more imperative to
attract and retain quality center staff, including directors with
academic qualifications and effective ties within the local host
community.

To achieve quality and stability in overseas center personnel,
without the option of high pay scales, Kalamazoo's Foreign
Study Office directors have worked to create good working and
personal relationships. They have avoided making demands and
generally backed the local center and university's policies in
dealing with Kalamazoo students.

Kalamazoo's Foreign Study Program administrators not only
granted authority to host country personnel, they related personally with these overseas directors and their families. In the
program's first decades, three or four visits per year to each
international center allowed the Kalamazoo directors to accept
invitations to family events such as weddings and christenings.
To show that this policy worked, Kalamazoo administrators cite
the fact that most overseas center directors have served for
years. Also Kalamazoo College has never been asked to leave by
any of its international partners.

Currently, in the mid-1990s, improvements in international
communication technologies have enabled Kalamazoo's Foreign Study Office personnel to cut the number of international

center visits to about two a year. This cost cutting measure has not diminished the amount of contact with center directors because FAX and, in some cases, E-mail is used.

The issue of academic credit was decided when Kalamazoo's overseas centers were first established. Since integration was the goal, class work was graded by local academics according to their university's grading system. Yet, since Europeans view a "C" more positively than do Americans, grade conscious students did not want their overall GPAs affected. Therefore, a nonthreatening process was adopted, i.e., the Foreign Study Office director reviews and certifies each student's work and the registrar assigns a Pass grade so long as the student has received the equivalent of at least a "C" from the host university.

Another issue presented itself when Kalamazoo's Africa programs were opened to non-Kalamazoo students. Adequate screening was needed, so the Foreign Study Office decided to require a telephone interview as a part of the application process. This would enable Kalamazoo program administrators to determine each student's suitability for program participation. Also, to help prepare all students going to Africa, a required week-long predeparture orientation is held on Kalamazoo's campus. This occurrs immediately before the students leave for their separate destinations.

Since the Foreign Study Program assumes international experience and language training are part of a good general education for all students, its administrators have developed strategies for recruiting natural science majors. Part of the response to this issue was the Foreign Study Office's policy of providing a variety of programs accommodating students with various levels of language expertise.

Also, an attempt was made to offer an option specifically for science students. From 1971 to 1976 Kalamazoo students could attend the Kernforschungsanlage Julich, a nuclear research center in Germany with excellent facilities. Eventually this program was cancelled due to lack of participation. Perhaps the needed language proficiency was too advanced.

Another attempt to attract science students was initiated in January 1994. Eight Biology and Environmental Studies students participated in a new program in Ecuador. This environmental studies program is sponsored by the College of Environmental Sciences in the Universidad San Francisco de Quito.

The issue of providing an overseas experience for natural science students has been specifically discussed at Kalamazoo. Natural science curricula is cumulative, sequential, and mandates many requirements. Thus, even when an overseas experience is supported by science faculty, a structural scheduling problem exists. At Kalamazoo the K-Plan's four quarter college calendar has helped science students fit study abroad into their academic programs.

A new situation has developed from the fact that about 40 percent of Kalamazoo's faculty are newly appointed in the last five years. To help increase awareness of and support for the Foreign Study Program, a Foreign Study Advisory Committee was created. This committee is designed to receive and discuss reports on programmatic issues, offer suggestions, and participate in the approval process for major changes, such as new program initiation.

Program cost created another general category of issues. As presently organized, the Foreign Study Program, with its general education goal, would not be possible without significant subsidies from the Light Trust. Yet this has not solved all budgetary concerns either for students or the college.

In the 1960s when the program was initiated, several faculty and administrators feared that making international study available to all students would result in a debilitating hemorrhage of resources off campus. The new college calendar was part of the answer because it allowed for anticipatory planning. Thus the fact that dormitory space would be available in the fall, with less the next quarter, could be incorporated into enrollment projections.

The situation assumed by those voicing the concern over the sending of too many students off campus never materialized. Instead, more dormitory space was needed since Kalamazoo College's enrollment went up dramatically, from about 1,000 students in the mid-1960s to around 1,500 by the early 1970s. This taxed the upper limit of the college's support system and the decision was made to limit enrollments to around the present 1,200. With hindsight, however, the upward enrollment trend put to rest the "empty beds on campus" issue.

The fact remains that, in spite of fortunate enrollments, trust subsidies, and careful planning, the program does produce a net flow of operating capital overseas. The educational benefits ultimately must be worth the cost as perceived by the Kalamazoo College community. This consensus seems to be holding after three decades.

Yet program cost is not only a macro issue. It also affects day-to-day administration. Program directors had to deal with budgetary problems caused by several factors outside of their control. One such factor was the fluctuating value of the U.S. dollar. A general tendency downward in the dollar's foreign exchange earnings has lasted for years at a time. Sometimes this increased a program's cost by 30 to 40 percent in one year. This amount had to be made up in some way. Increasing fees was not an option since, by policy, students were billed the same as on campus charges for tuition, room, and board. Thus the difference had to be made up by cutting costs and drawing more from program reserves.

Another financial externality has made an increasing impact on the program. Gradually, financial aid has increased over the years until it comprises a much larger percentage of overall fiscal support for Kalamazoo's student population. Since a portion of what students actually pay is credited to the Foreign Study Program account, the relative decrease in these funds has cut significantly into the program's operating capital.

The response to all these fiscal constraints has been conservative budgetary policies and frugal, anticipatory program administration. Because of this approach, a reserve had been built up in Light Trust funds over the years. Also, the opening up of several African programs to non-Kalamazoo students represented an effort to raise revenues.

Another aspect to the financial issue is the student point of view. While program fees make the Foreign Study Term very attractive, additional costs associated with overseas programs provide disincentives. Independent travel is encouraged but must be paid for by each student. Other costs include domestic airfares to the point of embarkation, and personal expenses not covered but still required for program participation, like bus fares for students with homestays outside of walking distance from their host universities.

The example of this need to use local transportation provides a case study of the kind of decisions often required of overseas study program administrators. One past response of a Foreign Study Program director was to provide funds for such program-related yet individualized costs. Students living too far away from class to walk received a local transportation subsidy. This ended during the 1980s because students were taking the money and not using it for bus or train fare. Students not receiving the subsidy had complained.

Another example of an administrative, cost-related micro-issue involves students who earn work-study support on campus. They lobbied for a comparable opportunity while on Foreign Study. This relates to an equity issue since the program should be available to all students, not just those with access to greater financial resources. This, after all, is one of the rationales for the Light Trust subsidy. In response, the program director arranged for paid part-time work while overseas for some students on some programs. This was dropped because many students opposed providing jobs for some and not others. They cited a concern over fairness.

A lesson for program administrators emerges in these examples of programmatic detail. These attempts to increase equity seemed to create the perception of less. This helps the case for standardization. Also, the examples illustrate the difficulties in administrating multiple programs at multiple sites.

One additional story more precisely illustrates the last point. As a Cold War policy, the German government used to finance one-week trips to Berlin for foreigners. Thus participants in Kalamazoo's German programs had a benefit those in other programs did not. This was often noted by students in other European centers. Since nothing could be done about this situation, the example shows that sometimes patient explanation over and over again is the only useful response. Foreign Study Program administrators recognize they must deal with such issues arising from program variations within and among countries. Such programmatic variety is needed to attain the Foreign Study Program's goal of providing access for all students.

Lessons Learned and Spin-offs

The following guidelines summarize Kalamazoo's three decades of program development via international centers.

1. *Program goals must fit the institution and its perceived mission.* Kalamazoo College prides itself on training future leaders. Well over a majority go on to graduate-level work or to advanced professional education. Therefore the Foreign Study Program's attention to quality and academic standards fit the college's ethos.

2. *Make programmatic decisions based on the goals.* The planning process must be seen as a series of choices concerning the proposed program's length, type, whether it is travel-study, university-affiliated, service or internship, or faculty-led. Other decisions involve the granting of credit and/or grades, relationship to on-campus curriculum, the role of language instruction, what accommodation to provide, either homestays, dormitories, or apartments, and organizing a local support network by determining the qualifications and role of host country personnel.

   As explained previously in this study, Kalamazoo made several decisions in designing the Foreign Study Program in its early years which have proven their worth over time. For example, the emphasis on languages and integration into host institutions was balanced with the addition of programs in English in the United Kingdom and at other locations.

3. *Carefully think through which program model would work best for which students.* If the college seeks to produce greater achievement levels for students in specific international specializations, such as languages, then the long-term social integration model provides the best training. On the other side of a hypothesized set of program models, the short-term, faculty-led group travel program would prove less risky for students who have little prior relevant academic training and no overseas experience. This model

often has proved less complicated to organize and cheaper to maintain.

Most institutions committed to international education offer versions of these two which may best be defined as a third model, a middle way between attempting to increase academic specializations and providing some international experience for the uninitiated. This third type of program retains the group structure while maximizing opportunities for student forays into host societies and educational institutions.

Applying this third approach should alert program administrators to issues the other two assume; for example, when to help students work through their problems and when to avoid excessive "handholding" under the guise of necessary support. Should a U.S. national serve as the program's local director or should a citizen of that country? What preparation qualifications and orientation activities should be required? The list could go on and on. To summarize, careful goal setting, program planning, and ongoing administration must be systematically interrelated and reevaluated.

Like other campuses with long-term, multifaceted, interwoven international education programs, Kalamazoo College has moved into a second and now third generation of spin-offs. Creative and unique, they reflect established and earned expertise. As noted previously in this study, the National Center for Western European Studies is perhaps the most noteworthy result of the college's years of international education development.

Building on the K-Plan's requirement that all students complete a Senior Individualized Project, the Foreign Study program has put its own stamp on the "Chamberlain Fellows Senior Program." Named after the Michigan foundation that provided initial and subsequent funding, seniors chosen for this honor use their awards to undertake internships and carry out research in countries they have specialized in via the Foreign Study Program. Internship and research opportunities are arranged individually by Kalamazoo's international center and partnership networks. Since 1992, the college has financed about half the budget for the Chamberlain Fellows Program with the foundation and other sources continuing to provide the other half. Six students initially received fellowships. This number had increased to eleven in 1993 and to fourteen in 1994.

As on other campuses with extensive student overseas programs, orientation and reentry remains a concern. At Kalamazoo several new initiatives have been tested. In 1991, the Western European Studies Center provided funding for an experimental summer interdisciplinary course open to selected students. Using multicultural content, this Comparative Literature course was designed to make student overseas experiences an integral part of their campus academic learning. It thus could serve as a vehicle for both orientation and reentry purposes. The course itself has not continued but elements of its cultural training have been applied in the Foreign Study Program's orientation and reentry seminars.

Kalamazoo College ranks high by any commonly accepted measure of campus internationalization. Its experience demonstrates what a dedicated, effective group of campus leaders can achieve over time. Although a key element of its success cannot be replicated on most campuses, i.e., substantial subsidies from a sizeable trust, the Foreign Study program can provide useful practical information applicable to other institutions; for example, administering overseas centers.

Pacific University

Animating Spanish Instruction Through Service

This small university, a half-hour west of Portland, Oregon, takes community service seriously. As a result, its Spanish language students have two service options, one domestic and one overseas. They can earn credit by tutoring local Hispanic school-age youngsters and/or spending a semester in Guayaquil, Ecuador on a program with a three-day-a-week service component. In the 1990s, about 50 percent of Spanish majors and minors had service placements in both programs and the percentage seems to be increasing. In 1993, all but one of the majors taking the Senior Seminar had participated in both service experiences. This trend has coincided with, and probably has contributed to, the rapid growth in the numbers of students taking Spanish.

Pacific University occupies a campus which reflects its sense of time and place. The old, refurbished wood frame houses at the edge of the campus connote a long history and mix easily with the modern buildings at its core. Pacific Northwest cedar and fir trees tower above the buildings. These are punctuated by an even taller and seemingly timeless mini-grove of three mighty sequoias.

A short, two-block walk takes people from the university community into the central business district of Forest Grove. In recent years, this town has become the home of an increasing number of Hispanic migrant and ex-migrant workers. Helping develop a response to their plight is consistent with the university's United Church of Christ affiliation and its social justice orientation.

The university itself has experienced rapid change in the late 1980s and 1990s. In the mid-1980s, it enrolled about 600 undergraduates, but by 1994 the number had increased to 1,000. Senior administrators plan for growth up to 1,200. In addition to undergraduates, in 1993 the university had approximately 700 graduate students and 130 full-time faculty. The growth in undergraduate numbers has enabled the university to admit students with rising GPAs and SAT scores while retaining its mission of providing educational opportunity; i.e., a little less than one third of the students have parents who did not attend college, and a large percentage of the undergraduates attended high schools with under 300 students.

The university has two colleges and three schools: the College of Arts and Sciences, College of Optometry, School of Occupational Therapy, School of Physical Therapy, and the School of Professional Psychology. In addition to the baccalaureate, the university awards several masters' and two doctorate degrees in Optometry and Psychology.

Pacific University takes pride in its pioneer heritage. It was established by the Missionary Society of the Congregational Church Association, which wanted to found "an academy that shall grow into a college . . . on the New England model." Oregon's territorial legislature granted a charter for an academy in 1849 and in 1854 a new charter added the words "and Pacific University." The first baccalaureate degree was awarded in 1863 to a man who became editor of *The Portland Oregonian* newspaper. Pacific University was the first institution west of the Mississippi to graduate Japanese nationals. Three received degrees in 1876.

Campus Context
Pacific University's succinct mission statement includes a commitment to service in international as well as local and domestic environments: "Pacific University provides an education of exceptional quality in the liberal arts and sciences and selected health professions to prepare students for service to a changing community, nation and world."

The university elaborates on its mission with a "Statement of Values." Here also international education is emphasized: Pacific University "pursues international awareness and involvement," and "strives for active participation and leadership in a rapidly changing world."

As indicated by its pride in graduating international students during the Nineteenth Century, Pacific University continues to encourage their role in campus life. In 1993, about forty-five international students attended the university. This figure does not include English Language Institute students. The Institute provides English as a Second Language instruction to about forty students who live with U.S. roommates in the residence halls. It also offers summer study. Its director reports to the vice president for student affairs/dean of students. International student advising is provided by the director of multicultural services. She also has the responsibility for Wellness Education and works in the university's Student Affairs Office.

Pacific University has affiliations with two universities in Japan, one in Hong Kong, and a technical four-year university in Ecuador. Students go to Europe on programs sponsored by other U.S. colleges. In the spring of 1994, thirty-six students planned to go overseas in the next academic year, with twelve of these going to Ecuador. A member of the Spanish language faculty, Nina Rukas, administers the study abroad program. She received her first course release for this purpose in the spring of 1994. Faculty at Pacific University normally teach seven courses during the academic year.

Pacific University offers majors in Japanese, Spanish, and Modern Languages with courses to the 400 level in French and German, to the 300 level in Chinese, and the 100 level in Italian. A Modern Language major takes thirty semester-hours in a primary language, twelve in a secondary, and three in English Literature or Linguistics. The major in International Studies requires a language through the 400 level and at least one semester of study abroad. Students also can minor in Peace and Conflict Studies.

These curriculum specializations are supported by international courses and components of courses infused throughout the curriculum from Art to Sociology. Most have an Asian emphasis. The art department offers three courses on the Art and Architecture of India, China, and Japan. Business includes not only the usual International and Comparative Economics courses, plus International Marketing, but Asian Economies as well. Anthropology has several courses on China plus on Chinese Americans. The East Asia focus continues in History's emphasis on China. Its courses cover Europe as well. Political Science listings include the standard International Relations plus Latin American Politics and Russia and Its Neighbors. The ecology component of international education is covered by courses in biology. The Sociology of the Family in the Sociology Department is cross-cultural.

Psychology provides a distinctive aspect to Pacific University's international curriculum. Courses with cross cultural perspectives are offered at both the undergraduate and graduate levels with the latter requiring a course in Human Diversity. Also at the graduate level, the education department requires Culturally Responsive Teaching and Global Issues courses of both elementary and secondary teachers. At the undergraduate level, elementary education majors must take both Cultural Geography and Global Issues. This is in addition to The College of Arts and Sciences graduation requirements, i.e., two semesters of a foreign language and one semester of cross-cultural studies.

For students wanting to teach English or another language, the foreign language department offers Methods of Teaching Foreign Languages and Teaching English as a Second Language, both at the 400 level. The former is taught by a member of the department and the latter by an instructor in the English Language Institute.

Two education department courses enable students to directly link their academic work with training for teaching or training for service. For prospective teachers, Teaching the Hispanic Child has a Spanish language faculty member as instructor. Mentoring Hispanic Middle School Students, taught by an Education professor, trains students who have chosen a service placement to tutor Hispanic children. These courses reflect close cooperation between Spanish and Education faculty. They also demonstrate how the university's curriculum and faculty encourage service. It provides a practical application for conceptualizations learned in class.

Service Opportunities and the Spanish Major

Strongly encouraged by Susan Cabello, a professor of Spanish, students have synthesized elements of a Pacific University education into what, to them, amounts to a well-designed program. They have linked three university programs, their Spanish language major or minor, local service placements organized by the Humanitarian Center, and the overseas study and service program in Guayaquil, Ecuador. Cabello is the senior member of the Department of Foreign Languages and served for years as its chair until 1993.

Some of the more sought-after among the Humanitarian Center's over 150 placement possibilities are tutoring "at risk" young people, mostly Hispanic. About twenty-five of the seventy-five to a hundred students in the center's service placements at any one time choose the tutoring positions. Credits can be earned in two ways: through departmental courses or via the center's Field Experience designation, which provides one credit for academic learning accomplished during forty hours of service. The center has also awarded credit to Habitat for Humanities groups which have gone to Mexico and Guatemala.

The Humanitarian Center has multiple, overlapping tasks. It was originally designed as the action arm of the Peace and Conflict Studies program and continues in this role. It is linked also with other majors and minors. As stated in the catalog, "The purpose of the Pacific Humanitarian Center is to help college students secure valuable experience in their major and minor courses of study." The university community views the center as fulfilling a general educational role. Its field experience provides ethical training and builds self-esteem. "The goal of the Center is to make public service the norm of every student's formal education rather than the exception."

The center, and the Peace and Conflict Studies curriculum, began in 1981 with a United Church of Christ (UCC) grant. In 1988, a CAPE grant (Consortium for the Advancement of Private Education) added to the service curriculum. The Hispanic courses noted above in the Education and Spanish Departments were first offered at this time. Another UCC grant was awarded in 1989.

In 1993, the Center was institutionalized when the university began paying its salaries and small operating budget out of its own funds. The half-time director, Mike Steel, spends the other half of his time as a professor in the English Department. The secretary is also half-time.

The Humanitarian Center's work with the local Hispanic community grew out of Pacific University's recognition that a different society lived right across the street. By the mid-1980s, senior administrators as well as faculty noticed that the campus "hispanicized" when university students vacated during holidays. From a section of town bordering the university, Spanish-speaking families used the campus for picnics while their children played. The basketball courts in particular attracted substantial community activity.

A university with Pacific's social justice commitment could not ignore problems right on its border. One house easily visible from the campus was said to be home for forty-eight people who collectively paid seventy-one dollars a day rent. The Dean of the College of Arts and Sciences at the time, Seth Singleton, challenged Pacific University's faculty to respond to the flagrant social problems pressing against their doorstep.

In response, The Humanitarian Center developed more Hispanic community placements. The center's director attributes the rapid growth in these placements to Drew Mahalic, an ex-professional football player who volunteered his time. For years until his departure in 1993, he organized a variety of activities. As a result, students teach migrants in literacy programs, counsel disadvantaged people of all ages, and tutor Spanish-speaking children in the school system. The first placements were in the primary grades and, based on the success at this level, middle and high school positions were added. By the mid-1990s, twenty to twenty-five primary schoolchildren were being tutored by university students at any one time.

It is estimated that about twenty percent of the students in Forest Grove high school are Hispanic. In the late 1980s, however, the official school district data reported that ninety-five high school students were not native English speakers. This was corrected when university students carried out a study which showed 356 as the actual number.

Dean Singleton also made another contribution to the university's development of Hispanic programs. In fact, his overall support for international education has been termed by some faculty as "crucial." He, Susan Cabello, and President Duvall travelled to Ecuador in 1989 to organize a program and sign an agreement with the Instituto Technológico Espirito Santo in Guayaquil, which has become the Universidad de Especialidades Espirito Santo. In 1990, a group of five students spent the semester studying Spanish, learning about Ecuador and Latin America, and engaging in service activities. Since then, the annual student groups have numbered around fifteen and, in 1994, twenty students had signed up. Besides the attractiveness of the programs itself, an additional factor is the fact that the Modern Language Department requires its majors to take one semester in an overseas program.

Students applying for the Ecuador program must have a minimum of two years of Spanish instruction. While there, they take Latin American Geography for two credits, Latin American History also for two, plus the Literature of Ecuador, Social problems of Latin America, and Spanish Grammar for three credits. All are taught by local faculty. The service placements carry two credits. Students receive two weeks of orientation upon arrival. Then they begin the semester's main activities of course work, often at night, and their three-day-a-week placements. Accommodations are provided by Ecuadorean families, one student per family.

Students report two placements as the favorites. In one, they tutor at a primary school, Corazon de la Patria, which previous students had helped build. The school is in an "invasion" neighborhood, a place where poor people from rural areas have taken over by building shacks. The second category of preferred placements involves accompanying a doctor or nurse to homes, the shacks in many cases, and providing basic health care. Often students administer shots and perform other nursing procedures they never would be allowed to in the United States.

The preferred Ecuador placements reflect Pacific University's curriculum strengths in the education and health professions. Also they strengthen the already existing tie between Spanish language instruction and the Education Department. Many language majors intend to teach and some go on for the university's M.A.T. in education.

The Ecuador program attracts not only Spanish majors and minors. International Studies majors also participate, often accomplishing the research required for their honors thesis. Whatever their field of study, virtually all students who have gone to Ecuador report overwhelmingly favorable responses. Their enthusiastic comments reveal the transforming nature of their experiences.

Academically, students home from the Ecuador program show a major improvement in their command of Spanish, according to a faculty member. They have also learned the literature, geography, and other program content very well. When asked why, one student attributed the thoroughness of her new knowledge to the fact that "most of the teachers did not speak English."

Yet, as with overseas service programs in general, most students think that personal growth is the most important result of their experiences. Some even say that their personality changed; for example, "I lost my shyness." Others report a new perspective, their "hearts opened up" and they greatly expanded the "capacity to enjoy life." "We are only half alive compared to those people," was one comment.

Some participants have been the first in their families to go to college and they felt they "had it hard" growing up. Yet they are the ones who often report learning the most about the real poverty they saw in Ecuador. Students also say they thought a great deal about the extreme contrast in Ecuador's lifestyles: They live with relatively wealthy host families while working with the poor in their placements.

As is often the case when people undergo such a transformation, returning to life in the United States takes some conscious effort; for instance, one student said it took her awhile to stop being "disgusted with everyone around me," because they were so "time conscious and not people conscious."

The loss of social control was how one student described the risk that she felt she took in going to work in such a very different society. She experienced the inability to judge the effectiveness of her actions and her interactions with people. This was scary. Also, "I had to deal with my ego a lot there."

Almost all Spanish language students go on the Ecuador program instead of the one in Spain. Upon returning, they want to continue volunteering and seek placements via the Humanitarian Center. In the words of one, "I realize I will always be a person who volunteers." Some returnees had Humanitarian Center placements with the local Hispanic community before going to Ecuador. Spanish language faculty report that there seems to be no pattern as to whether students become committed to service before or after their Ecuador experience. Anyway, trying to determine cause and effect misses the point: Pacific University maintains a series of mutually reinforcing Hispanic service opportunities with the enthusiastic encouragement of Spanish language faculty, among others.

Pacific University's Spanish language instruction is the third element in the ad hoc Hispanic Studies culture-service-language "program." Enrollments in Spanish courses suffered a precipitous decline in the early 1980s followed by explosive growth by the end of the decade and continuing into the 1990s. During the 1980-81 academic year, seventy-nine students took Spanish courses. The low of twenty-seven occurred in 1983-84, springing back to fifty-eight in 1984-85. Since then, major increases occurred each year with the enrollments reaching 325 students during 1991-92. The number of Spanish majors also increased from one in 1989 to seventeen in 1993. By that same year, the university employed two full-time Spanish language faculty, and three part-time instructors.

The whole Foreign Language Department experienced growth and revitalization during the same time frame. Inspired by a workshop on teaching languages led by Claire Gaudiani, now president of Connecticut College, department chair Susan Cabello wrote a National Endowment for the Humanities consultant grant. It brought a University of Texas at Austin faculty member, Janet King Swaffar, to campus to help design an action plan.

This plan proposed to revise Pacific University's language curriculum using the proficiency guidelines developed by the American Council on the Teaching of Foreign Languages

(ACTFL). Faculty would be trained in proficiency-based methodologies and apply them in their courses. Cabello then wrote a second successful NEH grant to implement the plan. The project funded faculty and curriculum development which coincided with increases in language course enrollments and number of majors. By 1993 there were twenty to twenty-five Modern Language majors, up from virtually none in 1987. Under the able leadership of Kazuko Ikeda, the department also experienced significant growth in Japanese.

Other, campuswide grant projects have supported new initiatives by language faculty. Adding instruction in Japanese was part of a large grant from the Matsushita Corporation. This grant also paid for the language laboratory and financed the purchase of camcorders. These have allowed students to videotape interviews with local native Spanish speakers. The videos have been used as teaching-learning materials.

Issues and Answers

A sea-change in the campus environment has reversed the 1970s lack of support for language instruction in particular, and international education in general. Eighteen years ago, when Susan Cabello first taught at Pacific University, the atmosphere was not friendly to foreign language instruction. Faculty as a whole, and especially senior administrators, were not convinced that language instruction was a needed or even valuable part of a good general education.

Cabello was the only full-time foreign language instructor, and one of only seven female faculty. Another faculty member taught German half-time while spending the other half of her time teaching courses for the English Department. The French professor's load also was reduced by two classes reallocated to the English Department. Throughout the 1970s, language enrollments were tiny since the language requirement had been eliminated.

During the 1980s, language faculty advocated reinstating the language requirement. There were pockets of sympathy for this position; for example, the physical therapy faculty thought language learning, and the cross-cultural thinking it implied, would provide important training for their students. Their graduates often had to work with members of various ethnicities. Their support was significant since the health sciences were, and are, a major force at Pacific University. They attract students with their graduate level programs and major contribution to the university's reputation. In addition to some campus support, the debate at Pacific University took place during a time of increasing national attention on international education.

Another major factor was a change in the university's administration. The new president in the early 1980s, Robert Duvall, proved to be an advocate of international education. The new College of Arts and Sciences dean, Seth Singleton, was as active and effective as he was articulate about the need for international curriculum and programs.

By the late 1980s, Susan Cabello's long vigil, hard work, and years of networking began to bring results. One language course was added to graduation requirements, and this was expanded to two by 1993. The grants described previously energized language courses and developed the service curriculum. Purely administrative decisions also helped; for example, applying financial aid to study abroad programs. By 1993, Pacific University employed six full-time foreign language faculty and four adjuncts. This record illustrates, yet again, the effectiveness of an able, hard working, respected, faculty member when actively supported by senior administrators and campus allies. Growth now continues under the guidance of chair of the department, Lorely French.

Another, more mundane, issue affected the informal Hispanic studies program as it developed. In Ecuador, homestay situations sometimes needed intervention, such as the behavior of an overly aggressive "brother" toward a female student. Such incidents, fortunately few, were handled ably by the host program director. In fact, homesickness and other personal student problems have been minimal in the Ecuador program. This has been attributed to the service component's high level of personal satisfaction as well as to the ability and sense of responsibility of its local administrator, Irma Guzman. She is the Universidad de Especialidades Espirito Santo's Director of Foreign Study. Her qualifications not only include an advanced degree in Psychology but also a year spent in the United States as a high school student.

Program planning must consider homestays as integral to the learning environment. In Ecuador, one student is placed per family and everyone involved commits to having at least one major Spanish conversation time a day. Family members often want to practice their English, which is fine as long as students also practice their Spanish. As a result, returnees from Ecuador have more highly developed conversational Spanish skills than those participating in programs without homestays.

Overseeing a program so far from campus produces some logistical problems. Effective communication, for example, is inhibited in Ecuador since mail delivery can be problematic. The program often uses personal couriers. The communication situation illustrates yet another reason the program needs an effective host country program director who has earned the confidence of the home campus.

Lessons Learned

Integration is the key to making the two service opportunities and Spanish language courses a complete learning experience. Students realize on their own how the three fit together in general. Yet able faculty must explain specifically how experiences during each part of the "program" reinforce, refine, and build on previous learning. Together the following points outline how to achieve the needed integration.

1. *The overseas program director must be very competent.* In the case of Pacific University's Ecuador program, Irma Guzman has fulfilled every needed role, from choosing local faculty to serving as a good listener for students with problems.

2. *Effective communications must exist between the campus and host country.* This has a cultural and personal as well as a logistical dimension. Guzman travels to Oregon at least once a year to discuss issues and maintain personal relationships.

3. *Able local placement personnel are also needed.* This is true in the case of Mike Steele, Director of The Humanitarian

Center. He, and the Center's secretary, work effectively with individual students and community placement supervisors.

4. *One person must serve as a linchpin.* In the case of this ad hoc program, Susan Cabello has acted as the informal "director." She as been the common denominator in designing and teaching the Hispanic service curriculum, assisting in establishing and administering the Ecuador program, advising students, building the language curriculum, writing grants, and networking on campus.

Pacific University's experience demonstrates yet again the creative programming that can result when senior administrators work closely with able faculty who are willing to accept responsibility well beyond their "position descriptions." Students also contributed by actually creating the "program." As a final point, the fact that Hispanic service opportunities and Spanish language learning have been linked at Pacific University must, in part, be attributed to the campus culture. Activities of the Humanitarian Center and the Ecuador program demonstrate that scholarship and service can be not only compatible but mutually reinforcing.

Ramapo College of New Jersey

Applying Telecommunications Technology

Ramapo College has long been known for the breadth and depth of its international education programs. A state college attended in 1991 by 2,800 full-time and 1,900 part-time students, Ramapo occupies a spacious wooded site at the northern edge of New Jersey. It lies on the fringe of the suburbs but well within the New York City cultural region. On a good commuting day, the college can be reached in 35 minutes from the "city," and in less time from northern New Jersey cities.

As usual for a small campus in a scenic environment, a visitor to Ramapo first experiences an almost cloistered calm. From the open spaciousness of parking lots surrounded by acres of grass, the visitor walks up a gradual incline to the heavily wooded main campus. From here, turning to the west offers an unencumbered view of low-lying mountains. In contrast, the two-story academic buildings cluster, largely hidden, amid large trees of varying ages and species. They reflect in the buildings' glass outer walls giving the impression that the products of human manufacture are merging with the natural beauty surrounding them.

Entering a building, however, quickly dispels this Thoreauvian image. Here a visitor encounters animated movement and conversation, the bustle of many people in a finite space. Part of the dynamism comes from the fact that these people reflect much of the variety of the human community. This impression of a city's compact closeness is reinforced by the buildings' functional internal architecture.

The scenery-city contrast provides a compatible atmosphere for international education programming. A global perspective seems natural in the college's physical setting. Also, the vital mix of ethnicities invoke a sense of cultural openness. Ramapo's programs achieve a synthesis of global and multicultural perspectives. The International Telecommunications Center, for example, uses the latest in communications technology to make information available from around the world. At the same time, it has enabled local ethnic communities to celebrate their achievements and share them with the larger population via local public television.

This center is perhaps Ramapo's most distinctive contribution to undergraduate international education since it widens the range of program possibilities. Yet it could only have been established on a broad base of prior initiatives.

Campus Context
Curriculum internationalization lies at the core of Ramapo's national reputation as a leader in international education. Established in 1969, the institution's faculty included many returning peace corps volunteers. These, plus other young faculty, were willing to create an innovative structure for organizing the college's curriculum. They also recognized the need to reflect the contemporary world in their courses.

By the early 1990s, faculty and administrators report that Ramapo's internal organization has helped create an environment conducive to change. Five interdisciplinary schools and one division, not the usual departments, organize Ramapo's curriculum offerings and faculty appointments. Therefore all peer decisions are interdisciplinary. The five schools carry functional designations combining disciplines, i.e., Administration and Business, American and International Studies, Contemporary Arts, Social Science and Human Services, and Theoretical and Applied Science. These are joined by the Division of Basic Studies. Students can choose an interdisciplinary major or a traditional one in a single discipline. The latter sometimes includes courses in more than one school; for example, history courses are offered in all of Ramapo's five schools.

The College's mission includes international or intercultural education in all of its "three primary goals." A Ramapo education is designed "to heighten knowledge, strengthen skills and sensibilities, and to prepare students to engage successfully in an increasingly interdependent and multicultural world." Secondly, "Ramapo seeks to . . . express the enriching diversity of contemporary society." The third objective commits the college to a "curriculum imbued with a global perspective."

Reflecting its strong international education mission, all students graduating from Ramapo must have taken at least one Global/Multicultural course. This requirement can be met with a variety of courses in all five of Ramapo's schools. In addition, all students must take a Senior Seminar several of which have international themes, such as Global Communications and Nutrition, Agriculture, and Energy: A Global Perspective.

The college offers several international majors and area studies minors. Students can major in international business, international studies, and environmental studies. Also, the American studies major requires the Introduction to International Studies course, one course in African-American studies, one in ethnic studies, and one chosen from several dealing with America in the world. Language majors cover French, German, Italian, Russian, Spanish, Chinese, and Japanese. In addition, Hebrew and Swahili were added to the Foreign Language offerings in 1993. Ramapo's minors include African-American Studies, Judaic Studies, Latin American Studies, and East Asian Studies.

Many international courses are infused throughout the Ramapo curriculum. Naturally, the School of American/International Studies, with languages and the bulk of the college's history and political science offerings, leads the others in numbers of courses. Yet each one of the five schools makes a significant contribution, including the Division of Basic Studies. This unit of the college teaches four English as a Second Language courses. The following lengthy list of courses may present ideas for curriculum development at other colleges and universities.

The School of Administration/Business requires all its students to take an international course, preferably in their junior year. They have a wide range of choices, at least one course in all major disciplines taught in the School; e.g., Finance contributes Multinational Finance, Accounting has an International Accounting course, Economics lists the usual such as Comparative Economic Systems, and World Political Economy is taught by a Business Administration faculty member. The social sciences also are represented in the School of Administration/ Business. Psychology contributes Multicultural Psychology, and

Political Science has two relevant courses, i.e., Canada/U.S. Economic Relations and Politics of International Investment.

The School of Theoretical/Applied Science focuses on environmental courses such as General Ecology, required of Biology majors, and Environmental Science's fifteen courses. These include Air Pollution, Biological Conservation, Appropriate Technology, and Environmental Law.

Area studies and intercultural communication summarize the offerings in the School of Contemporary Arts. Art lists Latin American Art, and Music highlights Music in Africa and the Americas, and Music in Asia and the Pacific. Communications presents two choices, i.e., Interpersonal and Intercultural Communication, and Intercultural-Ethnic Communication.

The School of Social Science/Human Services includes Environmental Economics and Economic Development taught by economics faculty. Law and Society contributes Comparative Legal Systems and Psychology lists Asian Perspectives in Psychology. Sociology offers five courses, including Third World Women and the Global Workplace. At least one of Social Work's courses deals with intercultural relations, i.e., Human Behavior and the Social Environment I-Cultural Diversity.

Most of the international courses in the School of American/International Studies reflect an area studies approach. History courses include several on Asia and Latin America. The Middle East and Russia also are represented. Anthropology includes a course on the United States and Japan. Political Science covers Russia, Developing Nations, Africa, East Asia, and the Middle East. Modern Italy, and separate courses on the French, Italian, and Spanish Cinemas are listed under Interdisciplinary Studies. The depth of Language offerings include civilization and business courses. Literature also presents an array of choices; e.g., Survey of Chinese Literature, Modern Novel in France, Chekhov Plays, and the Literature of Vietnam. Two other courses also show the extent of the Literature faculty's contribution to curriculum internationalization at Ramapo: Both the Patterns of Myth and Folklore I—Creation and Fertility, and Patterns of Myth and Folklore II—The Hero's Quest are thoroughly multicultural.

In addition to curriculum, international educators often note the cultural diversity on campus. Ramapo's faculty and administrators take pride in the college's ethnic mix. In 1991, U. S. minorities were reported as 16 percent of the student body, with African-Americans the largest group at 9 percent. These figures would have been higher if only calculated for daytime students. International students, numbering 154 in 1991, also made a contribution to campus diversity. The largest single group, thirty, came from Kenya. These international student figures reflect a recruiting effort since only fifty-nine attended the college in 1985-86. The international student advisor works in the Division of Student Affairs.

Ethnic diversity at Ramapo includes more than those generally classified as U.S. minorities. Various other self-identified cultural groups are represented, such as Italian and Jewish. In addition, the college has tried to hire faculty with varying cultural backgrounds, although no specific data are available. The overall figure of seventy percent, however, is cited to indicate those faculty who "have had substantial experience in the study of other cultures and use that experience to emphasize the international and multicultural dimensions of subjects they teach." (As quoted in a pamphlet, "A Window on the World: Ramapo College and the Challenge Grant.") Faculty in all of the college's major academic areas maintain international research interests. In the Division of Basic Studies most of the faculty have had substantial overseas experience.

The college's initiatives in another category of international education, student overseas programs, reflect the fact that much of its student population works throughout the academic year. Thus Ramapo has emphasized faculty-led summer programs, and their quality has attracted student participation from other campuses. In the summer of 1992 a total of 154 students, sixty of them from Ramapo, chose among studying language and culture in Italy or Puerto Rico, history in the United Kingdom, environmental issues in Costa Rica, development in Kenya, and archeology at a dig in Israel. A new program to China, organized by a faculty member originally from Shanghai, attracted twenty students in the summer of 1993. As the newest additions, programs to Madrid and Russia will be initiated in 1994.

The college hopes that summer programs will build interest in longer-term experiences, and there is some evidence this is working: In the 1991-92 academic year, eleven Ramapo students went overseas on semester programs sponsored by other institutions. Also, an International Cooperative Education program provides Ramapo students with positions in firms overseas. Placements have been made in Canada, the United Kingdom, Germany and the Soviet Union.

Ramapo's summer study abroad programs are organized in cooperation with institutions overseas. Such arrangements often include the college's hosting international scholars. The overseas universities send four or five faculty or graduate students a year to Ramapo to teach or carry out administrative responsibilities. In the spring of 1993, for example, international scholars from Russia and China were serving as adjunct faculty. In addition, the University of Urbina in Italy sent two doctoral students. Ramapo provides housing for all its international guest faculty and administrators in the "White House," a building on campus. They share a car and organize its use as well as the purchase of food and other necessities. Usually their income comes from teaching two courses and making presentations.

Visiting scholars are always interviewed before activities are organized for them at Ramapo. Since plans are often made years in advance, a Ramapo faculty member or administrator can meet with a prospective visiting scholar while travelling oversees on college business. If such face-to-face discussions are not possible, the scholars are interviewed by phone. Sometimes a committee of Ramapo faculty and administrators uses a speakerphone and conducts a group interview. The International Telecommunications Center has assisted with these recruiting audioconferences. By the mid-1990s Ramapo's screening policy had proven invaluable in sorting out a long list of potential visitors.

Administrators of the study abroad and the international scholar programs report to the Center for Intercultural Education. Directed part-time by a faculty member, John Cassidy, curriculum development comprises the center's primary mandate. As described in Ramapo's catalog, the center also sponsors conferences, publishes monographs, and works with the director of grants administration in the preparation of proposals. The director is assisted in his responsibilities by a faculty advisory board. In addition to the Center for Intercultural Education and the International Telecommunications Center, which will be described in the next section of this case study, Ramapo has two other special facilities relevant to international and intercultural education, i.e., the African-American Studies Institute and the Institute for Environmental Studies.

Given its level of faculty and administrative activity, it is clear that at Ramapo a constructively charged atmosphere seems to stimulate new initiatives. Many faculty have demonstrated the energy, commitment, and competence necessary for carrying out successful grant funded projects. These have produced ongoing programs. Ramapo's president, Robert Scott, has made international education a highlight of his administration. He delivers conference presentations, writes articles, and personally contacts funding agencies.

A three-year challenge grant ended in 1989. It funded the largest of Ramapo's internationalization projects, called "Window on the World." The State of New Jersey provided $3.5 million for activities covering the whole range of international education program categories. Written and directed by Clifford Peterson, a political scientist, and Walter Brown, an Anthropologist, about ninety new courses and course revisions were added to the curriculum.

A statement of other challenge-grant-funded activities reads like an international educator's wish list. The project purchased thousands of media and library items, built a state-of-the-art language laboratory, expanded study abroad programs with some including experiential components, funded faculty overseas research and development, organized cultural events and student volunteer opportunities with local ethnic communities, recruited international students and provided them with summer programs in English and American Studies, held workshops with high school teachers and local businesses, and provided student internships with many of the international corporations both foreign and domestic operating near the campus. Approximately 4,000 such businesses are reported within a fifteen-mile radius of Ramapo College. Yet establishing a new International Telecommunications Center marked perhaps the project's most distinctive achievement.

International Telecommunications Center

The center consists of two television studios, three satellite dishes, and several rooms for taping, meetings, class instruction, and offices. The center's director, Kathleen Sunshine, oversees the work of eight other full-time and several part-time staff, including occasional graduate interns from the City University of New York, and Ramapo student aides. Four part-time staff are dedicated to the campus television network and the fiberoptic, two-way, interactive video network which connects Ramapo to other colleges and thirteen secondary schools. The ITC Director reports to the vice president for academic affairs.

The director's professional background and personality are as distinctive as her name. With a Ph.D. in literature, and teaching plus administrative experience as associate dean of Ramapo's School of Contemporary Arts, Sunshine has had to master the technical knowledge required by state-of-the-art telecommunications equipment. To achieve this, she taught herself by applying her characteristic energy and intensity.

The International Telecommunications Center either administers or is developing a wide variety of programs. All are designed to make "distance education" a reality in helping to internationalize Ramapo's curriculum. Through its programs, the center's director has broadened the conventional definition of distance education. As she has observed,

> It's not having one person disseminating information via satellite or compressed video. We're defining distance education as people becoming resources to each other even though they are separated geographically. With a course like Modern British Fiction you could use a living British author by having the class read the book ahead of time and then interview the author. ("Ramapo College of New Jersey Internationalizes Curricula Through Distance Education," *Applied Business Telecommunications*, August 1990, pp. 7-8.)

The center transmits international signals directly into the college's language laboratory for use as culturally authentic classroom materials. Other courses in, for instance, business or political science, can use satellite-received telecasts after they have been translated. These voiceovers are produced by international students or visiting scholars on one of the college's several exchange programs. French Canadian advertisements provide one example in marketing and advertising courses. This role for international students and scholars in the Center shows the benefits derived from the interaction of varied international education programs.

Frequent audioconferences provide a second category of center projects. In the 1992-93 academic year, over 130 conferences allowed Ramapo students to talk to people in other countries. The ITC Director provides the vast majority of the initial contacts and reports that about one-third of Ramapo's faculty make use of the audioconferencing capability.

One of the earliest classroom uses of audioconferencing enabled a forestry class to discuss international deforestation and other issues with an official in the UN-affiliated Food and Agriculture Organization in Rome. In one of the most exciting of these early conferences, a communications class discussed mass media with a Cuban, the Director of International Broadcasting for Cuban National Television. The videotape of the students reveals an extraordinarily high level of attentiveness and prior preparation. The interchange with the Cuban broadcaster produced much material for follow-up class discussion.

More recently, students in the Comparative Legal Systems course interviewed attorneys in Italy, Germany, and Saudi Arabia in succession. Also, in Contemporary German History, people in the city of Leipzig told their own stories about the impact of German reunification. Students of all Ramapo's modern languages have live conversations with native speakers. This experience is available at all levels of language instruction from first-year to more advanced; for example, Business Italian.

A third variety of Center activities involved the production of half-hour programs for local public television stations. Formatted like ABC's "20/20," this "Intercultural Perspectives" series highlights the activities and points of view of local cultural groups; for example, one program included footage of a Chinese church and discussed how the Chinese community provides useful social services, like meals for the disadvantaged. The production of these programs has been temporarily suspended until additional financing is located, mainly to provide salaries for needed personnel.

Ramapo students and faculty producing their own videotapes comprise a fourth center project. Examples include compiling visual records of student travel-study programs to a Costa Rican rainforest and a Sea of Galilee archeological dig. Such activities also illustrate how international education programs can reinforce each other enhancing both; in this case, student study abroad experiences and the International Telecommunications Center.

A fifth category of center activities broadcasts Japanese language instruction from SERC, Satellite Education Resources Consortium. Headquartered in Nebraska, SERC relays its signal via satellite into secondary schools in 24 states. Ramapo's International Telecommunications Center provides the New Jersey downlink and channels SERC programming via cable into area high schools and Ramapo's language laboratory. The Center also organizes support services, such as native speaker tutoring by phone. These native speakers are often wives of Japanese corporate executives in nearby subsidiaries.

New technological capabilities have been added to the Center since it began operation. Ramapo is part of Bergen ITV, a countywide, two-way fiberoptic interactive television network linking thirteen high schools and three colleges. Ramapo's satellite downlink enables network members to participate in videoconferences and special events produced for nationwide distribution by various educational, business and government institutions. In addition, courses and teacher training events are also shared.

As its last major program, which became fully operational in the fall of 1993, the center operates Ramapo's internal cable network. The purchase of four new satellite dishes enabled this system to go on line. The expenditure was authorized by the student organization as well as the Office of Student Services, and financed from the student activities account.

Some of its channels are part of the usual packages for which licensing fees are paid, including channels like ESPN, USA, CNN, etc. Yet the system also provides three local channels. One allows students to produce their own productions. This provides opportunities for hands-on experience as technicians and programmers, in addition to increasing the opportunities for developing performing arts and creative writing expertise. A second channel has news and information featuring the Data Service, also available on monitors in the student center. The third channel can be programmed by students through the video club and Contemporary Art courses. It also shows films or other media assigned by Ramapo faculty.

This last center program illustrates the depth of learning possibilities when an operating system is creatively administered. Students helped install the internal cable system, just as they fulfill ongoing roles in other center programs. Thus the center provides communications majors specializing in broadcasting with practical experience. They do not have to rely on off-campus internships. As a related spin-off, two communications courses have been added in the School of Contemporary Arts, Broadcast and Telecommunication Systems Management, and Documentary Video Production.

The center's director reports that for the 1993 academic year over one-half of her operating budget came from sources outside the college; for example, the Nebraska consortium provided financing for salaries as well as about $30,000 for equipment use. In addition, during the same year, $100,000 in audioconferencing equipment was donated by Teleconferencing Technologies Inc., a company that had been a major center supplier. Equipment donations were also received from Sharp Electronics and Sony Corporation of America.

Two groups help provide the center with policymaking, communication, and support networks. The Faculty Advisory Board, an interdisciplinary group of about ten faculty, meets two to three times a semester. The Professional Advisory Board meets as often and consists of about fifteen representatives of the local business and media communities. This group includes

the education director of a New Jersey public television company, and executives from Sharp, Sony, Bell Atlantic, a video
production company, and a manufacturer of communication
equipment.

Issues and Answers

According to the center's director, addressing one key issue
would provide the means to alleviate other constraints. A lack
of personnel is central to the nondevelopment of many new
projects. There is a limit to what can be done by part-time student workers.

In 1991, the center hired a program assistant with funding
from the Nebraska consortium. Yet able though this person has
proven to be, the program possibilities have grown exponentially, it seems, while at the same time the center's institutional
funding has decreased with that of all New Jersey higher education. Even the position of program assistant was threatened in
the spring of 1993's budget process in spite of the fact that
funding for his salary came from an external source.

To illustrate, many faculty want to move beyond the current
ad hoc practice and make audioconferences a permanent addition to their courses. In addition, other faculty would like to use
audioconferences in their classes given the enthusiastic student
reaction to this methodology. Unfortunately, this expansion of
center services is hampered by the lack of personnel.

This problem also has prevented follow-up on several com-
mercial ventures that would raise funds; for example, setting up
videoconferences for local subsidiaries of multinational corporations. Such entrepreneurial activity requires an investment, in
this case in personnel. The center's director could be freed
from daily administrative tasks in order to negotiate contracts.
Also, she can only do this secure in the knowledge that she has
the staff to carry out contracted services quickly and effectively.

Other undeveloped possibilities include internships with the
equipment companies supplying the center, and making videos
for businesses, educational institutions, and other community
organizations. In fact, the lack of personnel problem become so
acute that in 1993 no "Intercultural Perspectives" documen-
taries were produced.

This situation is ironic because the very success of the International Telecommunications Center has produced its main difficulty. More projects require more personnel. Yet, the technological prerequisites and administrative precedents exist to implement many of the director's creative plans.

To an outside observer the notion that growth in ITC activities has been limited has something of a surreal quality given the scope of its current activity and the fact that operations only began in 1989. Given its short duration, the center's program expansion seems explosive. Yet so much more could be done and the contacts already exist. In this media age, possibilities seem limited only by capacity and imagination. The center's deficiency lies only in the former.

One other issue has been addressed and overcome to a large extent. Initially, faculty seemed hesitant to apply the new technology in their courses. They voiced worries about the time required and fears concerning technical feasibility. Perhaps these comments masked a lack of knowledge about the kinds of media available for classroom use, or about the technical process involved.

Yet, for an increasing number of faculty, the concerns have subsided. The ITC director spent much time with individuals making specific suggestions as to curriculum applications. Also, the examples of a few pioneers showed how useful international media and audioconferences could be in increasing student learning and in-class animation. Still, an ongoing reward system is needed for faculty development. This would ensure that new learning and creative course applications will continue to expand in number and quality.

Lessons Learned and Future Plans

Some of the following guidelines apply to international education programs generically, not only to those using the latest in communication technology.

1. *Engage in extensive campus networking.* The ITC director, after noting specific courses in which the center's programs may usefully be applied, not only wrote to the relevant faculty but met with them.

2. *Patience is essential.* Realize programs will develop slowly as faculty and administrators learn applications of the new technologies.

3. *Given the importance of off-campus networking, travel and establish relationships with relevant corporations as well as educational institutions.* This results not only in expanded programming but in donations of equipment, time, and money.

4. *Bridge the technology-academia gap.* The director and key personnel must be able to communicate effectively with both "worlds." They need to make decisions as to equipment requirements as well as to suggest classroom applications.

5. *Rely heavily on audioconferencing, at least initially.* This technology is cheaper and lends itself to a great variety of classroom applications.

Depending on funding, the International Telecommunications Center plans on producing more half-hour "Intercultural Perspectives" programs for local public television stations. In addition, negotiations are underway to rent its fiberoptic network to local police and fire departments. This will allow them to provide low cost training countywide.

Plans are nearing completion for two collaborative projects with universities in Russia. Funding is contingent on grants to the U.S. Information Agency. If implemented, these will enable Ramapo to provide technical assistance on distance learning to Volgograd and Kiev Pedagogical Universities.

The grant aspect of this initiative illustrates an additional category of future uses for the center. Curriculum grant proposals currently under discussion at Ramapo all incorporate the center's capabilities and networks.

One other potential result from international networking deserves mention. Mexico's University of Monterrey and Ramapo College are planning to each produce videos on doing business in their respective countries. These will then be exchanged as international business educational materials. In this context, and as a spinoff of ITC's audioconferences, two

Ramapo professors were invited to the University of Monterrey as visiting faculty.

Many of these points illustrate the relationship between the International Telecommunications Center and Ramapo's prior international education efforts. Years of relevant development has resulted in a density of programs at Ramapo. They provided the foundation for the specialized, high cost, and very visible International Telecommunications Center. Faculty could have objected to the center's cost, even given the fact its equipment was purchased with outside funding. Yet the center has received general support. Faculty as well as administrators see its utility and have developed vested interests in its programs and international networks. The ITC is an integral component of the campus' ongoing international education plans. Its capabilities enhance the possibility that future program refinements will have increasing subtlety and sophistication.

While most institutions cannot match the International Telecommunication Center's expensive technologies, there is a replicable lesson to be learned from Ramapo's experience. The institution has achieved program takeoff. International education programs generate new initiatives as a matter of course. Also, as one of the new initiatives, the ITC demonstrates the fact that significant campus constituencies will support major, expensive innovations if they are firmly based on years of successful international education programming.

Saint Olaf College

Offering a Multicountry, Comparative Experience

Just outside a small town in central Minnesota, Saint Olaf College's beige and brown stone buildings grace a high hilltop overlooking miles of farm country. The distinctive color and composition of the buildings has given rise to the rumor among successive generations of students that some alumnus gave the college a stone quarry. The large campus with its widely spaced buildings cover the ample top and sides of its scenic hill. It is easy to forget that the college, located forty miles south of Minneapolis-Saint Paul, is within commuting distance of a major metropolitan area.

The heavily wooded campus conveys a contemplative atmosphere. It is a place where, a little after 8:00 a.m., a small cottontail rabbit could peacefully browse for its breakfast amid administrators arriving for work. Joining the rabbit, two sparrows hop and pick their way to a morning meal. This scene makes the natural environment seem as much a part of the college as the stone buildings provide the academic environment.

Founded in 1874 by Norwegian immigrants, the college was named after Norway's patron saint, the eleventh century king who is credited with securing the country's monarchy and the position of the Christian church. In a way, this reflects a transformation theme which has been given new life. During the last twenty-five years and for successive generations of Saint Olaf students, education has come to mean a change in cultural perspective. They see themselves as world citizens as well as part of a specific cultural heritage. The faculty explain this as wholly consistent with the college's founding purpose; i.e., to provide students a liberal arts education with its free inquiry and liberation from the confines of a single experience.

Several conversations with faculty, randomly encountered while on a walk across campus, leave the impression that the world can be seen from Saint Olaf's hilltop vista. They express their commitment to providing the college's 3,000 students with a global perspective, not only in their courses but through participating in study abroad programs. They freely discuss their own learning resulting from leading groups of students on off-campus programs.

Over 130 of Saint Olaf's approximately 275 FTE faculty have ventured off campus, teaching more than 300 interim courses. In addition, forty-seven faculty have led one of the college's three distinctive multicountry, five-month travel study terms which begin in the end of August and continue through J-Term. Student participants in these overseas terms learn not only through observation and from their faculty leaders. The terms' curriculum also includes four courses taught by academics in at least two host countries. In this way, a comparative approach is consciously designed into what the college community has designated as "field supervised programs."

The first field supervised program began in 1965 when a faculty member and a group of Saint Olaf students ventured to Asia. This remains one of the college's three such programs offered every fall; i.e., Global Semester, Term in the Middle East, and Term in Asia. These three major learning and programmatic endeavors have provided the cornerstones for a wide variety of off-campus multicultural and international programs offered Saint Olaf students.

Conceptually, the college's far horizon is very far indeed since its curriculum and study abroad programs provide a path to the world. By graduation, about 65 percent of Saint Olaf's students have taken a course overseas, while 35 percent have had a multicultural experience in the United States. Due to the fact that many students participate in both kinds of programs, the figure given for graduates with off-campus, cultural learning is about 75 percent.

Campus Context
Many colleges have offered faculty-led overseas programs since the 1960s. Yet at Saint Olaf they have engendered many more study abroad options and substantial curriculum international-

ization. By the 1980s, international education had become part of the college's identity.

This is evident in the first sentence of the "Mission of the College," a statement approved by the faculty and adopted by the Board of Regents in 1987: "St. Olaf, a four-year college of the Evangelical Lutheran Church in America, provides an education committed to the liberal arts, rooted in the Christian Gospel, and incorporating a global perspective." The statement's last paragraph reads:

> St. Olaf College strives to be an inclusive community, respecting those of different backgrounds and beliefs. Through its curriculum, campus life, and off-campus programs, it stimulates students' critical thinking and heightens their moral sensitivity; it encourages them to be seekers of truth, leading lives of unselfish service to others; and it challenges them to be responsible and knowledgeable citizens of the world.

Graduation requirements include three or four language courses and two courses in multicultural studies, defined as "study of cultures outside the western tradition and cultural diversity within United States society."

The curriculum offers several international and multicultural specializations including majors in American racial and multicultural studies, Hispanic studies, Russian studies, Asian studies, and in five languages, French, German, Norwegian, Russian, and Spanish. Japanese and Chinese also are offered. Concentrations, i.e., approved interdisciplinary programs with a minimum of four courses, are offered in environmental studies and intercultural studies. This last program lists subsections on Africa and the African Diaspora, Latin America/Latino Studies, and The Middle East and the West. The college catalog also lists areas of emphasis, defined as a minimum of three related courses. One of these is international economic analysis.

As usual at an internationalized college, courses with international content are infused throughout the curriculum. At Saint Olaf not only the Departments of History, Political Science, Romance Languages, and Sociology/Anthropology list multiple international courses. The art department offers several courses on Asian art as well as European. The religion department has a course on every major world religion. Music also lists several alternatives such as "Ethnic Music" and "Asian Music," and biology students can take two ecology courses. In addition to the usual International and Development Economics courses, a specialized course on the "Cultural and Institutional Underpinnings of Japan's Economic Miracle" is offered in the Economics Department.

The catalog lists at least one international course for most other departments. The following illustrate the scope of the college's curriculum internationalization: "Social Welfare in the Global Community" in Social Work, "Cross-Cultural Psychology", "Asian Philosophy", "Movement and Dance as Cultural Expression" in the Dance Department, and "Post-Colonial and Third-World Literatures" in English.

The scope of the college's international curriculum is paralleled by a wide variety of international off-campus programs. Both short-term as well as semester and year long programs, traditional courses in overseas universities as well as service and internship experiences are offered. Together they cover all the major regions of the world. In the 1993-94 academic year, students could choose among fifty-one semester- and year-long plus sixteen interim options. About 575 students went overseas during that year.

The breadth and depth Saint Olaf's international education has provided the basis for a series of grant-funded projects establishing the college's position as a leader in the field of international education. The college has achieved international education takeoff since new ideas and refinements are implemented as a matter of course, some of these through grants.

In the 1980s, projects receiving outside funding were designed to provide not only Saint Olaf's faculty and students with more sophisticated teaching-learning strategies, but to serve as a laboratory to test the workability of the newest ideas in international education. The college was one of the first in the country to initiate Languages-Across-the-Curriculum projects, funded by the Fund for the Improvement of Postsecondary Education and the National Endowment for the Humanities. Saint Olaf also has received an award from the Joyce Foundation to fund individual faculty development projects overseas.

Given such comprehensive internationalization, it is not surprising that every applicant interviewed for a faculty position is asked about her/his international experience and expertise. A negative answer does not in and of itself veto a leading candidate but international qualifications are considered important and may make the difference in some cases.

Saint Olaf's international education profile also includes international students. A total of sixty-three attended in the 1993-94 academic year. Some became interested in the college as a result of meeting its students and faculty on Field Supervised Programs. Others learn of Saint Olaf from international affiliates of the Lutheran Church. Each year Saint Olaf hosts about fifteen students and faculty through exchange agreements with universities in Germany, Thailand, Scotland in the United Kingdom, Japan, Tanzania, and China. In addition, native speakers in the language houses are admitted to Saint Olaf from Costa Rica, France, Germany, and Norway. The appropriate language departments assist in the admissions process and the scholarships and stipends are administered by the Office of International Students and Scholars.

The recognition that international students contribute to campus internationalization has led to discussions about devising a systematic recruitment plan. An assistant director for international student admissions was added to the staff of the Office of International and Off-Campus Studies during 1993. This created the Office of International Students and Scholars which reports to the Director of International Off-Campus Studies. A separate and sizeable account for International Student Scholarships has existed for years.

The funding for the Office of International and Off-Campus Studies and International Students and Scholars, including all its programs, comprises 6 percent of the college's total operating budget. Although its staff of eight assist each other when needed, three, including the half-time international student advisor and a three-quarters-time secretary, are assigned international student responsibilities. Five others administer off-campus programs with one professional managing travel arrangements and another handling budgets plus international scholars; about five scholars arrive each year as a result of agreements with universities in China, Thailand, and Tanzania. The director reports to the dean of the college. She has faculty status which enabled her to initiate and codirect the first Saint Olaf interim to South Africa in January 1994. The Political Science Department chair served as the other codirector.

A faculty member in Art History served as the first director of international programs while the second and third held administrative positions. The fourth director holds a masters in International Relations from Yale and a law degree from Rutgers in New Jersey. She has spent much of her career in the developing world as a manager of projects for various non-profit agencies, for instance Africare's work in Zambia. Her credentials also include teaching at the School for International Training in Vermont, and administering the Carter Center's Voter Observation Project in Zambia. She has published articles on development issues in Africa as well as on international education programs.

Field Supervised Programs
The chair of the religion department will be leading 1994's Asia Term. While a Saint Olaf undergraduate, "a few years ago," he met his wife on the Middle East Term. This illustrates the fact that Saint Olaf's multicountry, comparative, five-month programs have retained their vitality for almost thirty years.

The field supervised programs possess various useful attributes. They continue long enough for students to begin to feel comfortable in new cultural environments while retaining the stabilizing effect of a group learning community. Since content and cultural experiences are inherently comparative, they guard against the overgeneralizations and excessive emotional identification or disenchantment that can occur when students first encounter another society. The programs also emphasize academic rigor by requiring the courses taught by professors at each university. Field Supervisors also are obligated to attend these classes. This assists in providing continuity since references to content from these courses can be incorporated into the course taught by the Saint Olaf faculty field supervisor.

A summary of each program's itinerary illustrates their depth, by spending substantial time in each location, while offering breadth by moving the base of operations to at least two additional countries and as many as nine. All three programs carry five courses. At the end of each term, many students travel independently to other parts of the world region they have learned about and lived in for the previous five months.

The Asia Term's partners are Chiang Mai University in Thailand, Chinese University of Hong Kong and East China Normal University in Shanghai. In 1994 the program will stay for one week at Nommensen University in Indonesia. Homestays are part of the experience on this program. The Middle East Term's four host courses are taught by Bogazici University in Istanbul Turkey, American University of Cairo in Egypt, Hebrew University in Jerusalem Israel, and Cadi Ayyad University in Marrakesh Morocco.

The Global Semester's itinerary includes some of the same universities offering courses on the other two terms, while adding additional locations. The first stop includes visits to the United Nations agencies in Geneva. Then on to Greece, Egypt, Israel, India, Nepal, Thailand, Taiwan, Hong Kong, and Japan. Four countries receive academic focus with a month in residence at The American University in Cairo, the Ecumenical Christian Centre in Bangalore India, Chinese University of Hong Kong, and Otani University in Kyoto Japan.

The Asia and Middle East Terms require a minimum of fifteen students while for the Global Semester the number is twenty-five. The maximums vary as well with thirty for Global and the Middle East and twenty-four for Asia. These figures are driven not only by budget but by accommodation availability at the various host universities.

The program fee for the Global Semester was maintained for 1993 and 1994 at $5,324 above the Saint Olaf comprehensive fee. In 1993, the Middle East Term cost $3,800 and, for Asia, the figure was $2,400 over the comprehensive fee. Program fees cover two meals a day as well as the usual transportation, accommodations, and field trips. Transportation to the point of embarkation is not included except in the case of the Global Semester. The field supervised programs comprise a large part of the total budget for semester and year-long programs which, in 1993, totalled $2.2 million.

The students applying for the three terms follow the same process as that required for all Saint Olaf off-campus programs: the application form must be signed by the program's adviser, the student's academic adviser, the two faculty writing the student's recommendations, the chair of the student's major department, and the program's field supervisor. For the field supervised programs all these, with a fifty dollar application fee, are due March 1. The Saint Olaf Abroad catalog promises selection decisions within thirty days.

The selection process for all Saint Olaf's off-campus programs occurs in the context of the college's policy of making off-campus programs available to every student. Good academic standing remains the only qualifying criterion for all but language programs. Yet if a specific program attracts many more applications than there are places, participant selection becomes competitive. In this case, various factors are weighed, such as the contribution the programs will make to the student's education.

All students applying for any program are interviewed personally by the program's faculty adviser. For the three field supervised programs, selection committees for each program make the decisions. The core group of these committees is comprised of the faculty advisor, the previous field supervisor, two students from the previous year's program, and the outgoing field supervisor. Often other relevant faculty, such as past field supervisors, are asked to participate. Sometimes deliberations involve a significant time commitment and degree of responsibility; for instance, the 1992 Global Semester attracted fifty-two applicants for thirty spaces.

All students going overseas are required to attend an orientation. For semester- and year-long programs, a two-day retreat is held in April at a YMCA camp in Wisconsin. Sessions are designed to accomplish a general objective, i.e., helping students to appreciate foreign cultures. Also more specific small group sessions provide detailed information about individual programs. Various techniques are used such as films, lecture-discussion sessions, talks by people from host countries and by students returning from study abroad. Health and safety issues also are emphasized. Students going on January interim programs attend a three hour evening orientation.

Letter grades are recorded for courses taken on off-campus programs but, generally, they are not computed in the student's grade point average. Interims and the course taught by field supervisors in the five-month term programs are the exceptions. The grades received for these courses are calculated in the participants' GPAs unless the student opted to take the course on a pass/fail basis. A field supervisor's teaching credit for the five month program is four courses, two-thirds of the normal six-course load.

Field supervisors are chosen two years in advance. Using a collegial, consensus-building process, the director of international and off-campus studies consults with prospective candidates and a variety of relevant faculty. Faculty who apply are interviewed by a committee chaired by the director, who presents a recommendation to the dean of the college. The dean then makes the appointment. Two people always accompany each program, the field supervisor and, traditionally, her/his spouse.

In addition to salary, field supervisors receive $1,000 to cover various idiosyncratic expenses, such as car storage. Other costs also are covered; for example, the fee for the required first aid course, and medical expenses such as inoculations. In recent years the spouse, as assistant field supervisor, also has all expenses paid.

Beginning in 1992, the assistant field supervisor received a monthly stipend which by 1994-95 was $1,000. This was in response to the fact that many spouses work. Leaving their employment for months without some remuneration was proving too significant a sacrifice for the families of potential field supervisors. Also, there is hope it will attract single faculty by allowing them to hire an assistant.

Faculty who choose to become field supervisors often have traveled abroad as interim course leaders or have attended conferences overseas with Saint Olaf support. It can take years for a faculty member to decide to direct a field supervised program. Constraints not only include a personal sense of academic preparedness. Family considerations often prove critical; i.e., the availability of the spouse to be an assistant field supervisor, and the ages of children.

Over the years, field supervisors have come from virtually all departments, including Art, Math, Physics and Dance. Religion has provided more faculty than any other department. To illustrate the fact that at Saint Olaf off-campus experiences are valued for faculty as well as for students, members of the physics department did not even question why one of their number would want to serve as a field supervisor, even though Physics offers no international courses. In fact, by 1994 two physics faculty had led the Global Semester.

Faculty who have led the five-month programs report that it really involves a three-year commitment. During the year prior to departure, course plans are made, individual research takes place, and students are selected. Upon returning, the spring semester is taken up with debriefing conversations, some programmatic detail, and working with the next field supervisor. Follow-up activities continue during the third year including presentations, incorporating new material into courses and academic papers, and attending relevant program meetings.

During the 1992-93 academic year, the International and Domestic Off-Campus Studies Committee began functioning, with policy oversight as its major task. It is composed of three elected faculty, two appointed by the dean, the director of international and off-campus studies, the associate dean of the college, and two students. It approves proposed off-campus interim courses and other programmatic issues as they arise.

Such responsibilities used to be carried out by a subcommittee of the college's Curriculum and Educational Policies Committee. The volume of off-campus programs had expanded to the point where their oversight required a committee with this as its only function.

Issues, Answers and Program Spin-offs

The constructive response to one problem that grew over time has already been explained. By the early 1990s, remuneration for the spouses of field supervisors demanded attention. Given the changing economy of the United States family, second incomes have become a reality. As explained previously in this case study, increasingly assistant field supervisors had to leave their own employment for the program's five-month duration.

To ease this financial burden on field supervisors' families, the 1992 change created the assistant field supervisor title, which carried with it a Saint Olaf salary and benefit package. One related issue has not surfaced as yet. Will the same policy be applied when the Assistant Field Supervisor is not a spouse?

Another "nuts and bolts" problem increasingly demands attention. The field supervised programs require an incredible amount of administrative time and financial outlay. They are holdovers from decades ago when they offered almost all the college's off-campus options. Also, for years, Saint Olaf programs brought the host institutions their only U.S. students in residence.

Many years and many programs later, global changes have required program adjustments. As one recent example, the cooperating university in Taiwan notified Saint Olaf that it could no longer host its students' one-month stay since its resources could more efficiently be used to support other international students in semester-long programs. This ended happily for now, since a university in Hong Kong accepted the Saint Olaf program.

Thailand's Chiang Mai University faces the same issue but, so far, it has made the decision to continue providing Saint Olaf the same three-month instructional and support services it has provided for the past twenty-five years. Its reason was stated simply: Saint Olaf had brought students when no other U.S. college came, and offered a student and faculty exchange. "You pulled us into the world," was how the university's dean of the faculty of humanities expressed it.

Compared to the college's many other types of overseas programs, the three multi-country, five-month terms seem unwieldy to an outside observer. In fact, their administration takes more staff time, proportionally by student, than do other programs.

Yet the strengths of the field supervised programs continue to far outweigh any administrative inefficiencies. They attract not only students but phenomenal faculty support. Attachment to these three programs appears even greater than that for most other off-campus experiences. Many, many faculty from most Saint Olaf departments, and their spouses, have learned first-hand the educational benefits and teaching satisfaction these programs uniquely engender. Program loyalty has become a family phenomenon. When an issue or even a small change is proposed, faculty and their spouses take notice and make known their points of view. When meetings are organized to discuss such changes, all sorts of people show up, and on time.

The fact that faculty across disciplines share the rather unique experience of having led one of the three multicountry terms has created a distinct campus culture at Saint Olaf. The "send-off" and "welcome home" potluck parties for each one of the three programs attract faculty, spouses, past and present students from many disciplines, all chatting freely together. Not only do faculty friendships cross disciplines, but the constant conversations have produced curriculum and programmatic effects. Trying new ideas has become commonplace, like the Languages-Across-the-Curriculum program which has become institutionalized. Further evidence is the fact that departments are willing to count for their majors courses taken overseas and containing content relevant to other departments. At other colleges this ambiguity could erupt into turf battles.

Discussions about the Global Semester and Asia Term are focusing on the financial problem resulting from the general rise in the value of the yen in relation to that of the dollar over past years. The steeply escalating costs of visiting Japan have reached the point where they cannot be made up for by cutting other program costs. Yet, because of its pedagogical value, dropping the Japan segment of the program remains a major point of discussion.

At least three issues are not specific to the field supervised programs. The first, staff development in the International and Off-Campus Studies Office, provides one response to the lack of opportunities for promotions and major salary increases. The director combs all budgets to scrape together financing for office personnel to not only attend conferences but to participate on panels. Giving professional presentations and writing papers are encouraged and assistance is provided where possible.

Another issue also relates to off-campus programs in general. Since Saint Olaf considers these cross-cultural experiences an integral component of educational excellence, the question consistently arises, how can they be made available to more students? In recent years, the answer has been to focus on specific groups where there is a lower percentage of participation, such as natural science students. One response has been to design discipline-specific programs, such as the actively publicized and always oversubscribed "Biology in South India," a study/service program. In addition, the Budapest Semester in Mathematics attracts enough students to send groups both semesters each year. Directed by a Saint Olaf faculty member, this consortial program recruits students from several colleges and universities.

Traditionally underrepresented "at risk" students present another group for which a specific program was designed. The successful 1994 J-term program in Costa Rica shows what needs to be done for this particular student population. Eight students of the twenty were from U.S. minorities. When they began their Saint Olaf career, they were promised their scholarships would include an overseas experience if they would successfully complete the first two semesters of Spanish on campus. The Saint Olaf treasurer served as mentor, took the Spanish courses too, and with his wife accompanied the group to Costa Rica. The faculty member who led the group overseas had taught the courses and, in the process, provided students with significant individual attention.

In specialized programs for "at risk" students, both mentor and faculty roles are needed. Both must provide much personalized attention and support, pedagogically and emotionally. Such a labor-intensive, specifically targeted program also requires a champion, someone who can make decisions and command resources quickly and effectively when problems arise. The Saint Olaf treasurer filled this need. The whole effort, from when the students first arrived on campus to their completion of the Costa Rican program, demonstrated that "at risk" students need an aggressive intervention strategy.

A last issue concerns budgets. Until the present, program budgets have been considered separate from each other. Those programs attracting a maximum number of students often have more funding than they need for extra field trips and other enhancements. The programs with a minimum number of students experience the opposite. There is general agreement that all share a common educational value. Therefore, the issue of budget equity arises.

One proposed change suggests that, to some extent, overseas programs should be managed like the college as a whole. Students in biology courses are not charged more than those in English courses even though the overhead expenses are greater. Yet, applying this approach to budgeting overseas programs would require a major attitude change among faculty, and administrators. As on most campuses, they think of each program as a self-contained unit; therefore, financing from one program should not be used to support another. This discussion will remain ongoing since the field supervised programs are increasingly expensive to operate.

Lessons Learned

Given some of the issues explained above, perhaps multicountry multimonth programs are no longer replicable in the 1990s. Yet their educational value could serve as a model; for example, one or two related overseas courses could be packaged as one program and, coupled with an on-campus curriculum, could provide comparative content and experience.

The following guidelines apply to overseas student programs in general.

1. *Involve faculty.* This is the major and abiding strength of the field supervised programs, without which they might have ceased to exist years ago.
2. *Create faculty development opportunities.* This point overlaps with the first but has a different emphasis. For maximum faculty development, their role should be more than serving as on campus program advisors who make an in-country visit now and then. Faculty ongoing, enthusiastic support comes from experiencing with students their educational and personal development. Also, interaction with academics in host universities benefits both students and

faculty. The resulting new knowledge is often applied directly in the campus curriculum.

3. *Hire a director with academic legitimacy.* This means that he/she has the assurance to make content and pedagogical suggestions to faculty.

4. *Systematically plan for the future.* The content of overseas courses should be integrated with the on-campus curriculum. Therefore off-campus programs must result from conscious design and not from a faculty member's idiosyncratic and temporary contacts.

5. *Encourage presidents and deans to visit overseas partner universities.* In 1993 the president visited host institutions in China, Hong Kong, and Thailand and the dean visited Turkey, Morocco, and Egypt. This not only reinforced their personal knowledge of study abroad's benefits, it also assisted in long-term program development by strengthening relationships with partner universities. The visits of the president and the dean clearly demonstrated Saint Olaf's commitment to the program at the highest administrative level.

The main factor contributing to the continued success of Saint Olaf's field supervised programs is faculty enthusiasm. They were faculty initiated and sustained through several generations of directors and campus administrations. Over the years, their success helped generate a vast array of all types of student overseas programs. This, plus concomitant curriculum development, culminated with the adding of a global perspective to the college's mission statement. Saint Olaf has become one of the few campuses in the United States where the concept of international education takeoff can be applied to the whole college and not just to specific programs or units.

University of California, Irvine

Retaining the Enthusiasm of Returning
Study Abroad Students

Overseas programs change undergraduates. Study abroad directors continually comment on the large percentage of students who return, particularly from semester- or year-long programs, not only with more knowledge but also with the experience of learning to be comfortable in a new cultural environment. They manifest the confidence and maturity such experiences produce and exude enthusiasm for learning and overseas study.

A prominent topic at international education conferences concerns how to continue and channel the energy of returning students. Conversations also take place about strategies for increasing the numbers of participating students.

Program advisors know that the most effective spokespersons for student overseas programs are previous participants. The University of California, Irvine has developed a program that accomplishes the goal of focusing the verve of returning students on increasing the numbers of future participants. This International Peer Advising Program also achieves other program development goals, such as recruiting more traditionally underrepresented students. Other colleges and universities have experimented with student-to-student orientations and program marketing strategies, but few have set up as structured a program as UCI's with its systematic training, paid student coordinator, and weekly meetings.

The UCI campus, one of California's nine research universities, was a ranch before its metamorphosis into a university. It is located in a rapidly growing suburban area adjacent to one of the largest industrial parks in the nation. Some personnel remember that not long ago part of the ranch was functioning with roundups held adjacent to the campus. University staff also report that the first UCI chancellor was an agronomist who planned the campus setting and designated where each of a wide variety of trees would be planted. A stroll through UCI does convey a sense of planning with two walking circles marking the campus center, one outside the other. The inner circle outlines a twenty-one-acre park with students and faculty striding purposefully across to reach classroom and office buildings located around the next circle. More three- and four-story buildings outline the third thoroughfare, an irregular circle, this one allowing automobile traffic. Dormitories, parking, the athletic complex, College of Medicine, and other outlying areas complete the campus setting.

The inner campus, with its now mature, strikingly beautiful trees, invites a walk. Having a park as the central feature connotes an appreciation for natural settings. This impression is reinforced by the fact that the UCI campus also contains a natural reserve at its western edge, the 200+ acre San Joaquin Freshwater Marsh. The university's friendly attitude toward the natural world may have influenced its choice of animal mascot, an anteater.

The University of California, Irvine opened in 1965 with 1,589 students and 116 faculty. By 1994 it had a student body of almost 17,000, 13,500 of these as undergraduates, and over 940 full-time faculty. The university consists of eight schools, the College of Medicine, and three departments, namely the Department of Information and Computer Science, Department of Education, and Department of Athletics and Physical Education. The five basic schools, Biological Sciences, Fine Arts, Humanities, Physical Sciences, and Social Sciences, are joined by the School of Social Ecology, School of Engineering, and Graduate School of Management. By the 1990s, the university had several attributes indicating significant internationalization, i.e., international and multicultural graduation requirements, and substantial ethnic diversity among its student population.

Campus Context
The statement of the chancellor, at the beginning of UCI's catalogue, includes the sentence, "A global perspective requires that we understand and respect cultural differences and value com-

mon goals." One of the underlying realities this statement reflects is indicated by the fact that UCI has the largest Asian population of any U.S. university on the mainland. In the fall of 1993, 47 percent of the undergraduate population was Asian. Other groups contribute as well, with 12 percent Hispanic, 3 percent African-American, and 1 percent American Indian. In the fall of 1994, 55 percent of the freshmen class identified themselves as Asian.

International students numbered 1,139 in 1993-94 with 305 as undergraduates. They are advised by two full-time international student advisers in the Office of International Services, part of the Office of Student Affairs and Campus Life.

In May 1989, the Faculty Representative Assembly voted to revise UCI's general education requirements. This action followed a two-year study by a campuswide Task Force on General Education. The new requirements are grouped into seven categories with the sixth and seventh devoted to international education, i.e., VI. Language Other Than English, and VII. Multicultural Studies and International/Global Issues.

The catalogue lists several ways to meet the language requirement, such as two years of language study, four years of prior training in high school, and testing out by examination. Another equivalent is completion of an approved course of study in an Education Abroad Program. To fulfill the Multicultural Studies and International/Global Issues requirements, students must take one course under each to be selected from two substantial lists. Students may also meet this requirement by participating in designated Education Abroad Programs.

The catalogue description of UCI's research specialities includes East Asian languages and literatures plus bilingual education. As this focus implies, several departments provide courses on East Asia, not only covering the region as a whole, but on specific countries. The departments listing such courses are Art History, Anthropology, Economics, Linguistics, History, Sociology, and Politics and Society.

Language majors include Chinese Language and Literature and Japanese Language and Literature, along with German, French, Russian and Spanish. The strength in these disciplines is indicated by specialized advanced courses such as Spanish-

American Theatre. The language department also provides English as a Second Language courses and students can apply up to twelve credits as electives toward the bachelor's degree.

The university offers two international and intercultural majors separate from disciplinary majors. The Comparative Culture major in the School of Social Sciences concentrates on the main cultural groups in the United States. This Comparative Culture major offers many courses on each U.S. group, as well as several general courses such as, Comparing Cultures and Philosophy of Culture. The second major, Environmental Analysis and Design, is available in the School of Social Ecology and it includes many globally oriented courses.

Several relevant minors are described in the UCI catalogue: Italian, Portuguese, Russian Area Studies, Global Peace and Conflict Studies, Latin American Studies, African-American Studies, and Chicano-Latino Studies.

Relevant courses and international subfields in departments usually considered heavily international include many aspects of the social sciences. Anthropology has areas studies courses on all the world regions as well as the countries of Korea, India, and Mexico, including a course titled Music of Greater Mexico. As well as the usual International and Comparative Economics courses, the department has several distinctive courses on Economic Anthropology, Japanese Economy, and International Money. Geography courses include Human Geography, and Environment and Resources. The linguistics department lists Introduction to Language and Culture, as well as Sociolinguistics. Courses in the Department of Politics and Society cover all major world regions and several countries in East Asia and Europe plus Canada. The department also has courses in most of the major subfields in International Relations plus a survey course on Basic Societal Issues. These include peace, economic justice, and the environment. History courses as well cover most world regions. China and Japan each have two courses with the history of these two countries divided at 1800. The department has a lower division course on Survey of East Asia: Traditions and Transformations. Included in its many upper division areas studies courses is one on Australia and New Zealand.

Several UCI majors include relevant internationally focused courses in their requirements. Sociology majors must choose one of two basic courses with one being Social Structures. This course includes material on the relationships between societies and nations. Students majoring in Art History also have the choice of one of two three-course sequences, either History of Western Art, or Asian Art. A Studio Art major must take Topics in Visual Culture, and Issues in Contemporary Art and Visual Culture. Both these three-course sequences cover multicultural studies as a "critique of the canon."

At UCI other departments not usually thought of as inherently international or intercultural also contribute to the university's relevant curriculum. Psychology lists Interdisciplinary Studies courses such as, Asian-American Psychology and Psychological Anthropology. Philosophy includes topics in Asian Philosophy and Geosciences offers three courses not for science majors, the first named Science of the Global Environment. Film Studies provides a National Cinemas Course which deals with several countries. English has Introduction to Multicultural Topics in Literature; the dance department has ensembles on Mexican and Spanish dance. The School of Biological Sciences, specifically the psychology and sociology behavior department, lists a lower division course on Peace and Technology in the Nuclear Age. It also has International Cooperation as an upper division offering. Several courses on pollution appear in the catalogue under the School of Engineering; for example, Pollution Control. Department of Education courses implementing its bilingual/cross-cultural emphasis are available in Spanish plus one upper division course, Perspectives on Multicultural Education.

The basic schools at UCI note in their sections of the catalogue that when participating in the Education Abroad Program, students can "make progress toward degree objectives while experiencing another culture." The Center for International Education is part of the Office of the Dean of Undergraduate Studies and administers UCI's student overseas programs. The university organizes its study abroad options into two general categories. The first, the Education Abroad Programs (EAP), are sponsored by the University of California and offered systemwide. They are all at least a semester long in duration. The second category, called the International Opportunities Program (IOP) provides counseling, information and predeparture preparation for students interested in international study, short-term employment, field research, volunteering and internships that are outside the University of California system. This includes programs sponsored by other universities or language schools.

The center's library offers students a vast array of program materials and a staff more than willing to follow up on requests for more information about a specific programs. One professional uses INTERNET's Gopher network to research which programs match a students' specific interests. Students have commented that the center is the "friendliest office on campus." It was center personnel who recognized the need for and developed the International Peer Advisor Program

International Peer Advisor Program
The idea for the program sprang from a convergence of several discrete events. The Center for International Education had been created in the late 1980s. Prior to this, the two long-term UCI employees who served as Education Abroad Program advisors were hidden away, literally, in a trailer at the edge of campus behind some trees. Materials were in a small box and data virtually nonexistent. About forty-plus students were participating. After professionalizing the operation, the number of EAP students doubled. Yet, given the size of UCI's undergraduate population and extensive international curriculum, especially in languages, the center's director decided EAP could grow by much more. Also the International Opportunities Program was established in 1988, which opened up many more potential options.

Another event occured at the state level in 1989. The University of California Academic Senate issued a *Report of the Task Force on Education Abroad and International Programs*. It deplored the near invisibility of EAP on many campuses and advocated more aggressive action by each university's study abroad office. More specifically, the report recommended that advisors should integrate overseas study with the campus academic community, and improve discipline-specific counseling with accompanying informational materials. These points echoed similar concerns and recommendations made in a 1978 report by the same body.

When the center's director, Barbara Bertin, was attending the 1989 annual conference of EAP advisors, one of the discussion topics concerned ways to increase the number of EAP students. Since Bertin was also UCI's director of general programs, she supervised the administration of another program in the Office of the Dean of Undergraduate Studies, namely the Peer Academic Advising Program. Its success had demonstrated how effective students were in influencing other students. Why not apply the same tactic to advising study abroad programs?

After writing a successful proposal to the Fund for the Improvement of Postsecondary Education, the International Peer Advisory Program began in 1990. It had multiple, interrelated objectives. Not only was the IPA Program designed to increase the numbers of students going on overseas programs, it also aimed to expand the demographic characteristics of the participants. About 75-80 percent of each year's study abroad students were U.S. mainstream females in the humanities or social sciences. Within two years this had changed markedly to include more ethnicities, nontraditional academic disciplines, and males.

The International Peer Advisory program (IPA) has several main components all of which have been institutionalized.

Selection and Training of International Peer Advisors

Applications to students studying abroad are mailed in early summer. Usually around thirty to thirty-five applicants respond by the deadline in mid-August. Fifteen are selected and attend the mandatory four half-day training sessions in mid-September two weeks prior to the beginning of fall quarter. Center for International Education staff serve as trainers.

Training session topics cover information about the center and its programs, especially the International Opportunities Program (IOP). The great variety of programs offered through

IOP makes the advising of students and matching their interest with a specific program more complex. In the words of one center staff member, "We don't train them to have answers, we train them to do their own research." The session does not provide IPAs with information to memorize but resources to use.

A day is devoted to developing advising and counseling skills. Another long training session coaches IPAs in public speaking and allows them practice time. This takes on great significance because preparing talks for delivery in classes, plus many other venues, is an important part of what an IPA does, and the task most IPAs find intimidating initially. The training also provides information about financial aid available for EAP students. Throughout the four days, a team approach is emphasized so that helping each other becomes routine.

Resource Development
During the first year of the program, IPAs and International Center personnel developed a set of twenty-two discipline-specific factsheets. These provide information on programs carrying credit in a wide variety of disciplines and are updated annually. They have proven invaluable not only for recruitment but also for training each year's new group of IPAs.

Three large binders were prepared called "Reflections From Abroad." These are collections of pictures and thoughts of students who have gone overseas to all the major world regions. Updated periodically, they are located in the center's reception area.

In addition, a thirteen-minute videotape was produced introducing the International Center, its study abroad options and services. Much IPA input went into the preparation of the video, "Globalize Yourself", and students first entering the Center can view it on the VCR in the reception area. Also, it is used frequently during long presentations as a focus for discussion. Most of the tape presents thirteen ethnically diverse students, with a variety of majors, explaining in a natural and engaging manner what their experiences meant to them. They describe their fears before going overseas, and how their study abroad experience fits their academic and future career plans.

International Peer Advisor Activities

The fifteen IPAs spend most of their eight to ten hours a week fulfilling assignments arising from their two main duties, recruitment and advising. Recruitment produces a wide variety of activities. International Peer Advisors make presentations in classes, dormitory meetings, student club meetings, workshop and conference panel discussions, advising sessions in schools and departments, and at campuswide events.

A systematic process is used in cultivating the relationships that produce good meetings. Preparation for dormitory presentations, for example, includes meeting with resident advisors at their early fall meeting. Their support is requested in setting up the sessions, as well as their positive reinforcement for study abroad. Follow-up includes setting the date and time, and preparing fliers and other publicity. No organizational task is left up to the R.A.s themselves.

Good relations with the staff of the Cross-Cultural Center are clearly important given the IPA program objective of increasing the level of underrepresented group participation. International Peer Advisors attend a CCC board meeting early in the academic year, make presentations at ethnic club meetings, and become involved in other activities as appropriate, such as the Cinco de Mayo celebration and Asian Heritage Week.

Article writing, graphic art work, and other publicity skills are part of an IPA's assignment. The campus has innumerable newsletters, and fliers announcing meetings seem to be needed all the time. Posters adorning a central campus walkway are a time tested UCI way of disseminating information.

These country specific meetings are led by two IPAs good at managing group dynamics. Prior to the meeting, they call returnees from EAP programs in the targeted country inviting them to come and talk to interested students. Collecting the names, addresses, and phone numbers of attendees is another IPA responsibility.

Since a positive faculty attitude toward study abroad is so essential, especially when IPAs make presentations in their classes, another IPA assignment includes discussions with individual faculty in their offices. For faculty not yet part of the Center's network, IPAs use their own experiences to point out the benefits of study abroad. For others, the visits are used to update information on specific programs related to the faculty member's field. Also, IPAs are expected to meet with the academic counselor of their own school once a quarter for an updating session.

Other activities can be added, bounded only by the IPAs' imagination and sense of propriety. Over time some of these have become routine, such as an activity called "brown bag advising." During the eighth or ninth week every quarter, IPAs sit at tables with resident advisors outside the Student Center to meet with interested students. In addition, IPAs are required to provide information for the Center newsletter sent each quarter to students overseas.

The advising role requires IPAs to sign up for a specific two-hour time each week at the center. Students first entering the center complete interest profile forms and then are seen by IPAs who discuss the center's resources and explore the students' backgrounds and interests. Also, IPAs set up appointments with specific students who want additional conversations about information or their concerns. During the second step in the process, prospective study abroad students meet with the center's professional counselors.

International Peer Advisors are assigned general office work as needed; for example, they cover the front desk during lunch times. When the deadlines for EAP applications approach, IPAs always assist in the office since this is one specific time that students and procrastination seem synonymous.

The IPA coordinator holds weekly meetings and all IPAs are required to attend. These meetings reinforce the program's common goals and team approach in a concrete way. Organized feedback allows IPAs to help each other with suggestions. This also occurs as new work assignments are made. The IPAs report enjoying the interaction with others with whom they now have a lot in common. Without the weekly meetings they know they would lose touch. Each individual IPA also meets weekly or biweekly with the coordinator.

IPA Coordinator's Role

Day-to-day administration of the program is handled by the IPA coordinator. During the first two years, a permanent professional staff member served as coordinator. Since then, each year a different former IPA has held the half-time job. It provides valuable administrative and a quality leadership experience for these outstanding undergraduate students.

Each coordinator has added a useful new dimension; for example, the 1993 coordinator attended the student leadership retreat in September. The 100 or so students present were those elected to campus-wide offices, editors of the student newspaper, and others who could provide good contacts for the IPA program. This coordinator, Christina, viewed such networking as part of the process of integrating international programs and issues into student campus life. She also emphasized the academic side of student experience in working with clubs and newspaper editors as well as faculty and academic advisors.

Predeparture Course

When the IPA program was initiated, it included development of the Global Issues and International Perspectives course listed under Social Science and Social Ecology. Carrying two units of credit, and taught on a pass/no pass basis, the dean of undergraduate studies serves as the instructor of record. He is also a UCI faculty member in the School of Social Sciences. The course is offered during every spring quarter for students who have been accepted on overseas programs and will be departing during the next academic year.

Faculty members lecture on global topics and issues, such as an overview of world religions, the status of environmental problems, women's role and status in certain cultures, cultural geography, economics and political sciences. Each lecture also locates America and Americans in its global perspective.

destinations. These sections are co-led by a center staff member and an IPA. Various guests are invited, including students, faculty, community people, all with a particular expertise helpful in preparing students for their overseas experience in the particular country. In 1992, the first time the course was offered, thirty-five students enrolled. The number increased to forty in 1993 and has increased since. The course has become a permanent part of UCI's curriculum and is recommended to those students who will be studying abroad.

The previously described activities were initiated in the early 1990s, a time of unforeseen problems faced by higher education in California. Recession, defense-related layoffs, and other economic factors have resulted in financial constraints as taxes diminished. One reaction was to raise tuition with student payments doubling during the first years of the IPA program. Consequently, students felt an even greater need to graduate as rapidly as possible. They generally regarded study abroad as potentially delaying graduation and as inherently expensive. A large part of the IPA's role was dispelling these myths by showing students that some programs cost about the same as remaining on campus, and most credits can be applied to meeting graduation requirements or to majors and minors.

Other student constraints are more complicated to address. As mentioned before, 47 percent of the undergraduates at UCI are Asian or Asian-American. They and other minority populations often have family obligations and responsibilities different from those of Anglo students. In addition, many UCI students are the first generation in their families to attend college where traditional expectations especially effect women students. Once parents see the benefit of study abroad, and women students can be freed from traditional home responsibilities, the issue of their safety abroad may arise.

Students also want to know that the credits earned overseas are directly connected to their college program. Many of these factors present seemingly unsurmountable obstacles, but a systematic approach to providing information and meetings with like students who have studied abroad, allows the IPAs to reach at least those students in traditionally underrepresented categories who may be open to participation.

In spite of the fact that the program was begun at a less than auspicious time, it has been successful. The level of overall study abroad participation doubled in four years. As the following figures show, substantial increases occurred most years.

Study Abroad Participation

Year	Number Of Participants
1989-90	133
1990-91	220
1991-92	242
1992-93	244
1993-94	278

The data below generally reflect increases in the variety of participation by gender, ethnicity, and discipline except in the case of Hispanics. The most significant growth was in the percentage of Asians and males choosing to study overseas.

Ethnicity

Year	Afr-Amer	Asian	Causa	Hispan	Other
1990-91	0%	25%	62%	8%	6%
1991-92	1%	19%	64%	11%	5%
1992-93	1%	30%	57%	6%	4%
1993-94	1%	35%	53%	6%	5%

Gender

Year	Female	Male
1990-91	76%	24%
1991-92	66%	34%

School/Program

Year	Bio	Eng	Fine Arts	Hum	Comp Sci	Phys Sci	Soc Ecol	Social Sci
1990-91	9%	2%	4%	32%	2%	2%	13%	35%
1991-92	5%	3%	11%	33%	1%	1%	10%	31%
1992-93	11%	3%	12%	28%	1%	2%	10%	28%
1993-94	11%	6%	9%	28%	1%	3%	6%	33%

As noted previously, Barbara Bertin, director of the Center for International Education, assumed overall direction of the IPA program. The first year the program was institutionalized, in 1993-94, expenses were the coordinator's $8,000 salary, and the $100 paid the IPAs each quarter. Given the latest round of financial cutbacks, the IPAs for 1994-95 will not receive any financial remuneration.

Bertin has a direct, confident style, enabling her to establish good relations with her staff. She knows the details of the several programs under her administration in her role as director of general programs as well as of the Center for International Education. Her enthusiasm seems contagious as she emphasizes her administrative role. Bertin takes pride in setting up processes that work.

As with many successful programs, the unforeseen and intangible benefits often evoke the most enthusiastic explanations from those most involved. International Peer Advisors note the sense of community and a new circle of friends as one reason they were glad to have participated. They also mention their upgraded skills, especially in public speaking. Yet they show the most enthusiasm when discussing another benefit as they see it: the respect they were shown by office staff, and particularly faculty and university administrators. In virtually all offices and classroom situations, IPAs report faculty and higher level administrators as interested and supportive.

Another set of comments concerned attitudes toward international students. One IPA said she knew what it was like being in a new country and it made her want to meet and get to know international students, helping them if needed. Her eargerness is expressed by her phrase "hunt them down." Many other IPAs nodded when this point was made.

These explanations as to the benefits of the IPA program can be multiplied several times over in the case of the coordinator. The job is not just a resume builder. Like the IPAs, which the coordinator was before her promotion, she had experienced an exponential increase in confidence in her own abilities.

Perhaps the personal growth and other reasons given for being an IPA all contribute to one general feeling on which they all agreed. They reported realizing they were part of the university in a meaningful way. They were no longer just recipients of services as students, but were able to offer some services of their own, and ones no one else could provide as effectively. Previous IPAs have summarized their experience as the "most meaningful thing we've done in college." Students serving as IPAs certainly had little difficulty reentering or readjusting to life at UCI.

Issues and Answers

The University of California has a highly selective admissions process and UCI students generally are intelligent, confident, and possess a variety of skills. This, plus their previous work with students, led program administrators to expect that the IPAs would be self starters. It seems, however, that youthful vigor and brainpower does not make up for a lack of program development experience. The need for detailed structuring of program activities soon became apparent.

As the first group of IPAs floundered, some becoming dispirited because "there wasn't enough to do," center staff responded with detailed planning. Some student ideas, and those from the staff themselves, became the basis for a systematic approach. Forms were prepared for collecting and reporting data. Position descriptions and how-to-do-it guidelines were written. An outline of the IPA's responsibilities became a five-page single-spaced document.

Policies were instituted where needed; for example, some IPAs the first year resisted talking in classes. Since one program objective was to provide personal growth opportunities, making classroom presentations became required with preparation for public speaking becoming part of the new training process. Handouts were written for the training session, such as one listing "presentation style elements." The pages on "hints and strategies" help students notice the impression they have on listeners and provide methods for making their talks more interesting.

Examples of the structure developed for program administration include the IPA application process. Students fill out a form, provide the names of two references, and attach a resume noting relevant work or volunteer experience. The form uses a variety of information gathering formats, such as asking applicants to "list your five greatest strengths in relation to this position." Every applicant is personally interviewed after returning home from study abroad in August. The list of questions for the interviewer includes some hypothetical situations; for example, "How would you respond if a student said," and this is followed by a variety of comments such as, "I'm afraid of leaving my family/friends for a whole year."

The advising process also became organized with an Interest Profile form filled out by each advisee and notations made during subsequent visits. Files were kept and check lists became routine. Record keeping became detailed, such as noting which classes were visited and when. Records of talks given at other events include this information plus attendance figures and lists of interested students, their addresses and phone numbers.

Out of the "chaos of the first year," as it was described by center staff, emerged a professionalized program. The structure enables students with a variety of abilities help each other instead of clashing in attempts to fit the program to their own strengths. Some students are adept at graphics, or writing, or computer skills. Others make good meeting facilitators while some thrive in public speaking situations. Many prefer the more informal dormitory setting. As the program progressed and the IPAs' role became more defined and categorized, students found their places on the team and encouraged each other to try new skills. Structure and teamwork need each other.

After the IPA program proved a success, a second major issue surfaced. Discussions were held on how to continue the program after outside funding ended. There was great reason for optimism since the undergraduate studies dean had previously taken action to back up his verbal support for international education. He had established the IOP program and served as professor for the study abroad orientation course.

Institutionalization became a reality when the Dean earmarked budgetary support for the Coordinator's salary and a stipend for each IPA. Unfortunately, the IPA salary had to be cut from $6.10 an hour for eight to ten hours a week, to a token $100 each quarter. Since the IPAs had been extremely positive about their experience, it was hoped they would need little financial incentive. This assumption proved true and will undergo an even greater test in the 1994-95 academic year.

Given additional decreases in the Deans' office budget, IPAs will be serving on a volunteer basis.

Lessons Learned

In reflecting on the Center for International Education's work and accomplishments, its Director cites *Abroad and Beyond* by Goodwin and Nacht. The authors present useful general guidelines which can be applied to the Center's role. Goodwin and Nacht outline three necessary stages to involving more students in study abroad programs and assisting them to integrate the experience into their general education. First, students need early exposure to international education themes and issues. They should practice the analytical skills needed to make such information meaningful to them. Second, their predeparture learning should adequately prepare them to gain the most out of their study abroad experience. Third, returnees need to relate their experiences to others, which helps them reflect adequately and develop new perspectives on their learning.

The staff at the Center for International Education at UCI would not say they have achieved complete implementation of Goodwin and Nacht's three objectives for all students on the Center programs. Yet this is probably true for the International Peer Advisors. For other colleges and universities thinking of initiating such a program, Center staff make the following recommendations.

1. *Listen to students.* They are the best source of current information on specific programs as well as ideas to motivate future student participants.
2. *Organize each task carefully.* Using a computer to create databases proved invaluable in keeping track of exactly which IPAs accomplished what assignments and when. The number of in-class presentations, dormitory meetings, and a myriad of other activities increase exponentially as the days go by. Checklists and other management tools help students monitor their own actions. Without such structure they can develop the impression that they are doing very little. The reports, individual student interest profiles, and other paperwork, as well as weekly meetings,

are not designed to reveal deficits but to document successful completion of tasks. Students actually take pride in recording the results of their efforts.

3. *Believe in the program.* There will be tough times, especially during the startup stage. Program initiators sometimes need conviction to keep going.

4. *Hire staff who have been overseas.* This does not mean on visits but on long term programs. They need to have gone through what the students will experience. This guideline certainly is true for the International Peer Advisors.

5. *Enter grant competitions.* In some institutional contexts outside funding may not be absolutely essential. Yet the program would probably not have been established at UCI without it.

6. *Create the position of coordinator.* Someone specifically hired to administer day-to-day details is essential for the program's success.

Several factors contributed to the International Peer Advisor Program's success. Its founder was a respected administrator with the authority and competence to organize something new. She had the complete support, and even the participation of the dean of undergraduate studies who served as professor for the orientation course. The center's staff, youthful, energetic, knowledgeable, and with international experience themselves, carried out the program with a needed attention to detail. In addition, successive generations of IPAs have proven committed and competent in fulfilling their role.

One change in the institutional context must be mentioned as possibly making a major contribution to the increased number of students in overseas programs. The new graduation requirements and the IPA program were initiated at the same time. Since approved Education Abroad Programs are listed as one way to meet the Language Other Than English, Global Issues, and Multicultural requirements, this well may have helped convince more students to study abroad. This point illustrates the importance of structural factors in international education program development.

University of California, San Diego

Initiating an International College

Undergraduates at the San Diego campus of the University of California can experience both the personal scale of a small college and the benefits of a large research university. Students attend one of five colleges, each designed for no more than 3,000 to 3,200. Enrollment figures from 1992 show that the plan works in practice since out of a total of almost 18,000 students, 14,280 were undergraduates about evenly divided among the five colleges.

Each semiautonomous undergraduate college has its own educational identity distinguished from the others by differences in general education requirements. Each college also has its own residence halls, faculty assigned from the universitywide departments, and administrative personnel under a provost. Thus many student services, such as advising, are provided by the individual colleges while all five share general administrative facilities, such as admissions. Buildings also are shared; i.e., the student center, the library, and classroom buildings.

The university's latest college is dedicated to international education. Called Fifth College until its name change in 1994 to Eleanor Roosevelt College, it offers a virtually unique case study of an international college designed literally from the ground up. The faculty group determining the college's graduation requirements were free from the sometimes overwhelming pressure of vested interests. Such interests often determine decision-making when an existing college internationalizes. Thus, Eleanor Roosevelt College presents a distinctive model for defining international education.

As the latest member of the UCSD institutional community, Eleanor Roosevelt College joins in the university's distinctive blend of both small college and research university approaches to education. This synthesis is derived from UC San Diego's unique history. The present university traces its origins to 1892 when a field station was established in La Jolla to survey Pacific marine animals. In 1912 this marine field station became the Scripps Institution for Biological Research, renamed Scripps Institution of Oceanography in 1925. Scientific research continues as a major emphasis at UC San Diego while a university has evolved.

In 1958, the Institute of Technology and Engineering was added which provided graduate level education. This expansion was quickly followed, in 1959, with approval for a general campus by the regents of the University of California. Thus UC San Diego became one of the latest of the nine research universities in the University of California system.

The director of the Scripps Institution at the time, Roger Revelle, wanted an innovative approach in adding undergraduate education to the university's mandate. The concept of a "family" of small colleges, each with its own facilities and academic identity, has been attributed to Revelle. Therefore, the School of Science and Engineering, later First College, is now called Revelle College. By 1994, the four other colleges were named John Muir, Thurgood Marshall, Earl Warren, and Eleanor Roosevelt.

The university moved to its present location in 1963, just a few blocks from the Pacific Ocean. Its undergraduate program began in 1964 with the 1,200 acre campus providing much room for expansion. By the early 1990s, UCSD consisted of five undergraduate colleges, the Scripps Institution of Oceanography, and three graduate schools; i.e., the Schools of Medicine, Architecture, and the Graduate School of International Relations and Pacific Studies established in 1987. The international emphasis was reinforced at the undergraduate level in 1988 when Fifth, now Eleanor Roosevelt College, began enrolling students.

The campus evidences both modernity and Southern California's past in its architecture and land use patterns. Quonset huts are still used which date from the location's previous life as a U.S. Marine base. At the same time, many buildings are contemporary in style. The campus' characteristic feature, a multi-storied glass library, resembles an inverted step pyramid. It was dubbed "the space ship" by students before supports were added to its narrow base.

With such varied architecture, tall eucalyptus trees provide the campus' unifying feature. The buildings seem to be planted among and around the trees. This reminder of Southern California's natural environment is reinforced by a large natural reserve on campus bordering Interstate 5. This main thoroughfare connects the U.S. west coast from the Canadian to the Mexican borders. The contradictory impressions of connection and environmental distance also are reflected on the Eleanor Roosevelt College campus. While a deep canyon separates one of its dormitory clusters from other buildings, E.R. College students join in planning and participating in co-curricular events designed to reinforce the college's unifying international focus.

Given California's ethnically and culturally diverse population, the founders of E.R. College believed they could attract enough students with an interest in learning about the world to justify a college with an international orientation. Enrollments, which have risen steadily since the College opened, bear this out. They had reached 1,672 students by 1992 and are expected to reach 3,000 as the university grows. This is the only undergraduate college at UCSD that will continue to increase enrollments.

Campus Context

In 1993, 45 percent of UCSD's undergraduates were classified as other than mainstream Americans. Asian-Americans comprised the largest group, at over 18 percent of total enrollments. Meanwhile, the number of undergraduate international students remained low at UCSD; in 1992 it was 267 out of 3,060 total international students and scholars. This reflects the fact that undergraduate international students are not recruited, a policy also followed by other University of California institutions.

The International Center administers many of UCSD's international education programs. International Student Services is part of its mandate. In addition to the usual advisory, host family, and English language services, the International Center houses a Resale Shop. The proceeds from the sale of a wide range of items, from clothes to home furnishings, goes into the international student scholarship fund. Besides space for the store, a room is devoted to storing used household appliances, cribs, pots and pans, and many other necessary household items in good condition for loan to visiting international families.

The Center sponsors many programs and activities designed to foster cultural interaction. The International Cafe takes place at lunchtime on Fridays when a different community group each week prepares and sells lunches for $2.50. The Wednesday coffee time allows international spouses and preschool children a time and place for interaction. The International Club sponsors events and excursions. The American English in Action Program trains volunteer tutors and matches them with individual international visitors to help them learn to communicate in American English. Ethnic dinners, potluck suppers, American Cooking Class, and several other activities round out the International Center's extensive support for international students and scholars.

In addition to international student services, the Center also administers UCSD's study abroad programs and reciprocal exchanges. The latter brought 102 graduate and undergraduate students to UCSD during the 1992-93 academic year. Also that year, 451 undergraduates participated in study abroad programs divided equally between those sponsored by the University of California and those sponsored by other institutions. In sending 149 students overseas, Eleanor Roosevelt College led the next in number of participants, Muir College, by over 50 percent. Three faculty members, assisted by staff from the Center, select the students for particular programs.

The work of the International Center takes place in a graceful, well-designed, multistory wood building located literally at the campus center. Roses, other flowers, and shrubs grace its courtyard, often occupied by tables and chairs. The center is as pleasant within as it appears from without. With its varied facilities it is the envy of international educators from other campuses. Its meeting rooms, lounge, offices, inside and outside patio eating areas, kitchen, small stage, display area, and resource room all complement each other and provide a pleasant atmosphere for center activities.

The International Center building was built with virtually all its funding coming from a community woman's group. The group's involvement began in 1961. The La Jolla affiliate of Zonta, a professional women's service organization, was influenced by the wife of a faculty member to help international students and scholars arriving at what was then the Scripps Institution and Institute of Technology and Engineering. The organization bought first one house, then another, to provide overnight accommodation, family care, and a meeting place. Then the decision was made to build a facility on campus.

The International Center was deeded to the university in 1971. The group of women, renamed Friends of the International Center, also raised funds for the Center's significant expansion which was completed in 1986. The Friends of the International Center also raises money for both study abroad and international student scholarships. It sets criteria, for instance, one international student scholarship in recent years was earmarked for students from Spanish-speaking countries. Another priority has been scholarship funding for underrepresented students to participate in overseas programs.

The International Center provides substantial office space for its staff. The Dean of International Education and director of the International Center oversees the work of twelve full-time and four part-time advisors and staff. The Study Abroad Office has four of the professional positions assisted by eleven returning students.

The Dean of International Education thinks that the university's decision to establish an International House was related to the decision to establish E.R. College. The administration mandated both at the same time. The International House is a residential facility for 170 U.S. and international students. In addition to the residents' own interactions, the apartment complex provides an enriched international atmosphere through a series of programs organized by staff and a resident faculty fellow.

The sense of community evidenced by the International Center fits with UCSD's educational philosophy. As stated in the

General Catalog, the university applies the small college concept, "which has served Oxford and Cambridge so successfully for centuries." Maintaining a small college atmosphere results from purposeful planning and differs from many U.S. university campuses where colleges and schools are discipline specific, such as engineering, business, the arts and sciences.

Yet at UCSD, disciplinary departments remain the academic framework for organizing faculty assignments and virtually all the curriculum. Undergraduates may select any major whatever their college. As with the other four, Biology attracts the highest number of students in a single major at Eleanor Roosevelt College. At the same time, UCSD's undergraduate colleges are designed to build on the traditional disciplines and produce the benefits of a multidisciplinary approach. Such an objective certainly provides a comfortable context for E.R. College's international focus.

The institutional setting at UCSD is compatible for E.R. College in another way. Two of the undergraduate colleges predating Fifth College include in their philosophy statements and graduation requirements elements familiar to advocates of international education. John Muir College has a U.S. cultural diversity requirement. Also its students must choose two year-long course sequences from three areas: the humanities, fine arts, or foreign languages. Thurgood Marshall College emphasizes cultural diversity with its three-quarter core sequence called "Dimensions of Culture-Diversity, Justice and Imagination." The third course in this sequence devotes time to Western and non-Western cultures.

The UCSD curriculum includes many international and intercultural majors and minors. Students can select a major from Chinese Studies, Ethnic Studies (U.S.), Italian Studies, Judaic Studies, Russian and Soviet Studies, and Third World Studies. The chemistry department has an Environmental Science major, and Biology offers a major in Ecology, Behavior and Evolution, which includes a course on Conservation and the Human Predicament. The Department of History includes Africa, East Asia, the Near East, Europe, and Latin America among its concentrations for majors. Political Science offers its majors concentrations in International Relations, Comparative

Politics, and Latin American Politics. Additional specializations are available at UCSD through minors in Japanese Studies, Latin American Studies, and Middle East Studies.

The Department of Literature provides the university's advanced language training by offering majors in French, German, Italian, and Spanish Literatures plus beginning and advanced courses in Russian. The linguistics department teaches the first year of the first four of these languages plus Portuguese. Chinese language courses are sponsored by the Chinese Studies Program, Hebrew by Judaic Studies, and Japanese by Japanese Studies. The Graduate School of International Relations and Pacific Studies offers Korean and Vietnamese. The English as a Second Language Program has one reading and two writing courses as well as a writing course for graduate students and a graduate level course on the Apprentice Teaching of ESL.

Several departments list many international courses which together not only cover specific issues and all the world regions, but several individual countries as well. The anthropology department offers courses on Latin America, Africa, the Near East, Southeast Asia, India, Melanesia, and China, including a course on Chinese Familism.

Sociology is one of the largest contributors of international and intercultural courses. Its majors are encouraged to develop an expertise on a country or world region. They also are required to take at least one course under each of two headings: Culture, Language and Social Interaction, and Comparative and Historical. These headings include courses on the Middle East, South Africa, China, Latin America, Israel, Africa, and a course on the Politics of Economic Development and Underdevelopment.

The other two departments with many courses, history and political science, cover various world regions in general and many countries in particular. History lists courses about Cuba, Mexico, Argentina, and Brazil. It also has distinctive courses such as, Machismo and Matriarchy: The Latin American Social Structure. The list of political science offerings includes Comparative Politics courses on China, Vietnam, Japan, the Soviet Union, China, Mexico, Britain, France, and Germany. The areas of Latin America and Central America also are represented including courses devoted to specialized topics such as Politics in the Andes and Organization, Resistance and Protest in Latin America. International Relations courses also have specializations like Immigration Policy and Politics.

Some departments not usually internationalized on most campuses have an international dimension at UCSD. The communication department requires its majors to take Introduction to Communication and Culture. It also lists several courses implying technological change, such as The Transformation of Global Communications. Health Care and Social Issues is an interdisciplinary minor with several anthropology courses listed. Music offers Folk and Popular Music which includes all of the world's major geographic regions. In addition to the usual International Economics courses, the economics department lists several specialized ones on International Monetary Relations, Japanese Economy, and Economics of the Environment.

Given UCSD's wide range of international curriculum choices, the idea of establishing an undergraduate college focusing on international education seemed logical to senior administrators and an influential cross-section of senior faculty. The product of their planning began teaching students in 1988.

Eleanor Roosevelt College
According to a university pamphlet, "the goal of Eleanor Roosevelt College is to prepare its graduates for living and working in the complex global community of the twenty-first century." Its general education requirements provide the intellectual means for "bringing the world into focus," whatever a student's major. The College's core curriculum consists of a six-quarter, two-year sequence of courses titled "The Making of the Modern World (MMW)." Together the six courses explain the historical origins of contemporary societies and institutions. One description explains that "MMW weaves together knowledge from many fields to bring you forward through time, from prehistory to the present, toward an appreciation of the varied tapestry of the world in which we live." The intensive curriculum experi-

ence is portrayed as an "intellectual odyssey during the freshman and sophomore years."

All but two of E.R. College's other general education requirements incorporate its international raison d'etre. The two are Quantitative Methods and Natural Sciences, both of which require two courses. The two-quarters writing requirement is integrated with two of Making of the Modern World's six quarters. These two quarters carry six credits instead of four. To fulfill the two-course fine arts requirement, one course must deal with non-Western music, theatre, or art. Students also must take three courses in a Regional Specialization covering any one of the world's geographic regions.

The language requirement applies to all E.R. College students, even those who are bilingual and biliterate. Such students cannot test out of the requirement or be exempted. They must take at least three quarters of a language "other than the one in which they were educated." To be admitted to E.R. College, students must have at least three years of high school language study. Most applicants have four, and to graduate from Fifth College, they are required to take another year which encourages advanced study. The language requirement is used to achieve another goal as well, that of preparing for overseas programs. About 50 percent of E.R. College students start a new language, mainly Chinese, Japanese or Russian.

Given the financial realities many students face, study abroad is highly encouraged but not required. Eleanor Roosevelt College administrators would like to see at least 50 percent go overseas but consider the present rate of somewhat over 30 percent an achievement. About half the students choose University of California programs but some arrange experiences on their own. Students are said to report that the Making of the Modern World was the best preparation for their overseas study.

Some of the students who apply to E.R. College are self-selecting. They have already been abroad or developed international interests in some other way. Yet a large percentage comes with no announced or demonstrated interest in internationalism, though they usually display a willingness to expand their international horizons after taking the General Education curriculum. About 45 percent, according to 1993 figures, have ethnic origins other than those considered the U.S. mainstream. The college's student service administrators work with students in planning co-curricular programs that build on their initial interests and enhance the international and intercultural atmosphere.

In 1993, a Celebration of Cultures series was initiated which highlighted a different world region each month. Administered from the Dean of Students' office with student input, a series of activities was organized on a monthly basis. Taking February as an example with Africa as the theme, events included two musical evenings, one session illustrating African storytelling, two plays, with one a South African play by the famous dramatist Fugard, a theme dinner, a film, a cultural study break, and two major events with varied entertainment including songs and art. Eleanor Roosevelt College administrators report that the entertainment events attracted 200 students or more, while 25 was the smallest number attending any one happening. Thus, the Celebration of Cultures will continue in 1994. It may be worth noting that events generally did not include formal presentations.

Discussions with administrators show how the international theme permeates the college in various ways. Strongly recommending that students study abroad, for example, has affected the advising role. Structured activities begin with the orientation for first year students. They not only listen to an information session on study abroad opportunities. In addition, they fill out an interest form to get them thinking and, it is hoped, planning. The form then is used in future advising sessions with individual students. Preparing for study abroad is a major part of advising at E.R. College. Academic advisors try to ensure that students get preliminary prior approval from relevant departments for their overseas credits. Therefore a filled-in form is a part of the application process. This is especially important for students participating in other than University of California programs.

UCSD's International House, which serves the entire campus and in which international and U.S. students room together, is physically located within the E.R. College area. For this reason, and because E.R. College has so many returnees from abroad, a disproportionately high number of International House residents are E.R. College students. As a side note, when E.R. College first opened, the residence halls were named after explorers. The college administration later corrected this situation. In fact, the residence halls at E.R. College often live up to a small college ideal, i.e., students with common interests learn from each other as they discuss major world and life issues until very late at night. Many Resident Assistants have returned from oversees programs, which also adds to the international atmosphere.

Most administrative staff have some international or multicultural experience. The acting dean of students in 1994, for example, had spent a year in Japan and came to E.R. College from the International Living Center at Cornell. Also the acting resident dean had been born in Egypt.

Many other student activities reflect international and intercultural education. Student organizations thrive, like the Multicultural Student Network and the Experience Abroad Club. A National Association of Foreign Student Advisors mini-grant financed an intercultural weekend retreat for students in the leadership program. The retreat continues with funding from various offices on campus.

Student demand is part of the explanation for the internationalization of E.R. College's student activities. There is so much intensity and focus to student interaction that constructive suggestions are not only made but are carried out; for example, the international trivia quiz in the College newsletter. This was enhanced by a monthly raffle for dinner at a local ethnic restaurant with one ticket earned for each right answer. According to one administrator, "International is what makes my work satisfying. When I run into the routine roommate conflict I know there is something more to my job."

As with its student services, E.R. College has internationalized other activities common throughout the university, its honors programs for example. At UCSD many departments have senior honors programs and colleges award Academic Achievement Honors certificates of merit. These are presented to students earning Provost's Honors for a full academic year during which they maintain a GPA of 3.5 or higher. Each college also sponsors other honors programs and, at Eleanor Roosevelt, relevant activities have an international focus. Entering students with high GPAs and SAT scores are invited to participate in the Freshman Honors Program. During the first quarter, faculty discuss their international research interests and career development using a seminar format. The faculty-student discussions during the winter and spring quarters are directed by specific topics each quarter; for example, "Our World and the Environment," and "Social and Political Challenges in Today's Russia."

Second year students with GPAs of 3.5 or higher can work on an independent study with individual faculty. The themes or topics must relate to the Making of the Modern World course sequence. Research projects may be designed to cover one, two, or three quarters. Many of these honors projects are selected for presentation at UCSD's Undergraduate Research Conference held each spring. Students also plan cultural and social events which comprise an important component of the first and second year honors programs.

Eleanor Roosevelt College's distinctive curriculum and co-curricular activities center around the Making of the Modern World. It remains the college core in more ways than one. Students as well as faculty and administrators share this perception. Some years students designed tee-shirts announcing, "I survived MMW." The six-course, intensive, highly structured MMW curriculum will be elaborated in the next section of this narrative.

Throughout their E.R. College careers, students perceive themselves as having gone through the hard MMW experience together. This has produced social as well as intellectual benefits. A UC-Los Angeles study revealed the strong sense of community resulting from the shared experience of taking The Making of the Modern World. In the words of a E.R. College student, "Not only do I believe that the course work was challenging and enlightening, but that being carried along with the same classmates for two years created a special bond of friendship and comradery."

A visitor to a MMW classroom notices an uncharacteristically vibrant atmosphere as students assemble before the lecture begins. As well over 100 students wander in they become interactive, some intensely so, and a crescendo builds. Virtually all become engaged in conversation. To prepare for examinations, study groups form spontaneously, more so than in the other colleges, according to a E.R. College administrator who has worked in one of them. The provost keeps in his office a wall sized matrix salvaged from the trash. Students had designed it to help organize their thoughts for an examination. It has seven cultures as headings in the vertical columns and the horizontal categories cover political, economic, technological and cultural characteristics. All the squares were filled with concepts and historical detail. This study tool illustrates the academic scope and sophistication MMW engenders. It has become what the Fifth College designers envisioned.

Planning for Eleanor Roosevelt College

By the mid-1980s, the undergraduate population at UCSD had grown too large for the existing four colleges. Campus growth was reflected in the addition of more than forty new faculty members in a single year. Expansion was seen as beneficial to the state, with increasing numbers of high school seniors applying for admission to the University of California system, and to the campus, since California funded its universities on a per capita basis at the time. In this atmosphere, the Dean of Graduate Studies wrote a memo in 1985 to the vice chancellor for academic affairs recommending that a new undergraduate college be established, and that it have an international focus.

In response, the vice chancellor formed a committee, chaired by the dean of arts and humanities, to implement this recommendation. In 1986 the committee proposed to the Academic Senate an outline curriculum for the new college, which included a language requirement and a one-year world civilization course. After this proposal passed, the search for the new provost began in the fall of 1986. James Lyon, a German literature specialist, was named in March, 1987. He assembled a group of eleven senior campus faculty members from the arts, humanities, social sciences, and natural sciences to design the college's core curriculum. Lyon likes to begin discussing how this process took place with a quotation from Robert Maynard Hutchins: "Changing a college curriculum is like moving a cemetery." Fortunately the committee had the advantage of not having to change an existing curriculum, but to invent a totally new one for the college.

Planning began in March of 1987 and lasted seven months. The committee contacted many colleges and universities around the U.S. to provide information for the deliberation process. The first plan presented and accepted by the Academic Senate was modified. The one-year, three-course sequence became two years and six courses. The Making of the Modern World theme was developed with John Dower, a historian of Japan, as a major contributor. Now at the Massachusetts Institute of Technology, he is remembered at UCSD for his fine teaching and deep commitment to undergraduate education, as are the others. His premise became one of course's key concepts: There is no world civilization but many civilizations.

The titles of the six courses indicate the Making of the Modern World's overall historical approach; Prehistory and the Birth of Civilization, The Great Classical Traditions in which India and China are treated equally with Greece and Rome, The Medieval Heritage including China and the Islamic Empires, European Expansion and the Clash of Cultures, Revolution, Industry and Empire, and Our Century and After. In addition to the large volume of information they cover, all six courses require major writing assignments. In the second and third, moreover, additional writing assignments, such as a weekly journal, enable these courses to fulfill the universitywide writing requirement.

The faculty committee designing E.R. College's core curriculum made several key decisions. The first set dealt with content: Western and "non-Western" material would be treated equally and the courses would be overtly cross-cultural. Thus, the first course on Prehistory and the Birth of Civilization was designed to be taught by anthropologists. Teaching the other five would be sociologists, historians, literature specialists, philosophers, political scientists and fine arts professors. All courses were historically based, interdisciplinary, and comparative.

Other committee decisions dealt with methodology. There would be no team teaching, since beginning college students often have difficulty integrating different course content from various professors, but guest lecturers could be invited to class. Faculty were to be encouraged to continue teaching the same course. The courses would require original readings, literature and primary documents from diverse eras and cultures. Since the courses were to focus on the historical origins creating the world as it is today, all regions and eras would not receive equal emphasis.

A catalog review showed that no other research university offered a course sequence like Making of the Modern World. The committee recognized that MMW's success depended on substantial faculty development. In the words of one committee member, "Every faculty member had to go back to school." Faculty drew heavily on each other's expertise, and teams formed to develop each course. Fortuitously, the Ford Foundation invited UCSD, as one of thirty-nine campuses recognized for excellence in undergraduate education, to apply for grant support. The university's proposal was for E.R. College development, especially its core curriculum. The $150,000 grant was matched by the university.

The MMW faculty's self-training process covered content and concepts from other disciplines. Yet faculty were not to neglect their own disciplines. Making of the Modern World was designed as interdisciplinary, not undisciplinary. Chronological history, for instance, was to provide the framework but not the only way to explain events. Faculty were to "reflect their own discipline as part of their job," according to one of the MMW's curriculum designers.

The faculty committee's search for a textbook revealed the innovative quality of Making of the Modern World. Course designers wanted both continuity and comparability. A text explaining the development of Western Civilization and not offering the same continuous approach to other civilizations would not be appropriate. Though faculty felt it necessary for students to have a basic text for the sake of reference, none of the texts adopted in the .irst three years of the course proved to be satisfactory. Not only did all break the historical flow of the

Indian, Chinese, and Islamic civilizations, most had too little information about them. None offered a well integrated history of the world.

Lectures provide continuity while extensive readings guarantee depth. Syllabi list secondary works as well as translated original sources. The Medieval Heritage course taught during the spring quarter, 1994, for example, required ten books including Ebrey's *Chinese Civilization, The Confessions of St. Augustine,* and resource works such as the *Times Concise Atlas of World History.* Since Medieval Heritage has an extensive writing component and carries six credits, students had to write three short papers and a weekly journal. They also took midterm and final examinations. Lecture classes met three times and section meetings twice a week. The professor, a specialist in ancient Western civilizations, noted that he learned a great deal in preparing to teach MMW's Medieval History course.

Issues and Answers
Staffing for Making of the Modern World has become an ongoing issue. Three lecture tracks are offered per quarter and, in the case of five of the six courses, several departments must provide faculty at the same time. In responding to the request for faculty, department Chairs have been known to point out that covering departmental courses takes priority. Grant funding helped initially, but later Provost Lyon had to recruit by appealing to the good will of departments and individual faculty. Some are committed to international undergraduate education. Also, large, guaranteed enrollments provide additional incentive. The university publishes enrollment figures by department, and this is a major part of the formula for funding allocations. In addition, some departments have attracted majors from MMW students. Anthropology, for instance, has seen both enrollments in its own courses as well as its number of majors increase as a result of teaching the first course in the MMW sequence.

Another initial problem concerned covering the wide variety of fields MMW requires. Most faculty in key departments were specialists in the early-modern or modern eras. The university had very few medievalists and no Islamist. Hiring temporary faculty was the first response, but since then relevant departments have been able to hire with MMW's needs in mind. History, for example, had a medieval historian by the early 1990s.

An administrative issue arose in E.R. College's early years, i.e., the question of what to require of transfer students. At first everyone graduating from the college had to take all six of Making of the Modern World's courses with no exceptions. Over time, however, outside pressures built on University of California universities to take more transfers and this position was adopted by the California legislature. Consequently Eleanor Roosevelt College modified its requirement: transfers must take MMW for one year, and they can choose three of the six courses.

A last issue is politically sensitive. The first reaction of some students to cultural learning can be a self-consciousness awareness of their own ethnicity. While healthy in most respects, it also has produced demands promoting one cultural perspective. This phenomenon has been called a "delayed-action time bomb" by one E.R. College administrator. Its practical effect has been a few students' advocating revisions in the content balance of Making of the Modern World. They have felt that MMW is still too Eurocentric and want more about their own culture; for example, some students feel that too much time is spent on Ancient Greece and not enough on the Aztecs.

The ongoing culture-based debate became crystallized during the search for Fifth College's new name. In the early 1990s, a committee of students and staff came up with many possible names and no consensus. The issue was on hold when Third College was renamed Thurgood Marshall in 1993. Then pressure began to build on Fifth College. Senior administrators wanted a decision, and the list was narrowed. The Executive and Policy Committee, an ongoing organization made up of staff, faculty, and students, solicited student feedback on proposed names, held open discussions and "town meetings," and then chose Eleanor Roosevelt. Although a woman, one with impeccable international human rights credentials, the name was not the choice of a small but ardent group of students.

Encouraging students to study abroad has been one response in the effort to produce graduates with maturity and balanced judgment who have experienced the world as made up of many cultures. Yet the key as perceived by students and administrators alike is still the Making of the Modern World, the "glue that makes our college," as asserted by one senior administrator. The importance of MMW was reinforced during the sometimes intense, often polite discussions about the name of the college and MMW's content. Students on all sides of the debate shared the perception that MMW set the context as well as the knowledge base for their positions. Maybe activism is an essential stage in the learning process for some students.

Lessons Learned

While most campuses will not be creating an international college from scratch any time soon, some of the decisions made at UCSD are replicable. Therefore, the following guidelines are designed to provide practical advice, particularly as applied to developing a core world civilization course.

1. *Ensure faculty good will, since they must design and teach the curriculum.* An effort like Making of the Modern World needs a group of able, experienced faculty willing to take on new challenges. Only the anthropologists had enough prior competency in teaching the first course. All faculty involved determined that they needed new knowledge.

2. *Money for retraining is vital.* For a major undertaking, good will alone is not enough. An incentive system is needed to provide MMW staffing. Chairs particularly need tangible rewards; for example, the political science department used to contribute more faculty to MMW but the number has been reduced since its enrollments and majors have increased. This has occurred in spite of the fact at least some of the department's new growth may be attributed to the E.R. College core course.

3. *Both the humanities and social sciences are needed.* A cooperative approach to designing curriculum brings its own faculty development rewards as well as benefitting the program.

4. *Make a case for having a voice in recruitment.* Since departments determine recruitment priorities, the E.R. College

provost has maintained good relations with chairs. Consequently, he has often had a favorable response when appealing to them for assistance. In the mid-1990s, Sinologists and specialists on Japan were needed, and history had indicated it had adopted these areas as priorities for the next hire.

5. *Recruit staff with some international or intercultural experience.* This makes a valuable contribution to the atmosphere at E.R. College.

6. *Encourage but do not require study abroad.* This experience does not appeal to all students even though it is needed. Therefore, strong encouragement must be maintained.

7. *Require languages.* This also does not attract all students but is essential for an international education.

8. *Success breeds success.* Eleanor Roosevelt College received another Ford Foundation grant in the early 1990s to develop upperdivision Languages-Across-the-Curriculum courses in the social sciences.

Future plans for Eleanor Roosevelt College include recruiting more traditionally underrepresented students. The vitality, cultural perspectives, and even the issues they raise, make a meaningful and possibly necessary contribution to the goal of intercultural learning.

Although the design of E.R. College was the work of a group of senior faculty, its creation relied on the ideas and active support of the university's senior administrators. A dean wrote the initiating memorandum, another dean chaired the first committee, and deans took part in its deliberations. Outside grant support proved essential to establishing the new college, and the contribution of its first provost, although yet to be fully assessed, has been highly significant. He has taken a good idea and made it an even better reality. This achievement required his enthusiasm, energy, years of experience on the UCSD campus, and the respect that accompanies an established academic reputation. This summary of factors resulting in E.R. College's success must include mention of the many faculty who managed to make coherent courses out of Making of the Modern World, and their students who worked hard as well.

University of Hartford

Contracting International Student Programs

This private comprehensive university, with approximately 3,700 undergraduate and 1,500 graduate students, links nine schools and colleges. Several of these were separate institutions before they merged to form the University of Hartford and they retain their distinctive institutional identities. In 1952 the Ward College of Technology affiliated with Hillyer College, a liberal arts institution. In 1957 these combined with the Hartford Art School and the Hartt School of Music to form the University of Hartford. In 1991 the Hartford College of Women joined the "federation." The university also includes four other institutions: the Barney School of Business and Public Administration, the College of Basic Studies, the College of Engineering, and the College of Education, Nursing, and Health Professions.

As the University of Hartford joins several schools and colleges, it also is located where three political jurisdictions meet, i.e., the cities of Hartford and West Hartford, plus the town of Bloomfield. Some campus buildings are subject to each of these three governments. Now and then this situation causes some difficulty; for instance, on an occasion when the wrong police were called.

Building the campus on its present location began in 1957 when the University of Hartford was formed. By 1979 the dormitories were completed which marked the change in university's student body from commuter to primarily residential. Located on a suburban site minutes from downtown Hartford, the campus presents an inviting, open appearance. Its low-lying brick buildings stake out the perimeter of the campus center, an undulating, spacious grass quadrangle.

The University of Hartford has a distinctive history. It was established by the coming together of several colleges at the nexus of three local governments. This theme of meeting, and of cooperation, continues with the international program activities of the University of Hartford's University Program Office. Beginning in 1990, the office has contracted with overseas educational institutions to a offer programs for their students.

The first such program was contracted with the Ecole Superieure Des Petites et Moyennes Enterprises (ESPEME), a business college in Paris. The first group of French students arrived in the summer of 1990 to have one month of academic training followed by a two-month internship. The experiential component and careful evaluation of the ESPEME program, plus the number of its successors, make it a useful example of specialized international student programs.

Campus Context
In the University of Hartford's federated context, international education is still evolving. With the enthusiastic support of its current president, Dr. Humphrey Tonkin, long a proponent of campus internationalization, two recent campuswide initiatives have taken place. First, in 1991, the Subcommittee on Internationalization, part of the University Strategic Planning Committee made up of faculty and administrators, produced a mission statement for the university's international education programs.

A second major step was taken in the summer of 1992 with the creation of the Center of International Studies. The center includes the former Office of International Student Services, previously administered under the vice president for student affairs, and the Office of International Studies responsible for undergraduate overseas student programs, formerly located under the associate academic dean for university programs. The center has three full-time staff and a faculty director, Susan Coleman, who continues to teach one business course per year. She also has a new mandate, i.e., initiating international curriculum development.

The University of Hartford includes international education in its graduation requirements. The All University Curriculum, adopted in 1987, requires all baccalaureate degree students to take four courses from four of five thematic areas: 1. Living in a Cultural Context: Western Heritage, 2. Living in a Cultural

Context: Other Cultures, 3. Living in a Scientific and Technological World; 4. Living Responsively to the Arts; and 5. Living
in a Social Context. A choice among four to six courses exists
within each of these categories. All are multidisciplinary and
many team taught by faculty from "all of the university's schools
and colleges," according to the university bulletin. In addition,
the College of Arts and Sciences has a one-year foreign language requirement.

The university's curriculum includes several intercultural and
international specializations. A Judaic Studies major, an African-American Studies minor, and a major in Political Economy.
The Department of Foreign Languages and Literatures offers
majors in French, Spanish, Italian, Japanese, and German.
Hebrew is offered through a local Hebrew college.

In addition, the university bulletin notes a wide range of
individual international courses in several departments. Examples of these include Art History's courses in Chinese and
Japanese Art, Music's World Music Survey, Philosophy's Islamic
Philosophy, Language and Literature's Latin American Studies
and Studies in Comparative Literature, Theatre Arts' Contemporary Ethnic Theatre, Religious Studies' Introduction to
World Religions, and Sociology's Peoples and Cultures of the
Caribbean.

The usual international offerings in Economics are joined by
Economic Growth and Development, and the biology major
requires two ecology courses. A strong geography department
includes a course on the Geographic View of World Events.
The standard courses on international relations in the politics
and government department are augmented by courses on the
Third World and Europe while History offers at least one
course on several world areas, i.e., the Middle East, East Asia,
Russia, and the Caribbean. The Barney School of Business has
international courses in management and marketing.

During the 1991-92 academic year, the University of Hartford
attracted 557 international students, 275 of these as undergraduates. This comprised 7.5 percent of the university's undergraduate student body. The English Language Institute provides the university's English as a second language services.
Located in the English and literature department of the College

of Arts and Sciences, its courses carry credit but cannot be applied to graduation.

During 1991-92, over 100 students participated in a range of student overseas programs. They studied in the United Kingdom, Australia, Italy, and Mexico at institutions affiliated with the University of Hartford. These long-term programs are augmented each year by short-term travel-study programs led by university faculty. In 1993, groups went on a January course called Landmarks and Legends in Italy, and on Discovering Britain in Oxford, the United Kingdom. Students also participate in consortial programs.

International education outreach programs at the University of Hartford are organized jointly by Jim Narduzzi, Associate Academic Dean for University Programs, in cooperation with faculty in relevant academic departments. These include summer "immersion institutes" in Spanish, French, Japanese, Russian, and Esperanto offered for anyone interested. All are administered with the academic unit on a revenue sharing basis.

One of the more recent initiatives illustrates further this working relationship between the University Programs Office and an academic department. In September 1992, the Institute for Foreign Languages was initiated as the vehicle for contracting language services with businesses in the Hartford community. The University Programs Office provided its staff and negotiating expertise while the chairperson of the languages department ventured into the community. Within weeks, this partnership produced two contracts with businesses to train small employee groups in Spanish and Russian. Currently, the institute is preparing to bid on translation contracts.

These initiatives follow the pattern that worked so well in the case of the earlier program contracted with an organization outside the United States, the Ecole Superieure Des Petites et Moyennes Enterprises in Paris.

International Summer Business Program for ESPEME

The Barney School of Business of the University of Hartford has its own M.B.A. program and facility in Paris with courses taught in English. Preliminary contacts between this unit and the Paris branch of the Ecole Superieure des Petites et Moyennes Enterprises (ESPEME), eventually produced this four-week undergraduate program on the Hartford campus for an average of thirty ESPEME students each summer.

Designed by Program Director Susan Coleman, an assistant professor of finance at the Barney School, and James Narduzzi, then Director of summer and special programs, the three-month program began in the summer of 1990. After its first pilot year, the program had two main components, one month of academic training and the two-month internship with an American subsidiary of a French company. The internship was organized by ESPEME.

The first month, held on the University of Hartford campus, has four components: 1. Academic instruction in accounting, finance, economics, management, and marketing; 2. "Real world" business experiences including guest speakers and field trips; 3. Intensive English language instruction plus information on American culture; and 4. Host family and community activities.

The program's title indicates its general purpose: "Business Decision-Making for the 1990s." The academic "course work" uses a case study methodology. Cases are selected to illustrate finance, management, and the other business areas covered by the program. Thus, students are encouraged to discuss issues as they arise in actual business situations. To provide context and perspective, selected Business School faculty lead class sessions applying their specific areas of expertise.

Classes are held four days a week and include daily language instruction, often using the university's laboratory facilities. Field trips or speakers are arranged on the fifth day each week with students visiting locations such as the stock and futures exchanges in New York City, small businesses in Boston's Quincy Market, a sports business such as the Hartford Whalers, Mystic Seaport as an entertainment business, a major corporation's local division, Pratt and Whitney or Otis Elevator, a health care facility, the state capitol, Connecticut Yankee Power, a nuclear power plant, and West Farms Mall.

Although a noncredit program, the director uses the American grading system for written analyses of case studies and other assignments as well as examinations. This allows students to experience more fully U.S. business education. No grades are given for the language exercises.

Organizing the logistics of the program is facilitated because the office of the associate academic dean for undergraduate programs also administers the campus conference center as well as the continuing and professional education programs. The French students, in the past all between the ages of eighteen and twenty-four, are housed in the university's apartments which have cooking facilities. Some do use these, but most purchase a meal plan.

After the four-week course on campus, the French students separate for various two-month internships, most of these in the United States. All are with U.S. and French companies or their subsidiaries. These work experiences are arranged by ESPEME generally before the students arrive in Hartford. This aspect of the program illustrates the utility of the working partnership between ESPEME and the University of Hartford.

The International Summer Business Program's budget provides for all costs incurred by the University of Hartford. This includes the administrative time and office expenses of both the University Programs Office and the Business School. These plus instructional costs, which also cover tutoring services by a graduate assistant, add up to a tuition payment of slightly less than $1,200. Food, when applicable, and housing costs are then added, with ESPEME paying the total by installments in French francs.

An extensive evaluation has documented the program's success in achieving its twin objectives, i.e., expanding knowledge about business, and developing new cultural perspectives about the United States. Evaluation data collection used two different processes. The first, a pre- and posttest with fifty multiple-choice questions, tested knowledge of business terms and concepts. As reported by Susan Coleman and James Narduzzi in the summer of 1991, students improved their mean score by 34 percent. ("Developing and Evaluating a Noncredit Business Program for French Undergraduates," *The Journal of Continuing Higher Education,* Susan Coleman and James Narduzzi.)

The second evaluation activity formed students into two pre-
and post-focus groups. Facilitated by the program's two planners, discussions addressed four general questions: 1. What are
your perceptions of American culture and way of life? 2. What
do you think characterizes American business and what are its
strengths and weaknesses? 3. How competitive is American
business relative to that of other countries, such as France? 4.
How would you compare American business education to that
in France?

The article by Susan Coleman and James Narduzzi, in the Fall
1991 edition of *International Education*, analyzes the results of
the focus group exercise. It indicates that even a relatively short
program of overseas study can lead to greatly increased knowledge as well as to some attitudinal changes toward the host
country. Based on their review of prior research on the study
abroad experience, the program's designers had sought to provide opportunities for positive personal contacts between
Americans and the students. Their data reflects the success of
this effort. The first question indicated the most noticeable
changes in student perceptions; for example, the evaluation
concluded there is less difference between the priorities of
Americans and French than the students had originally thought.
They also noted their surprise that people of such different
ethnicities could work well together.

Issues and Answers
The three general issues which surfaced requiring varying
responses were cultural, financial, and academic concerns of
University of Hartford business faculty.

Barney School of Business faculty in its Paris MBA program
provided valuable input in making the summer experience
attractive for ESPEME students, particularly in regard to the
academic content. Yet student criticisms reflected underlying
cultural issues.

An instructional issue rooted in cultural differences emerged
early in the program. The focus on decision-making and the use
of a case study methodology necessitated student interaction.
Yet lectures with little student participation characterize most

French classrooms. Therefore students had to learn to discuss. With time and encouragement, they readily adopted this new behavior and the American instructors learned to explain overtly what they expected.

Cultural perceptions also surfaced concerning the program's logistics. A major student complaint concerned the food; they found it distasteful. Since the students were housed in University of Hartford dormitories, a meal plan was included in program costs. Given the scope and intensity with which the first group of students objected to the food, during the following years they were given the choice of using dorm cooking facilities or buying the meal plan. Since most chose the former, criticisms were substantially reduced.

Such a programmatic solution could not resolve a smoking issue since the university designates its buildings as nonsmoking. Fortunately this problem proved minor and students became accustomed to going outside.

The refusal of ESPEME to renegotiate the budget has become a concern requiring administrative readjustments. Payment is in French francs and remains the same each year. One year the exchange rate favored the University of Hartford, and ESPEME benefited the next. Yet the inability to adjust the budget to real costs has necessitated minor program variations. Learning from this experience has been applied in the University of Hartford's other international negotiations. New program budgets have a ceiling and a floor built-in so annual adjustments can be made as a matter of course.

The program directors had to devise a strategy to deal with one more issue area, academic concerns. Some University of Hartford business faculty wanted reassurance as to the students' academic qualifications. They also noted other, practical, matters, such as spreading thin the Barney School faculty's time. These concerns needed attention because, even though the ESPEME program was noncredit and in the summer, these factors would not necessarily characterize future programs.

Although untenured, the ESPEME program director had earned the respect of her colleagues. Not relying on this alone, she took specific actions. For example, each summer she requested twelve to fifteen of the business faculty to present their speciality and paid them market-competitive honoraria.

These positive experiences in interacting with the French students helped when the next program placed international students in regular semester courses. An externality, a change in the institutional environment, also diluted potential objections to this new program. The number of students taking Barney School courses was leveling off, and even declined. While these points do not apply specifically to the summer ESPEME program focused on in this study, they illustrate a reality program administrators should keep in mind: successful programs often produce spin-offs. Given this interrelatedness, effective responses to issues raised in the first program inevitably proved useful for the spin-offs noted in the next section.

Finally, an instructional issue was raised by the ESPEME students which proved easily remedied. Students requested more materials relevant to American business during the English as a Second Language section of the program. Such cultural authenticity was supplied with the *Wall Street Journal* and actual business memoranda, among other handouts.

Lessons Learned and Spin-offs
The successful International Summer Business Program, tailored to a specified group of international students, produced substantial benefits for the University of Hartford. These are indicated below along with academic results. In addition, specific programmatic guidelines are listed as recommended by the program's directors.

1. *Well-designed, short-cycle programs can produce a substantial improvement in knowledge and attitudes about the United States.* The focus group evaluation process revealed that the French students arrived with the usual "Dallas-Dynasty" view of the United States. Upon completion of the four-week program, they were able to analyze the American business environment with some sophistication, including its cultural context.

2. *An effective curriculum model has many applications.* The University of Hartford's special programs office has used the

ESPEME course design in at least fifteen subsequent program proposals.

3. *A successful international student program provides a useful recruitment tool.* The summer ESPEME program brought increased visibility in France for the University of Hartford. It has provided a positive context for graduate program recruitment.

4. *Program administration should be centralized under an academic director.* Even though another person organizes program logistics, such as accommodations and field trips, the academic director should be involved. Fragmented authority creates difficulties for integrated programs. Host families and dormitory experiences have cultural academic implications and should be incorporated, overtly, into the learning process. Director involvement in all aspects of the program provides an additional administrative benefit, an early warning system and at the decision-making level which allows for a quick response.

5. *Deal up front with any perceived conflict between academic credibility and client-centered decision-making.* Even noncredit programs should be designed and directed by a faculty member, and reflect substantive, academic content.

6. *Draw on the expertise of faculty and staff experienced in working with the program's projected student population.* Input from Barney School of Business personnel in Paris assisted in designing the ESPEME summer program.

7. *Build in both formal and informal assessment processes.* Administratively, this expedites effective problem solving. Programmatically, it provides convincing evaluation data. Professionally, it produces analytical and not just descriptive information, and thus more useful published articles.

8. *Point out the financial and public relations benefits to the institution.* While these may be obvious, verbal and written reports to top-level administrators provide them with needed documentation. In the case of the summer ESPEME program, use of the university's conference facilities and administrative overhead financing brought in additional revenues. Also, presentations by business, and

other speakers from the community, brought positive visibility for the university's curriculum and faculty.

9. *Be prepared for cultural differences in negotiating styles when designing programs with international partners.* In common with most university administrators in the United States, those at the University of Hartford needed specific answers to detailed questions within relatively short time frames. This contrasted with the less hurried French style, and its penchant for first dealing with substantive issues. Program organizers were caught in the middle. Not surprisingly, they successfully maneuvered using patient explanations.

As alluded to previously, the University of Hartford's University Programs Office has negotiated several other international programs within just the last few years. The summer course for ESPEME students led to a semester program for INSAM, the Institut Superieure des Affaires et du Management, a unit of the Ecole Superieure Libre des Sciences Commerciales et Appliques in Paris. In the fall of 1992, twenty-one INSAM students arrived at the University of Hartford. The English language, host family, and speaker-field trip components supplemented a finance course taught by Susan Coleman. The group then divided to attend regular University of Hartford business courses as part of the program.

Another international program administered by the University Programs Office was initiated during the 1992-93 academic year. Growing out of an idea originated by a group of local businessmen, who continue to raise its funding, the YEES program brings Russian business graduate students to the University of Hartford. Students in this Yankee Eastern European Entrepreneurial Studies Program spend an academic year taking eight MBA courses and then having an internship experience. The sponsoring group of businessmen selects the six to ten participants each year. Seminars and site visits enhance their training.

The University Programs Office initiated two more programs for international students in 1993. The Otis Graduate Studies Program, financed by Otis Elevator Company, provided support for eleven students from countries formerly part of the Soviet Union. Like YEES students, they take regular graduate level business courses and attend YEES' enrichment activities such as seminars and site visits. Also, in the summer of 1993, a group of K-12 educators from Kuwait arrived at the University of Hartford for a two month program. Much of their time was spent visiting school districts. In addition, the university organized academic components at the program's beginning and end.

The University of Hartford's specialized international student programs, particularly its first such program, ESPEME, illustrate what can be accomplished when a imaginative administrator with entrepreneurial skills works well with an innovative faculty member. As a factor, overseas contacts are necessary but not sufficient to produce a successful program. Also, the university's senior decision-makers gave a well-positioned administrator both the responsibility and authority to produce new initiatives.

University of North Carolina at Asheville

Creating Campus-Community Cooperation

The University of North Carolina at Asheville seems isolated from its host city by dense woodlands. Contrary to the impression made by this physical separation, the university has built an extensive network of multifaceted programs in cooperation with community groups.

The first of these, and the most distinctive, focuses on a computer simulation. The Inter-Nation Simulation was first applied as one of the instructional methodologies in the War, Peace and World Politics course. The enthusiasm of students taking this course led to their working with local high school teachers and students in applying the simulation in high school classrooms. Called the Simulation Service Program, this outreach effort proved a forerunner of another large-scale program using the annual series of Great Decisions booklets. Published by the Foreign Policy Association, these provide information on international issues. These two programs illustrate how the university has employed its international studies expertise to develop effective working relationships with high schools, community colleges, and community-based organizations.

Historically strong in the liberal arts, the University of North Carolina at Asheville is attended by approximately 3,000 students. It offers a masters degree and is classified as a comprehensive university. The university has several preprofessional programs like Forestry and Nursing which require transfer to other North Carolina state institutions.

Campus Context

Achievements in international education outreach have been accomplished in a generally supportive campus environment.

The UNC-Asheville's reputation as a quality liberal arts institution has attracted a well-respected faculty. Many helped design and now teach courses in the Integrated Humanities Program. For over ten years this curriculum has consisted of four team taught humanities courses required for graduation. In turn, the program has attracted new faculty, many with international knowledge and experience. According to data from a 1992 survey, 40 to 50 percent of the college's present faculty possess international expertise.

The General Education Requirements reflect several international education elements. Before graduation students must take at least two foreign language courses. Two courses in the four-course humanities sequence cover "The Modern World" and "The Future and the Individual." Also, the Political Science course on War, Peace and World Politics is listed as one of the choices, along with nine other courses, which can fulfill the two-course social science requirement. One of the others is also international, i.e., Comparative Economic Systems.

An international education needs assessment process, carried out by a Global Perspective Task Force in 1990, reported that 22.6 percent of the college's courses had "moderate-to-substantial" international content. Modern language offerings include majors in French, German, and Spanish. Russian and Italian courses are available through the intermediate level. In addition, specialized international curriculum programs are made available through two minors in International Studies and Africana Studies.

Various departments have international courses. In History, Europe is heavily emphasized plus two courses on China are offered. Political Science has courses on Africa, the Middle East, Latin America, and Politics in the Third World. Political Science and Economics courses also cover the usual international systems topics. The mass communications department has an International Mass Communications course and the major in environmental studies includes a course on Tropical Ecosystems.

Faculty focus groups began in 1991 with about thirty faculty attending twice a month during the academic year. Lectures and seminars concentrated on Africa the first year followed by Eastern Europe and Latin America in 1992 and 1993.

In 1992, student diversity included the 6-7 percent of the student body from traditionally underrepresented U.S. groups, mainly African-American. Also included are the fifty to sixty international students, about 2 percent of the student total. A full-time advisor provided minority and international student services in 1991-92 under the supervision of the multicultural affairs director, a faculty member with a half-time release from teaching. In 1992-93 this changed and international student advising became the half-time responsibility of a person in Student Services, with Outdoor Recreation taking up the other half. This proved to be a transitory move because in 1993 a new position was created combining in one person a half-time residence hall director and half-time international student advisor.

Study abroad programs attract approximately 100 students per year. Many go to Oxford University in a program jointly administered with North Carolina State University. Another UNC at Asheville overseas program, this one at Cambridge, attracts fifteen to twenty students every summer. Many of these are prospective teachers because the state of North Carolina has mandated education majors to have a summer overseas experience. Students also participate in a variety of programs sponsored by other institutions.

The university has a scholar exchange agreement sponsored by the chemistry department with a university in Nanjing, China. The Spanish department also participates in a faculty and student exchange with an Ecuadorean university.

Coordination of study abroad programs and international agreements is the responsibility of the International Studies director. Curriculum responsibilities are included in this position since the director advises students taking the International Studies minor. In addition, she organizes special campus events and processes requests from faculty interested in opportunities overseas. In 1993 Heidi Kelly took on the half-time director's position. As a cultural anthropologist she also teaches half-time, which amounts to two courses each semester. She had been on the faculty three years before applying for and being offered the position of director. The director of International Studies reports to the vice chancellor for academic affairs.

Also in 1993, George Yates, a management department faculty member, became director of Community Outreach. This position organizes events with the Sister-City Program and the World Affairs Council. The latter organization's activities are extensive as will be described later in this chapter.

The UNC-Asheville's mission statement provides a rationale for programs linking the campus and community: the University, "seeks to apply its resources to enrich cultural life, enhance the conduct of public affairs, and contribute to the constructive development in the community." This commitment flows from the institution's origins in 1927 as a county junior college. In 1963 it became a four-year state university dedicated to "the development of quality liberal arts education."

The Simulation Service Program is one tangible example of this community orientation. Learning from its development can produce information useful for other campuses contemplating major outreach initiatives.

Simulation Service Program

A creative simulation of the international system fostered the earliest of the UNC-Asheville's international education activities both on and off campus. Successive generations of the Inter-Nation Simulation have been used for about 25 years, going back to the old precomputer days. Now computer assisted, the simulation enables students to engage in their own foreign policy making. This decision-making model of the international system was pioneered by the work of Harold Guetzgow at Northwestern University in the 1960s. The most recently updated version, Inter-Nation Simulation IV, is available from C.W. Brown and Company. Written by a UNC-Asheville faculty member, Bahram Farzanegan, this most recent version received the Best Software in Political Science award from the American Political Science Association in 1991.

This computer package allows great pedagogical flexibility. Countries represented by student delegates may be real or hypothetical. The situations they face, their budgetary allocations, military and economic sectors, can be manipulated by the faculty director. Thus the simulation can emulate either an historical situation or a scenario devised by the instructor.

The use of this simulation by college students in the Political Science 180-War, Peace and World Politics course has spun off a major outreach program. When first integrated into the course, students became so enthusiastic they advocated making it available to local high schools. This annual activity began in 1973. By the late 1970s, hundreds of high school students were coming to the UNC-Asheville campus on a Saturday in April to interact as country delegations.

A simulation laboratory enhances their experience as well as that of the college students. Built in the late 1970s expressly for this international negotiating experience, the laboratory has proven its worth over the years. Its facilities and capabilities include closed-circuit television, videotaping, meeting rooms linked by an intercom system, a large central area for "international" negotiations, and an observation room with one-way mirrors.

Several innovative characteristics are woven throughout this high school outreach program. Its very title, Simulation Service Program, implies one of these. Enthused by the War, Peace and World Politics class simulation, college students earn credit by holding workshops for high school teachers. Since 1975, UNC-Asheville students have traveled to local high schools and used on-site computer equipment to demonstrate the Inter-Nation Simulation software package. Participating teachers have followed up this in-service training by using the simulation in their own classes or as an after school activity. The college students often become interns for these teachers as they expand simulation activities within their schools.

High school students trained in using the simulation meet every year for a culminating event. On a Saturday in the spring, the UNC-Asheville campus hosts an "international" negotiation. As "delegates" from one country, each high school team decides on a policy response to a specific scenario. This situation is designated by the UNC-Asheville faculty member who directs the program. As the delegations negotiate "internationally," they also must allocate resources to specified domestic sectors, such as the military. The computer processes the results of these allocations which become the basis for the next round of decision-making. College students provide the staffing for this conference and up to sixteen teams participate each year. Billed as a competition, the winning team members are offered UNC-Asheville scholarships.

For two decades, Bahram Farzanegan, a Political Science faculty member, has administered the Simulation Service Program. As a graduate student in the 1960s, he helped develop the Inter-Nation Simulation. He introduced it in his War, Peace and World Politics course after accepting the UNC-Asheville teaching position.

Until 1988, Farzanegan received no pay or course releases for his programmatic activities. The college initially did provide about $250 in financial support for student mileage costs. Such funding has expanded to around $3,000 to cover materials purchases as well.

In the early 1980s recognition came with the title Director of Community Services and a reporting line to the vice chancellor for academic affairs. This title changed in 1988 to Director of International Studies. Since this signified additional curriculum responsibilities it carried a half-time release from teaching. In 1992, Farzanegan resigned this position but continues the Simulation Service Program as one of his courses.

Other Campus-Community Programs
The nationwide Great Decisions Program provides another major vehicle for UNC-Asheville's international education outreach. Previously under the direction of Bahram Farzanegan and now administered by George Yates, the college sponsors the World Affairs Council of Western North Carolina which provides speakers on topics in the Great Decision booklets. The Council organizes meetings at eight geographic locations in cooperation with local co-sponsors such as community colleges, retirement and civic groups. Visiting experts from inside and outside the region serve as speakers as well as UNC-Asheville faculty who receive honoraria. Over 1,000 people attend sessions each year on a fee-paying basis. Thus the program generates a modest income after expenses.

The World Affairs Council of Western North Carolina has existed since 1990. The high number of attendees and cooperating groups shows it has tapped a hitherto underdeveloped community interest.

Support for the World Affairs Council comes from another of the college's community programs, the North Carolina Center for Creative Retirement. Retired diplomats, military officers, engineers with extensive overseas experience, and retirees from other relevant as well as non-relevant occupations attend meetings. The center has approximately 1,500 dues-paying members and has "exploded with lots of energy in carrying out many projects," according to a UNC-Asheville senior administrator. He also describes the retirees as "dependable as the sun."

Some of the same people also have formed a Senior Academy to offer their services as speakers and advisors. Drawing on these retirees illustrates how an academic institution can strengthen its activities by cooperating with its particular local community.

This brief sketch of UNC-Asheville's international education outreach activities provides an example of effective campus-community interaction for their mutual benefit. Faculty and college students, high school teachers and their students, retirees with international experience, and interested citizens, all have contributed in developing useful programs. The college's international studies content expertise and pioneering simulation methodology have provided a solid foundation for effective outreach programs. In turn, the expertise of community people has enriched college faculty and students. The Mentor Program for political science majors provides an example of how the campus-community network comes full circle.

This program takes the form of a UNC-Asheville course. When first offered in 1990, twelve students enrolled. Course requirements included discussions of readings, a research paper, presentations by retirees from international careers, and weekly meetings between each student and her/his chosen professional mentor, a retiree. Mentors were matched as closely as possible to the student's career interest. Bahram Farzanegan, the course instructor, reports an enthusiastic response from all involved based on oral and written evaluation statements.

For over twenty years, one international studies/international education activity has built upon another at UNC-Asheville. A search for the key reason leads to the one person who helped write the simulation years ago and has upgraded it ever since, teaches the War, Peace and World Politics and Senior Mentor courses, and organized the Simulation Service Program and World Affairs Council. Bahram Farzanegan has done all this and more. He has twice served as political science department chair. His energy, enthusiasm, and endurance seem boundless. The results of his efforts show creativity plus his ability to generate, administer, and build sustainable programs.

Programmatic success must also be attributed to support from the college's top administrators. Building the simulation laboratory represents two of the most significant commitments an institution can make, namely substantial financing and space allocation. While the facility has been used for various purposes, it remains under Bahram Farzanegan's direction. The windows of his second floor office look down on the whole lab area. Thus instructors can observe student interactions while avoiding the intervention their presence would create. The lab also serves as a major site on the campus tour for visitors and prospective students.

Other evidence exists of commitment to international education outreach. In the mid-1980s, college administrators authorized Farzanegan's setting aside funding for an additional faculty position, made possible by increasing political science enrollments, and using it for programming. At the time he was the political science department chair, the college was using this "distinctive funding" process to support other programs as well. In the case of international education, it provided initial financing for the World Affairs Council as well as the ongoing Simulation Service Program. Not only did these activities result in favorable publicity for the college, but the latter program helped recruit good students.

Issues and Answers

Initiating the Simulation Service Program gave rise to its first problem, convincing high school teachers and administrators that the initiative was well intentioned and to their benefit. Bahram Farzanegan met with everyone involved from superintendents of schools, to principals, to teachers. Probably several factors were at work; for example, the fact that college students would be working with the high school teachers, actually instructing them, caused some hesitancy. Also, the program may well have stimulated the latent suspicion that condescending initiatives from institutions of "higher" learning were imposing new demands on secondary education.

Besides persistence and the fact that the simulation worked well in the classroom, two programmatic choices helped convince the reluctant. First, the teacher volunteers and the students assigned to work with them already knew each other. While now in college, these students had previously been in the high school classrooms of the teachers with whom they were now working. Based on these personal relationships, the high school teachers caught the student's enthusiasm for the simulation.

A second move, securing outside funding, also helped establish the program. In its first year, 1973, an Asheville business group gave about $5,000 to cover workshop expenses. Fostering computer literacy provided a common objective for both business and education. Full legitimacy came in 1975 with a grant of $12,000 from the North Carolina Department of Public Instruction for additional teacher training workshops.

Solving the legitimacy issue created a practical difficulty. By the late 1970s the program had grown too large. Most of the high schools in western North Carolina wanted to take part and already the fifteen to sixteen participating annually were creating logistical problems. High school teachers ran the simulation in their own classes as training for the spring interschool negotiation. In the age before desktop computers and modems, UNC-Asheville students were using the college's main frame to process each "country's" data changes after decision-making sessions in the high schools. Some students were driving over

fifty miles one way to bring the data to the college for processing and to return the results to the high school the next day.
Consequently, they cut classes.

The volume of participants also required a steady increase in
administrative time. This proved unworkable since the program's director carried a full-time teaching load. Consequently,
the number of high schools was limited using distance from the
college as the criterion.

Lessons Learned

The following offers a checklist and specific suggestions for
developing successful outreach programs. Notice that these
recommendations all involve intrainstitutional relationships.

1. *Work with top administrators.* Maximum institutional benefit
   for minimum cost assures their support which is essential
   in the long run. The Simulation Service Program brings
   the university some positive visibility and good students.
   The World Affairs Council is self-sustaining since participant fees cover materials and speakers and retired people
   volunteer their administrative services.
2. *Take steps to ensure at least tacit faculty support.* When possible, incorporate faculty expertise into the program; for
   example, in the 1970s, when he organized two series of
   roundtable discussions for local television stations,
   Bahram Farzanegan invited UNC-Asheville faculty to participate. Currently, they receive honoraria for speaking at
   World Affairs Council sessions.

   In working with faculty, use academically acceptable
   terminology. The designation "games" was dropped from
   "simulation games" very early on. At the time, the NAFSA
   analogy proved useful in explaining the pedagogical relevance of simulations.
3. *Do not expect overt faculty approval.* This actually does not
   contradict the previous guideline. Passive acceptance
   should be distinguished from active support. Outreach
   programs can continue with the former rather than the
   latter.

4. *Institutionalize the program from the start.* This can be accomplished by establishing a budget line item no matter how small. Also written documentation should be prepared incorporating the new program into the ongoing activities of a unit of the university.

5. *Establish systematic procedures.* International education outreach programs at UNC-Asheville rely on a delegation of responsibility. College students, high school teachers, and volunteer retired persons carry out program activities at many sites in western North Carolina. Therefore administrative procedures, contacts, and time lines need to be preestablished, regularized, and clear-cut.

The successful outreach programs at the University of North Carolina at Asheville were initiated because of a faculty member's energy and expertise. They quickly took root and grew in the supportive community environment. At various times, senior administrators made key supportive decisions, such as in the construction of the simulation laboratory. By 1993, community outreach programs at UNCA had outgrown administration by one person. Now two carry out the activities described above: the director of Community Outreach and the originating political science faculty member.

The University of North Carolina
at Charlotte

Venturing a Business-University Partnership

A few miles out of town on its 1,000 acres, the University of North Carolina at Charlotte has grown with the city. Both Charlotte and its university now occupy positions of regional, and in some respects, of national prominence. In the late 1980s the city emerged as the country's third largest banking center. By 1992, Charlotte hosted 324 subsidiaries of foreign owned firms within the metropolitan area alone. This represented a 220 percent increase since 1980.

During the same period of time, the university's international business programs flourished. Originally administered by the UNC-Charlotte's Office of International Programs, they helped establish the university's national reputation as a leader in international education. In addition, the university itself grew from over 10,000 students in 1982 to about 15,000 in 1993. Its capabilities developed to the extent that the state has authorized planning for doctoral programs in selected fields.

The university's physical setting facilitates growth. The panoramic view from the library's tenth floor observation area reveals the benefits of a suburban location. Ample space for expansion is evidenced by the fact that most campus buildings are relatively new and have two or three floors, the library dwarfing them as the only high-rise. A pleasantly landscaped yet relatively compact inner campus is bordered by hundreds of heavily forested acres, and all easily accessible from the interstate. This natural appeal is reinforced by a pond, overlooked by the Cone University Center. As a reminder of urban life and the frugality of state-financed institutions, visitors must pay to park in various lots around the campus.

The generally horizontal architecture is interrupted by an isolated edifice. A narrow, round carillon tower, rises abruptly to dominate the campus center. With the library it is one of the highest structures for miles, until the high-rises of downtown Charlotte. The tower contrasts sharply with, and thus calls attention to, the campus image of inviting openness, of accessibility to the Charlotte community.

Identifying itself as North Carolina's metropolitan university, UNC-Charlotte considers campus-community cooperation as central to its purpose. The university mission statement reads, in part, "to provide for the educational, economic, social, and cultural advancement of the peoples of North Carolina through on- and off-campus programs and collaborative relationships."

The University of North Carolina at Charlotte's international education programs represent the university both in their rapid, purposeful growth and in their community orientation. Program administration is centralized in the Office of International Programs, prior to 1992 the Center for International Studies. As one of the country's earliest multipurpose undergraduate international education centers, the office has worked with Charlotte's business community since it was established in 1975. Initially, this meant corporate funding for student scholarships and other OIP activities. Then the relationship expanded in 1977 with the initiation of cooperatively planned and mutually beneficial international business seminars.

These seminars coincided with the beginning of the effort by Charlotte's business leaders to establish the city as a major hub for domestic and international business. The Office of International Programs and its business constituency grew together. In the 1980s other local colleges began offering general programs similar to OIP's, so the office made a transition to specifically negotiated, customized business training workshops. It also produced significant new spin-offs; for example, the Corporate Sponsors Program and the Japan Center, described later in this case study. Its longevity, plus the scope and success of its programs, distinguish the Office of International Programs from other undergraduate international education centers.

The History of International Education at UNC-Charlotte

The University of North Carolina at Charlotte began in 1946 as Charlotte College, a two-year, liberal arts, state institution designed originally to educate returning World War II veterans. By the mid-1950s, it had grown to a four year college and in 1965 became part of the state university system with the addition of professional schools. In the 1990s, UNC-Charlotte had six colleges: Arts and Sciences, Architecture, Business Administration, Education and Allied Professions, Engineering, and Nursing.

Rapid growth also characterized UNC-Charlotte's international education programming. In 1975, Earl Backman, a relatively new assistant professor in Political Science, received a half-time release from teaching to establish a Center for International Studies, the forerunner of the Office of International Programs. It took on curriculum internationalization as the first task but the new director, a visionary and ardent spokesperson for international education, recognized the potential of an "integrated" approach.

Centralizing international programs in one administrative office would provide the mutually supportive environment needed for rapid growth. Earl Backman recognized that spreading study abroad, international student and scholar support, English as a Second Language instruction, curriculum internationalization, and community outreach among disparate university units would stunt program development in the long run.

Backman's vision became reality when advising international students and study abroad became part of the Center's responsibility in 1978-79. That year students traveled overseas on the first UNC-Charlotte sponsored program.

In addition, outreach activities were initiated in 1975. Harold Josephson, an assistant professor of history and another new UNC-Charlotte faculty member, began going to local businesses to organize a Great Decisions Program. This now involves more than twenty different communities, one of the largest such programs in the country. In 1984 he took charge when the center's first director left for a position at another university.

Thus business-university cooperation became an integral component of UNC-Charlotte's international education activities from the very beginning. This pioneering achievement is noteworthy, not only because it comes early in the formal effort to internationalize U.S. higher education, but also because such outreach was a rare occurrence at what was then primarily an undergraduate institution.

The Office of International Programs has been the most active UNC-Charlotte unit in establishing connections with Charlotte's business community. This fact has not escaped the attention of a succession of the university's top administrators. Perhaps partially as a result, they consistently have supported international education while noting that OIP's business outreach programs have helped implement the university's mission.

Campus Context

International education was incorporated into the core of the institution's identity in 1991. As stated in the second paragraph of the UNC-Charlotte catalog's Purpose Statement, "It is the distinctively metropolitan-oriented university of the state and focuses special attention on global literacy and international education." This is given added definition in the last paragraph which states that "policies and practices of The University are designed to promote . . . knowledge of and experience with cultures and circumstances that differ from the familiar in location, time, or values."

To implement this objective, the university's curriculum has an international/multicultural general education requirement, several specialized programs, and courses infused throughout various departments. To graduate, students must take at least one among several designated courses with "a cross-cultural and/or international emphasis."

International curriculum specializations include majors in Afro-American and African Studies, International Business, Geography, and Environmental Science, in addition to an International Studies minor. Indicative of student enthusiasm, in its first year the International Business major attracted forty students. Foreign Language majors are offered in French, German, or Spanish. Japanese is taught on a regular basis through the "advanced intermediate level" and courses can be taken "on demand" in Portuguese, Italian, Hebrew, Greek, Danish, Chinese, and Arabic. The university also awards a master's degree in Teaching English as a Second Language.

International courses also are offered in the history, political science, religion, English (including literature) and anthropology departments. They cover Europe, Russia, Northeast Asia, and Latin America. In addition, the environment and developing world issues are covered in the Departments of Geography and Earth Sciences, and Economics.

Over the years, the office has stimulated new international curriculum through grants and faculty development funds. The center administers an International Travel Grants Program which initially used funds from a university foundation. After a series of recommendations the program's budget was increased by the early 1990s to $30,000. Used for research and other professional activities overseas, this OIP program is not designed to cover all expenses. It provides an incentive for faculty to apply for matching funds from departmental or other travel budgets. In 1993, the International Travel Grants Program was shifted to state funding and fifty-six faculty participated from twenty-two departments in all six colleges.

As another OIP program experiencing substantial growth, international student services assisted 303 undergraduate, 200 graduate, and forty-three exchange students from seventy-three countries in 1992-93, for a total of 546. The English Language Training Institute has also expanded to the point where its classes had to be capped for the first time in 1991-92. It employs six full-time personnel and from ten to fourteen part-time instructors. During the spring of 1992, 103 students from nineteen countries enrolled in the Institute's wide variety of non-credit courses.

The office's contribution to the university through effective international student services has been noted. Evidence for this may be found in the beginning of the catalog, under "General Information," where UNC-Charlotte proudly asserts, "With a significant concentration of international students at the undergraduate level, UNC-Charlotte has one of the most active international studies programs in the country for an institution of its size."

As in most universities, UNC-Charlotte sponsors its own study abroad programs as well as channeling students through consortial arrangements. The combination of such programs attracted over 140 students in 1992-93. The center administers exchange agreements with universities in France, England, Spain, Korea, Russia, Taiwan, Germany, China, and Japan. Summer programs expand the number of countries to include Italy and Costa Rica. Professional school majors also participate, particularly those in engineering, business, and architecture.

The College of Architecture sends some of the largest groups due to its innovative summer field programs in Italy and Spain. The program in the Italian province of Tuscany deserves particular mention. Since 1988, students actually have engaged in designing restoration and "recuperation" projects for historically significant buildings in small Tuscan towns.

Another OIP initiative, the International House, occupies one wing of the new residence hall and it has become a campus mainstay. Beginning in 1990, 180 students pair as roommates, one international student with one U.S. student whose course of study includes an international specialization. Speakers and other special activities were organized by OIP for the first two years, then Student Life took over the responsibility.

The aforementioned programs are noteworthy for their variety, level of participation, and self-generating finances. This also is true of OIP outreach activities. Besides the international business seminars and workshops and their spin-offs described below, outreach programs include the annual Great Decisions presentation/discusssion sessions, Student Town Meetings, which each fall are attended by over 500 high school students, and the International Festival in September. As one of OIP's first initiatives, this one-day event now attracts over 10,000 people to its ethnic displays, demonstrations, foods, music, and dance.

When the center became the Office of International Programs in 1992, its director was promoted to associate vice chancellor for international programs and its program coordinators became directors. Five directors were responsible for Study Abroad, International Students and Scholar Services, the Charlotte World Affairs Council, the Japan Center, and the English Language Training Institute.

In 1993 the Office of International Programs operated with a budget of over $1.5 million and a staff of eighteen full-time personnel, plus part-timers and student workers. Only $200,000 came from the state, covering a variety of expenses and four salaries, those of the associate vice chancellor, the directors of Study Abroad and Foreign Student Advising, and one secretary. The rest was earned through revenue generating programs with the English Language Training Institute as the largest single source. Grants, corporate contributions, and program fees provided other sources of funding.

International Business Seminars and Workshops
In 1977, the Office of International Studies became one of North Carolina's regional leaders in assisting U.S. firms that wanted to export. The first training sessions were small-scale and covered technical information, such as how to prepare letters of credit. The demand quickly grew, however, both in numbers of participants and in the topics they wanted covered.

A representative sampling of topics shows the scope and variety of OIP organized seminars: "Doing Business with Canada," "Doing Business with the Japanese: What's Myth, What Matters," "Help Dispel the Mystique Surrounding Foreign Trade: Letters of Credit and Other Payment Methods," "Markets of Opportunity: A Global Perspective" (highlighting all world regions). These one-day seminars were supplemented by some with multiple-day schedules, such as "U.S.-China Trade: Piecing Together the Puzzle," covering two days, and a four-day workshop series on "International Trade: Opportunities for the Future." Most are held on campus at the Cone University Conference Center and all are cosponsored by local businesses, business organizations, and/or other educational institutions.

Seminar agendas reflect certain similarities which, taken together, could serve as a model for other such ventures. Whatever the seminar topic or length, virtually all speakers are practioners, successful businessmen mostly from the Charlotte area but some from other parts of the country or overseas. Occasionally UNC-Charlotte faculty appear on a program to provide cultural or historical background. Every seminar includes successful cases, practical technical sessions, such as legal considerations, trade financing, or customs procedures, and at least one presentation on local resources or sources of information. All "doing business" seminars also devote at least one session to a point of view from the country in question, often delivered by one of its official representatives.

Over the years, seminars have attracted from twenty-five to over 100 attendees. Three to four a year are held, on average, and financially they break even to the extent of covering the salaries of relevant Office of International Programs personnel. Since these people have other OIP responsibilities as well, the international business seminar program helps support other functions. Seminar fees vary according to length and level of outside support. They range from thirty-five to ninety-five dollars, with a majority around forty to sixty dollars for a one-day program.

One OIP activity, administered under its seminar program, is distinct from the rest both in its clientele and in the fact that it occurs annually. The Student Conference on Careers in International Business is held in February of each year. In 1993, the sixth such event was attended by over 400 students and faculty from thirty-two colleges and universities in three states, North and South Carolina plus Virginia.

Not a career fair, the conference charges a twenty-dollar fee and invites speakers to lead concurrent afternoon sessions from many employment sectors, such as banking, transportation, finance and accounting, foreign-owned corporations, and government agencies. Students make the most enthusiastic comments about the lunch session, although not for the reason perhaps first assumed. Tables at lunch are organized by field or area of interest with six students and a businessperson, or other practitioner, assigned per table. The entire event is subsidized by corporate sponsors.

By the early 1990s, many other educational, business and civic organizations were marketing international business training seminars. Thus, the Office of International Programs has had to create a new niche. The result has been to customize, i.e., to work with individual companies in designing specific training sequences. This development enabled OIP to establish client relationships and match its regional, national, and international information networks to the specific needs of the Charlotte business community. Thus the office draws on its years of developing personal contacts and program experience to bring together various elements of its clientele.

To illustrate, a one-day training seminar on documentation for international shippers was organized for Federal Express clients in the fall of 1991. It was underwritten by Federal Express, thus allowing a low conference fee of twenty dollars. In the next year, bankers from other countries were invited to Charlotte to learn about the procedures of the U.S. banks with which they were doing business.

Spin-offs

Years of effective mutual programming has resulted in good relations between OIP and Charlotte's business community. This coordination has been enhanced by projects funded by the U.S. Department of Education's business-higher education grant program, Title VI, B. These have also supported curriculum development in UNC-Charlotte's Belk College of Business Administration. In 1984, the year Harold Josephson became director of the Center for International Studies, the college's faculty included one international business specialist. By the early 1990s, after two grant projects written and administered by the Center, an increase in the number of courses and student interest had justified the addition of five more faculty and the international business major.

This addition to UNC-Charlotte's curriculum has impacted study abroad, again demonstrating the benefits of an "integrated" approach to international education. Programs on international accounting in London and international business in France are supplemented by courses at several of UNC-Charlotte's exchange partner universities.

Effective OIP-business community collaboration has produced at least five significant spin-offs. First, the Charlotte World Affairs Council was nine years old in 1993. It has steadily increased in size to over 800 members with forty corporate sponsors.

Beginning in 1990, an annual World Citizens Award dinner is held in late spring. This $150-a-plate gala event attracts over 700 of Charlotte's business, civic, and education leaders. Billy Graham was the first recipient, and in 1993, the CEO of NationsBank Corporation was honored. The World Citizens Award is presented to prominent Charlotte area citizens of international stature who "promote international understanding and awareness, and increase the international visibility of the Carolinas."

The Corporate Sponsors Program has existed idiosyncratically since 1975 but became systematic in the 1980s. It collects donations from local and area businesses for student scholarships, community and campus lecture series, and other international activities as they develop.

The associate vice chancellor for international programs serves as editor of the North Carolina World Trade Association's quarterly newsletter. The document is published by OIP in cooperation with the U.S. Department of Commerce. The association also provides student scholarships for Charlotte area institutions of higher education.

As the latest of its outreach programs, the Japan Center has developed even faster than previous OIP initiatives. The Center, which began in early 1992, is directed by an energetic woman with an entrepreneurial bent. Within one and a half years, this lecturer in Japanese language in UNC-Charlotte's Department of Foreign Languages has attracted corporate funding to carry out an amazing array of activities. A partial list includes breakfast and luncheon seminars for business leader networking, on-site seminars for U.S. companies on Japanese language and culture, a conference on intercultural management styles, a conference for the Southeast Association of teachers of Japanese, K-12 teacher workshops, a "Japan in the Schools" program, an art exhibit exchange between Japanese and North Carolina high schools, a host family and tutoring program, a Japanese movie festival, Japan Night featuring a dinner and culture presentation, host family and tutoring programs for Japanese students, and an information/resource center in the Office of International Programs.

The Japan Center developed swiftly at least partly because of the supportive community climate in Charlotte. Japanese firms comprise the second largest number of international subsidiaries in the Charlotte area, second only to German-owned companies. Also, the number of U.S. firms doing business with Japan is increasing constantly. Thus, both U.S. and Japanese business people recognize the need to bridge cultures. They want, and have been willing to support, an institution which facilitates their meeting and engaging each other in the context of mutual learning. Through its events, the center provides a communication forum. In turn, the center has stimulated interest in Japan on campus and among other community groups, such as in the schools.

The success of OIP's business-university cooperation may be attributed to several factors. First, as explained in reference to the Japan Center, the business environment in the Charlotte metropolitan area has provided a secure and expanding operational base for international business-oriented programming. With 2.3 million people, Charlotte hosts hundreds of foreign-owned firms, extensive banking facilities, and increasing numbers of U.S. exporters.

Second, UNC-Charlotte has contributed effective support networks. University administrators have supported the centralization of international education programs and allowed OIP to retain discretionary control over its program-generated revenue. Also, substantial numbers of knowledgeable and interested faculty have contributed their expertise to curriculum internationalization and program development. They have made effective presenters, grant writers, researchers, and program consultants.

Third, the capabilities, policies, and personality of OIP's director, now associate vice chancellor for international programs, have created an environment where success seems commonplace. He has encouraged and supported potentially effective new initiatives on the part of his staff and others throughout the university. While fulfilling his own role as innovator, he has not hesitated to inspire and help others as well.

The experience of the Japan Center's director provides a case in point.

The latest example of the associate vice chancellor's supportive style is provided by a teacher who wanted to start something new. She was willing to work part time until her efforts provided enough funding for a full-time position. Her new program involved following leads and organizing two- to four-week summer institutes for students and educators from other countries. She has proven so effective that the first summer's earnings may justify her working at 100 percent time.

Four, such encouraging leadership has produced an exceptionally able and entrepreneurial staff. This, in turn, creates the needed administrative support for all OIP activities.

Issues and Answers

While entrepreneurial revenue generation has proven successful and allows creative OIP decision-making, it also creates a planning problem. Formulating an annual budget with so many staff dependent on external funding sources produces particular pressures, to some extent different from those in most other UNC-Charlotte units. Thus far, there has been no significant shortfall, due, in part, to solid financial planning, and also to the fact that national recessions have not had a major effect on OIP program participation.

This ongoing situation is part of OIP's operating reality and no major shift is contemplated in the balance between state- and program-generated funding. Yet, the associate vice chancellor for international programs has made a decision that the state should fund the additions in staff required by OIP program expansion. The latest OIP reports point out the need for such assistance. Existing staff, though able, are stretched thin. Therefore securing a new, state financed, support position has become the top OIP priority.

A second OIP personnel need has led to the request for a part-time faculty associate. This person would help oversee curriculum development, design, write and administer grant projects, and help plan future international education initiatives.

The 1991 capping of English Language Institute courses should have sent a message. It constituted a concrete act implementing the "managed growth" policy OIP has announced in recent years. In practice, this seems to mean maintaining the current level of programming until more personnel can be hired. In addition to the two positions noted above, new personnel are needed in both study abroad and international student/scholar services.

Yet even if state financing were available for new staff, the lack of available space "remains a constant source of frustration," as stated in a recent OIP report. The space crunch has become a vital issue with no answer in the foreseeable future. Many units of the university are experiencing the same problem; therefore, it seems, progress must await the construction of new buildings.

Another major issue, and OIP's response, has been explained previously. As other education, civic, and business organizations became competitive in offering international business training seminars, OIP developed specialized products. This "customizing" takes more planning time since it requires tailoring seminars to the client's specific needs. This also puts pressure on existing OIP staff.

The issue of campus politics accompanies most attempts to foster change. At UNC-Charlotte, resistance to curricular revision surfaced in the professional colleges particularly. It has diminished over the years with grant-funded projects as one of the most effective vehicles for change. In preparing a proposal, the vice chancellor for international programs has proceeded carefully. His policy guideline has proven effective, i.e., establish a cooperative relationship by helping to implement decisions the colleges make themselves. It should be noted, however, that the associate vice chancellor has not been shy in approaching the colleges with recommendations.

Business Administration has been impacted more heavily than other UNCC colleges. The Office of International Programs' international business outreach activities and student scholarships helped create an environment which encouraged the college to internationalize its curriculum. Events sponsored by OIP resulted in the interaction of Belk College faculty and administrators with Charlotte's international business community. The effect of this took time but in recent years the College of Business Administration has embraced internationalization wholeheartedly.

Also, Phi Beta Delta's campus activities helped create a campus climate favorable to internationalization. This International Honor Society recognizes scholarly achievement in international academic fields and encourages scholarly interchange between U.S. citizens and those from other countries. Thus, Phi Beta Delta testifies as to international education's academic validity. The honor society's membership includes U.S. faculty and students with international expertise as well as international scholars and students. Thus the structure of the organization itself provides a working demonstration of international cooperation. Graduate students from UNCC's professional colleges' have joined, thus creating additional advocates for internationalization.

Lessons Learned and Future Plans

The first three points refer to the development of an international education center responsible for initiating and administering campuswide programs. The remaining seven provide guidelines for organizing an international business seminar program.

1. *An international education center cannot operate effectively over time without the simultaneous support of faculty and the administration at the highest levels.* Faculty-led initiatives can shrivel over time without supportive policies from the administration. The same can happen to top-down programming if it occurs without a strong faculty base.

2. *The administration must provide resources and structure rewards as part of the institution's incentive system.*

3. *Funding for faculty development is essential.* Effective campus internationalization depends on curriculum revision. This not only requires some faculty to expand their own expertise. Approval of new curriculum means a significant number of faculty must see the need even if they do not teach international courses themselves.

4. *Know the local community, its needs and capabilities.* Successful outreach requires frequent and ongoing interaction

with community leaders. The associate vice chancellor for international programs estimates that such interaction takes about half his time.

5. *Build strong ties.* Do not ask for funding without providing useful services, such as staff support and visibility.

6. *Formalize relationships.* In the beginning, the Office of International Programs had an International Business Advisory Committee, with five UNC-Charlotte business faculty and twenty community leaders. This committee was critical in the early years and provided ideas, speakers, and practical suggestions.

7. *Begin modestly and well.* Business leaders have little time to allow second chances. Visit and plan downtown, becoming comfortable in the business environment. It actually is different from academic programming.

8. *Use an appropriate mix of faculty and practioners.* Each has a role and both are necessary constituencies.

9. *Involve the university's administrative leadership.* Administrations often perceive themselves as representing their universities and consider local community interaction as part of their responsibilities. This perception has proven very strong in the case of UNC-Charlotte chancellors and other high-level administrators because they consider outreach, particularly with Charlotte's business community, as part of the university's mission. Therefore they have responded positively when asked to speak at OIP events, review proposals, and meet to plan future initiatives.

Currently, OIP plans for the immediate future involve on campus programming. A Japanese Studies minor has administration and faculty support, particularly now that eighty students in Japanese have created sufficient demand for advanced courses. Another proposal will present a multiyear plan to expand the International Studies minor, with over forty students, into a major. Present plans call for the major to require three years of language training and a study abroad experience.

Integrating international studies into professional degree programs remains an OIP priority. A grant to the National Science Foundation has been funded which will provide development assistance for faculty self-training projects, new curriculum, and related study abroad programs in engineering.

As one of its ongoing efforts, OIP continues to focus attention on the need to establish international expertise as a priority for recruiting new faculty. This has proven a long term process since departments exercise virtual autonomy in hiring decisions. Thus, they must become convinced individually of the need to include international criteria.

The experience of UNC-Charlotte's Office of International Programs provides a resounding endorsement for an integrated approach to international education. Curriculum, co-curriculum, and outreach program growth has been characterized by a mutual push-and-pull incentive process. Such interconnected programming can be replicated on other campuses regardless of type and size.

This centralized approach worked in Charlotte due to the quality of its director, an active, able administrator with legitimacy from his faculty status, a cooperative mode of operation, and a record of resounding success. His business community programs and networking earned the support of the university's top administrators. Beginning with a central office also proved crucial because it meant that the benefits of successful business outreach and English as a Second Language programs could support other international education initiatives.

University of Rhode Island

Melding Engineering and German

As a land grant institution, the University of Rhode Island's mission includes the application of knowledge "in the daily life of the nation." Also, as one of the nation's research universities, its faculty engage in the "scholarly acquisition of new knowledge." This dual purpose is reflected in both the academic quality and practicality of the University of Rhode Island's International Engineering Program.

This program merges German and Engineering; it does not simply juxtapose them. It requires extensive language courses of its participating engineering students which have been designed specifically for them. Open only to engineering students, these specialized German courses incorporate culturally authentic, technical information as instructional materials. Both disciplines are integrated also in two other requirements of the program: A six month internship in a German speaking country is followed by a cross-listed German-Engineering course. Taught by Engineering faculty fluent in German, this course provides engineering instruction in German.

The practicality of this program to prepare students for today's international economy, fits with the university's ongoing mission. First established as Rhode Island's agricultural school in 1888, the campus was built on a farm purchased by the state. The restored farmhouse still stands. Given its growth over the years in both size and scope, the state legislature changed the designation in 1951 to the University of Rhode Island.

Thirty miles south of Providence, the university occupies a spacious campus linking the town of Kingston with its rural surroundings. The four-floor, grey granite buildings at the campus center evoke a sense of solidity as they overlook a large tree-lined grass quadrangle. Other campus buildings reflect many architectural styles, including converted late nineteenth-early twentieth century houses.

The University of Rhode Island enrolls about 12,000 undergraduates and 3,700 graduate students. It has approximately 720 full-time teaching faculty. The university consists of eight colleges; Arts and Sciences, Business Administration, Engineering, Continuing Education, Human Science and Services, Nursing, Pharmacy, Resource Development, and the Graduate School of Oceanography. Its strong marine programs have led to its designation as one of the country's national Sea Grant universities.

The International Engineering Program illustrates the creative application of in-depth expertise available at a major university; for example, four engineering faculty fluent in German. Also, it reflects the close cooperation of faculty in varying disciplines, despite the fact that individual faculty spend much of their time in specialized research. All involved, whether from German or Engineering, consider IEP not as a dilution of either but an enhancement of both.

Campus Context

International education curriculum at the University of Rhode Island includes a General Education Requirement as well as specialized majors and individual courses infused throughout various departments and colleges. The graduation requirement is two courses or the equivalent in a foreign language or culture. Majors include Comparative Literature, Latin American Studies, French, German, Italian, Russian, and Spanish.

These degree programs are augmented by Minors in International Development administered by the College of Resource Development, International Business Studies, and African and Afro-American Studies. Also, the university offers courses through the intermediate level in Chinese, Hebrew, Japanese, and Portuguese. The catalog also lists two "Irish" courses which cover Gaelic literature using English translations.

A wide variety of other international courses are offered within various departments. Under History, the catalog includes a course on every world region and several with a Third World focus. Political Science offers international relations courses plus courses on Africa, Europe, Asia, and Israel. In Anthropology, Latin America and Africa are emphasized with one course on the Irish. English offers two courses on African Literature; Economics includes Growth and Development; and, in the department of Resource Economics, several international courses are listed such as International Trade and Natural Resource Products. Sociology has a course on Population Problems and Religious Studies has Comparative Religion.

The list goes on with international courses in disciplines not usually noted for their internationalization. The Textiles, Fashion Merchandising and Design department offers a course on Textiles: A Global Perspective; Theatre's contribution is Theatre Architecture in Western and Non-Western Drama; Women's Studies includes Women in Irish Society; and Film Studies has an Italian Cinema course. Also the catalog devotes a separate page to listing many, many courses on Environment and Pollution issues in 21 departments and colleges from Animal and Veterinary Science through Marine Affairs and ending with Zoology. The University of Rhode Island also sponsors a specialized research Institute for International Business.

The list of Study Abroad programs at the University of Rhode Island names 14 affiliated institutions overseas, six in the United Kingdom, two in Japan and Canada, and one each in France, South Korea, Venezuela, and Mexico. In addition, each year the university sponsors faculty-led programs. In 1993, about 60 students participated in such travel-study opportunities to Spain and England. The program in Spain included a hike to the place of pilgrimage at Santiago de Compestela. The summer programs are administered by the Continuing Education Office as part of summer school.

The Study Abroad Office Director reports to the Dean of University College, a non-degree granting institution within the University of Rhode Island. University College advises students before they are accepted as majors in the degree granting Colleges.

Throughout the academic year, about 230 students go to the university's international partners or on consortial programs. The study abroad office also assists another 30 students who participate in the National Student Exchange Program, which sends them to institutions in the United States.

The Study Abroad Office provides each student going overseas with a pre-departure handbook. Most of them also attend at least two of the three or four non-credit orientation sessions. Re-entry sessions take place once a semester.

The Coordinator of International Student Services in the Student Life Office oversees advising for the approximately 1,000 international students, of which 99 were undergraduates in the fall of 1993. The university offers partial tuition support for international students based on need, called the Suddard International Grants. A gracious old house serves as the International Student Center, a meeting place for study, co-curricular activities, and social events. Approximately 800 domestic multicultural students also contribute to the university's student diversity.

An example of international education outreach at URI has continued for fourteen years. In cooperation with the Goethe Institute and the German government, the university's College of Continuing Education sponsors the Deutsche Sommerschule am Atlantik, the German Summer School of the Atlantic. Held on campus, the "school" offers intensive German language courses at all levels for teachers, business professionals, community people, as well as students. Many cultural events supplement instruction adding information on German life. This outreach program shows the entrepreneurial tendencies of URI's German language faculty, a trait that produced a creative new program merging Engineering and German in the mid-1980s.

International Engineering Program
The program originated serendipitously. John Grandin, the future program's director and faculty member in German, found himself living next door to the College of Engineering's new Dean, Hermann Viets, who had grown up in Germany. In conversations they found themselves agreeing that the United States often leads the world in technological expertise but lacks the ability to communicate effectively in global markets. Professional education should provide U.S. students with all the tools

necessary for productive, fulfilling, and rewarding careers in the changing world economy.

They set out to pioneer a program providing students with needed international and professional knowledge plus skills. A committee of language and engineering faculty was appointed by the Provost in the mid-1980s. Fortunately for IEP's future design, five of the engineering faculty were fluent in German. In addition, others had research contacts with colleagues overseas. The joint committee first determined the feasibility of a new program. Then it designed one. The Provost approved the product of the committee's deliberations, but committed no support. Without a major grant, little could be done.

It would take a major financial commitment to free up faculty in both engineering and German to offer the unique courses and test them in the student market. Therefore, beginning in 1986 and for its first three years, IEP was funded by a grant from the U.S. Department of Education's Fund for the Improvement of Postsecondary Education.

As Grandin described IEP's design, it was to "unite sciences and technology with the humanities," yet there appeared to be no practical way to do so within the existing university curriculum structure. Therefore, a new program was needed.

> After wrestling with the apparent reality that there is no room for meaningful change within the current curricular format, the University of Rhode Island committee began to look at more basic change. By extending the undergraduate program one year, it would be possible to incorporate rigorous foreign language and intercultural study as well as an internship abroad into the engineering program, with no sacrifice to the technical subjects. Even though some of our committee doubted that students would opt for this kind of opportunity if an extra year would be required, we concluded that there was no other way. (John Grandin, "German and Engineering: An Overdue Alliance," in *Unterrichtspraxis*, Fall, 1989, p. 147.)

Students completing this five-year program earn two degrees, a Bachelor of Science in Engineering and a Bachelor of Arts in German. Because of its quality and degree of innovation, in 1992 the Program received the annual Educational Innovation Award from the Accreditation Board for Engineering and Technology.

To recruit the first student group, a mailing was sent to all 275 incoming freshmen engineers and to most sophomores as well. Over 80 returned the postcard indicating their interest. The second mailing of registration materials yielded 47 students, enough for two sections of beginning German, GER 101-German for Engineers. Predictable attrition brought this number down to 25 the second year, but this was much higher than the committee had dared to hope. The second year's publicity effort yielded two sections again, totalling 39, about 15% of the incoming engineering students.

By the summer of 1990, fifteen interns were placed with regional engineering firms. Subsequently, all but one of these completed their internships in Germany during the next academic year. Eight worked overseas in the fall of 1990 and six more during the first half of 1991. The first six IEP graduates in 1991 received varying engineering degrees, two in Chemical, one in Industrial, and three in Mechanical Engineering.

Twenty-two University of Rhode Island students had graduated with IEP's dual degrees by 1994. Also, by the end of the summer of that year, 40 had completed IEP internships. Most graduates are employed in private business and some have gone on for advanced work in engineering.

The IEP design required building a specialized German language curriculum. Each year's level of courses posed specific curriculum development issues. The first year courses have two objectives. The first is to introduce spoken German, since students will be living in Germany as part of the program. The German text selected emphasizes oral skills through short dialogues. It teaches every-day German using the words and grammar needed for functioning in Germany at a survival level.

The second objective for IEP's first year German courses is to begin development of a working facility with the vocabulary of mathematics, computer science, and the natural sciences. Integrating these disciplines requires learning the grammar and vocabulary needed to do algebraic problems, once the numbers are mastered. Since Grandin was the first instructor for these introductory courses, he noted that, "It is a bit unusual (and sometimes a bit taxing) for the German instructor who has long since dismissed algebraic terms from daily thought to see the blackboard of the German 101 class filled with geometric shapes or mathematical formulas."

Although some authentic technical materials are used during the first year, many more are incorporated into the intermediate level of German instruction. As listed in an article by John Grandin, Kandace Einbeck, and Walter von Reinhart, the sources for useful materials include professional journals, vocational texts, reference works, popular magazines or books, and business publications. The same article provides examples of several materials actually applied in the IEP German courses. One of these, a chart from a German textbook for electrical engineers, explains the color coding used for resistors. The narrative explains how this graphic can be used in several different levels of German instruction. ("The Changing Goals of Language Instruction," in *Languages for a Multicultural World in Transition* edited by Heidi Byrnes, National Textbook Company, Lincolnwood, Illinois, 1992, p. 155.)

The IEP program integrates several bilingual faculty into its third year German conversation courses. They discuss topics in their own disciplines. Such topics are not always science or engineering related: Lectures on seismic oil exploration and electromagnetism are mixed with talks such as by the Chair of the Philosophy Department on the basic elements of logic.

After returning from their overseas internships, Students take a cross-listed capstone course taught in German by an Engineering faculty member. This course is taught every other year, not always by the same instructor, and attracts from eight to ten students.

To first establish IEP's internships, Grandin and Viets visited twelve firms in Germany in as many days and returned with twelve internships. All these German and U.S. companies, and businesses providing subsequent internships have working relationships in the United States. By IEP's third year, unsolicited inquiries began to arrive directly from Germany, usually from firms with American subsidiaries. Since then, the list of companies with internships has grown longer than the number of students ready to fill them. Ongoing personal contacts are needed to retain the quality of IEP's internship component.

Therefore, the program director visits participating companies in Germany once a year, often with the Dean of Engineering.

Each internship pays a stipend either directly or in non-cash benefits, such as meals and housing. The aim is to provide students with enough to cover their room, board and some spending money. Some German firms have their own housing and others help locate suitable accommodations. A local Rhode Island newspaper article reported that returning interns say the companies pay plenty to live on.

Student participants must have a sufficient level of professional preparation to work in actual engineering contexts. They are placed according to their engineering subject areas; i.e. mechanical, computer, electrical, civil, industrial or chemical engineering. In some cases a more specific student-position match has been possible, such as in automotive design or aviation; for instance, a civil engineering student with a specialization in environmental problems has worked with water purification specialists in a German chemical company.

Student interns earn six German credits for significant progress in language proficiency. This is determined from their biweekly journals written in German and an oral examination upon returning to the university. Grandin, and in recent years the IEP program's Associate Director Kandace Einbeck, correct and return the students' writing using E-mail and the INTERNET system where possible.

Since its initiation, the program has developed a two-phase internship design. Because some Rhode Island firms have interests in Germany, they have provided internships during the summers before and after students leave to work in Germany. As an example, Brown & Sharpe offers internships both at their local facility and in Germany as an investment in long-term recruiting. Four other U.S. companies in New England also provide these ongoing summer internships for selected students. In the summer of 1990, 15 students were placed in regional engineering firms.

There is convincing evidence of student enthusiasm for IEP. The numbers signing up for the German for Engineering courses remains steady or is increasing. Students further along in the program have begun a new student organization, the

Society of Students of International Engineering. Accepted by the University of Rhode Island's Student Senate, this organization arranges guest lectures and other events.

Local newspapers have taken note of IEP and its students' experiences. In highlighting the program, they have provided a steady stream of favorable articles. This positive publicity for the university has supplemented its use of IEP for recruiting purposes.

The Advisory Board for the International Engineering Program had 12 members in 1993 from U.S. businesses with German subsidiaries and German businesses with U.S. subsidiaries. Most provide IEP student internships. A representative from the Consul General's office in Boston was also a member. The Board meets an average of once a year.

The administration of IEP continues to be directed by John Grandin, a published expert on Kafka. His writing ability and creative bent served the program well beginning with the initial FIPSE grant. He has proven an astute program developer and prolific grant writer, having written three more successful proposals funding the IEP spin-offs described below. He also had published three articles on the program by 1993. Grandin speaks of his undergraduate education at Kalamazoo College as having a major effect on his life. As a Philosophy major, he took German and discovered the excitement of learning about another part of the world.

The International Engineering Program has a German faculty member as the Associate Director, as noted above. Also its Engineering Academic Advisor, Richard Vandeputte, manages the technical portion of the program for the College of Engineering. Admission to the IEP program is administered by this college and, in 1993, its new Dean Thomas Kim was continuing the strong support for the program begun by Hermann Viets.

University operating budgets cover two IEP program elements. The College of Engineering funds the German travel to oversee internships. The Language Department and College of Arts and Sciences covers the salaries of the two non-tenure track faculty teaching IEP's German courses. Initially these people were grant funded. Students pay for their own travel and the Director, Associate Director, and Academic Advisor do not receive course releases specifically for the International Engineering Program. Six courses per year is the normal course load for University of Rhode Island faculty. The program has no budget line of its own. The university's senior administrators have expressed support for international education in general, and have approved IEP as one of the institution's authorized programs.

The International Engineering Program has generated several spin-offs, most supported by U.S. government grant programs. A second Fund for the Improvement of Postsecondary Education grant allowed Grandin to initiate a Languages-Across-the-Curriculum project. Financing from the Undergraduate International Studies and Foreign Language Program is supporting the internationalization of the undergraduate business curriculum. A third project will take place in the summer of 1995. This German-Across-the-Curriculum summer institute will be funded by a successful proposal to the National Endowment for the Humanities. Participants will come to the University of Rhode Island from colleges and universities across the United States.

In addition to these grant funded projects, another spin-off has been private business support. A scholarship fund has been initiated at a meeting of the IEP Advisory Board. As soon as the idea was introduced, $2,000 was pledged, and this was followed within a few weeks with another $30,000. The goal is $100,000.

Issues and Answers
According to the Director, IEP had "no real hurdles" only "things to deal with" as the program developed. The faculty involved evidenced a problem solving dedication because they wanted a successful program. Not all faculty in the Language Department were supportive, however, and some remain uneasy since they perceive educating engineers as rather far removed from the disciplinary role of language instruction.

One strategy in dealing with the often latent doubts was requiring two 400 level German Literature courses of IEP students during their fifth year. Another factor eroding opposition is the fact that German enrollments have doubled since the program began. Two full-time, non-tenure tract instructors have been hired. Also some opponents among the engineering faculty have changed their minds since the IEP program has attracted good engineering students to the university. Interest exists in the College of Engineering to expand into other languages, and this has met with some positive responses among French language faculty. Yet, when John Grandin was appointed Language Department Chair by the Dean, the issue of what is appropriate language instruction surfaced again.

Internship administration has emerged as a major issue because this aspect of the program has proven more time consuming than originally planned. The director must provide more information about students to prospective employers and about jobs to students. Such detailed communications have proven effective as demonstrated by the fact that, in spite of the inevitable occasional disappointments with housing or work assignments, no intern has come home early or changed jobs.

One addition was made after the first round of internships. A specific contact person was designated in each company hosting an intern. Also, all involved learned to sharpen their expectations. The process was tightened up and now students write letters of application and provide information about themselves to their prospective employers. The matching of interns with assignments has become akin to a professional job search. The Director and Associate Director have collected information on the companies so students can learn about them before applying, and especially before leaving the United States. Also students meet with their predecessors in the internship as part of their orientation. This benefit flows from the fact that a majority of the internships are now with the same companies that previously have hosted IEP students.

Student recruiting never became an issue because the process was carefully thought through when IEP began. Forming introductory German courses expressly for interested students has allowed the time and academic preparation necessary to ensure the success of the other program elements, such as the internship.

Another issue also cannot be categorized as a problem but it has taken much time and effort; i.e. locating source materials for teaching engineering subjects in German. Also the program had to ensure that incentives existed for team-teaching the specialized German for Engineers courses on an ongoing basis. Such instruction was essential because students had to achieve the level of language proficiency needed to work with native German speakers in a professional capacity. Fortunately, the University of Rhode Island has a policy of rewarding faculty for their participation in team-taught courses. Thus faculty contributing in the German for Engineers courses can accumulate credits toward earning a course release for their individual research.

Lessons Learned

This list of practical suggestions reflects the International Engineering Program's environment at the University of Rhode Island. As such, they may prove instructive on campuses where similar conditions exist.

1. *Build in vested interests for both parties.* Here "both parties" refers to two levels of partners, both external and internal to the university. First, it means the university and participating businesses benefited. Second, IEP enhanced the programs of both the German and Engineering units of the university.
2. *Define the program as helping to carry out the university's mission.* In the case of the International Engineering Program, its goal coincided with the University of Rhode Island's identity as the state's land grant educational institution. The program clearly was part of the university's effort to assist in Rhode Island's economic development.
3. *Secure grant funding.* Faculty need to be recognized and rewarded. In IEP's case, grant funding was not only crucial in initiating the program, but it also provided a forum for national recognition.
4. *Leadership should come from faculty at least in their mid-careers.* The IEP Director had the rank of Professor, thus reflecting the quality of his teaching and his research and publication record. Other participating faculty also had earned the respect of their colleagues. Their achievements lent legitimacy to IEP's curriculum innovations.

These points highlight the key factors in the International Engineering Program's success. Several faculty, with the director as the crucial element, have carried the program from its inspiration as a conversation topic through to its full implementation. The director has expanded his activities in developing several refinements and spin-offs. Outside funding also proved essential. Lastly, IEP program students recognized the value of taking on additional course work.

University of Richmond

Fostering Curriculum Change Through
Faculty Overseas Seminars

This comprehensive university occupies a spacious campus at
the edge of Richmond, Virginia. It was founded in 1830 as
Richmond College, a four-year liberal arts institution for men.
Other liberal arts facilities were added as the Westhampton College of Women in 1914 and the Graduate School of Arts and
Sciences in 1921. Professional schools also became part of the
university. In 1870 the T. C. Williams School of Law was
founded and in 1949 the E. Claiborne Robins School of Business opened for graduate and undergraduate study. More
recent additions are the University College for continuing education in 1962, and, in 1989, The Jepson School of Leadership
Studies, the first of its kind in the United States. The University
of Richmond retains a relationship to the Baptist General Association of Virginia. In 1992, the 222 full-time faculty taught over
3,700 students, 2,876 of these as undergraduates.

A visitor enters the university from a winding road through
an upper-class suburb and then acres of woodlands. The campus occupies 150 acres graced by a lake and many species of
trees. The variously shaped, neo-Gothic buildings in the campus
core rise at angles from each other. Built of red brick, they are
outlined in marble and highlighted by varieties of arches and
spires. Together they evoke a cloistered seriousness of purpose.

The university's administration has made a commitment to
fostering ongoing internationalization. Perhaps the most telling
evidence is its financing of annual Faculty Seminars Abroad.
The provost considers providing faculty with an international
learning experience as the key to curricular change. For three
weeks each summer, a group of eight to twelve faculty travel to
various sites in a chosen region of the world. The seminar
begins on the campus with approximately two months of read-

ing and meetings with experts on and from the region. Members of the university faculty as well as outside speakers address the group. When overseas, participants meet with business leaders, journalists, government spokespersons, and academics, as well as share field experiences.

This summer program began in 1989 at the suggestion of the international education director. Actively supported by the administration, the initial group was financed with a local foundation grant of $20,000. The success of this effort has led to a distinctive and possibly unique, ongoing program since the Faculty Overseas Seminars are now institutionalized and supported wholly from the university's budget.

Campus Context

International education content and programs are implied in the University of Richmond's statement of purpose. As presented on the first page of its undergraduate catalog, the university includes as one of its "educational objectives," "to convey to students a representative portion of that body of knowledge that has accumulated and endured through the history of cultures."

One of the School of Arts and Sciences' graduation requirements implements this purpose by obliging undergraduates to take an Interdisciplinary Core Course, "Exploring Human Experience." This 1990s addition to the university curriculum taught by faculty from varied disciplines, uses primary texts from four world traditions, the Western, East Asian, African, and Middle Eastern.

The University of Richmond's statement of purpose also offers a list of commitments designed to achieve the objectives. Two of these allude to the value of a multicultural campus and international education programs: "A diverse, largely full-time and residential student body that participates in a broad range of university activities," and "Opportunities for social commitment and public service, internships, travel and study abroad, and other appropriate learning experiences outside the campus."

In addition to the graduation requirement noted above, Arts and Sciences undergraduates must demonstrate proficiency through the intermediate level in either a modern or an ancient foreign language. The university offers modern language majors in French, German, and Spanish, and many courses in Japanese and Russian. Also students may major in International Studies and choose one of seven concentrations in Africa, International Economics, German Studies, Latin America, Modern Europe, Politics and Diplomacy, and Russian and East European Studies. In 1993 this major, which had been in existence for five years, attracted about 150 students.

Since the International Studies concentrations are inherently multidisciplinary, their scope implies that courses with a significant international component exist throughout the Arts and Sciences curriculum. Illustrations include Music of Non-Western Cultures, Modern African Literature, Sociology's course on Population, and Introduction to Comparative Literature. The history department course listings in the catalog cover every major world region, and even some subregions such as the Modern Balkans. Also the university offers a Geography course.

The Office of International Education coordinates the International Studies major, develops and carries out international linkages and exchanges, administers the university's summer study abroad programs, organizes co-curricular campus events including an annual film series, and advises international students. These numbered fifty-seven in 1993. The university funds merit scholarships which are open to international students. The office also advises all students (generally forty to sixty per semester) who study abroad, participating in approved programs. All study abroad procedures are centered in the office.

Three people staff the office, all working full-time; a director, who has faculty status, her assistant, responsible for international student and study abroad advising, and an administrative assistant who provides secretarial support. One graduate assistant and up to six peer advisors support the staff.

Other office responsibilities include the development and administration of a growing number of student and faculty exchanges. In operation are exchanges with universities in the United Kingdom, Japan, and Germany. Also each year international visitors are invited on an ad hoc basis; for example, the campus hosted two writers-in-residence in 1989 from Ghana and Russia, a Fulbright scholar-in-residence from Jordan in 1992-93, and a Polish theatre critic in 1993-94.

In 1992 the international residence concept became a reality when a small house was devoted to that purpose. The board of trustees approved a second one in 1993. International students have U.S. roommates and their accommodations are organized according to clusters of languages. Thirty six students lived in the residences in 1993. They accept a responsibility for participating in programs serving the whole campus. The students organize a program including culturally specific field trips, dinners, dance parties, game nights, films, and other learning enhancements.

In 1993, ten summer programs provided groups of students with overseas courses and experiences. Most were in Europe and six involved language training, with one of these in Saint Petersburg and another in Japan. One program emphasized the relationship between environmental issues and cultures in Australia. The two located in developing countries also included language study, Shona in Zimbabwe and Spanish in Costa Rica. In 1993 about 100 students participated in these University of Richmond faculty-led programs. It is estimated that approximately 25 percent of Arts and Sciences graduates have had an overseas experience.

Also during the summer, groups arrive from other countries for short-term conferences. During 1993 two student groups from France and Japan, accompanied by their teachers, spent time at the university. The director of international education assisted the summer conference manager in the planning process. They encouraged conversations between the groups' leaders and University of Richmond faculty, students, and staff.

According to the provost, the goal is to make international education part of the "fabric of the University of Richmond." As noted previously, faculty development via an overseas experience provides a pivotal part of this long-term process. About 20 percent of the faculty had participated by the fall of 1993.

Faculty Seminar Abroad

As administered by the Office of International Education, this program is designed to encourage faculty to internationalize their curriculum by internationalizing their own knowledge and definitions of their disciplines. The program does not accept faculty whose research interests focus on the part of the world to be visited during any particular summer. Providing research opportunities as such is not the goal. Instead, the presentations, readings, and experiences are designed to stimulate new disciplinary applications and cross-disciplinary dialogue for faculty with a wide variety of specializations. The aim is to change the campus by challenging "what people perceive as possible," to use the director's phrase.

The emphasis on a multidisciplinary approach to faculty development was consistent with the university's internationalization process. This began with an ad hoc faculty committee in the mid-1980s. The group, itself multidisciplinary, recognized the general need for international education and focussed on designing the International Studies major. The committee produced a report recommending the current interdisciplinary major and the creation of an Office of International Education. Campus internationalization was set as the long-term goal. Two key, mutually reinforcing guidelines emerged from the discussions, the need for a campus-wide process and for an interdisciplinary program. It was felt that faculty should be encouraged to move beyond the dominant narrow academic reward system with its emphasis on specialization.

In 1987 the office was established and Uliana Gabara became director. She had taught Russian language and literature since 1984. Gabara also speaks Polish. Both languages are part of her cultural background. The new director initiated discussions leading to Faculty Seminars Abroad as a means of faculty development, and thus of campus internationalization. She not only organizes each faculty seminar and establishes its focus; she also leads each faculty group. Her quiet confidence, academic and administrative competence, plus her cultural background, go a long way toward accounting for the success of the five seminars to date. In his report, a faculty participant noted, "I have seen

Dr. Gabara handle a surly train porter at 4 AM in Budapest, and charm university presidents in China. I know of no one else on campus who could accomplish these diverse tasks."

The first three-week seminar travelled to Eastern Europe and included Yugoslavia, Poland, and the Soviet Union. The second visited Hungary, Czechoslovakia, and the still existing German Democratic Republic. These were followed by seminars in China, West Africa, and the Middle East. In 1994 a Latin American experience is planned.

The itinerary of the 1993 seminar illustrates each program's scope. Jordan, Syria, Yemen, and Israel were visited, with a talk by a Palestinian academic on "A Palestinian View of the Current Situation" included in the last country. Presentations covered antiquities and history as well as current events. Nine faculty participated from eight departments: Modern Foreign Languages and Literature, Sociology and Anthropology, English, Mathematics and Computer Science, Art, Philosophy, History, and Economics. The over $40,000 price tag was provided by the University of Richmond. Prior to the Middle East seminar, the provost had participated in two seminars.

Each seminar requires its participants to meet several times during the two months prior to departure. They read from a jointly constructed reading list, plus hear and discuss presentations by noted specialists from on- and off-campus. Planning for the next summer's seminar begins each fall using local experts and following leads with calls around the United States and, literally, around the world.

The application and selection process begins with the announcement of the location and dates of the next summer's seminar in the provost's newsletter. Applicants must explain their rationale for participating. The process is completed by Christmas break with selections made by the university's deans, provost, and director of the International Education Office. More applications were received than there were positions for the first seminar, and the number has increased each year.

The preparation phase during each spring takes the form of a "mutual teaching exercise." This includes informal discussions, suggestions of speakers, sharing bibliographies, establishing a reference section in the library with relevant resources. Also, useful articles make their rounds to each participant. All this culminates with the seven sessions described previously. Participants are also encouraged to develop contacts for meetings abroad.

A final report is required in the fall after the seminar and these vary from a few pages to article-length. Participants also give a talk and this is well attended by faculty who took part in prior years. Something that could be called a shared seminar spirit has developed among many faculty. One of the reasons for this phenomenon is revealed in several faculty reports. They note their experiences as "life changing."

The seminar is designed as a multidisciplinary experience. Participants compare their differing scholarly observations and comment on varying disciplinary-based methodological perspectives when presented with content information about the countries to be visited.

The Faculty Seminars Abroad provided invaluable faculty development during the period of creating the new core course "Exploring Human Experience." For this team-taught course, faculty members from various departments undertook to go beyond their discipline and into new cultures. The Seminar Abroad served as a means for offering broad knowledge and familiarity with the realities of the new cultures. Thus, when East Asian texts were introduced into the core course, the seminar went to China, and when Middle Eastern texts were added, it went to the Middle East. This was true for Africa as well.

An unanticipated consequence of the multidisciplinary, group nature of the program has benefitted the university. New across-campus friendships have not only strengthened the support network for international education, but have contributed to the university itself by creative curriculum cross-fertilization.

The majority of participants were nontravellers prior to their seminar experience. In many cases, they have changed their vision of what is possible for them as scholars and as individuals. Subsequently some participants have designed overseas research projects, whereas before they had not thought of the possibility. The world has opened up for them. Several have taken their families on overseas holidays, previously not considered an option.

One U.S. historian has turned into a world traveler. Since going to Central Europe and China, he has visited Vietnam on a Council for International Education Exchange program and then presented his research in a conference paper. Students have benefitted directly since he has incorporated information from all his learning in the university's core course, as well as his courses in U.S. diplomatic history.

Upon returning from the seminar to West Africa, the university's sports psychologist wrote about what the U.S. can learn from the role athletics plays in Ghana. His source for this information was a counterpart at the University of Ghana. He will not only write a conference paper and journal article; he also wants to establish an ongoing exchange relationship with the University of Ghana.

A faculty member from the art department used a Ghanaian proverb to summarize the seminar's effect on his professional growth: "Hunt in every forest, for there is wisdom and good hunting in them all." One faculty report explained the experience this way: "When everything is so different, strange, and new, the sense of being alive is profound." These comments show why some faculty are beginning to comment that an overseas experience should be a graduation requirement for all students.

The overseas seminar program has helped campus internationalization in both predictable and unpredictable ways. To illustrate the latter, the program has developed into a useful faculty recruitment incentive. In addition, a growing number of faculty with cross-cultural experiences have become advocates of greater diversity. In the 1980s, the university employed only three or four foreign-born faculty and administrators. Now four or five people from Latin America and three from Africa join several from European countries. The number of such faculty has quadrupled in the last ten years.

The seminar, and other activities which have increased cultural awareness, also have provided support for diversification in general, including women and U.S. minorities. On a related note, the seminar has had an impact on international student recruitment. As a result of contacts with institutions abroad, several students have applied to the University of Richmond after meeting its faculty while on their overseas program.

Issues and Answers

From available evidence, only one issue has developed which requires a response. The amount of time needed to organize this program puts a heavy burden on the Office of International Education, given its other responsibilities and staffing. The director has responded with creative uses for student workers, and in the process is training them with real administrative experience and enthusiasm for work in the field of international education. Their work in the office requires research and organizational skills. It is "not a casual job."

The director reports that one potential issue has not surfaced. All participating faculty have proven to be good travellers. When the inevitable logistical problems presented themselves, faculty responded with understanding and patience. Everyone has returned to campus appreciating their experience and with a new level of commitment to their own academic work in particular, and to international education in general. By including their own newly acquired knowledge in their courses, faculty participants have consciously linked the overseas experience to the goals of a liberal arts education. This reinforces the university's emphasis on teaching as its primary enterprise.

Lessons Learned

Not surprisingly, some of the following points relate to the value and functioning of a central coordinating office.

1. *Visibility is important.* This includes the campus location of the office itself and its use of the university's information sharing networks. Since the Office of International Education moved to the library building in the center of campus, students now "drop in," whereas they did not before. This converts into expanded program participation.

    The office's newsletter, prepared every semester, includes information on every aspect of its work. Also, the director makes international education program announcments in almost every issue of the weekly newsletter sent from the provost's office. She makes sure these include notices to the faculty of specific topics international students can help address in classes.

2. *View international students as an important part of the university's academic life.* Providing faculty with information about their knowledge creates an important role for them as resources. Thus, these students feel less marginalized because they are making a contribution to the university's academic life.

3. *Nurture connections to various administrative offices as well as academic departments.* Use both formal and informal strategies. Drawing upon such personal networking can become useful when issues arise, such as how particular administrative offices, food and health services for example, interact with the varying cultural styles of international students.

   The publications office provides a particularly important vehicle for informing the university community about the value of international education programs.

4. *Develop a faculty inventory data base.* Include international interests as well as specializations. This can help in various ways, such as suggesting linkages with specific international students. The packets given to new faculty contain cards for them to fill out with the heading "Faculty Inventory of International Expertise and Interests." As a side benefit, the inventory alerts new faculty to the importance attached to international education at Richmond.

5. *The director of international education should continue teaching and carrying out other faculty responsibilities.* This remains valid no matter how difficult it is to combine academic and administrative duties. At the University of Richmond, the international education director continues to teach one course a year in the International Studies program.

6. *Always use a consensual process.* This is as true in interacting with administrators as with faculty. Such a process produces a useful side effect with both groups: it blunts the potential accusation of "empire building."

7. *Work with a faculty international education committee.* At the University of Richmond this campuswide, eleven-member, policy-making group has monthly meetings and deals with a variety of issues from approval of new study abroad programs to international student recruitment and cultural programming.

8. *Use national and international networks.* Consortia, area studies centers, and E-mail connections with overseas universities all prove essential over time. Widespread communication links assist in making decisions as detailed as assessing the relative value of credits and grades received on overseas programs. They also provide general information, such as what approach to take in preparing conference presentations.

The broad scope of the University of Richmond's international education activities has been achieved in a relatively short period of time. This demonstrates the effectiveness of a central office, an able staff, and its leadership under a creative, competent director. The director attributes her success to the "students' interest in international studies and in study abroad," and the fact that faculty have taken a direct role by proposing the creation of the International Studies major, for example. The active support of senior administrators also has proven crucial.

The University of Southern California

Focusing a University Curriculum

In one sense, the University of Southern California exists as an enclave in Los Angeles. As one of the fifty-six-member Association of American Universities, USC represents U.S. higher education at its most prestigious and prosperous. This reality contrasts with another since South-Central Los Angeles lies just across the street. Iron gratings on dormitory entrances and first floor windows serve as reminders that Los Angeles and its problems hover just outside.

The university reflects the L.A. metropolitan area in another way. A walk across campus shows the university alive with conversations in several languages. Rows of tables advertise ethnic group clubs, artistic events, social justice causes, and lectures by prominent human rights advocates. The university seems to have achieved a synthesis combining academics and multiculturalism.

This impression is supported by data on student ethnicity. In 1991 over 14,600 undergraduates attended the university, 8.1 percent as international students. Also that year U.S. minorities comprised 43.6 percent of first year students, up from 38.4 percent in 1990. Of these, 21.6 percent were Asian-Americans, 7.5 percent African-Americans, 4.3 percent Hispanic-Americans, and 0.2 percent Native-Americans. If this trend continues, in three years at least half of USC's undergraduates will be other than Euro-American. Human variety has become part of the USC experience.

The campus reflects a southern California image. A visitor passing fountains and flowers along broad thoroughfares must remain alert for students on skateboards, rollerblades, and bicycles. Both traditional and modern sculptures grace the fountains. One is surrounded by a well-tended rose garden. The student cafeteria offers plastic-wrapped sushi and California rolls, and long lines form at the espresso bar. Highrises, club buildings, and a four-story book and department store reinforce the impression of a city within a city. The University of Southern California consists of thirteen professional schools, with programs for undergraduates as well as graduate students, five graduate schools, the College of Letters, Arts and Sciences, a Law Center, three departments in the health professions, and an Institute of Safety and Professional Systems Management.

The elitist stereotype of a large research university includes the perception that its faculty have little time for, or interest in, university wide program development. Yet such an effort proved successful at USC. A multidisciplinary faculty committee, aided by students and administrators, organized a South Africa Semester. In the fall of 1989, this cooperative effort focused campus attention on both the artistry and anguish of southern Africa.

Not only its size and scope differentiate this theme semester from others. The South Africa Semester sought, and to a large extent achieved, a sense of shared enterprise through an analysis of a controversial issue. Whereas the intense argument over divestment had set sectors of the campus community against each other, intellectual discussion of apartheid and other issues affecting the southern African region created a sense of a common academic purpose.

Choosing a region of the world in great controversy involved the danger of reducing its complexity to a negative polemical debate. To avoid this result, the theme semester's planning group wanted students to learn as much as possible through their own experience and critical thinking. To achieve this result, faculty used culturally authentic information from the region itself. Poetry and other literary works were adapted to classroom use. Also the performing and visual arts became part of the semester's activities. The semester's planners drew upon faculty overseas contacts and resources to locate artists and their work.

Campus Context

As with any of the country's large research universities, the point at USC is not whether a variety of international education programs exist but which areas receive emphasis. In addition to undergraduate international majors in anthropology, geography, French, German, Russian, and Spanish, specializations are offered in East Asian area studies, East Asian languages and cultures, international journalism/East Asian area studies, ethnic studies, slavic languages and literatures, comparative literature, international relations, and Judaic studies in the Department of Religion. International minors show even greater variety encompassing cultural anthropology, environmental engineering, environmental social sciences, peace and conflict studies, Russian area studies, Russian language, Russian literature, and Italian.

Additional language offerings reflect the curriculum's area studies majors. Courses in the East Asian Languages and Cultures Department cover Chinese, Cantonese, Korean, and Japanese, with all but Cantonese offered through the 400 level. Judaic Studies includes Hebrew, and the Spanish department also offers Portuguese through the advanced levels. The Department of Slavic Languages and Literatures lists courses in Polish and Serbo-Croatian through the 200 level. The classics department includes three courses in Modern Greek.

International education is reflected in the general education requirements of the College of Letters, Arts and Sciences. Generally graduates must demonstrate foreign language competence through the third semester, although some departments require more. One non-Western culture course is required as well as Western Culture I. Many departments mandate an additional course, Western Culture II. This core is also required by several professional schools, i.e., Education, Business Administration, Fine Arts, and Public Administration. Graduates from the Schools of Accounting and Music must take a non-Western course but not a foreign language.

International courses are distributed throughout the curriculum including the professional schools. Business Administration offers several courses in International Finance as well as Management in a World Perspective. The School of Cinema lists Television History of the International Cinema and the Department of Nursing includes Transcultural Nursing. The

School of Engineering contributes Energy and Society, but not for major credit.

International courses appear in USC's catalog under several departments in the College of Letters, Arts and Sciences. Communication Arts and Sciences has a Cultural Dimensions of Speech Communication course. The biological sciences department lists two ecology courses, and Philosophy offers Oriental Philosophy. Religions of the East and Moral Perspectives on War and Peace are in the religion department as well as several on specific Asian religions. Geography has two courses on Latin America, one general and one on Mexico, as well as two issues courses, one on conservation and another on population.

Courses in the usual departmental mainstays of international and intercultural education cover all the world's major regions. This is true for Anthropology, Political Science and International Relations. The last also has courses on specific countries, Japan, China, France and the former Soviet Union. In History the focus is on Asia with two courses also on Latin America. Speciality courses also are listed, such as Mexican Migration to the United States. Political Science's specialized courses include the Politics of Peace and Women in International Development. Sociology has several international offerings, i.e., Environmental Sociology, Soviet Society, Development and Sociology, and Change in the Third World. Economics courses cover the Middle East, Latin America, and East Asia, besides the usual offerings on trade and world economy.

The University of Southern California sponsors two international research-curriculum development centers in cooperation with the University of California at Los Angeles, i.e., the East Asian Studies Center and the International Studies Center. These are U.S. government-funded. The School of Business Administration hosts a national center of International Business Education and Research, also federally funded. Another major USC unit, the School of International Relations, was established in 1924 as the first such school in the United States. The 1991-92 catalog lists twenty full-time faculty, and International Relations attracts over 800 majors and minors.

The Office of Overseas Studies administers the university's undergraduate study abroad programs. These include the Madrid Center, a Paris Center run cooperatively with Sweet Briar College, and many consortial and individual USC departmental programs. The office has six staff members with one serving as the full-time manager of the Madrid Center.

According to the Office of Overseas Studies report in September of 1990, 309 USC undergraduates went overseas during the year, 155 on semester and year-long programs, and 154 during the summer of 1990. Most attended programs in Europe with the Madrid Center receiving the greatest number, 62. Seventeen went to Tokyo, five to Tel Aviv, and none to the developing world, although the catalog lists programs in Kenya, Zimbabwe, Russia, China, Korea, and Mexico.

International student services are provided by the Office of International Students and Scholars. The reporting line of this office has shifted in recent years. It was administered under Student Affairs and then became the responsibility of the dean of the Division of Humanities in the College of Letters, Arts, and Sciences. Its director now reports to the vice president for student affairs. The office has eleven full-time staff supported by twenty student assistants. In 1993 they worked with 1,274 undergraduate international students.

International education outreach is given focus and direction by the School of International Relations with its Center for Public Education in International Studies. The center was begun in 1981 by Steven Lamy, then a new SIR faculty member.

Under his direction, the center has provided extensive K-12 teacher training nationwide, and initiated a program to internationalize some USC freshman writing courses with a grant from the U.S. Department of Education's Undergraduate International Studies and Foreign Language Program. Lamy also has served as a consultant for the PEW Foundation's Initiative in Diplomatic Training. In the process, Lamy has established himself as one of international education's leading advocates and consultants throughout the United States. The center's latest endeavor, the Teaching International Relations Program, will develop and test creative innovations in college teaching.

The outreach activities of the School of International Relations help implement one of USC's stated objectives. While research, the "creation of new knowledge," remains the university's pivotal focus, "the university also has a role of service to its communities," according to its catalogue.

It was this sense of responsibility to the Los Angeles community that helped motivate a multidisciplinary group of faculty to organize the South Africa Semester. They also shared a commitment to teaching excellence, which expressed itself as a felt need to respond academically to the divestment issue, one very prominent on campus in the late 1980s. The divestment campaign had crystallized student and faculty interest in apartheid as well as in the Southern African region in general. This provided the impetus for the strikingly successful program which has led to multiple spin-offs.

South Africa Semester

Other campuses have sponsored theme semesters, yet USC's South Africa Semester is noteworthy for its scope and multi-layered faculty support network. Faculty in fourteen departments taught eighteen relevant courses, enrolling over 1,800 students. Another 1,000 students in designated sections of the Freshman Writing course also studied and reflected on South African issues.

A partial list of courses infused with relevant issues includes Social and Ethical Issues in Business, Cinema and Television/Drama in Southern Africa offered by the School of Theater, Environment and Ethics in the Geography Department, Problems in African International Politics in the School of International Relations, Contemporary Moral and Social Issues offered by Philosophy, Religion's South Africa: Religion and Ethical Issues, and Third World Cities taught by an Urban and Regional Planning faculty member. All courses involved in the semester were electives. In a sense, this includes the Freshman Writing course sections since not all of them covered topics related to southern Africa.

In response to the divestment issue, and at the request of faculty and student organizations, the university's president appointed a South African Initiatives Committee. Four members of this committee served as a planning group and actually organized the semester's activities. The core four represented various university units, i.e., Carol Thompson—Political Science, Herbert Shore—Drama, Steven Lamy—International Relations, and Barbara Soloman—Dean of the Graduate School. Carol Thompson and Herbert Shore were chosen by the committee as cochairpersons and supervised the half-time administrative assistant and the $20,000 budget provided by USC's president.

The idea for a South Africa Semester originated in the realization that it would serve as an appropriate academic response to a controversial issue. Not only had apartheid become a major foreign policy debate in the United States, but a student-led divestment campaign had brought the controversy home to the University of Southern California. Divestment rallies attracted 200+ students instead of the anticipated twenty or so.

In discussing this issue, faculty in several departments discovered they not only shared a common position on divestment, but expertise and interest in Southern Africa. There had been theme semesters in the 1970s on Latin America and the European Middle Ages. Why not use this method to channel the highly charged debate on South Africa into positive learning?

Given the issue's political delicacy, the planners adopted an appropriate goal and process, i.e., the students' right to learn through open discussion. This not only proved rhetorically effective, but set the tone at planning meetings. The South Africa Initiatives Committee's openness to various points of view convinced a wary administration that the semester would provide a nonpolemical, academically valid educational experience. Also helpful in this regard was the fact that Barbara Soloman, a member of the planning committee, had direct access to senior administrators as dean of the graduate school.

Courses and co-curricular activities were designed to enable students to actively participate and draw their own conclusions. Faculty chose instructional materials and classroom activities which allowed various voices from southern Africa to speak for themselves; for example, *No Life of My Own* by Frank Chikane was required reading in Religion 265—South Africa: Religion and Ethical Issues, and one section of Composition 102 built a series of assignments around a consideration of the Afrikaans play *Deep Ground*. Methodology as well as content received much thought and discussion in preparation for the semester.

As stated by Barbara Soloman, the goal was "to broaden and deepen understanding of the southern African region generally and the problems of apartheid in particular." Carol Thompson adds, "Students should not just know but also understand." This implies program planners thought in terms of an education of human involvement which must engage emotions and senses as well as intellect.

To achieve this objective as far as possible without leaving southern California, students needed an "immersion" experience. The campus had to be transformed. Song, dance, art, and drama enriched the entire semester. Students could learn through sight and sound about the beauty, artistry, empathy, dignity and courage of the region's people. The drama of human suffering was necessarily a part of the semester's content. Yet program planners also wanted students to experience South Africa as a land of promise and hope with people of vision and compassion.

Since the "right to learn" had emerged as the key educational goal of the semester, the visual and performing arts became a vital part of its planned activities. Theater, films, music, and art provided emotional intensity through artistry. They also supplied authentic voices since visiting artists from the region came to campus. These guests represented diverse points of view. The imagery and information from southern Africa itself meant instruction did not simply rely on the interpretations of experts from outside the region.

Treating co-curricular activities not as supplemental but as an integral part of the semester's experience also reflects the importance of the visual and performing arts in southern Africa. In the words of the planning committee cochair Herbert Shore, "An artist is a transformer of the world, helping us to understand it." In Africa the arts are viewed as modes of exploring the social situation, the lives that people lead, and projecting alternative possibilities. In southern Africa especially, an artist is not separate from the people but is an integral part of society. Thus the arts become the major means of expression for a repressed people.

Consequently, USC's South Africa Semester saturated the campus with co-curricular activities. "It seemed as though something was going on all the time," according to one planner. Twenty films were shown from the commercially produced *Cry Freedom* to the experimental *Mapantsula* made by black South Africans. A festival of black township plays on videotape was held including *Bopa*, *Woza Albert*, and *Sarafina*.

The USC School of Theatre produced *Born in the RSA* and the premiere in English of *Deep Ground* by the young, recently acclaimed Afrikaaner playwright Reza de Wet. These were cast with students in the conservatory acting program, professional and community actors, and were directed by members of the theatre faculty. Athol Fugard, the famous playwright/director/actor, accepted an invitation to come to USC for the South African Semester. He rarely, if ever, accepts an engagement on a university campus, but in this case made an exception. In celebration of his reunion with South African actor Zakes Mokae, they appeared together in "An Evening with Athol Fugard," and read from Fugard's works. The evening ended with a long excerpt from his play *My Africa, My Children* which had not as yet received its premiere performance on the stage. Athol Fugard and Zakes Mokae also lectured on campus, conducted workshops and classes, and met with groups of students in informal sessions. The School of Theatre also produced *The Island* and *Sizwe Bansi is Dead* by Athol Fugard. After each performance, cast, directors, and audience engaged in discussions of the plays, the experiences out of which they came, and the issues involved.

The planners did not neglect music and dance. Two groups brought the sights and sounds of South Africa to the campus. The first, Vukani Mawethu, illustrated universality as well as distinctly African culture since the performers were American as well as international students from South Africa. The second, Themba, an a cappella and dance group from South Africa, performed on the steps of the bookstore to close the semester. Food enhanced the spirit of celebration at the music and dance events.

The visual arts also were well represented. Malangatana Ngwenya visited the campus for a week. As a painter, poet, and theater artist from Mozambique, Malangatana conducted workshops in the School of Fine Arts, lectured in the School of International Relations and Department of Political Science, and worked with students and faculty in the Division of Drama. He also engaged in activities at the William Grant Still Community and Cultural Center. This center, named for and endowed by the African-American composer, is sponsored by the city of Los Angeles' Department of Cultural Affairs and is located in South-Central.

The William Grant Still Center is dedicated to African and African American arts and culture. It thus promotes the arts in the "African diaspora." There, Malangatana conducted a workshop, gave a lecture demonstration, and taught classes for children in which they learned to create works of art out of materials that they found in their surrounding environment. These works were exhibited at the center. Malangatana also launched a major mural project with collaboration between African-American and southern African artists.

Malangatana's appearances inspired substantial community support. No major grant funded the semester or its community outreach, but financial support for individual art exhibits and theatrical events was provided by various sources including the California Community Foundation, a private nonprofit, the L.A. Department of Cultural Affairs, a city agency, and ARCO, the multinational corporation. In-kind contributions were also made by local schools and the William Grant Still Center.

The visual arts also contributed a poster exhibition in the USC bookstore with its extensive three floors of windows. This was the first time that the university had allowed such a display in this prominent location. The bookstore is central to the campus and visible from the public cafeteria with its outside tables.

The semester culminated with a keynote speaker who also addressed classes and participated in a final celebration for all participants, students, faculty, administrators, and guests. This speaker, Martin Luitingh, is a lawyer who for years brought human rights cases before the South African Supreme Court.

The scope of the semester's activities calls for comments concerning its administration. As noted above, USC's President provided for a twenty-hour-a-week support person for one year. Also, a $1,000 speakers' fund came from the same source. Yet obviously this does not come close to reflecting actual costs either in financial outlays or administrative time.

The key was a redirection of university funds in response to faculty planning. Each activity during the semester was sponsored by a specific university division. Faculty volunteered with an extraordinary willingness to contribute their time and energy. Many individual efforts added up to the whole and, in a real sense, a whole that was larger than the sum of its parts.

Extensive faculty development occurred for the low price of a series of biweekly lunches. Here faculty taught each other by sharing content information, instructional suggestions, and knowledge concerning the location of resources. Some participating faculty had no background on South Africa, others were specialists. A package was handed out consisting of basic data about the region, relevant articles, and a resource guide. Another strategy organized via these information sessions was lecturing in each others' courses. In addition to this informal learning process, some faculty engaged in individual self-instruction; for example, an education professor, an expert on West Africa, received a grant to go to South Africa.

Issues and Answers
Since the South Africa Semester was a multidisciplinary program and not housed in one university unit, two logistical issues arose. One problem dealt with financing, and the second with information, i.e., how to let faculty and students know about the semester in advance so they could participate by revising courses or signing up for them.

These issues often exist with multidisciplinary programs but they proved particularly difficult at USC because of its revenue center concept of operation. Each university unit carries responsibility for its own budget; i.e., its budget is tuition generated. To pay for its own expenses, individual units must earn enough through student enrollments or, in the case of administrative offices, by the number of individuals served. Thus, deans have even more authority and responsibility through their budgets than in other university systems. Since the South Africa

Semester was not within the jurisdiction of any dean, no budgetary unit took responsibility for its funding or for publishing information on courses and co-curricular activities.

The planning group responded in the only way it could, by requesting each relevant revenue unit to fund and publicize each activity which fell within its jurisdiction. This added immeasurably to the time it took to administer South Africa Semester activities. Yet such decentralized sponsorship also proved a strength by spreading involvement and interest.

To include as many faculty as possible, the planning committee devised a biweekly lunch strategy. This became the key vehicle for sharing information, including suggestions on teaching activities and topics for particular courses. These lunches became a substantial budget item and proved the only means of systematically transmitting detailed information. Lunchtime discussions provided the curriculum structure, the base for the semester's wide variety of activities.

The revenue centers established an unchangeable context and functioning within this structure imposed very real administrative constraints. It took a remarkable coordination effort by the planning committee to make the South Africa Semester a success. The committee often relied on personal contacts with faculty in various schools and divisions. This probably created more awareness of the semester and its goals than if faculty coordinators had relied on the usual hierarchical communication channels.

In addition to the logistical issues just explained, the highly politicized controversies at the core of the South Africa Semester's content caused another concern. At the earliest planning stage, the university's administration feared that the semester's instigators may use it an academic cover for hammering away at the divestment issue. Even if this did not happen, senior administrators seemed to feel that a whole semester of activities would build effective momentum for divestment.

Planning sessions allayed this latent suspicion by their openness to a wide variety of points of view. After all, the semester's avowed goal was to provide information and perspectives so students could make up their own minds about the region's controversial issues. Participating faculty practiced what they preached and did not become advocates for a predetermined position. Activities were not designed to reinforce one conclusion but to produce culturally authentic information and academic debate. Perhaps it is useful to note that at no South Africa Semester activity was violence threatened, and extra security was never assigned.

One particular procedural decision helped provide the university administration with accurate information as to the committee's process and objectives. The assistant to the president was a member of the overall South Africa Initiatives Committee, the planning committee's parent organization. As an interesting addendum, the University of Southern California's board of trustees never voted divestment.

Lessons Learned and Spin-offs

Practical guidelines emerging from the University of Southern California's theme semester can apply to institutions of any type and size.

1. *Be prepared for a long-term commitment both before and after the semester.* Not including the conceptualization of the semester, the actual organization took over one year. Also, spin-offs should be part of the plan as well as procedures for their maintenance.
2. *Design a multifaceted program involving faculty campuswide.*
3. *Make co-curricular activities an integral learning component.*
4. *Go beyond strictly academic boundaries by involving the local community.* This definitely does not mean planning activities for community groups but implies working with them from the beginning.
5. *Choose a linchpin,* a faculty member willing to work even harder and for much longer than others involved and who expects no return except personal satisfaction and the gratitude of colleagues, in other words, a Carol Thompson.
6. *A major success with long-term effects can occur without major grant support if a respected group of able, dedicated faculty take on a multiple-year commitment.*

Perhaps predictable from the South Africa Semester's success, several spin-offs continue to the present. Among these are two Freshman Writing Seminars about southern Africa, a full-time professorship funded by the Henry Luce Foundation, and about five graduate fellowships a year for South Africans to complete one year of study at USC including midcareer internships.

One of the South Africa Semester's cochairs, Herbert Shore, received a grant from the university's Fund For Innovative Teaching. This enabled him to develop two intercultural studies courses offered by the School of Theater which remained in the curriculum after the semester was over. In addition, Shore and William Rideout of the School of Education collaborated in designing a series of thirty-two half-hour programs, "Voices from Southern Africa," using short stories from southern Africa by authors of diverse backgrounds and views. These were presented not as dramatizations of short stories, but as readings modelled on the region's oral traditions. The School of Education took on the responsibility of preparing educational materials and study guides so that the whole package could be offered by National Public Radio. This collaboration between the School of Theatre and the School of Education evolved into the informal Joint Program on Southern Africa (JOPROSA).

Herbert Shore is now on the Steering Committee of the Center for Multiethnic and Transnational Studies in the Office of the Provost. Founded by C. S. Whitaker, former dean of social sciences and communications, the center receives support from the Henry Luce Foundation as well as the university. The center does not only fund research, it also sponsors new curriculum and co-curriculum activities as well as outreach programs.

One of the center's first major projects was the "Los Angeles Year." Modeled on the South African Semester, it offered some thirty-two courses and numerous co-curricular events. The center has a three-quarters-time faculty director, a full-time administrative assistant, and five resident fellows. These are supplemented by work-study students and graduate research assistants.

As a consultant at the University of Transkei in South Africa, Steven Lamy, another member of the South Africa Semester's planning committee, developed and taught new curriculum for the university's School of International Relations and Diplomacy. He also conducted workshops for its faculty on teaching using the case study methodology. Thus the University of Southern California was one of the first U.S. universities to work directly with what has been described as a "multiracial university with a black center of gravity" in South Africa.

The quality of these spin-offs, and scope of the original activities, illustrate the success of USC's South Africa Semester. Its distinguishing characteristics are replicable on almost any campus: It was faculty-led, dealt with a highly controversial issue, devoted as much attention to pedagogy as to content, and, in its attempt to teach through culturally authentic perspectives, treated both the visual and performing arts as integral to the semester's experience.

Warren Wilson College

Transforming Development Education

Warren Wilson's contribution to international education emerged from its deeply rooted and still vibrant heritage. The International Development Program grew naturally from the college's commitment to combining academics with work and service. Students participating in the International Development Program carry out a voluntary work project overseas. This program, among many others, helps implement the college catalog's contention that a Warren Wilson education "provides a strong sense of purpose, place and participation, and supports diversity, intimacy, and personal development."

Just outside of Asheville, North Carolina, Warren Wilson College lies nestled in North Carolina's Blue Ridge Mountains. With its approximately 530 students, the college describes itself as providing "an opportunity for learning, working, and living in an environment where the contribution of each person counts." This small undergraduate liberal arts institution emphasizes academic quality yet its educational role does not stop here. In the fifteen-hour-a-week work program all students earn a $2,040 annual work fellowship which is deducted from the total cost of attendance at the college. Thus students provide most of the campus' workforce. They join one of sixty-four work crews, all of which are designed to teach responsibility, leadership, practical living, and interpersonal skills. Thus the college defines education broadly. It establishes a community in which academics and practicality reinforce each other.

Begun in 1894 by the Presbyterian Church, Warren Wilson first served as a secondary school for boys called the Asheville Farm School. Fifty years later it merged with a girls school and, in 1942, added a junior college division. In 1966 it became an accredited, independent, four-year liberal arts college.

The campus consists of a 300-acre farm, about 700 acres of forest, and twenty-five miles of hiking trails. The sixty-acre central campus houses not only students but 70 percent of the full-time faculty and 50 percent of the staff. This produces a strong sense of coherence, commitment, and community. Even the campus appearance reinforces a sense of personal scale as the mostly low-lying stone and wood buildings fit comfortably into a gently rolling hillside.

Warren Wilson has retained the essence of its original purpose via an eighty-hour community service requirement for graduation. Inherent in the college's initial and ongoing mission, service joins and strengthens academics and work to produce a socially conscious, holistic education. These three elements are applied creatively in the International Development Program. As explained in its official description, "this program allows students to combine the college triad of academic study, work, and service in a supportive group setting (eight to twenty students)."

Campus Context

Adopted by the Board of Trustees in 1990, Warren Wilson's mission statement includes three elements compatible with international education, i.e., international students, multicultural education, and environmental issues. Objective three of the statement asserts that the college fulfills its mission by "serving students from the region, nation, and world who represent personal, cultural, and racial diversity." The sixth objective states that the college is "furnishing students with opportunities to understand and appreciate a variety of cultures." Another section of the mission statement reflects an additional commitment: "Warren Wilson College invites to its educational community individuals who are dedicated to personal and social transformation and to stewardship of the natural environment."

The mission is implemented in various ways. Graduation requirements include one four-credit course in Global Issues. Of the recent freshman seminars students can choose from to meet their graduation requirement, many have had international orientations; Thinking Globally/Acting Locally, Environmental Issues for the 90's which deals with global issues, War in the Modern World, and Ways of Knowing: Sustainable Society.

The college also offers a minor in Intercultural Studies with three required courses, i.e., Introduction to Geography, Intercultural Communications, and Special Topics: Global Issues. The new Human Studies major offers a concentration in Global Studies. The social sciences department lists the courses taken on the college's overseas programs, such as Asian Studies and International Development Practicum, as well as other specializations including Mahatma Gandhi: Experiments with the Truth.

The modern languages minor has courses in Spanish and French, and the modern language department also provides Self-Instructional Japanese to prepare students for attending Kansai Gaidai University in Japan via Warren Wilson's exchange program. Self-Instructional courses are offered only when someone fluent in Japanese is available to serve as drill leader. Student progress in these courses is measured by an outside examiner. The department also offers two English as a Second Language composition courses for credit.

Other departments encourage students to learn about the world and its people. An ecology course is required of all biology majors. Anthropology contributes Introduction To Ethnic Music for two credits and, for the usual four credits, a course covering worldwide Folk Tales and Storytelling. Students choosing a two credit art course called Raku study Zen philosophy in its cultural context. Biology's 100-level course for non-science students, Field Natural History, emphasizes various ecosystems. Economics offers International Trade, Environmental Economics and Economic Development. History has Latin American Civilization plus four courses on Russia, while Political Science lists International Relations, Comparative Government, and the Politics of Developing States. The college also offers a religion course on Eastern Religions.

Warren Wilson has a Peace Studies Program which, although not a major or minor, lists eight courses through the 400 level under its own designation. These include Introduction to Peace Studies, Martin Luther King and His Legacy, Lifestyles of Nonviolence, the Vietnam War and Its Legacy, The Palestine Question, and Resolving Conflict Local and Global.

International students are encountered on most walks across campus since they comprise about 8 percent of the student population. Many have scholarships and, like U.S. students, all are assigned to one of the campus work crews, thereby reducing room and board costs. The international student advisor, located in the dean of student affairs' office, also has faculty rank in the modern language department and teaches the two English as a Second Language courses.

Campus diversity is valued by people throughout the Warren Wilson community, senior administrators, faculty, staff, and students. During conversations, many people in all roles note the fact that several of the about forty-five full-time faculty were born in another country. Also, they estimate that at least one-half of the other faculty have extensive overseas experience.

Warren Wilson has an active international education outreach program in the form of the Intercultural Resource Center. Overseen by Joan Moser, an anthropologist, a main center activity is the circulation of kits and exhibits. These consist of collections of artifacts, as well as videos, slides, and printed materials from various world culture regions. They include hands-on objects as well as museum quality works and prints. The kits are used by public schools and local community groups as well as in classes on campus.

Bill Mosher, the intercultural studies advisor and professor in South Asian Studies, is particularly proud of the center's India collection. Three or four times a year an India Fair is held in local schools, mainly at the seventh grade level where non-Western history is taught in North Carolina. With materials from the resource center, these fairs set up booths where youngsters can learn something about India through activities such as dressing in Indian clothes, and using block printing to decorate tee shirts. Also Indian food is cooked and videos shown at these fairs.

Through its study abroad programs, Warren Wilson has provided its students with access to major areas of the world. Students can spend a semester or a year in Osaka, Japan under an agreement with Kansai Gaidai University. Several times the Discovery Through Wilderness off-campus program has taken a student group to an international location, for example, Canada, the Bahamas, and Jamaica.

Yet it is the International Development Program that systematically introduces students to the cultures, peoples, and issues in the developing world. Each year about thirty-five to forty-five students travel overseas in various faculty- and staff-led groups. True to Warren Wilson's personal style and informal processes, the designation "international development" has been interpreted in various ways by the individual faculty and staff who plan and organize each student group. The groups to India led by Bill Mosher, for example, focus mainly on cultural learning while groups to other countries have accomplished a work project in cooperation with local people. It is the latter which will be described in detail below. Yet the distinction between the India location and others has become somewhat blurred in recent years with its addition of a service component. Also, the developing world as a unifying theme may be modified in the 1994-95 academic year because a group is planning a project in Scotland.

International Development Program
Each year since 1985, at least one work project has been accomplished in the developing world by a group of Warren Wilson students. This activity is directly linked to learning on campus prior to departure. Thus the International Development Program provides the structure for a combined campus and overseas learning experience while allowing individual faculty and staff the flexibility to design specific group projects.

After completing the on-campus courses required for each service-work-academic experience, a student group and its leader travel overseas, usually for one eight-week term, although a sixteen-week semester program is possible. Students interact cooperatively with local people to build useful infrastructure at the village level, such as compost toilets in Mexico, a health center in the Dominican Republic, and an irrigation system in Nicaragua. This "supervised group service work and field study" earns credit for two courses in the social sciences department, i.e., International Field Study and International Development Practicum.

Predeparture requirements vary with each project depending on the country location and work objective; however, one course, Journal Writing: Exploration of Cultural Patterns, is always encouraged. This course provides training in journal keeping as a means of using reflection to connect academic concepts with observed behavior. If the work project will take place in a Spanish-speaking country, predeparture course work usually includes a modern language course called Introduction to Spanish for International Development.

While on the overseas portion of the program, students pay for their own travel in addition to tuition. Travel costs vary from about $2,000 per student to around $2,500 for the India program, which lasts a whole semester. The college pays the faculty or staff member's full salary as well as contributing to other expenses. The program attracts students of various economic means because living in villages substantially reduces accommodation and food costs.

The college's academic calendar, adopted in 1975, facilitates the International Development Program by allowing the overseas service experience to take either eight weeks or a full semester. Warren Wilson has two seventeen-week semesters, each of which has two terms of eight weeks separated by a one-week break. Usually, students take two four-credit courses each term. This pattern has the benefit of reducing the number of courses at any one time and allows for a more intensive learning experience. It also facilitates the International Development Program because students returning from eight weeks overseas easily fit into Warren Wilson's normal course schedule.

Precedents had occurred prior to initiation of the International Development Program. Intermittently since 1973, faculty-led student groups had ventured to India and Mexico. The Discovery Through Wilderness program also had contributed to Warren Wilson's experience in sponsoring student groups overseas. Faculty had taken students not only to various parts of the United States but to the other countries mentioned previously in the "Campus Context" section. Warren Wilson personnel also cite other precedents such as the long-running

Appalachian Studies Program with its field studies component, and the college's community service requirement. The college counts the International Development Program experience as the equivalent of the year's 20-hour, off campus service requirement.

The program began when a group of Warren Wilson faculty and administrators wanted to design an ongoing overseas program for larger numbers of students. Previous efforts had been intermittent and attracted small numbers. Bill Mosher was a member of the group as was Joan Beebe, the then dean of the college. Beebe wrote a successful grant proposal requesting funding from the U.S. Department of Education's Undergraduate International Studies and Foreign Language Program. With part of the grant's financing, Warren Wilson hired a consultant, Chris Ahrens, to help organize the first overseas project. Grant support also allowed faculty to design the predeparture orientation and other curriculum the program needed.

Ahrens' prior experience included two decades of development work with international nongovernmental organizations, such as CARE, as well as with international governmental organizations such as the World Bank. In addition, he had worked with agencies within the United States to provide low income housing. His years of personal experience in producing effective appropriate technology projects in Latin America, Africa, and Asia, and his knowledge of Spanish, made Ahrens exceptionally qualified to make the necessary contacts and design an effective program. His wife Ollie also brought useful knowledge and skills to Warren Wilson. Not only had she development experience parallel to that of her husband, including facility in Spanish, but also she was able to teach mathematics on campus. Thus one administrative act produced two effective additions to the Warren Wilson community.

The Dominican Republic was the site of the first project. The island had been hard hit by hurricanes in recent years causing much damage not only to crops but to housing. A Dominican Republic government agency had planned, financed, and organized the building of well-designed housing to withstand hurricane-force winds and water, but people in one particular village were tiring after building about fifty homes. The group of fifteen Warren Wilson students provided the "vim and vigor," as Ahrens has described it, to finish the last twenty-five houses. The students lived in two of the buildings already constructed.

Before they left Warren Wilson, the students participated in a program piloting the orientation sessions and predeparture courses which now are a part of each overseas work project experience. They learned Spanish, trained in building the kind of housing the project required, and learned about the history and people of the Dominican Republic.

When the students returned to campus, most were very vocal about their extraordinarily positive shared experience. Some had slides and pictures. They not only took advantage of these, but created opportunities to use them in talks about their new learning. This produced something of a chain reaction as other students began asking when and where the next overseas project would take place.

The process used to develop a project is relatively informal, which works well given Warren Wilson's size and emphasis on community. An individual faculty or staff member takes the responsibility for planning and organizing a project, then recruiting students. The International Programs Committee meets to coordinate the various projects. Made up of faculty and staff who have led student groups overseas or who teach related courses, the committee reviews and approves the project proposals and course syllabi, which include descriptions of both on-campus requirements and the overseas projects. A review of syllabi shows that they consider the academic and work elements as a whole learning experience.

One example of a specific program illustrates the process. In 1992, a group worked in Nicaragua for eight weeks as a follow-up to a Habitat for Humanity housing project. With villagers on Nicaragua's east coast, the group built a retaining wall and extended a water pipe to provide new houses with a source of clean water.

The supervisor of Warren Wilson's campus plumbing crew, Dennis Ash, led the group. Previously, he had accompanied a group to the Dominican Republic which needed plumbing expertise in building a health center. At that time Ash was an independent contractor. Subsequently he took a full-time position at the college. Interested by his Dominican Republic experience, he paid his own way to Nicaragua following up on contacts, and designed a project for students.

In defining its requirements, the syllabus for the International Field Study course in Nicaragua began with the two terms prior to departure. It also included on-campus discussions and report writing during the term after completion of the overseas project. Thus the syllabus describes a year-long sequence of activities and notes that they all will be reflected in the student's grade. Upon its return, the Nicaragua group made a formal presentation to the campus community with a slide show and readings from student journals.

Predeparture weekly discussions were required and continued for a whole semester. They focused on readings, videos, and talks by specialists on Nicaragua. Predeparture information was described as covering the country's culture and history, as well as its social and political institutions. The syllabus also noted that two courses must be taken before the term overseas, the Spanish and Journal Writing courses noted above. An annotated bibliography was attached to the syllabus with the notation that it was the predeparture reading list.

Field research for the required paper occured in Nicaragua while the writing as well as reference research took place back on campus. A long, annotated list of general topics was included in the syllabus, with the suggestion that students could choose a narrower topic related to one of the general themes, or another subject in consultation with the group leader.

While in Nicaragua, students read newspapers and magazines plus other material relevant to their research project. A course objective stated that while in the country, students would be able "to understand social and economic development issues from the point of view of those living in Nicaragua."

Ten students participated in the Nicaragua program. Three examples of their individual research projects illustrate the kinds of topics students choose, virtually all related to their individual interests and prior knowledge. One paper discussed some of the economic and social factors involved in Nicaraguan fishing as well as the techniques used. This student referred to articles in a Nicaraguan magazine and spoke of his experiences while going out on boats with villagers from both coasts. Another student wrote on conditions of Nicaraguan women, comparing the situation before and after the fall of Somoza. While some legal changes were beneficial, the student concluded that restrictive cultural practices remain. A third paper described Nicaragua's deforestation and resulting erosion problem and includes specific information on tree species with an analysis of which best survive hurricanes.

The objectives of the second course syllabus, International Development Practicum, stated that it would enable students to reassess their own cultural and personal assumptions by learning about people of a different culture. Also students were to learn about cultural dislocation and adaptation, as well as about developing group process and community building skills. Course content would include the conceptual frameworks related to these objectives. Achievement of the objectives would be measured by the personal journal, which would receive a grade.

The Nicaragua group illustrates the cooperative nature of the International Development Program. Various academic, physical work, and group process skills are merged into a whole experience. Dennis Ash, the supervisor of the campus plumbing crew, led the Nicaragua group while Bill Mosher, chair of the International Programs Committee, took overall responsibility for grading the students' journals and papers. Learning at Warren Wilson is multidimensional, whether on campus or someplace else in the world.

Several groups have been led by Ian Robertson, the Dean of Work. In the case of the Kenya program, for example, students camped for eight weeks in a rural area and finished a water project initiated by CARE. Water holding tanks had been built but needed gutters for channeling water to where it could be used. Robertson and the students built two and sealed them using materials found locally. In this case, the leader graded the papers and journals since he has an advanced degree from the United Kingdom and adjunct faculty status.

The list of destinations in recent years shows how much of the world is open to Warren Wilson students via the International Development Program. During the 1991-92 academic year a group went to Kenya, as noted above. Nicaragua was the destination during 1992-93 and in 1993-94 groups went to the Cameroon, Guatemala, and Mexico. In 1994-95 the program will send groups to Chile, India, and potentially to Scotland. By the early 1990s, the India Program included a village-level service experience. Covering two terms, one semester, participating students take formal courses as well as studying development issues by living and working in a village.

In the 1980s, groups accomplished worthwhile projects in Sri Lanka, Mexico, Honduras, Costa Rica, and the Dominican Republic. Future work sites are planned for Indonesia, Jamaica, and Palestine as well as the countries previously hosting Warren Wilson students. Group leaders include faculty, supervisors of work crews, and the Minister to Students who also has a doctorate in professional psychology. The fact that this individual, Andrew Summers, has led student groups overseas greatly facilitates his discussions with students experiencing reentry problems.

All group leaders emphasize the fact that the International Development Program has two content objectives. The first, learning about another culture, involves interacting with its people as well as readings, and discussions. The second objective allows students to learn about the development process not only as an academic set of issues but as they impact the lives of village people. If only learned in the classroom, these issues can become a discouraging litany of seemingly unsolvable problems. After participating in the program, students realize that effective solutions do exist, at least at the local level.

Students who have participated in International Development work groups report that the experience had changed their academic focus and, in some cases, their career plans. An environmental studies major, for example, now wants to study the effects of environmental issues on the developing world, especially the use of waste disposal sites by developed world companies. Another student reports that he became much more open to people from other cultures as a result of his experience. A third noted that he has changed his future plans. He may seek to work with a church agency in the developing world. Another student developed an interest in preserving local cultures and wanted to help accomplish this in the United States. The list could go on and on.

One of the most significant lessons students learn is humility. One, who had worked on a project in the Yucatan in Mexico, remarked, "We weren't there a week before I realized we had come so that the Mayans could teach us appropriate technology. They're the masters of it."

In addition to the depth of learning achieved by all involved, students, faculty, and staff, the International Development Program also has produced unanticipated benefits for the college. Usually one or two students from each overseas location seek admission to Warren Wilson.

The International Development Program reflects at least two underlying assumptions, i.e., a specific definition of development and a commitment to the experiential learning methodology. With reference to the first premise, the program operates with a human-centered definition of development which emphasizes working with villagers who have defined their own needs. The projects are designed to solve a practical problem in daily living as decided by local people, can be sustained by the village's existing technological capabilities, and are environmentally sound.

The program's second premise assumes that students learn most effectively about global issues by experiencing their impact. This is also true in learning about the attitudes and behavior of people in other cultures. In a village experience, students realize various approaches to international education can be separated only academically. In daily living they are intimately interconnected. This illustrates the wisdom of Warren Wilson's goal of educating each student "as a whole person."

Issues and Answers

In the decade since the International Development Program began, Warren Wilson faculty and administrators have discussed and responded to several issues. The first concerns the fact that the process used to organize projects means some disciplines have been left out.

Given Warren Wilson's size, sense of community, and bottom-up administrative style, projects are developed informally and therefore idiosyncratically. A faculty member or work crew leader has used his own contacts to set up projects in a specific location overseas. Then he has gathered together a group of students, most of whom he already knows from courses or his own work crew. Since there is no overall, systematic planning in the selection of locations and projects, students emphasizing certain disciplines, such as French, have not had as many opportunities to participate in group overseas learning. This becomes significant because the International Development Program is virtually the only vehicle Warren Wilson students use for group study abroad experiences. Thus the strength of the program, its relying on an individual's energy, initiative, international contacts, and personal relations with students, also has resulted in the program's restrictiveness.

Several leaders of past student groups are discussing ways to provide assistance for other faculty and staff on campus to develop their own connections and projects. More inclusiveness would strengthen additional on-campus curriculum programs as well as provide increased numbers of students with opportunities to learn about the world for themselves.

Two other issues involve practical aspects of managing the International Development Program. The first involves financing. The college pays the group leader's room and board costs. Even though often the leader's plane ticket is free because ten students or more participate, the increase in the number of groups per year has put a strain on the international travel budget. Presently, the International Programs Committee is discussing a proposal to charge students a laboratory fee to help cover the group leader's travel costs.

A second practical concern arises because often groups venture to remote areas. Given the fact that this locates them far from professional medical care, group leaders take the three-week Wilderness First Responder course. Other precautions include making sure students have taken the necessary shots and recommended preventative medications. Yet two people developed malaria symptoms upon their return to campus, one was the leader of the Cameroon group, and another was a student who traveled to India. Both had taken preventative medicine.

In spite of extensive orientations, which deal with cross-cultural issues among other topics, a few students have evidenced cultural insensitivity when overseas. While on campus, discussions about appropriate behavior in another culture seem abstract, but when it becomes a living reality, problems can arise. One example occurred in Guatemala. The student group included two strict vegetarians. Before departure, they seemed to understand that their food choices would be limited in rural areas, but much discussion ensued after their arrival. Their view was value-based, but so was that of their host families. While the students were committed to eating lower on the food chain, to their hosts they seemed ungrateful both as guests receiving hospitality and as accepted members of the family.

An additional problem is pointed out by those at Warren Wilson with International Development Program experience, i.e., providing students with the time to write quality research papers. Most of the actual writing is accomplished after students arrive back on campus since grades are due two weeks after the term spent overseas. Unfortunately, this means students are still trying to finish their reports well into the beginning of the new term. In some cases, the resulting paper is less than it could be.

In response, group leaders have attempted to provide students with time during the few days before they leave the host country. Yet, this also presents difficulties. Most students have become comfortable in, and fond of the host country and want to experience as much as possible before leaving. They often resist writing during this precious time. As yet no solution has been proposed to this dilemma.

As with all the issues, the last is ongoing. The International Development Program, as a form of experiential education, has its ardent supporters at Warren Wilson, but also detractors. Those insisting that traditional classroom instruction has greater academic validity have caused the program's supporters to strengthen its academic basis. Having to justify the program's course work in the same terms as other courses on campus, and measure the learning achieved using tried and true academic procedures, has produced strong syllabi and an attention to the quality of student reports, other papers, and journal entries. Unfortunately, according to some overseas group leaders, the amount of time students now spend writing, researching, and on class discussions in the host countries, might more usefully be spent in traveling to acquire a greater variety of observations.

Lessons Learned
Three of the following five guidelines involve predeparture activities.

1. *Require extensive orientation seminars.* Program planners should include not only written information on the country destination, but detailed discussions about the kinds of experiences the participants will have. Warren Wilson's group leaders invite one or two people to the orientation sessions who have already been on the program, or have spent some time in the country and can answer very specific questions. Films, videos, and visuals in general are also highly recommended.
2. *Make students responsible for their own logistical planning.* Students begin to think of themselves as travelers when they not only report on the culture of the soon-to-be-host country learned from readings, but also discuss alternative airfares, medical requirements, and information needed to fill out necessary forms, such as their own blood types.

   In addition to these usual orientation activities, Warren Wilson students also go camping together and engage in other community building activities. Given their task when overseas, the group needs to develop good working relations among its individuals. Some groups even practice the skills they will need to accomplish the group work project overseas, such as laying building blocks. Chris Ahrens, who helped initiate the program in the 1980s, has established an appropriate technology training center on his property near the college. Some groups visit not only to practice the physical skills they will need, but to learn about the development principles underlying the building project.

3. *Organize the work group early.* Time is needed to accomplish all the practical planning, academic, and community building tasks noted above. Group leaders also mention another reason to organize the group early. Students register in April for the fall semester's courses. Since each overseas project has required courses, participating students must sign up to take them the semester before departure if they had not been taken before.

   This early registration process means advertising and filling the work group occurs before freshmen come to campus. Administratively this makes sense because group leaders would rather not have to reject new Warren Wilson students, a situation which would occur otherwise. Faculty and staff would not have had the opportunity to get to know first year students, and observe their work behavior in the Warren Wilson community, prior to recruiting for specific international work projects.

4. *Plan projects where known, personal contacts exist.* Given the cross-cultural and other difficulties which arise, as in more traditional study abroad programs, added to the issues which surface on the International Development Program's intensive work project, resilient host country support is needed. Strong personal relationships provide understanding and problem solving flexibility.

5. *Decentralized administration works.* Warren Wilson personnel who have led student groups recommend the current project planning process. It allows projects based on individual contacts and initiative which also benefit from the guidance of the International Programs Committee. The committee has proven invaluable by helping those who will be leading future student groups to be freed from their campus responsibilities while overseas. The committee also has provided academic leadership by preparing a model syllabus still used by group leaders.

In summary, several factors have produced Warren Wilson's successful International Development Program. Student energy and enthusiasm must be noted as significant as well as these same qualities in the faculty and staff who have organized projects and led student groups. The program has earned the support of a succession of deans of the college. Yet the fact that Dean Joan Beebe was an active organizer and proponent of the program in the mid-1980s, and wrote the successful grant application, must be highlighted. Even on a campus with Warren Wilson's culture, the distinctive characteristics of the International Development Program meant it needed the advocacy of a senior administrator willing to take a risk. On the other hand, the point also must be made that the college's ethos, its balanced emphasis on academics, work, and service, created the environment where the program could take root and flourish. In addition, the outside consultant's exceptional qualities need mentioning, and he continues to play a meaningful role. Lastly, grant funding proved invaluable in the initial phase of program development.

Wheaton College

Encouraging Faculty Development Through Service

Picture an ideal physical setting for a small liberal arts college in a New England town, and Wheaton's campus probably provides a close approximation. A small stone wall borders one entrance. To the right, the eye is drawn to a large, wood frame structure dating from the early nineteenth century. Other campus buildings stand at a respectful distance. Not far beyond the wall, a picturesque pond, complete with ducks and a weeping willow, weaves past a low-lying modern dormitory. A short walk to the right reveals a traditional campus "quad" with large trees, grass, and ivy covered brick buildings. The campus' varying architectural styles reflect several historical periods since Wheaton's beginning in 1834. They also attest to the college's ability to adapt.

Wheaton was founded as a woman's seminary by Judge Laban Wheaton as a living monument to his daughter. In 1912, after changing societal and educational trends resulted in precipitously decreasing enrollments, Wheaton adopted a four-year curriculum and was granted a college charter by the Massachusetts legislature. Adapting again to a changing environment, the college became coeducational in 1988.

With over 1,250 students and 100+ full-time faculty, Wheaton is larger than at any time in its history. Its long tradition seems to have engendered confidence not insularity. In the 1980s, the college redefined its mission by adopting "Making a Difference in a Complex World" as its theme. This heading on the college catalog's first page summarizes Wheaton's commitment to life-long learning and skill development through community service, appreciation of diversity, international experience, and collaborative classrooms. Since Wheaton's administration saw faculty as crucial in making the refurbished mission a reality, an imaginative new faculty development program was initiated in 1983, the Faculty Overseas Internship Program.

Transforming Wheaton and its students meant transforming the faculty. Initiated in 1983, the Faculty Overseas Internship Program was designed to provide an opportunity for faculty to complete a service project in a "non-Western culture," one not directly related to their academic expertise or prior experience. They go as volunteers and learners for four to eight weeks. Program planners hoped the new knowledge would inspire participants to integrate it into their courses and ongoing professional growth. To a large extent this expectation has become a reality.

Campus Context

Wheaton offers an extensive international curriculum. The General Education Program, approved by the faculty in 1986, sets the tone. By graduation, all students must take one course covering "Perspectives on the non-Western World," one course on "Cultural Diversity," and two semesters of a foreign language.

The catalog includes a lengthy list of international specializations, remarkable for an institution of Wheaton's size. Majors are offered in Asian, Hispanic, Italian, German and Russian Studies, as well as in International Relations. Students can select minors in African Development, Latin American, and Environmental Studies as well as in International Economics. In addition to majors in Spanish, French, German, and Russian, Japanese and Italian also are offered.

This array of area studies programs indicates the depth of international courses which are infused throughout several departments. The art department alone lists six courses in Asian art. Courses in the history department under the subsection "National Histories" cover three pages. These, plus political science department courses, cover all the world regions needed for the area studies majors and minors. Literature courses on these areas are included in Spanish, German, Italian, French, and Russian.

Two departments usually not in the international education mainstream offer courses fulfilling the General Education Program's multicultural and international requirements. The psychology department contributes Infancy Across Cultures to the "Cultural Diversity" component, and the music department lists Anthropology of Music as meeting the "Perspectives on the Non-Western World" requirement. In addition, Introduction to Western and Zen Psychology is among five introductory course selections from which psychology majors must choose one.

A sampling of other departmental offerings shows the depth of Wheaton's curriculum internationalization. The education department offers Multicultural Education, a course meeting the "cultural diversity" requirement. It also provides English as a Second Language instruction in a course called Introduction to ESL Tutoring. Economics offers, besides the usual International Economics, Economic Development, referring to the developing world, Comparative Economic Systems, and a senior seminar on International Issues. The Natural Sciences weigh in with Environmental Science and Ecology of Tropical America in the biology department, plus Chemistry and Our Environment and Current Problems in Environmental Chemistry offered by the chemistry department.

Extensive international/multicultural course offerings help Wheaton in "Making a Difference in a Complex World." As explained in its catalog, this commitment shows the college recognizes that "students' contributions stretch far beyond campus boundaries . . . being a responsible citizen of a world made smaller by technology and scarce resources means learning to appreciate diversity: the differences that exist among people in other countries, within the U.S., and even on the college campus."

Other elements in Wheaton's identity statement show the college has achieved a synthesis in its commitments to global education and to community service. "Convinced that responsible world citizenship begins with responsible community citizenship, Wheaton promotes the value of public service by offering a host of volunteer opportunities." The college's Faculty Overseas Internship Program is consistent with this combination of global and service educational objectives.

Given its international/multicultural orientation, Wheaton offers several study abroad options. These are available mainly through consortial networks, such as the program in Russia administered by Wheaton's Russian language faculty. This program is organized by the American Collegiate Consortium, headquartered at Middlebury College. Such "Junior Year Abroad" and semester programs combine with specialized options organized by Wheaton faculty to attract about sixty students a year.

One program, sponsored by the anthropology department, provides majors with an field experience in Ecuador during January. In 1990, Wheaton sent eleven students to East Africa on its first overseas summer study program. For several summers Wheaton students have served as camp counselors in Turkey, organized by Robert College. For four years two students and a faculty member traveled to Chiang Mai in Thailand. There, at the Yupparat School, they taught English as a Second Language and were informants on U.S. culture.

Several campus units are responsible for international program administration. A director of international programs coordinates study abroad options as well as administering the Faculty Overseas Internship Program. She reports to the dean of academic advising as well as working directly with the dean's supervisor, the provost and academic vice president, Hannah Goldberg. The provost has had responsibility for the Faculty Overseas Internship Program since it began.

The responsibility for providing international student services is shared by the Office of Admission and the English Department. The assistant director of admission also serves as the international student advisor. She assists from eighty to one hundred international students each year, mostly from Asian countries. The English Department offers two semesters of English as a Second Language for credit. They fulfill the first-year writing and foreign language requirements for non-native speakers of English.

Faculty Overseas Internship Program

As part of Wheaton's Global Awareness Program in the early 1980s, this distinctive approach to faculty development was designed to help refocus the college identity. The themes of service and multicultural/international education helped give Wheaton a direction and new momentum.

After ten years, the original Faculty Overseas Internship Program guidelines have proven their worth. Since the program was designed to stimulate change, its policies and practices were carefully considered. Faculty volunteers engage in a summer service experience for up to two months. They are placed in a developing world location where they have no prior experience. Thus they learn contrasts with Western cultural perspectives.

Assignments may apply academic skills but are unrelated to research specializations. Faculty participate as learners, not as specialists. The hope is that they will return to Wheaton and convey to their students and other members of the Wheaton community the enthusiasm that flows from a fresh perspective. Thus Faculty Overseas Interns will exemplify the kind of education Wheaton offers.

An additional program requirement is designed to help stimulate ongoing faculty interest in the country they serve in: At least two participants go to the same location. It is hoped their shared experiences will prove mutually reinforcing after their return to campus.

The Global Awareness Program, the faculty internship component, and its policies and objectives, were the inspiration of Wheaton's first female president, Dr. Alice Emerson, 1975-1991. A 1980 visit to China convinced her that students at a liberal arts college should become aware of diverse cultures and related perspectives, as well as of the interdependence of all peoples.

President Emerson raised private funds for the first two faculty to travel to Korea in the summer of 1983. Then she convinced the Exxon Education Foundation to provide $50,000 to finance on-campus events discussing international issues as well as the travel costs of six Faculty Overseas interns, two to Thailand and four to Kenya.

Additional funding was pieced together from various sources to send faculty to the Seychelles in 1985 and 1986, and to Egypt/Israel in 1987. Following a hiatus in 1988 and 1989, the program resumed in 1990 with Thailand as the destination.

This country continued hosting Wheaton's faculty through 1993. The 1993 group was the first financed by the Alice Emerson Fund. This fund raises money in honor of the Faculty Overseas Intern Program's originator upon her retirement as Wheaton's president in 1991.

Through the summer of 1993, twenty-two faculty have served as interns in six countries. This amounts to almost one-quarter of the college's full-time faculty. The costs per participant have varied from a low of about $3,000 to a high in the range of $6,000.

Perhaps two of the more dramatic examples of faculty interns as agents of change occurred in the English and psychology departments. A teacher of poetry and creative writing, Sue Standing, spent six weeks in Kenya in 1984 producing an issue of a monthly children's magazine in Nairobi, and then encouraging children to write their ideas using poetic forms in a rural village. According to a Winter 1985 article by Elaine Leitert Birkholz in Wheaton's alumni magazine:

> She found them shy at first about writing anything original, as they were accustomed to learning more by rote. But they were willing to try the writing exercises she asked them to do, and she was soon rewarded with some very original and interesting verse.

Examples of the children's poetry include, "Life is as invisible as air," "I fear dogs as much as a child fears hot soap," and "Time is like a wind that blows but you can't see it."

While in Kenya, the American poet mastered a working knowledge of Swahili, enough to converse and study her new anthologies of Swahili poetry. The education of Wheaton students has benefited from the enthusiastic introduction of Kenyan poetry and novels in two creative writing courses, Poetry and Advanced Writing. She has also introduced an African Literature course. Standing has returned to Kenya twice since her internship.

A psychology professor, Paul Sprosty, travelled to Korea in 1983 as one of the first interns. He served as discussion leader for corporate mid-managers to help improve their English skills. His reaction illustrates the effect hoped for by the program's originators:

I love Korea. Of all places! But that affection in retrospect is perhaps not surprising. I have lived longer in Korea than in any other place outside my home. And the blend of the familiar and the unfamiliar, the forbidding and the easy, was just right to stimulate exploration and encourage change, rather than withdrawal in self-protectiveness or a breezy scooting over the surface which might have occurred in situations more threatening or more accessible.

This faculty intern has continued to build on his Korean experience to produce a new course, Introduction to Western and Zen Psychology, and infuse other courses, for example, teaching Zen Buddhist and Confucian theories of personality in Personality—The Study of Lives.

For most participants, the experience of spending weeks adjusting to life in a completely "foreign" place propels them to produce new insights and useful innovations long after returning to Wheaton. Although the result is not often the volume of curriculum development as the two faculty previously noted, the program has stirred deep, long lasting personal and professional reactions in other participants. Faculty Overseas interns from the Departments of Political Science, Music, Economics, Mathematics, Art, History, French, Chemistry, Education, Sociology, and Theater all have their own stories, from vignettes to sagas.

Although often resulting in new teaching material, curriculum development is not the stated goal of the program. Wheaton provides no funding for classroom application and this results from a conscious decision. Faculty letters of application to the program are required to include a project, but this does not necessarily have to include the development of new curriculum. This is to allow maximum creativity in what individual faculty expect to achieve and what difference they will make when they return to Wheaton, two subjects which need to be addressed in the application letter; for example, a math professor returned from Kenya with a new awareness of the impact of culture on behavior. He, therefore, makes an indirect but useful contribution to Wheaton's "Making a Difference" objective.

The selection process remains relatively informal. Faculty submit application letters to the provost in response to a notice announcing the location and type of service possibilities for the

next summer's program. Sometimes several faculty apply, sometimes some cultivation of interest is needed. A faculty-staff
committee then makes the selections.

The location of projects has developed idiosyncratically based
on individual contacts; for instance, contacts in Kenya evolved
from a Fulbright professor at Wheaton one year. His wife, a
Montessouri teacher, organized the program and hired a coordinator, an American living in Kenya, who provided language
training and an orientation once the interns arrived. In the
case of the Seychelles, as another example, the country's ambassador to the United Nations was a Wheaton alumna.

After the faculty group is designated they share in orientation
activities. These include conversations with previous interns,
especially those who have gone to the same country. Briefing
books are provided with survival language training, some cultural information, logistical hints such as maps and transportation services, a list of contacts provided by previous interns and
the program's in-country coordinator, and other specifics such
as suggestions for appropriate gifts.

Participants are required to keep journals and produce a
report during the fall semester after their return. Since their
experience is considered an institutional investment, interns
may be asked to serve as speakers to alumni and other groups.
They also are expected to give a luncheon talk for the campus
community. Faculty interns represent the college in various
ways while overseas; for instance they often provide contacts
for the Office of Admissions.

Those involved with the program report that all interns have
adapted well to their new environments and have provided
valuable service. The program's success may indicate the effectiveness of emphasizing human interaction rather than physical
conditions because providing American-style comfort was given
a low priority. The experiences of the two faculty noted previously are cases in point. To the Psychology professor, home was
a Korean college dormitory room. To carry out one of her service activities, the poet lived in a rural Kenyan village without
running water or electricity.

Several interns have returned to their original country sites
while others have ventured to other developing world

countries. Host informants have visited the Wheaton campus as guest lecturers. In one instance, a Kenyan history professor spent a full semester at Wheaton as a Fulbright scholar.

While not always producing immediate, direct, tangible results, the program has had a profound effect on Wheaton according to its proponents. It has helped create a climate for change. Wheaton's 1984-85 curriculum review process provides evidence. The faculty's adoption of both diversity and non-Western requirements in the General Education Program "would not have occurred," according to one administrator present at the time, without the leadership of the faculty interns. Ten had participated in the program by the fall of 1984 including senior and untenured faculty, males and females, social scientists and humanities specialists.

Issues and Answers
Those responsible for the program's administration report no major problems. Enthusiastic responses of returning faculty provide articulate and convincing testimony as to the soundness of the program's original design. Yet it does require time consuming administrative detail. One of the program's strengths lies in the individualization of each location and placement; however, this also makes it labor intensive.

Thus far there is no pressure for greater standardization. This is probably because the current levels of funding and prospective faculty participation keep the program manageable. Most groups have consisted of two faculty. The highest number, four, occurred during the summer of 1984. After Exxon Foundation support ended, financing depended on a combination of gifts and grants. The Alice Emerson Fund has alleviated this situation.

An ongoing issue concerns "mainstreaming" the program's effects, making them a part of student learning. Responding to this objective has produced several spin-offs.

Lessons Learned and Spin-offs
Wheaton's experience shows that a modest, well-designed program can produce substantive results.

1. *Accept diffuse, intangible program objectives.* This approach maximizes faculty creativity and individual initiative. To work, such a program should be legitimized by an academically sound rationale and have clear guidelines. The Faculty Internship Program has had a significant impact on that area of experience that influences all others, attitudes and perceptions. Faculty journal entries provide ample evidence for the transforming power of their experiences. Thus the acceptance of nonmeasureable objects, viewed by some as a weakness, has proven itself as a strength.

2. *Articulate clearly how the program's objectives relate to the larger goals of the college.* Faculty interns were well aware that their activities formed part of Wheaton's evolution as an institution emphasizing service and international education.

3. *Plan for substantial, long-term expense.* Although the Faculty Overseas Internship Program produced immediate curriculum benefits, its more substantive contributions to Wheaton's change process took several years. To maximize effectiveness, this type of faculty development program should be ongoing. This makes it expensive both financially and administratively.

Long-term change in unforeseen ways was part of the plan. Acceptance of unpredictability has been rewarded by several noteworthy spin-offs, some involving the campus ethos, some leading to new programs. This lends credence to the notion that if able people gain new perspectives, they will apply them constructively and effectively.

A major spin-off was explained previously, i.e., enthusiastic, knowledgeable, and articulate support for revising the General Education Program. In addition, the faculty internships have stimulated student interest in experiential opportunities overseas. Wheaton received a Dana Foundation grant which provided funds to support financial aid students as they gained meaningful work experience. The successful proposal to the Dana Foundation requested that two of these work positions be located overseas. This initiated the Thailand program mentioned previously.

In the early 1990s, a Mellon grant to introduce Japanese instruction through the intermediate level is attributed to Wheaton's international education efforts, with the faculty development program as a distinctive component. Also, a Huelett Foundation grant will provide International Relations majors with overseas internships. The goal of making this a requirement is linked to the grant program's larger purpose, i.e. providing specialized international career training. Additional program elements include assistance for developing courses offering more specialized language training, and preparing special housing, complete with speakers and other enhancements, for students upon their return.

The progression of Wheaton's international education programming can prove instructive. The general approaches in the 1980s have provided the foundation for more specific programs in the 1990s. The Faculty Overseas Internship Program continues to play a valuable role throughout the process.

This program owes its initiation and continuation to senior administrators. A president originally advocated the idea, secured outside funding, and, some years later, was instrumental in establishing an endowed fund. Also, the provost has exercised direct administrative oversight since the program began. Another factor should be noted, i.e., the willingness of faculty participants to make the most of their experiences and to engage in follow-up activities, such as curriculum revision.

Whitworth College

Coordinating International Education Programs

Whitworth College, with its heavily wooded campus and low-lying brick buildings, offers its approximately 1,200 undergraduates and 500 graduate students a sense of self-contained serenity, common purpose, and permanence. Located at the far northern edge of Spokane, Washington, the campus seems secluded even though it is just minutes away from both the gracious lifestyle and neon garishness of a mid-sized U.S. city. Because of its graduate school, the college is classified as a comprehensive university.

Over the last two decades, the college has used a central coordinating office to expand steadily its overseas programs. These originated in the late 1960s with faculty-led courses abroad. From 1975 these have been coordinated by Dan Sanford, as Asian specialist and member of the history and political studies department. He also negotiated many early agreements with international partner institutions, adding new opportunities. In the 1980s, these programs rapidly increased in both quantity and in number of participants, thus enabling Whitworth to provide approximately 50 percent of its graduates with an off-campus multicultural experience. Of these, 30 percent go overseas.

In 1989, the operation became the Center for International and Multicultural Education, which included international student advising. Under Dan Sanford's direction, the center stimulated creative new curricular, faculty development, and outreach initiatives. These all share the center's key guideline: new programs and projects must prove effective with minimal resources.

Campus Context

Adopted in 1980, Whitworth's Educational Philosophy and Goal Statement included a sixth objective which validated past international activities. It also contributed to the campus ethos and thus supported further growth in international education. This objective reads, "Multi-Cultural Understanding—the college advocates an understanding of other cultures within the nation and the world. We prize the richness that comes from cultural diversity within our community." This was viewed as strengthening the college's long-standing mission statement, part of which specifically sets international education goals: "The college emphasizes cross-cultural and international study in response to the Christian tradition and the challenge of global realities."

Whitworth's curriculum covers three internationalization categories—a graduation requirement, specialized majors, and courses infused throughout a broad cross-section of departments. The general graduation requirements list includes an eight-hour foreign language requirement and an approved "Other Culture" course. Students are encouraged to fulfill the latter with an off-campus course either taken overseas or "dealing with a cross-cultural encounter" in the United States.

The college offers five international, non-language majors; International Business, International Studies, International Political Economy, Peace Studies, and Cross-Cultural Studies. The Department of Modern Languages offers Chinese, Russian, and Japanese through the intermediate level as well as four years of French, German, and Spanish. Students can take upperdivision courses in Chinese, Russian, and Japanese by attending partner universities overseas.

A sampling of international courses in various departments includes a biology course on the Human Ecology of Africa, China and Latin America, World Music Traditions in the music department, Speech's Intercultural Communications, and the Sociology of the Middle East.

In 1993, eighty-five international students are attending Whitworth, 7 percent of its undergraduate population. Their countries of origin have become increasingly diverse with fewer from Asia and more from Europe. In addition, countries not previously represented are now sending students; for example, Nepal, India, and Malaysia. Many of these students have been referred by Whitworth graduates who are working in their countries. Another trend has developed in recent years; international students are coming from countries where Whitworth has thriving partnership programs.

Whitworth's English Language Program courses carry credit that can be applied toward graduation. Six courses are offered regularly in the basic program and students can take twelve specialized courses as needed, such as American Studies and Class Visitation, meaning auditing a Whitworth course to practice note and test taking.

The college's most recent project in the category of faculty development supported non-language faculty as they improved their language skills and incorporated language study into their courses. Funding for this Language-Across-the-Curriculum project was provided by the Fund for the Improvement of Postsecondary Education. Twenty-two faculty participated, and all their self-development projects included overseas experiences.

This project illustrates one of the latest initiatives of Whitworth's administrative unit responsible for coordinating all the college's international education efforts, the Center for International and Multicultural Education.

Center for International and Multicultural Education

The Center serves as "the administrative core of all international programming." This statement by its long-time director connotes coordinating as well as directing functions. He employs the full repertoire of administrative skills, which includes using gentle persuasion with some faculty and departments who have organized their own programs in the past. In most cases, however, faculty have relied on the Center's expertise in its direct administration of programs. This capacity to vary the method of leadership illustrates one major reason for the Center's success, the flexibility and diplomatic nature of its director. For example, a faculty/student committee, the International Multicultural Education Committee, makes important decisions, such as approving faculty to lead specific programs in a given year.

The center's staff consists of a director, a secretary, and two program coordinators, one who organizes programs sending Whitworth faculty and students overseas, and the other with responsibility for international students and faculty coming to the college. It offers the full range of study abroad opportunities including experiential as well as classroom programs lasting from a few weeks to one year.

The year programs are individualized and rely on overseas partner institutions for administration. These often provide Whitworth students with service opportunities. All semester programs send student groups overseas with accompanying Whitworth faculty members. The majority of students go on Jan-term programs which include service and travel-study experiences. Among the best attended are Theater and Fine Arts in London, Marine Biology in Belize, and cross-cultural training for education majors in various countries, including Korea, Jamaica, Mexico, and the United Kingdom.

The center also maintains faculty and student exchanges flowing from fourteen formal agreements with universities in China, Korea, Japan, Thailand, Mexico, Germany, Spain, England, France, Italy, Ukraine, and Liberia. In addition, regularized working associations exist with units of other overseas academic institutions in Russia, China, Taiwan, Costa Rica, Jamaica, and Korea. Besides the usual student and faculty exchanges, the partnerships and associations produce additional activities; for example, short term visits of music and athletic groups.

Although sharing a common pattern, Whitworth's relationship with each overseas partner has evolved differently. The exact nature of the exchange programs, i.e., the students' courses of study, faculty teaching and research exchanges, and co-curricular activities, varies with each overseas partner. All, however, operate as actual exchanges with citizens from both countries involved. This illustrates the Center's programmatic flexibility, its ability to establish a structure without imposing uniformity.

Administratively the center reports to the college's highest academic officer, now called the provost and dean of the faculty. It cooperates closely with the English Language Program, located in the same building. In the 1980s, this relationship proved financially useful. Since the English Language Program was, and still is, a revenue generator, its overhead income placed in the general fund, was used by a supportive dean to justify the budget of the center staff.

Just prior to the formal establishment of the center in 1987, the director made the decision, supported by the dean, to hire a person with a master's degree and overseas experience to carry out administrative as well as secretarial duties as a replacement for the secretary who had resigned. This move freed the director for program development. Consequently, international partnership agreements increased from two to eight in a little over a year, with four more added later. In 1989 a second growth period occurred with the addition of one other position, a transfer from elsewhere on campus.

The center's growth shows that program expansion and the addition of personnel can be mutually reinforcing. Acquiring a professional staff person preceded growth, which then justified additional staff. Investment in personnel, in some instances, must happen first.

The center's main responsibility was academic off-campus student programs, international student advising, and the negotiation and administration of international partnership agreements. These activities provided a solid basis for curriculum change, faculty development, and outreach endeavors. Originating in the late 1980s, at least five major spin-offs show what can be accomplished by a centralized operation with the confidence of both faculty and administration.

1. The college's Summer Language Program was expanded in 1991 to include a talented youth program allowing high-achieving high school students to take French, German, Japanese, or Russian at the college level. The six-week courses carry college credit and employ Graduate Teaching Fellows as well as the college's regular faculty. The program was created and is coordinated by Kathy Cook, the center's coordinator for off-campus programs who also serves as a part-time French instructor.

2. The Graduate Teaching Fellows Program invited applications from graduate students in Whitworth's partner institutions to teach their native language at the college in exchange for an adjunct's salary and a tuition waiver. They

take graduate courses in the Master's in Teaching English
as a Second Language Program.

3. The previously noted FIPSE-funded project provides support for faculty to learn languages relevant to their teaching, engage in an overseas experience, and to include the
   languages in their teaching.

4. The Whitworth Institute for International Management
   offers a master's degree program as well as other services
   to Spokane's business community. These activities flow
   from the college's participation in the Spokane Intercolle-
   giate Research and Technology Institute, a consortium of
   the area's educational and business institutions.

5. Gradually, Whitworth faculty and administrators have
   incorporated international knowledge, skills, and experience in their hiring criteria. Some faculty have been chosen in recent years expressly to fill the needs of the international and multicultural programs.

These examples demonstrate that Whitworth has the institutional capability to create new international education programs on an ongoing basis. Initiatives of increasing subtlety are
generated based on an established network of interactive programs.

As the mechanism for this accomplishment, the Center for
International and Multicultural Education has remained true to
at least three of the director's administrative principles. First,
programs should reinforce each other; for instance, all of the
five previously mentioned new efforts will increase foreign language capabilities on the campus.

Second, the programs should fulfill more than one need at
minimal cost. The Graduate Teaching Fellows program, for
example, has enabled Whitworth's international partners to
provide their ESL graduate students with course credit and
teaching experience at a U.S. institution while incurring very
little cost to themselves. At the same time, Whitworth could
develop its own foreign language offerings at almost the same
cost as hiring an adjunct instructor locally.

Third, insofar as possible, tuition dollars should remain on
the campus. The range and curricular relevance of Whitworth's

off-campus programs means that, of the approximately 200 students presently participating, only one or two are on other institution's programs. It should be noted that grant funding has not played much of a role in the center's development. In most cases, its director has not waited for external financing before putting a new idea to work.

The Center's Evolution
A brief history of the center shows how faculty-initiated overseas programs evolved into a multifaceted center organizing a wide range of international education endeavors. In 1973, Whitworth formally established a study abroad office with a senior student assistant. This person's work was supervised by a faculty committee chaired by the center's present director, Dan Sanford. Also that year, the college adopted an off-campus internship graduation requirement which included international/multicultural programs among others.

Whitworth took the next step in 1977 when Sanford was granted a one course release from the standard seven-course teaching load. A half-time secretary replaced the student worker. As chair of the oversight committee, Sanford's role took on curriculum implications since he joined department chair meetings. The next year the faculty voted to make the graduation requirement specifically multicultural. It would be fulfilled with either an international or a domestic program "with international implications," to use a faculty member's phrase.

During the mid 1980s, the center became a reality following the same gradual decision-making process that characterized the 1970s. In 1984, Sanford became a director with more course releases and, a year later, the half-time secretarial position became a full-time coordinator with the beneficial results described in this study's previous section. As well as quadrupling the number of overseas partnerships, this freeing the director from daily administration allowed him to take on curriculum and faculty development responsibilities.

All this culminated in 1987 when the center was established. It combined off-campus program coordination with international student advising and administration of the summer English

Language Program. The center's personnel consisted of the faculty director, two program coordinators, and a full-time secretary. Curriculum development discussions led to a successful application to the Fund for the Improvement of Postsecondary Education and the resulting Languages-Across-the-Curriculum project initiated in 1988. One more half-time person joined the center when a regional consortium moved to Whitworth in 1992, the Northwest International Education Association.

The center has played a pivotal role in Whitworth's progress toward campus internationalization. Therefore, the question should be addressed as to how was such a focused approach achieved? The interaction over time of at least four factors provides an answer: faculty initiatives in leading student groups overseas, knowledgeable support and leadership at the highest administrative levels, a clearly articulated global perspective shared by the college's international education advocates, and consistent, capable leadership in the form of a key individual who was one of the originating faculty and has served as director of the center.

Whitworth's international education activities originated with the first faculty initiated, organized, and led student group in 1968. In succeeding years faculty from various disciplines participated; e.g., English, Literature, Asian History, Languages, and Political Science. All wanted to provide their students with one of their own most significant learning experiences, field work overseas.

In the 1970s, Whitworth's president for ten years guided the college with a set of ideas accepted today as human-centered global literacy, although then they often seemed iconoclastic. President Lindaman incorporated a "one world" concern for ethnic fairness and the physical environment with a perceived over-militarization of American foreign and domestic policy. He applied this definition of Christian stewardship in his own decision-making; for example, he held firm in opposing the sale to developers of property left to the college despite substantial criticism.

In the 1980s, during the time the center was formally established, the dean of the faculty carefully and consistently supported international education. Dean, and doctor of theology,

Darrell Guder saw the future as requiring bilingual and bicultural knowledge and abilities. Fluent in German and with many years experience in Germany, Dr. Guder advocated that faculty themselves become examples of international education. He also understood the administrative value of a centralized operation.

Throughout the last twenty years, the campus credits one person for patiently and persistently attending to the daily details of building international education programs, the director of the center for most of its period of existence. Dan Sanford earned the respect of colleagues as a political scientist specializing on Asia and as a classroom teacher. Also, as associate dean from 1986 to 1988, he was chosen Administrator of the Year. In the 1970s Sanford received one course release from Whitworth's usual seven-course load. By the late 1980s this had increased to three courses. His personal style reflects a quiet self-assurance, lack of self-aggrandizement, calmness, commitment, and competence. These traits have enabled him to make the center the key to Whitworth's growing international education program.

In Whitworth's case, establishing a center did not precede but followed a high degree of campus internationalization. In turn, it added to the continuing trend. The factors explaining its development clearly emerge as separate influences only with hindsight. In events as they unfolded, cause and effect intertwined becoming indistinguishable.

One other factor needs noting: from the first, faculty involved were willing to do extra. Whitworth's international educators report that faculty and staff work on programs because of their intrinsic worth. According to Sanford, "People made it happen."

Issues and Answers
In the early years the faculty's contagious enthusiasm for the benefits of overseas learning characterized Whitworth's programs. Subsequently, in the late 1980s, a disturbing trend has accompanied the increasing effectiveness and visibility of the center. Gradually, faculty have opted out of program planning and recruitment, assuming the Center would do more. They

continue to exercise policy oversight and make specific decisions since they participate on the Center's advisory committee
and serve as team leaders for semester programs. Yet for some,
the lack of concern for programmatic specifics has produced
more detachment than before.

This lack of direct involvement in the details negates effective
sources of program rejuvenation through faculty suggestions
and their overseas contacts. The busy center staff have little
time to cultivate new leads and rethink existing processes. Of
particular concern, recruitment depends on active faculty support and increasingly this key role is left up to the center's staff.

In response to this situation, world area faculty committees
were organized in 1989. They were designed as vehicles for
renewal by stimulating new initiatives and interest in existing
relevant programs. These committees also have provided continuity by including new faculty.

Even given Whitworth's seemingly thorough commitment to
international education, justification for study abroad programs
has proven an ongoing issue over the years. If analyzed on a
strictly financial basis, off-campus programs seem an external
drain on scarce resources. Practical arguments must be made in
response. The pedagogical point that overseas experience is
intrinsic to a good education should be stated, but it needs to
be supplemented by a cost-related pragmatism. At Whitworth,
attracting students, and their tuition dollars, has become the
most useful argument.

The Center has worked with the admissions office by sharing
relevant information and collecting data. Surveys taken by new
students on why they chose Whitworth have included an item
on overseas programs. Yet monitoring their responses over
time is not enough. To ensure entering students will include
this item, the center supplies admissions personnel with information on programs to include in their recruitment efforts.
Anecdotal material has proven the most memorable and therefore the most effective in eliciting student responses. Providing
such information remains a constant process since admissions
personnel change often. The results have proven well worth the
substantial investment in time and energy.

Maintaining the campus' international education support network does not only involve faculty, students, and admissions counsellors. Presidents and deans change over time and the new ones require orientation. Formal visits to Whitworth's overseas partners provides one means of acquainting new campus leaders with the benefits of the college's international programs.

A third issue reappears regularly. Over time, pressures build to increase both general education graduation requirements and required courses for majors. Cumulatively, this means students have fewer options and they find it harder to fit overseas study into their schedules.

Presently Whitworth has a General Education Task Force charged with analyzing the graduation requirements and specific overseas courses and experiences. The Task Force is charged with determining whether some international credit bearing activities are the equivalent of on-campus courses used to meet the requirements. Faculty have been surveyed to provide the task force with relevant data on the overseas programs.

A fiscal procedure also presents the center with one of its ongoing issues. Each year international programs, whether revenue generating or not, must turn all remaining finances back to the general college account. This creates difficulties in multiple year planning.

This issue hasn't been tackled directly. At present, the center's director is attempting to make the case that at least a small amount should be committed to a multiyear, ongoing program, i.e., a scholarship fund to pay the plane fares of students going overseas in their junior year. Student retention is the selling point.

Lessons Learned

Whitworth's international programs provide pragmatic lessons for small colleges which must remain budgetarily circumspect. Its experience demonstrates the possibility of achieving a major impact within a consensus-based decision-making structure and employing minimal resources.

1. *Make openness and involvement with faculty colleagues a central policy.* Even good programs can shrivel without the support of major cross-sections of the campus community.
2. *Engage an all-campus advisory committee in as much decision-making as good administration allows.* Therefore the director does not stand alone as an international education advocate.
3. *Persistently use persuasion and promotion with all sectors of the campus community.* Levels of enthusiasm will wax and wane in various units of the institution. Yet up-to-date knowledge of the latest programmatic successes proves invaluable to international education supporters wherever they many be at a given time.
4. *Present reports which illustrate the programs' cost effectiveness.* Also show how they serve retention and recruitment goals.
5. *Keep clear and follow lines of communication and approval with supervisors.* This point may seem obvious, but too many assumptions can be made by default in the rush of enthusiastic program development. Keeping program initiation, policies, and administrative decisions in tune with the campus' overall direction requires vigilance and awareness. Top-level administrators need information about programs and how they fit with overall policies when they represent the institution to the community. The communication of such information also sets precedents when new presidents, vice presidents and deans take over.
6. *Join regional consortia.* Sharing conceptual and procedural ideas proves important in two ways: first, as a forum for presenting your institution's accomplishments to like professionals, it results in feedback and favorable publicity. Second, consortia meetings and conferences provide information on new and tested programmatic innovations. On the personal level, informal discussions with colleagues from other campuses reinforces the common commitment. These benefits also come with national memberships but the travel to regional meetings can occur more often. Far from needlessly draining scarce resources, the benefits gained from regional associations are well worth the time and travel money.

As discussed previously, the immediate future will produce closer integration between student overseas programs and graduation requirements. Also, the center will give priority to new programs which generate income; for example, American Studies for international students is in the discussion stage.

One such program ready to get underway will administer a contract with the American University of Rome. Whitworth will recruit and process all U.S. applicants for the Italian university's one-year music program for international students. Participants will pay Whitworth's tuition. The college, in turn, will pay the American University of Rome's fees after deducting expenses. As well as earning revenue, Whitworth hopes to attract students to its own music program.

These plans illustrate the growth potential a central office can deliver. They are just the latest evidence of the center's ability not only to provide effective programs for its own campus but also to enrich a much wider community. Center programs have enlarged Whitworth's working constituency in the Spokane area and beyond.

The development of Whitworth's Center for International and Multicultural Education illustrates several points about how a campus can become internationalized. It shows the need for a long time frame and the value of patience. The center did not suddenly become a central coordinating and administrative unity with a full complement of mutually reinforcing international education programs.

Yet, Whitworth did not achieve takeoff until the center came to life with sufficient personnel. To achieve this fortunate result required a combination of factors. During the crucial 1980s, both the president and dean actively made decisions providing for program growth. They consciously rejected benign lip service. The emergence of a campus consensus as to who should direct the center is another essential component of Whitworth's success. The college seems to have avoided debilitating, long-term, internecine conflict over this issue.

Finally, years of discussion and effective programming also created a consensus as to the content of international education at Whitworth. Its curriculum and program development demonstrate the workability of combining international and multicultural programs both conceptually and practically.

Worcester Polytechnic Institute

Engineering International Education through a Project-Based Curriculum

Implanted atop one of Worcester's hills and spilling down its steep side, Worcester Polytechnic Institute seems solidly fixed as part of two worlds. From WPI's hilltop unfolds both an urban landscape and a small college setting. A secure and serene college atmosphere merges with the everyday world of Massachusetts' second largest city. Here a program seems appropriate which requires students to apply their educational expertise to help people with everyday technical problems.

The college's closely grouped buildings of various styles and shapes impart a sense of planning, of effective space utilization. Such conscious action also is indicative of WPI's curriculum. Since the early 1970s, graduation requirements have included three projects obliging students to work individually on real world problems. These three are the Major Qualifying Project (MQP), the Interactive Qualifying Project (IQP), and the Humanities Sufficiency, requiring five courses and a culminating project.

To complete the Interactive Qualifying Project, students must define, investigate, make recommendations, and report on a problem which arises from the interaction of science, technology, and society. Resulting projects apply a broad definition of technology, i.e., a process which can be repeated, enhancing efficiency and output. The aim is to produce socially aware engineering graduates with practical problem-solving experience. For an increasing number of students in the last decade, this experience has occurred overseas. Thus, this science and engineering college with about 3,000 undergraduates has evolved a distinctive study abroad program.

The IQP as part of the WPI Plan

During the late 1960s, Worcester Polytechnic Institute was suffering through the enrollment effects of prevailing social attitudes. Technology was linked to an unpopular war and to environmental degradation. This negative perspective was reinforced by the perceived practical problem of fewer engineering jobs due to government cutbacks. Social relevance was adopted as a coping strategy on many campuses, even major research institutions such as MIT.

Faculty at WPI, most notably William Grogan, soon to become dean of undergraduate studies, decided that the threatening financial situation due to falling enrollments called for dramatic action. Before becoming dean, William Grogan had been in the electrical engineering department since 1947. He, plus other respected campus leaders, became fervent advocates of fundamental change. Consequently, in 1970, the United States' third-oldest private technological college redefined its mission and dramatically restructured its curriculum and calendar.

The structural change divided the calendar into five seven-week terms. This enabled students to work full-time for seven weeks on the Major Qualifying and Interactive Qualifying projects. The new calendar meant students could fulfill these new requirements and still complete their heavy engineering and science course loads in four years. With the five-term system, students could take one of them each year to complete their projects while using the other four to take a year of course work.

Time and distance should not dim the significance nor the drama of WPI's restructuring. Two and a half decades ago the goal was fundamental change. In 1968 the planning group appointed by the president, a retired lieutenant general who had helped negotiate the Soviets out of Vienna, assumed the task of refocusing the college's future.

After presenting a selection of dramatic alternatives for the college to consider, the appointed committee resigned to allow the faculty to elect its own committee. The faculty elected a second group, with about the same personnel, who took on the task of redesigning the college from the ground up. They approached the issue like a design problem with the specifications calling for graduates who were "humane technologists," to use a WPI term. This meant "understanding people, communications, themselves," in the words of William Grogan.

To produce these humanist technologists, WPI instituted a humanities minor, called a "sufficiency," and the Interactive Qualifying Project. To graduate, students are required to complete a coherent emphasis in the humanities consisting of five courses and a project, the equivalent of one course, and all related thematically. Two social science courses were adopted as an additional graduation requirement.

As originally designed, the investigative and planning work for the Interactive Qualifying Project would be accomplished by teams of students, usually three. Thus their preprofessional experience will emulate what engineers do when on the job, solving real problems in a team effort. Also, in communicating with each other and with the people who have the problem they are attempting to solve, students develop their interpersonal skills. This team approach remains the main IQP methodology, particularly for students completing international projects.

The whole WPI Plan was presented to the faculty in May 1970. They adopted it by a vote of ninety-two to forty-six with almost every department head voting with the opposition. Perhaps this was in reaction to that part of the plan which mandated five-year terms for department chairs renewable for only one additional term.

During the next several years faculty development was funded by grants from the National Science Foundation, the National Endowment for the Humanities, as well as from the Carnegie, Slone, Mellon, Lilly, and Rockefeller Foundations. This, over time, worked to reinforce the other factors supporting the new model; these included continued support from the top, a new president having taken office in 1970, and the assurance, competence, and dedicated enthusiasm of the change agents.

According to a February 1992 article in the *Engineering Science and Education Journal* by Lance Schachterle, associate dean for undergraduate studies, and Maria Watkins, then codirector of the London Project Center,

The decision to educate engineers about the impact of their professions on society through a project rather than through courses had at least five important consequences:

1. By working in teams, students learn to draw upon different disciplines as well as how to assess their own strengths and weaknesses.

2. Since supervising faculty also come from a variety of disciplines, students see that engineers are concerned with societal as well as technological issues.

3. Sponsoring agencies for projects can teach by supplying feedback and a real world problem as well as benefit from the students' work.

4. The project model guarantees a renewable source of topics sponsored by a wide variety of professional organizations.

5. Given the openendedness of real-world programs, students learn the ambiguities and trade-offs that characterize problem-solving.

In recent years more and more students have chosen projects at one of five centers and more than ten sites overseas. Such extensive international operations need solid on-campus support. Developing a multifaceted global education program on campus became a major WPI objective beginning in the late 1980s.

Campus Context

Worcester Polytechnic Institute has incorporated global education into its institutional identity. On page four of its undergraduate catalog, WPI is introduced as a "Global Technological University." The following explanatory statement gives substance to WPI's claim and places the college at the forefront of U.S. undergraduate international education:

WPI students must prepare to live and work in the global community of the next century. Technology creates and demands a global perspective. Professionals no longer can study, develop and live in ignorance of other cultures, as professional practice and commerce increasingly cross over national boundaries. WPI thus emphasizes real-world project experience, and provides extensive opportunities for studying the kinds of global issues that will dominate professional and political life in the 2000s.

This educational objective flows logically from the college's formal mission and goal statement. As endorsed by the faculty and board of trustees in 1987, and found on the catalog page immediately preceding the global commitment, WPI's goal statement includes the following wording: "A WPI education encompasses continuous striving for excellence coupled with an examination of the contexts of learning so that knowledge is won not only for its own sake but also for the sake of the human community of which the people of WPI are a part." In this age of global interdependence the whole world has become one of these "contexts of learning."

Curriculum internationalization comprises another category of international education. A major curriculum development project from 1992 through the first half of 1994 reflects WPI's recognition of its need to prepare students who increasingly choose to complete their Interactive Qualifying Projects overseas. Funded by the U.S. Department of Education, the project is building on the base of WPI's established curriculum covering Europe to add courses on Latin America and Southeast Asia, the two world regions where the college has established new project centers.

Previously, international courses emphasized European studies; for example, Introduction to Russian/Soviet History, Introduction to European Economic and Social History, Modern France, and European Technological Development. After one year of new curriculum development, such courses as Introduction to Spanish American Literature, Latin America in Global Perspective, and Introduction to ASEAN Cultures will join Religions of the East, which has been taught for some years.

By 1994, eighteen new courses will have been added to WPI's international offerings. Besides covering two world regions, they will also introduce students to multicultural and developing world issues. In addition to new courses such as Economics of Development, Modernization and Population, and International Environmental Policy, existing courses will be revised including History of Ideas and Moral Issues in the Modern Novel.

All new international curriculum development is occurring in the Departments of Humanities and Social Sciences. Some questioned the addition of so many international courses in so short a time at an institution dedicated to science and engineering education. Yet data on two new courses taught in the spring of 1993 reveal a groundswell of student interest. The first time Topics in International Politics was offered, forty plus a waiting list signed up. The second new course, Latin America in Global Perspective, attracted twenty-five students, with only a two-week advance notice.

New language course development is designed to strengthen the two languages already offered at WPI, Spanish and German. Presently these languages are offered through the second year. Students can take third year courses and other languages via a consortium of local colleges.

The list of new and existing international courses is heavily weighted in the humanities which reflects graduation requirements. To graduate, students must complete the humanities sufficiency's five courses and a project. The social science requirement was set at two courses because it was thought in the late 1960s when the present project requirements were formulated, that students would voluntarily prepare for their IQP projects with social science courses. Therefore the formal requirement could be held to a minimum. In practice, students often prepare for their overseas experience by taking humanities as well as social science courses while fulfilling their humanities sufficiency.

Fitting the new international emphasis within existing graduation requirements reflects the fact that science and engineering programs necessitate heavy course loads. Given this context, the pattern has evolved that most students completing their IQPs off campus take a course called Social Science Research for the IQP. This counts as one of their two social science courses needed for graduation.

The college's new International Scholar transcript designation provides students with the opportunity for an international specialization. Students apply who concentrate their humanities, social science, and IQP requirements on international studies.

In 1992, nineteen students in the class of 1994 were designated as International Scholar candidates. They submitted successful applications and participated in seminars, a series of lectures, and informal meetings with speakers both internal and external to WPI. These special activities were designed to develop a peer group with global competencies and perspectives as its distinctive characteristic. One such activity involved participation in simulations, one on international terrorism written and facilitated by Moorhead Kennedy, and another on development in Peru produced by Technoserve.

In addition to curriculum, international students influence the on-campus environment. In 1992 over 200 undergraduates, about 8 percent of the student body, were from forty-six countries. The college contracts English as a Second Language services externally and its international student advisor is the associate dean of student life.

The international student advisor also coordinates WPI's Swiss, German, and Swedish exchange programs. In this capacity he advises two to three IQPs per year. His academic qualifications will soon include a Ph.D. in African history. Worcester Polytechnic's exchange agreements bring several visiting scholars per year to campus. This program is administered by the college's personnel office, i.e., Human Resources Office.

In 1991, Worcester Polytechnic appointed a Global Program Officer to coordinate international education initiatives. When appointed to this position, Hossein Hakim, a bicultural member of the Electrical Engineering faculty, initially received 25 percent-released time for his new responsibilities. This was increased to 50 percent when he began administration of the curriculum development grant. His diplomacy, competence, and commitment has earned him the respect of the administration, the liberal arts, and the engineering faculty. With his professional engineering expertise as well as extensive international knowledge and skills, he successfully bridges the liberal arts—technology gap.

The Global Program Officer reports to the associate dean of undergraduate studies who is also chair of the interdisciplinary studies division. The projects administrator, who coordinates international IQP projects, also reports to the associate dean, a former humanities faculty member. Locating academic international activities in one office facilitates coordination, especially since all involved share the same office suite.

Thus an international education center is evolving at Worcester Polytechnic Institute. This development occurred after a year of meetings during 1990-91, and an extensive report to the college community outlining a "WPI Global Perspective Program," a plan of action, and an implementation schedule. The collection of written materials, hardware and software has grown to the point where the catalog section "Resources Available to Undergraduates" lists the Global Program Resource Center along with all WPI's extensive laboratory facilities such as the Fluid Dynamics and Thermal Processes Laboratory, and the Optical and Electron Metallography Laboratories.

The Global Program Officer's functions were broadly defined but in practice he has provided the energy and initiative to write and administer grants, as well as to formulate plans and reports. Particularly worthy of note was his preparation and presentation of WPI's "Globalization Initiative" to the board of trustees meeting in the spring of 1993. Here the board took note of the institution's global education commitment as well as its implementation as the "Strategic Plan, 1990-2000."

Part of the rapid development and accompanying aura of success of WPI's global education efforts was due to the rapid preparation and funding of three grant proposals in 1992. A working group of faculty, the Global Program Officer, and the associate dean of undergraduate studies produced the U.S. Department of Education curriculum development project already noted. In addition, a second successful proposal was submitted for a U.S. AID university linkage grant. This five-year project, directed by a faculty member in chemical engineering, has already established the project center in Guayaquil, Ecuador. The third project, funded by the Xerox Corporation, will provide support for the project center in Puerto Rico. This is administered by a social science faculty member.

The IQP Goes International
The college's unique study abroad program, i.e., internationalization of the IQP requirement using centers and sites in other countries, remains at the heart of WPI's international education efforts. In 1992-93, 118 students completed their IQPs at these centers and sites. In addition, seventeen others partici-

pated in traditional programs established by exchange agreements; six more students used their own overseas contacts to
work on IQPs. Thus a total of 141 WPI students studied abroad
during the 1992-93 academic year.

At WPI, project centers are distinguished from sites. They
attract enough students to support a full-time in-country coordinator as well as a faculty member working full-time during the
entire seven-week project period. This usually requires five
three-person student teams during each seven-week period a
faculty member is in residence. International off-campus centers are located in London, Venice, Bangkok, Puerto Rico, and
Ecuador. Two other centers are in San Francisco and Washington, D.C.

A project site has fewer students and the faculty member
overseeing the students' work visits but does not reside at the
location. Ongoing supervision is provided by a local resident
academic who has a part-time WPI appointment. Sites have
been established in Ireland, France, Belgium, two locations in
Germany, Switzerland, Russia, Sweden, Hong Kong, Taiwan,
and Canada.

In addition, a number of IQPs per year with international
topics are completed on campus; for example, students work
with Heifer International, a private voluntary organization with
a local affiliate, to tackle a specific issue arising from work in
the developing world.

As early as 1973 WPI began study abroad programs in London and Zurich. Until the recent U.S. AID and Xerox grants,
WPI has used its own resources to develop overseas program
locations. The college intends, in the long run, to encourage
enough student and faculty interest to turn more sites into full-
blown project centers.

In addition to centers and sites, WPI also has exchange
agreements. According to these agreements, some of the universities serving as project sites also provide WPI students with
classroom study. Several of these universities offer advanced
language study. Students can apply this formal language
instruction toward WPI's humanities sufficiency requirement.

Worcester Polytechnic's program ensures students multiple
cultural and academic supports at every international location.

All projects have a designated faculty advisor who will be working with the students while they are carrying out their field work. In addition, local nationals share program responsibilities for academic and project work as well as for logistics, such as accommodations. All this assistance is needed as students learn to function professionally in what are to them new societies.

Established international IQP project topics are available at each location; for example, in London students choose from issues in engineering training and licensing; in Venice they devise responses to protect historical and artistic artifacts from environmental threats; in Bangkok and Taipei they study the impact of mass transit systems on Asian cities. Such organized choices help students in their application process.

Matching student interest with available international projects follows the same process as that used for IQPs in general. A variety of initiatives are available already or faculty can develop topics and advertise to attract students. Students also can propose topics based on their interest and contacts, and community organizations or businesses can sponsor projects based on their own needs. In practice, most international IQPs originate with the needs of public and private organizations.

Completed applications are due in the Projects Office by mid-December. These include a transcript, two suggested topics with an essay of up to five pages on one of them. Then a faculty member interviews each student.

The student proposals are matched with project proposals from overseas sponsoring agencies. Then specific project proposals are offered to the students. They must include the commitment by a WPI faculty member to act as the project's advisor. Extensive advice and counseling by faculty and administrators facilitates this stage in the process. Students then make their final selections one term before departure and develop full proposals, including timetables. Accordingly the students communicate with the in-country supervisor reflecting this further refining of the proposal. Ideally, students receive feedback before their departure.

Students are advised to plan ahead and, prior to going overseas, take humanities and social science courses about the part of the world in which they will be working. At the least, during the term prior to their departure, students engage in orientation activities directed by their faculty advisor.

In order to attract the broadest representation of students, WPI attempts to keep international program costs in line with on-campus programs. The same tuition is charged. Also, housing and food prices are negotiated to approximate on-campus room and board. Students supply only the air fare and spending money. Also, a specific category of financial aid is available for study abroad students.

One noteworthy aspect of the international IQP project program demands mention. All projects present actual problems needing practical responses. None are contrived or make-work activities. Students work full-time, sometimes putting in fifty to sixty hours a week. They must make an oral presentation to the agency as well as write a formal report before leaving the country.

Ample evidence exists as to the quality of WPI student reports and recommendations. Since the reports go to the agencies as well as WPI faculty, the approximately 100-page documents usually meet exacting standards of professional communication. Over the years, many student recommendations have proven useful.

To cite a few examples: WPI students suggested ways to improve efficiency at the Action for Blind People in London, which supports a workshop where the visually impaired fabricate polyvinyl chloride products. When adopted, one of the student recommendations has achieved greater mobility for the blind workers. The United Kingdom's Department of Energy has used the results of a project to achieve international collaboration to foster safety research and development in the offshore oil and gas sector. The WPI students designed a lecture and live demonstration on flight at the Royal Airforce Museum.

As a final point, the IQP overseas project network provides excellent faculty development opportunities. As project advisors, WPI faculty interact with counterparts in other countries. This takes place in a highly useful professional context. In reviewing the work of their students, faculty share in experiencing the practical applications of their academic expertise. They also learn to function in another society.

International project advising also leads to new content learning by faculty. In serving as IQP advisors, science and engineering faculty are introduced to social issues in international settings. Humanities and social science IQP advisors gain a familiarity with technology as a component of contemporary issues as well as of another culture.

Issues and Answers

In 1970, the adoption of a project-based curriculum was not greeted with unanimous acceptance. One of the concerns voiced then was echoed in the late 1980s when global education became a major WPI focus. Doubts continued as to whether enough valid topics will be developed to fulfill all the worthy and notable goals expected from the IQP, especially in its internationalized version.

Another ongoing concern involves faculty expertise. Do faculty advisors of IQP projects possess the wide knowledge of both the societies and engineering or sciences required by the student topics? The answer, of course, must be "no," and then the issue becomes one of academic validity. The response to this concern has emerged from years of practical experience. The quality of student work demonstrates the ability of faculty, at the undergraduate level, to learn "on the job."

The faculty advising international IQPs are not alone. Each overseas project center and site has at least one local academic with WPI adjunct status to assist students. In practice, this person also helps WPI faculty in their own learning. Thus the residential international center concept has proven effective not only in providing academic, logistical, and emotional support for students, its original purpose, but in providing other valuable and unforeseen services, such as faculty development.

Establishing residential centers in international locations also answered another pattern seen by global education advocates as a problem. From the mid-1970s, traditional exchange agreements existed between WPI and universities in other countries but few students were participating. If ten spent the one or two semesters overseas it was considered a banner year. About six usually went to Zurich, London, or Limerick, the locations of WPI's university partners.

Beginning in the mid-1980s, WPI tested the residential center model in Washington D.C. Based on its success, the college initiated the London project center in the 1987-88 academic year. This reflected a realization by WPI administrators and faculty interested in global education that science and engineering students experienced difficulty in leaving campus for extended periods of time. Program planners thus decided that the WPI Plan's seven-week terms could foster Interactive Qualifying Projects overseas as well as in the United States.

The biggest problem anticipated in establishing the London center concerned whether British agencies could be convinced that U.S. students would prove useful to their operations. Would enough British managers realize that the students would prepare professional level reports and make useful recommendations? Worcester Polytechnic's IQP had no equivalent as far as anyone in the British and WPI planning group knew. Yet, of the fifteen agencies visited, all but one responded positively. The fourteen British organizations agreed. Only the U.S. embassy declined to participate with the comment that the program would never work.

If any latent doubts existed that science and engineering students would react positively to IQP internationalization, the rapid expansion of international project centers should have dispelled them. With each new center established, the required number of students apply. This "Field of Dreams" response supported seven centers in 1993-94, five overseas and two in the United States.

Faculty exhibit positive responses as well as students. Each new expansion has been greeted with enthusiasm by a solid core of interested faculty. The high level of faculty and student participation has necessitated planning three years in advance for some overseas project centers.

Yet faculty are overstretched. Project advisors for each international center or site handle the heavy work load involved in processing individual projects. Also, they are the main campus contact throughout the year as projects develop. The Projects Office on campus deals with student applications but does not work with the students or overseas center personnel once they have been accepted. At present, these faculty receive little assistance in handling a myriad administrative details; however, the Global Program Officer has recommended that a position be created for an on-campus administrator to handle WPI's expanding international network.

The rapid increase in overseas centers and in student participation has stimulated a need to expand WPI's on-campus international curriculum. Faculty travel to and residence in project centers and sites has served well as a means of faculty development. Yet the institution's commitment and level of existing programming has reached the point where a stronger academic base is needed. Students both going to and returning from project work overseas should be able to further develop their growing international expertise with course work.

The existing grant funded curriculum development project is part of the answer. The rest can be found in WPI's long term plans, currently under discussion, to add faculty positions covering some combination of WPI's four chosen areas of emphasis, i.e., Asian and Latin American studies, plus development and multicultural issues.

A final ongoing issue concerns maintaining and increasing the quality of student work. In a brief seven weeks students must learn to function effectively in another cultural setting, complete field research, plus write the report and develop useful recommendations. Given all these demands, they must be deterred from indulging a tendency to put off the writing and recommendation stage until returning to the United States.

Therefore, the program requires all projects to be completed before departure. Students on each three person team must orally present their work and recommendations to the relevant agency as a final task. This requirement is feasible because sufficient academic, logistical, and personal support is provided at each off-campus center and site. The process has proven its effectiveness because off-campus students have a much better record of timely project completion than do those who remain on-campus.

Lessons Learned and Future Plans

This checklist includes practical guidelines for both international education programs in general as well as large-scale campus wide initiatives.

1. *Think carefully about the incentives and disincentives embodied in the institutional structure.* The calendar and graduation requirements must provide a favorable context for the international program.

2. *Top-level support is vital.* At WPI, faculty are "strongly encouraged" by every administrator to advise IQPs. The provost examines the record of faculty participation as IQP advisers. Upon occasion, if a faculty member refused over time to participate without a valid reason, a letter was sent by the provost taking note of this failure to fulfill the obligations of WPI faculty. As a result, a substantial majority advise IQPs with many accepting international topics. Clearly visible, active, and tangible support for global education has come from the president and provost.

3. *Begin with a small, dedicated faculty group.* New initiatives need not attract massive support. Acceptance accompanies success.

4. *Involve students in their own learning.* A passive methodology is used in most classrooms. Yet the success of the IQP, and especially of its internationalization, shows that students respond well to learning by doing. Also, the team approach, plus interaction with businesses, community and governmental agencies, all teach how to work with others, a skill needed in most occupations. When this project experience occurs in a new cultural setting, international education becomes practical and its lessons unforgettable.

5. *Cooperate with all on-campus administrative offices.* Mutually benefiting, reciprocal relationships are worth the time spent in their development. Sooner or later international programs could use assistance from placement, alumni,

admissions, advising, and the library, to name just a few; for example, samples of enthusiastic student responses to their overseas experiences have proven useful to WPI's admissions office while its data and sessions with incoming students have helped publicize the college's international programs.

6. *Document successes.* Data collection can prove useful in so many ways, from justifying next year's budget to disproving a detractor's doubts.

7. *Faculty members should serve as program directors.* A respected faculty member can approach all campus units non-threateningly but with authority. The director should retain some teaching responsibilities thereby balancing an administrative and faculty identity. Both are needed to be effective in various campus contexts. Given WPI's science and engineering emphasis, the campus has been well served by having an engineering faculty member with liberal arts capabilities lead the internationalization effort.

8. *Develop a reward structure.* Sooner or later faculty must know that their international activities will be taken into account when promotion and salary decisions are made. If not, they will devote their time to research and publication even if initially they engaged in international faculty development activities with enthusiasm. This remains one of the issues under discussion at WPI.

When asked about the future of global education at WPI, one influential decision-maker responded, "Globalization is *the* strategic plan." Specific short term implementation strategies include encouraging students to meet their Major Qualifying Project requirement overseas. Precedents exist since a few are completed each year at present. In addition, efforts are being made to hire faculty with international expertise.

Also, in the short run, a structural change needs to be carried out. Plans are underway to expand the Office of Global Programs. A full-time assistant director, with a master's degree and study abroad program experience, will be hired to organize predeparture orientations and reentry activities as well as providing faculty with administrative support relative to the project centers, sites, and exchange programs. Also, the Office of Global Programs will ask for a full-time secretary.

Worcester Polytechnic Institute's long-term plans include increasing the number of faculty positions in a combination of Latin American and Asian studies, as well as developing world and multicultural issues. Also, the setting of institutional global education goals is under discussion, such as graduating a certain percentage of students with an overseas experience. The expansion of overseas student opportunities reinforces another WPI goal, i.e., the evolution of existing project sites into full-blown centers. Added together, these plans would enhance WPI's already established position as a perhaps the country's only "Global Technological University."

At least two generations of risk-taking, visionary administrative and faculty leaders have brought WPI to its position of national leadership. The first built the foundation in the 1970s by creating the project-based curriculum. In the 1980s, the second initiated an internationalization process with momentum. Several factors account for both these changes: the usual fortunate combination of an able faculty member working closely with a group of colleagues and senior administrators responded to real needs in the interest of the institution, and was supported by a succession of well-planned grant projects.

Learning from Success

The incidence of sustainable international education programs has increased over the last fifteen years or so. The probability that this growth will continue seems high since reports of new program sightings are increasing rather than decreasing. The necessary factors are coalescing on an ever greater number of campuses. Yet on the macro level, the pessimistic pronouncements of international education's notable proponents retain their validity. As Ernest Boyer concluded in 1987:

> After visiting dozens of colleges and speaking with hundreds of faculty members and students, we are forced to conclude that a dangerous parochialism pervades many higher learning institutions. While some students have a global perspective, the vast majority, although vaguely concerned, are inadequately informed about the interdependent world in which they live. They lack historical understanding and have little knowledge of significant social trends that will consequently shape their lives.[1]

Likewise, viewing developing world issues from an overall, macro level yields similarly sad conclusions. Yet micro-observations reveal many steady, sustaining rays of hope emanating from specific village projects. Encouraging success stories also radiate from many campuses, many more than this book could include. They do more than brighten an otherwise bleak landscape. Successful, sustained program development has become self-generating.

This concluding chapter will provide a mountaintop view of the international education landscape. Having studied a sample of the healthiest programs, it is possible to determine the field's stage of development and growth in both dimension and diversity.

This chapter's summaries and conclusions are organized into four sections. The first, "Identifying Patterns of Institutional Internationalization," discusses international education's goal in an overall, institutional sense. It differentiates colleges and universities based on the introductory chapter's general programmatic definition of international education as either a condition or a process. The second section, "Essential Elements," uses the twenty-five case studies to generate guidelines for initiating and sustaining programs. Several key factors previously presented at conferences as well as in books and articles are evaluated to determine their relevance.

The "Preferred Content Choices" section offers a discussion of international education's content by analyzing the curriculum choices made by the twenty-five institutions studied. It may seem odd to deal with the content issue not before but after presenting guidelines on what is needed for successful programs. This decision emphasizes an assumption made by many international educators, i.e., that content and program, substance and process, are intertwined in practice. The fourth section, "Observations and Recommendations," points out perceived gaps in content and deficiencies in program. It also offers general recommendations for moving the field forward.

The twenty-five case studies provide a useful basis for a comparative assessment because they cover the major undergraduate international education categories. In addition, their sponsoring institutions represent all general classifications of U.S. higher education. The matrix on the next three pages lists each of the twenty-five programs by name and identifies its programmatic and institutional category. Further, virtually all of the twenty-five case studies fit the rigorous criteria defined in chapter one. Thus, far from random, their selection deliberately focuses on success and representativeness.

Identifying Patterns of Institutional Internationalization

All the institutions studied were capable of sustaining a distinctive international education program with replicable characteristics. Yet on some campuses, faculty and staff involved in international education exude enthusiasm for more programs. They discuss international education as a dynamic, ongoing process with much more needing to be accomplished.

On other campuses, faculty and staff seem satisfied with their existing international programs. They provide their students

Figure 1
The Twenty-five Programs Organized According to Program Type and Institutional Classification

Insti-tution	Curric-ulum	Co-curric-ulum	Student Overseas	Inter-national Students	Faculty Develop-ment	Outreach
Community Colleges						
Brookdale Community College				Guayaquil Learning Center		
Capilano College						Asia Pacific Management Coop Program
Private Liberal Arts Colleges and Universities						
Davidson College				Dean Rusk Program		
Earlham College				Ethno-graphies		
Goshen College				Study Service Term		
Hollins College				Human Development in Jamaica		
Kalamazoo College				Foreign Study Program		
Pacific University	Service Opportu-nities & Spanish Major					
Saint Olaf College				Field Supervised Programs		

Figure 1 (continued)

Insti-tution	Curric-ulum	Co-curric-ulum	Student Overseas	Inter-national Students	Faculty Develop-ment	Outreach
Warren Wilson College			International Development Program			
Wheaton College					Faculty Overseas Internship Program	

Private Comprehensive Colleges and Universities

Augsburg College			Center for Global Education			Center for Global Education
University of Hartford				Int'l Summer Business Program for ESPEME		
University of Richmond					Faculty Seminar Abroad	
Whitworth College	Center for International and Multicultural Education					
Worcester Polytechnic Institute			Interactive Qualifying Project			

Public Comprehensive Colleges and Universities

Eastern Michigan University	Language and International Trade					
Grambling State University	Humanities and General Education Requirements					
Ramapo College			International Telecommunica-tions Center			

Figure 1 (continued)

Insti-tution	Curric-ulum	Co-curric-ulum	Student Overseas	Inter-national Students	Faculty Develop-ment	Outreach
UNC at Asheville	International Simulation					Simulation Service Program
UNC at Charlotte						Business Seminars
Private Research Universities						
University of Southern California	South Africa Semester					
Public Research Universities						
University of Rhode Island	International Engineering Program					
UC, Irvine			International Peer Advisor Program			
UC, San Diego	Eleanor Roosevelt College					

with specialized curriculum choices, overseas programs, and international student advising. Often they have a relevant graduation requirement in languages or multicultural studies. Yet because on many of these campuses responsibility for international education programs is scattered among various campus units, planning and coordination remains ad hoc, leaving the benefits of synergy difficult to achieve. Individual programs often flourish but have limited spin-off possibilities or effects on each other.

The majority of the sample twenty-five campuses fit the first model. Faculty and staff view international education as a dynamic, campuswide process. Institutional initiatives are ongoing and designed to increase the involvement of students, faculty, administrators, and members of the community. At these colleges and universities, expanding international education is not measured by numbers alone and qualitative issues receive attention. The issues most discussed reflect such concerns as whether international students constructively interact with U.S. students to the educational benefit of both, and whether study abroad programs actually produce students who can explain the behavior of people in another culture with its own perspectives. These standards are difficult to achieve and assess, but more and more educators at heavily internationalized colleges and universities are attempting to devise strategies addressing them. On the other hand, the task of measuring success is easier for institutions using the second model which considers international education as a condition, i.e., a set of programs. They simply count the participants.

Some of the colleges and universities studied have achieved a density of interactive programming where spin-offs are produced as a matter of course. A partial list of institutions where such takeoff has occurred include Earlham College, Kalamazoo College, Ramapo College, Saint Olaf College, the University of California San Diego, the University of North Carolina at Charlotte, Whitworth College, and Worcester Polytechnic Institute. The programs at these colleges and universities differ in tone, texture, and technique yet they share the goal of ongoing, increasingly sophisticated program development on a campuswide basis.

This list includes colleges and universities both large and small, public and private. It indicates the inaccuracy of an assumption, occasionally discussed by international educators, that the kind of institution limits where international education takeoff can occur. One of these speculations considers the necessary density of interrelated programs as easier to achieve on smaller campuses. This common sense assumption may seem valid given the many examples of small colleges in the sample twenty-five.

Also, this reasoning continues, large universities are less likely to consolidate and therefore interrelate international education programs because faculty, given their heavy emphasis on academic research, are not directly involved in noncurriculum programs such as study abroad. Therefore, the programs tend to remain isolated with relatively static levels of student participation from year to year.

The generalization did not prove true for at least three large universities in the sample. At the University of California San Diego, the International Center under a dean administers international student advising, study abroad, and outreach. At the University of Southern California, faculty took upon themselves administration of the South Africa Semester, which involved campuswide curriculum and co-curriculum programming and community outreach. Also, the University of North Carolina at Charlotte has an office which includes international student advising, study abroad, and outreach plus curriculum and faculty development responsibilities. These examples illustrate that size and a research emphasis does not necessarily inhibit coordinated, interrelated international education endeavors.

Community colleges comprise another type of higher educational institution where coordinating programs in the various categories of international education remains difficult to achieve. Such institutions tend to be large, have highly mobile student populations for short periods of time, and enroll a large percentage of older students who have family and other responsibilities. Therefore, they have difficulty in sustaining student overseas programs. Also, the fact that community colleges do not have majors and minors means international curriculum programs can seem like anomalies on many campuses. On some, however, international certificate programs have worked well.

While this study does not provide enough information to negate the perception that community colleges have built-in debilitating difficulties, Brookdale has the basis for expanding both its programs and numbers of participants through its International Education Center. It needs additional personnel and the active support of senior administrators that it had in the 1980s.

Whether an institution is public or private is sometimes proposed as another variable significantly affecting international education programs. Private institutions seem to have greater programmatic flexibility, at least according to faculty and administrators on publicly supported campuses. Private colleges lack the political pressure from legislatures and interest groups. On the other hand, international educators at private colleges often must attend to the views of specific constituencies, whether religious, business, or networks of alumni, which exercise influence through their presence on governing boards.

Some international educators on small private campuses think that large state-supported institutions may have it easier when it comes to funding program initiation and development. On the other hand, the large state supported universities perceive smaller institutions as having access to greater financial support due to the perception that higher tuition charges produce the possibility for more discretionary spending. Evidence from the programs in this book supports neither of these contradictory assumptions.

Large, state-supported universities as well as small private colleges both have successful programs which struggle for lack of funds. The case studies from the University of Rhode Island, University of California-Irvine, Eastern Michigan University, Hollins, and Warren Wilson Colleges provide clear examples of shared financial concerns. On the positive side, funding was not noted as a constraining issue at the University of California San Diego and Earlham College.

To summarize this discussion, systematically comparing information from the twenty-five case studies supports the contention that the type of institution may be a conditioning factor in creating and maintaining programs but it does not determine their scope, scale, or success. Further evidence is provided by comparing from campus to campus the major issues that emerged over the lifetime of the twenty-five programs. As the following matrix demonstrates, there is no relationship between the type of institution and the general problems that required action. The issue categories on the matrix were derived by con-

Table 2
Issues By Institutional Classification

Issue Category	Private Liberal Arts Colleges (9)	Private Comprehensive Colleges & Universities (5)	Public Comprehensive Colleges & Universities (5*)	Research Universities (4)	Community Colleges (2)	Total (25)
Academic	13	8	6	4	2	33
Administrative	13	3	5	3	0	24
Financial	8	4	4	2	3	21
Perception	2	1	1	1	3	8
Health & Safety	2**	0	0	0	0	2
Totals	38	16	16	10	7	88

*Includes the University of North Carolina at Charlotte which is awaiting its designation as a doctorate-granting university.
**Relates specifically to study abroad programs.

solidating information taken from the "Issues and Answers" sections in the case studies. In some cells in the matrix there are more responses than number of institutions because each respondent noted several issues.

The following discussion explains the kinds of comments that are included in each issue category on the matrix. "Academic" issues summarizes concerns some faculty voiced on several campuses about academic quality. Interviewees mentioned such topics thirteen times. To these are added twelve comments about academic processes, such as whether to assign letters or pass/fail grades, and how much course time to devote to a specific learning methodology. The need for faculty development was noted five times. The remaining issues mentioned were the need for better student preparedness for their overseas experiences and increased curriculum support for study abroad programs.

The category of "administrative" processes and procedures was differentiated from "financial issues" because interviewees themselves made the distinction. Administrative issues summarizes such comments as whether to have one person responsible for a program or a collegial working group. Two interviewees preferred the former while two others advocated a collegial model. In pointing out issues requiring a response, several commentators cited the need for tightening administrative procedures, such as requiring deadlines and forms. Others noted their actions taken to expand participant diversity. The two comments about the need for quality personnel administering overseas programs are also included in this category.

The "financial" category includes budget constraint problems, mentioned twelve times. Five of the interviewees linked financial constriction to their understaffing problem, while three others made this connection indirectly. The "perception" category includes the three instances where cultural differences were reported as producing problems. Other comments also alluded to a need for attitudinal adjustments, such as local businesses having to recognize their international potential, and the hesitation of senior administrators to support the program. Fortunately the last issue was mentioned only once.

The two matrixes in this section indicate that institutional type does not provide a useful predictor of the kind of program which will be successful nor of the issues it will engender. This conclusion underlies the assumption made in the next section, i.e., that the factors producing successful international education programs apply to all types of colleges and universities.

Essential Elements

The twenty-five case studies provide an empirical basis for indicating how to create and continue successful programs. The list of recommendations in Table 3 on the following page is compiled from the Lessons Learned sections ending each of the chapters.

Individual interviewees made several other noteworthy points not mentioned by any other respondent; for example, ensure academic validity, design effective short cycle programs and they can teach cultural differences, require languages, attend to health and safety issues, use a variety of instructional methodologies, and hire staff with overseas experience.

Table 3
Lessons Learned Summary

General Comments	Number of Times Noted
build widespread faculty support, also administrative (two comments)	12
empower an able director	11
design a clear administrative structure, institutionalize (two comments), establish leadership in a central office (one comment)	11
cultivate community involvement, including overseas	10
create a faculty development and reward system	8
plan long-term	7
listen to students, give them responsibility for their own planning	6
maintain senior administrative support	6
ensure a quality host country director and local support network	5
appoint an advisory committee and keep an open process	5
plan the process, use an integrated approach, build in vested interests, start modestly	5
relate to campus ethos and objectives	4
point out benefits to the institution	4
evaluate	3
know the host culture	2
design an interdisciplinary program	2
write a grant	2
do not rely on grants	1

The above list overlaps some of the suggestions generally made in the literature on international education, however, they add greater specificity. Also some new guidelines are indicated. The framework for the following discussion is taken from the "lessons learned" section in *Beyond Borders*, as noted in this book's introduction.

The fact that the largest category of responses urges program planners to develop strong faculty support highlights the importance of the Johnston and Edelstein prescription to "engage faculty colleagues." Their admonition, "Know your institution," applies as well, since working cooperatively with administrators on a campuswide basis is also covered in the twelve comments.

Another lesson learned by a significant number of respondents indicates that the ability of the director is one of the keys to successful program development. The applicable recommendation in *Beyond Borders* includes two pivotal factors: "Leadership makes a difference; this refers to both the program's creator as well as supportive senior administrators." Interviewees distinguished the role of the program's director from that of senior administrators. The latter were mentioned six times while the qualities of the director received more attention with eleven references.

Yet active support by senior administrators proved a significant factor in the development of most of the twenty-five programs. Regardless, when asked specifically to list guidelines for others contemplating the initiation of a program similar to theirs, respondents mentioned heeding student input as often as ensuring the support of senior administrators. Perhaps in the case of many successful programs, top level administrative approval has become a given.

Interviewees, when describing the capabilities of successful directors, most often included energy, initiative, the willingness to take on added responsibility, leadership, creativity, combining relevant knowledge with administrative sense, and a demonstrated capacity to mobilize faculty, administrators and students. Often the ability to write successful grant proposals was added to the list. Several respondents also noted the fact that successful directors were faculty members. This observation is supported by evidence from the program descriptions. Twenty of the twenty-five directors were faculty and all but three had begun their careers on their campuses as full-time teaching faculty. Two of the remaining five were senior administrators with doctorates, and another had a Yale degree in law and a masters in international studies.

Clearly academic credibility matters, as well as the earned respect of colleagues. The twenty faculty directors represent various disciplines with no real pattern emerging, although the largest number, seven, have doctorates in a modern language, comparative literature, or linguistics. This situation exists because several of the programs studied directly involve languages. Four directors held degrees in political science while two were sociologists. Four were bicultural, having grown up in a country other than the United States.

One factor mentioned relatively often usually does not appear on lists of suggestions for future program designers. Eleven respondents drew attention to administrative processes and structure. They discussed, sometimes at length, such guidelines as establishing clear policies and procedures. Such recommendations were advocated by those involved in curriculum as well as in other kinds of international education programs. The fact that these points were not only elaborated in the Issues and Answers sections of many of the case studies, but also prescribed as Lessons Learned, means administrative matters should not be taken for granted. Perhaps they should be given prominence in compiling future lists of recommendations.

Following up on the need for attention to administrative issues, it may be useful to point out that fifteen of the twenty-five program directors report to the college or university's highest academic officer. This indicates that international programs should be administered on a campuswide basis.

Also, seven respondents commented on the need for long-term planning and commitment. Such statements are compatible with the attention given to systematic administration as an important factor contributing to successful programs.

One respondent made particular note of the leadership role a center can exercise in effective program administration. Fifteen of the institutions studied have centers or offices carrying out programs in at least two of four general categories of international education, i.e., curriculum and faculty development, study abroad, international students, outreach. At four colleges and universities the center has responsibility for all these categories. Multipurpose centers operate on all but one of the campuses where a case can be made that campuswide international education takeoff is occurring. This reinforces the attention that the "center" issue receives in articles and conference discussions.

The *Beyond Borders* statement finesses the factor of whether a college or university should have an international education center: "Select an appropriate campus home; a wide range is mentioned such as a center, separate colleges, existing curriculum, student life programs." This implies various administrative arrangements can produce effective programs. Such a conclusion is vindicated by evidence from the twenty-five case studies. If, however, the goal is campuswide, self-sustained growth in the number and type of programs, then establishing a center becomes essential.

A significant number of interviewees recommended the cultivation of community involvement and good relations. The ten times this was mentioned referred to curriculum and study abroad programs as well as outreach. Again, this issue area often is not noted in lists of recommendations but, perhaps, should be addressed specifically.

Another guideline receiving substantial interviewee attention advocated ongoing faculty development and systematic incentives. One respondent also discussed at length the need to incorporate international expertise into the faculty recruitment process. As with the previous recommendations, the advice to include a faculty development program was made by those involved in various categories of international education programs.

Given how many times outside financing was needed to initiate the programs studied, it is surprising that grant writing does not appear higher in the list of recommendations. Perhaps interviewees assumed that new programs require new funding sources. Fifteen of the twenty-five programs studied needed extrainstitutional funding to begin activities. Two depended on a special endowment, five applied to private foundations, and the rest used public support, in one case from a substantial state grant. The U.S. Department of Education's International Studies and Foreign Language Program proved essential for four programs, the Fund for the Improvement of Postsecondary Education financed two, and the National Endowment for the Humanities funded one. Five more colleges and universities wrote successful grants to strengthen and enlarge the program once it became established, two securing public financing, two private, and one both. In all, outside financing was a major factor on twenty campuses.

Concerning outside funding, the relevant Johnston and Edelstein guideline states, "Funding is necessary but not sufficient; more successful programs do not depend exclusively on external support." This is technically true in the case of the twenty-five programs, however, it may be misleading. Clearly institutional support and the institutionalization it implies should be stressed. Yet, based on the case study evidence, outside financing must receive equal emphasis because of the vital role it often plays in program initiation.

Another common topic in recommendation lists calls upon international educators to, as Johnston and Edelstein put it, "Create an international ethos on campus." As discussed in the Introduction, Maurice Harari for years has pointed out the importance of campus culture, or ethos to use his word, in developing international education programs. He contends that the ethos must change for full-scale, campuswide internationalization to take place. Even though only four respondents mentioned this point specifically, the case studies provide ample evidence supporting Harari's contention.

Mission statements indicate whether an institution has incorporated international education into its identity. According to their own statements, thirteen of the colleges and universities have adopted international objectives as part of their purpose. Three others use relevant phraseology, such as support for the human community, or diversity, or study abroad. Two more print a letter from the president or chancellor in the beginning of their catalogs identifying respect for human diversity as one of the institution's objectives. Together these add up to seventeen of the twenty-five institutions.

Changing the campus culture as a necessary and conscious part of international education planning should not to be construed as connoting the need for a revisionist mentality. Sometimes it seems that international educators picture themselves as revolutionaries. Their imagery alludes to storming the barricades of ethnocentricity and ignorance as they lead the forces of constructive change and educational enlightenment to a better tomorrow. This approach may not be what Harari had in mind.

An evolutionary approach has proven effective at several of the institutions studied. On these campuses, the adoption of international education as part of the college or university's mission seemed a natural development. It occurred after years of operating successful, mutually reinforcing, international education programs directly related to the institution's traditional, accepted vision of itself. On these campuses, the new international and multicultural commitment is seen as reinforcing the institution's original identity. What happened was not wholesale conversion but the emergence of an international dimension from a preexisting commitment. For these colleges and universities, international education was not considered an appendage; it grew from within.

One of the Johnston and Edelstein recommendations implies a concern about academic quality, i.e., "Attend to the challenge of pedagogy." Evidence from the case studies reinforces this admonition. As recorded on Figure 2 found earlier in this section, an academic issue of some kind was raised thirty-three times in the Issues and Answers sections of the case studies. As the largest category of concerns, academic quality and process issues affected all twenty five colleges and universities.

The twenty-five program descriptions also provide evidence that another point of contention sometimes discussed by international educators is a nonissue. Some international education proponents contend that a bottom-up administrative process is best for creating and continuing successful programs. Others argue with equal intensity that top-down procedures ensure the involvement of senior administrators and produce better results.

A case can be made for either. Top-down proponents base their argument on the fact that senior administrators can assign personnel and provide budgets to accomplish their objectives.

On the other hand, those advocating a faculty-initiated program development strategy point out that strong faculty support is needed for virtually any kind of international education program to be effective in the long run. They say that faculty as a group respond better if the leadership comes from their own ranks.

The cases in this book indicate that the best strategy may be relative to the institution's established administrative style. There are clear examples of both initiation patterns, as well as several programs which resulted from a relatively equal combination of both faculty and senior administrative leadership. Besides, all respondents agree that both are needed to sustain effective programs.

The colleges and universities where senior administrators actually took a direct part in making specific, detailed administrative decisions, at least in the program's start-up phases, are Wheaton College, Brookdale Community College, Capilano College, and Davidson College. On others, faculty initiatives provided the key impetus, eventually supported by senior administrators, e.g., Whitworth College, Saint Olaf College, Earlham College, Augsburg College, Ramapo College, Grambling State University, the University of Southern California, and the University of North Carolina at Asheville.

Three needed strong, active, close cooperation at all levels because of the scope of the planned change, including a redesign of the college calendar. Such a structural overhaul occurred at Kalamazoo College, Goshen College, and Worcester Polytechnic Institute. Since the goal was the creation of a new college, the University of California San Diego also required strong leadership from both key sectors, senior administrators working closely with a group of respected faculty.

One last point involves differentiating a program's initiation phase from its continuation. The issue arises over whether a different set of factors are at work during the former as distinguished from the latter; for example, the role of senior administrators is presumed by some to be different during the two phases of a program's development.

Attempting to make distinctions between the phases of program development seems a nonissue because, in all but one of the twenty-five cases, program initiation and its ongoing administration are attributable to the same set of factors. Only at Brookdale Community College can the initiation process be clearly distinguished from the Ecuador program's subsequent history. In the beginning, senior administrators were key players, making some program decisions as part of their own administrative activities. After they left the college, the director had to carry on and convince new senior administrators, with the help of important campus allies, that the Ecuador center should be sustained.

Preferred Content Choices

Several prominent leaders in the field of international education have cited a lack of systematic program development as one of the field's major problems. Each campus has acted separately to internationalize. Such entrepreneurship has resulted in artful creativity and responsiveness to local needs. On the other hand, according to these leading international education advocates, the resulting idiosyncratic programs seem to lack direct interinstitutional comparability.

Richard Lambert concludes in his quantitative study, *International Studies and the Undergraduate*, that the existing variety of programs produces "overlap, confusion, duplication, gaps, and a range in quality."[2] In the case of study abroad, "Our essentially decentralized and uncoordinated response to student demand and individual institutional initiatives has created an amazing structure of several thousand different programs maintained by various institutions and organizations and spread across some 95 countries."[3]

As for international studies courses and concentrations,

> the particular mix of international courses that students get is almost random. It is unlikely to cohere into an integrated whole, or fully serve the goals of general international education as defined by any of the currently available statements of what an educated citizen of the next century needs to know.[4]

Other prominent international education spokespersons have echoed Lambert's concerns. Sven Groennings, for instance, notes that internationalization has led to "a disorderly development, lacking clear definition, boundaries, and agreement. . . . It is a many-splendored chaos with momentum."[5]

In the earlier stages of international curriculum development, local campus initiatives proved useful in piloting a wide a variety of programs. Another response to the criticism of chaos in the field points out that international education, like the world, should allow conflicting definitions and perspectives, even contradictions. It takes a wide variety of programs to learn about the world, its peoples, and its problems. International education as a field should include peace and social justice approaches, such as at Augsburg College, Goshen College, and Pacific University. It must also encompass education for careers in business and engineering, e.g., at the University of Rhode Island, Eastern Michigan University, and Worcester Polytechnic Institute.

International educators recognize that their field is not a discipline with interrelated theoretical assumptions and concepts, or with a canon to debate. Yet it has more structure than just the coincidence of dealing with the world outside of the United States, or whatever the home country. Actually, the most commonly accepted definitions of international education share two general conceptualizations, i.e., interdependence and diversity. Besides agreement as to these general concepts, the field has developed specific approaches which organize the international curriculum on most campuses.

Three approaches appear again and again, i.e., area studies, for example Latin American studies, issues like environment studies and peace studies, and general programs analyzing trends in the world as a whole, such as international studies, intercultural studies, international relations, and global studies. Besides these three content approaches, international educators have refined three programmatic categories for curriculum internationalization: graduation requirements; specialized programs, mainly majors and minors; and infusion, that is, locating international and multicultural courses throughout an institution's departments. A comparative curriculum review of the twenty-five campuses shows substantial agreement as to what comprises an international curriculum.

Table 4
List of Institutions with International/Multicultural
Graduation Requirements

Institution	Multicultural	International	Language
Augsburg College	X		X
Davidson College	X		X
Earlham College			X
Eastern Michigan University*	X	X	
Goshen College	X		
Grambling State University		X	
Kalamazoo College			X
Pacific University			X
Ramapo College*	X	X	
Saint Olaf College	X		X
University of California, Irvine	X	X	X
University of California, San Diego	X (3 of 5 colleges)	X (one college)	
University of Hartford	X (choice of 4 of 5 categories with one "non-Western")	X (College of Arts & Sciences)	
University of North Carolina at Asheville		X	X
University of North Carolina at Charlotte	X		
University of Richmond	X (School of Arts & Sciences)		X (School of Arts & Sciences, ancient or modern language)
University of Rhode Island*	X		X
University of Southern California	X (College of Letters, Arts & Sciences)		X (College of Letters, Arts & Sciences)
Warren Wilson College	X		

Table 4 (continued)

Institution	Multicultural	International	Language
Wheaton College*	X		X
Whitworth College	X		X

*indicates institutions allowing a choice of one or the other requirement

Twenty one of the colleges and universities studied have international/intercultural graduation requirements, at least for a major school or college if not for all the institution's graduates.

The preponderance of multicultural course requirements indicates a growing consensus that culture-based knowledge and skills lie at the core of general education. Thus cultural diversity, one of international education's two overall concepts, is influencing curriculum choices. The cultural approach also is reflected in, and reinforced by, the resurgence of modern language requirements.

The second programmatic category, specialized curriculum programs, consists of international and intercultural majors and minors, for the most part. Since they are multidisciplinary, their underlying content rationales and conceptualizations borrow from established disciplines, and link them to create a new whole. According to the list of programs in Table 5 on the following page, area studies has emerged as the most prevalent choice for educating students about the world.

The choices colleges and universities make when designing international and intercultural majors and minors are not random. They follow established patterns. An area studies approach includes, at a minimum, the culture/history and major language(s) of the world region or country selected as the program's focus. Political, economic, and increasingly environmental issues often are included as well.

Likewise, a consensus is developing not only about what issues to offer as majors, but about the content each one includes. According to the list on the next page, colleges and universities tend to sponsor mainly three international issue

Table 5
International-Intercultural Majors

Area Studies	General Studies	Issues
Russian and Soviet (4)*	International	Environment/
U.S. Ethnicities (3)	Studies (7)	Ecology (5)
Judaic (3)	International	
Italian (2)	Relations (3)	Third World
Asian (2)	Intercultural	Politics or
African/Af. Amer (2)	Studies (2)	Economics (3)
African Amer. (2)	International	
East Asian (2)	and Area	Peace (2)
Hispanic (2)	Studies (1)	
Chinese (1)		
Japanese (1)		
Latin American (1)		
Hispanic Ministries (1)		
American (1)		
German (1)		
Scandinavian (1)		
Intl. Journalism/		
East Asian (1)		
Totals: (30)	(13)	(10)

*Number of institutions

majors, i.e., programs dealing with the environment, peace studies, and the developing world. Minors show some additional variety since a research university in the sample twenty-five offers minors in health care social issues and in an internationalized women's studies program. Otherwise, the minors available at the twenty-five institutions parallel the majors listed above.

A review of the core courses and electives available in international studies, and other general approaches to international curriculum programs, shows less content commonality. Some international studies programs require a modern world history course; others do not. Most include some form of multicultural material in their required courses, and in many programs students must take economics as well. Yet there is less consensus as to what content topics international studies does and does not include than in the other two approaches to international majors.

Besides engaging in a nationwide discussion defining an international studies curriculum, undergraduate international educators should be clear that the range of area studies majors actually teach the cultural knowledge and skills objectives they all profess. Students can become so involved with learning the specifics of Scandinavian or East Asian history and languages that they may not be aware of learning general multicultural concepts and perspectives, or cross-cultural skills.

The languages offered at the twenty-five colleges and universities show that the designation "less-commonly taught languages" is still relatively accurate, at least at the undergraduate level. The variety reflected on the lists in Tables 6 and 7 exists not only because the sample twenty-five includes research universities. Several of the rarely taught languages are offered by Capilano and Augsburg Colleges.

Study abroad programs also have commonly accepted programmatic categories, i.e., classroom/field trips, and internship/service, designations which are not mutually exclusive. In addition, they offer three varieties of living experiences: in dormitories, home stays, or group accommodations such as flats or houses. Generally, study abroad programs complement

Table 6
Language Majors

Language	Number of Institutions
Spanish	20
German	19
French	18
Russian	7
Japanese	4
Italian	4
Chinese	2
Norwegian	2
Modern Languages	2
East Asian Language and Culture	1
Slavic Language and Literature	1
French Education	1
Spanish Education	1

Table 7
Nonmajor Language Courses

Language	Number of Institutions
Chinese	13
Japanese	13
Russian	8
Italian	7
English as a Second Language (for credit)	7
Hebrew	5
Portuguese	4
German	4
French	3
Spanish	3
Arabic	2
Greek (modern)	2
Cantonese	1
Korean	1
Swahili	1
Thai	1
Danish	1
Bahasa Indonesian	1
Dutch	1
Polish	1
Serbo-Croatian	1
Ojibwe (Chippewa)	1

a campus' curriculum offerings by providing first-hand learning about what has been or will be covered more abstractly in classrooms on the home campus. The issue for international educators is the same as that noted above for curriculum programs, i.e., whether students actually learn what faculty think they do. In the case of study abroad experiences, this means multicultural knowledge and perspectives. Earlham College, among others, has moved on in its program development to respond to this issue. As described in the relevant chapter, Earlham's study abroad programs require student ethnographies.

The existence of patterns in international curriculum development also extends to courses infused through the curriculum of many departments campuswide. Disciplines usually interna-

Table 8
Departments with International Courses

Discipline	Number of Institutions
Art	13
Biology	16
Chemistry	4
Communication	8
Education	13
Engineering	3
English/Literature	14
Fashion Merchandising	1
Film	3
Geology	1
Music	10
Nursing	3
Psychology	8
Philosophy	7
Religion	15
Social Work	3
Sociology	19
Theatre and Dance	7

tionalize predictably; psychologists apply a culture approach, Religion introduces courses on Asian religions or world religions. On some campuses, such courses have been taught for decades and are considered an inherent part of the discipline. On others, such courses are newly introduced as part of curriculum internationalization.

Courses offered by the twenty-five colleges and universities studied include a few exceptions to a discipline's usual approach to internationalization. One college, for example, lists a psychology course called Environmental Psychology. Appropriate Technology and Population, and Community Ecology are two courses available in a biology department. Chemistry's contribution is usually Environmental Chemistry. Yet in one instance, a course for nonmajors called Chemistry in Societal Context is offered.

Several departments are not listed above because their contributions to an internationalizing curriculum are considered a normal part of their disciplines. Of these, Anthropology, Business, Economics, Geography, History, Modern Languages, and Political Science, only Geography is not present in all twenty-five catalogs. Human Geography courses in some form are offered only at seven of the institutions studied. Also, eleven catalogues do not list at least one of the usual international business courses; however of these, all include at least one international economics course.

As indicated on the above list, Biology and Sociology are becoming mainstream international disciplines, at least on the sample twenty-five campuses. At two institutions Sociology carried a large percentage of the area studies major's courses. Other fields becoming integral to curriculum internationalization are English and Comparative Literature, Art, and Religion.

Observations and Recommendations

The previous sections indicate that international education is developing identifiable patterns and processes both as to content and program. Although much progress has been made, information from the twenty-five case studies also reveals several issues which deserve attention. The following discussion covers five points with one focusing on content and the others noting programmatic concerns.

Cultural Diversity and International Interdependence

Material in the above section on "Preferred Content Choices" implies that international education and multicultural education could be considered as mutually reinforcing if not integrated endeavors. Such an assumption underlies the area studies approach. To illustrate, Whitworth College's undergraduate international education programs are administered by the Center for International and Multicultural Education.

As far as program directors are concerned, being practical people they usually treat international and multicultural as belonging together, as part of each other. Interviewees never differentiated multicultural from international education nor seemed to consider separating them as an issue. Yet when naming a major employing a general approach, "International studies" was chosen more often than "Intercultural studies." Perhaps this indicates that the former is considered more general than the latter because it includes international political and economic systems in the curriculum's content. Some campuses demonstrate even greater inclusivity by using the term "global," thus implying that the program treats world cultures, issues, and perspectives as transcending country borders.

Assuming a merger, or at minimum an overlap of multicultural and international education explains why U.S. ethnic studies majors and courses are noted throughout the various case studies. Knowledge of and respect for different cultures can be learned within as well as outside of the United States. In learning about cultures as well as other multicultural and international topics, the United States should be considered as a part of the world.

In the last few years, the relationship of multicultural to international education has received much attention. Whole conferences have been organized around the issue. Since the ongoing discussions have produced no general consensus, and since both movements have developed established vested interests as separate programs on many campuses, perhaps sorting out how they relate both conceptually and programmatically will remain an ongoing discussion. Every academic field is enlivened by such unresolved dynamic tensions.

Virtually all definitions of international education include interdependence as well as cultural diversity as an overall theme or concept; for example, a generally educated person should be able to describe and analyze issues resulting from the political, economic, linguistic, environmental, and cultural interdependence of the contemporary world. Often technological interdependence is noted as well thereby indicating that engineering education also has inherent international content.

Yet the conceptual emphasis on global interdependence has not been translated into an identifiable curriculum. Institutions requiring all their graduates to take a course in "international studies" may assume that the courses listed will adequately explain the world's increasing interdependence, or dependence from a developing world perspective. A review of the course descriptions, however, shows interdependence issues as at best often more implicit than explicit.

As Table 4 in the previous section shows, fourteen colleges and universities in the study cover cultural diversity by requiring at least one multicultural course before graduation. At five other institutions students must take an international course, and three more have both multicultural and international general education requirements. If it is assumed that international implies a consideration of interdependence, then eight out of the twenty-five include this basic international education concept in the learning their graduates should have accomplished.

The discrepancy between cultural diversity and global interdependence requirements occurs perhaps because interdependence lacks a natural constituency. Domestic ethnicities and area studies graduates consider their own groups and world regions as distinct and deserving of a separate curriculum identity. Also, explanatory concepts and a pedagogy have not been developed as fully to explain interdependence as they have for multiculturalism.

Recommendation: Review systematically the general education curriculum to determine whether international requirements and what is actually taught reflect the institution's definition of international education.

Campus Culture
Research detailing the development of the twenty-five programs in their campus environments leads to a growing realization that a program's type and objectives seemed to merge with the campus' identity. Interviewees often did not note this point explicitly, probably because of the fact that the program reflected the campus culture and therefore seemed natural to those involved. Such an unconscious acculturation reflects the most effective form of socialization. An outsider, however, is struck with the fact that on campus after campus, the most creative and distinctive contributions to international education are so integral to the particular campus culture.

This conclusion does not imply that the general type of program, and some of its specific procedures, cannot prove instructive for directors on other campuses. The observation does connote that conforming to the institutional culture and structure counts and carries more significance than is often acknowledged. This may well be why directors of successful programs tend to emerge from within an institution.

One of the most striking characteristics of international education is its enlightening, enlivening, and engaging flexibility. The case studies show that successful, sustainable programs take root in a variety of institutional environments, e.g., those dedicated to academic excellence and research, those committed to providing an academic and practical basis for a socially responsive citizenry, and those preparing students to lead full lives in the professions. Whatever an institution's self-image, international education can enhance and extend it.

Recommendation: Consciously relate proposed new programs to the campus culture.

Faculty Development

Most campuses in the study do not maintain ongoing, systematic faculty development programs specifically to foster international expertise and experiences. Perhaps related is the fact that very few have data on the international expertise and experience of their faculty and administrators. In order to internationalize their teaching, many faculty must learn new conceptualizations in addition to applying their disciplinary concepts and approaches to new material. Thus the lack of an institutionalized faculty development process becomes a definite deficiency. As several respondents remarked, curriculum internationalization cannot be achieved without an internationalized faculty. Besides supporting faculty development programs, senior administrators should incorporate international expertise into the hiring and reward structures.

Recommendation: Establish an ongoing faculty development program.

Evaluation

Most programs have not built in a continuing, systematic evaluation process. Some can provide data on participant reactions to specific courses, study abroad and outreach programs; however, very little evidence exists as to whether all these activities actually produce the requisite knowledge, skills and perspectives. The debate continues as to whether courses and programs measure up to the claims of their faculty and administrators. More than useful, such studies are needed.

The University of Hartford's summer business program for French students provides an exception due to its substantive, content-oriented evaluation process. Two assessments were built in, the first consisting of a fifty-item pre- and posttest on business terms and concepts. The second required systematic note-taking of focus group discussions. In these discussions, the participants gave their responses to structured questions about cultural perceptions and comparing U.S. with European business practices. Data from each separate process, and the resulting conclusions, were disseminated in two articles, one in the *Journal of Continuing Higher Education* and the second in *International Education*.

The few examples of one-time evaluations show how their results can be used effectively to solidify and strengthen programs. Goshen College and Brookdale Community College provide noteworthy examples. In the case of the latter, the program underwent intense scrutiny as part of the institution's accreditation process.

Adopting a systematic evaluation process will increase the workload of program directors. This may be construed as undeserved cruel and unusual punishment. Judging from the case studies, many international education programs are understaffed and their personnel overworked; for example, directors often must continue teaching and research while maintaining programs and developing new ones. Overseas programs particularly seem to produce myriad detail and continual problem solving situations. Consequently, extra support must be made available for piloting substantive evaluation procedures. Then they can be incorporated into ongoing program administration.

Several respondents noted a national need for a comparative assessment as to which topics and teaching strategies are more effective in accomplishing particular international education objectives. An ongoing, systematic national discussion should be undertaken comparing program evaluation data, along with student learning data, without the protectionist distortion of turf defense.

Recommendation: Incorporate evaluation processes into ongoing program planning and administration. Engage in a comparative national assessment process. Outside support could prove necessary.

Integration and Coherence

Many campuses continue to maintain international education as bits and pieces of programs resulting in hit and miss results. A substantial proportion of U.S. students graduate even from heavily internationalized colleges and universities without the basics of an international education. Also, student participation in one course or program may be an isolated experience, unreinforced by other learning. On several campuses attempts are ongoing to integrate the international curriculum with overseas programs. In some instances outreach programs, and even international student and visiting scholar recruitment, are planned to augment the international curriculum foci. Such articulation between international curriculum and supporting programs seeks to produce a coherent, multidimensional education.

Recommendation: Draw attention to the need for international content in general education requirements. Integrate the international curriculum with student overseas, outreach, and other relevant programs.

Suggestions

Most interviewees shared a common characteristic, i.e., their animated interest in and involvement with various campus, local, and international communities. They perceived their activities as relating the college or university to a larger constituency. Directors of curriculum as well as of outreach and student overseas programs reflected this attitude. Perhaps the content of international education evokes this wider vision and added responsibility.

Respondent remarks indicate that international program directors need not wait until years of effective endeavors convince a sufficient number of administrators and faculty that incorporating international objectives into the college or university's mission makes sense. They can move the process along by using a designed strategy. International educators can connect the college or university with local, national, and international constituencies. In this way, program directors can be recognized as providing information, publicity, name recognition, and even students.

Consciously employing this strategy has an impact on how international program directors spend part of their time. Administering effective programs becomes only a part of their role. They also have an additional, organizational task, referred to in the literature on complex organizations as a boundary-spanning role.

Boundary units can prove invaluable in open, complex, decentralized organizations. Theorists use these adjectives to classify institutions of higher education in contrast with less porous organizations, such as manufacturing firms, as well as other businesses, single-goal organizations, and many government agencies. Open organizations are heavily dependent on interactions with their environment and must keep in close touch with external constituencies. In other words, they must be attentive to their boundaries.

International education directors can serve as a bridge and buffer for their institution as it interacts with its environment. In this linkage function they join other university offices, such as public relations, admissions, development, and academic programs with major outreach components. In carrying out boundary-spanning activities, program directors should intentionally insure a two-way communication flow between the institution and its constituent communities, as well as with the outside world in general. In this way, they help keep education relevant and responsive within the college and university. At the same time, they assure external constituencies that the institution is fulfilling its larger social role, i.e., helping to educate the general public. Effective communication between a campus and its outside community also enlarges the institution's constituencies, often encompassing new worldwide connections.

The program directors at a majority of the twenty-five colleges and universities consciously capitalize on their community contacts, however in different ways. They remarked directly on how their community liaison role helps their college or university. The following examples, while not inclusive, illustrate the practical benefits of highlighting the boundary spanning role.

- Interviewees at Whitworth College noted that some of their programs, developed mutually with community businesses and groups, positively represent the college. The community-based programs provided a favorable climate for discussing international education with new generations of senior administrators.
- International educators at Whitworth, Saint Olaf, and Kalamzaoo Colleges alert their campus communities to the fact that international students are often recruited through the contacts of their overseas partners and programs.
- Several directors emphasized how positively campus administrators and community contacts view their advisory committees made up of local community leaders. Active involvement and advise by such committees on specific programs occurs, for example, at the University of North Carolina at Charlotte, Davidson College, the University of Rhode Island, Eastern Michigan University, and Ramapo College.
- In implementing the goal of providing "distance education," the International Telecommunications Center at Ramapo College has developed several cooperative ventures with local community groups; for example, its production of a series of one-half-hour programs for local public television on the activities of ethnic organizations.
- Employment of graduates becomes one of the factors drawing the favorable attention of some senior administrators. At Eastern Michigan University and the University

of Rhode Island, programs linking languages with professional education have included internships. These have produced constructive interactions between business firms and the university to their mutual benefit. Also, in many cases, students have been hired after graduation by the same companies where they worked as interns.

- A new provost at Grambling State University mentioned that she had been favorably predisposed toward the university even before visiting the campus because of its reputation for extensive faculty development in the field of international education. Grambling's Southwestern International Studies Consortium had sponsored Group Projects Abroad and curriculum development activities for many colleges and universities.
- At the University of California, San Diego, the Friends of the International Center raised the funds necessary to build the center. This volunteer organization of local women continues direct support of the institution in various ways; for example, collecting scholarship donations for international and study abroad students.
- Pacific University's Humanitarian Center provides service learning placements in the local community. Many students volunteer as tutors for Hispanic children and youth in the public school system. Spanish language faculty encourage their students to participate in this as well as in a service program in Ecuador.

These examples demonstrate how international programs can bridge the campus and community by articulating and carrying out elements of the institution's mission.

The variety and significance of these examples reinforce the analyses of organizational theorists. They see the boundary spanning role as important, but not all university administrators and faculty recognize this initially. There is a danger of marginalization if senior administrators and a cross-section of faculty have not reached a consensus that the international program operates close to the core of the institution's *raison d'etre*. Thus imagery is important. International education must be seen as bridging boundaries but not as located at the edge. It should be considered an integral component of the college or university's ability to achieve its overall purpose.

International educators can usefully employ a buffering tactic specifically discussed by sociologists of organizations. Referred to as "symbolic coding," program directors can use a vocabulary that links the organization's mission and activities with those of its outside constituencies. International educators can help translate the university's sense of its mission to those outside and explain outside events to those inside.

The mission statement of the University of North Carolina at Charlotte, for example, commits the institution to providing "educational advancement" for North Carolina's population through "collaborative relationships." This phrase has been given form and focus by the Office of International Programs through its seminars for members of the local business community. Similarly, words in the mission statements of some colleges convey great symbolism, such as "service." In several case studies, service has been translated into programs linking the college and community in a common purpose.

Related to the coding function is the "uncertainty absorption" concept introduced by James March and Herbert Simon in *Complex Organizations*. Since organizations develop a vocabulary and classification schemes which permit easy internal communication, any idea or practice that does not fit into the established system may not be clearly transmitted. Thus boundary spanning units "absorb uncertainty" by summarizing and editing communications from the outside thereby making new information intelligible to an organization's members. International educators can help their intrainstitutional constituencies deal with the unfamiliar. Accomplishing such a useful task can give a college or university a stake in the success of their international education program. The South Africa Semester program at the University of Southern California took a potentially explosive issue, South African divestment, and produced a focused, creative, campuswide learning experience.

Another technique exists for hastening a college or university's recognizing that international education is important. Directors of international programs can present themselves as agents of constructive change. They can make a positive contribution whatever the current campus issue. Precedents from the field of international education already exist for improving faculty development and instruction, two issues around which a consensus may have formed. Directors can provide examples of relevant, effective programs in various institutions which, of course, just happen to involve international education. At Ramapo College, for example, the International Telecommunication Center has encouraged faculty to apply a variety of classroom methodologies, e.g., audioconferences with relevant specialists in other countries, culturally authentic telecasts in various modern languages originating overseas, and students demonstrating learning through the production of their own videos.

Most international educators view themselves as change agents. The twenty-five case studies cover a wide range of change. At Goshen and Kalamazoo Colleges, adopting a commitment to international education meant a major structural overhaul of requirements and calendar. At others, change was defined as an added program. Some interviewees viewed their programs as designed to foster the long term goal of internationalization. To illustrate, the faculty development programs overseas at Wheaton College and the University of Richmond were explained as one of the most effective ways to internationalize an institution over time. Capilano College seeks to produce a similar result through a different faculty development process. The college negotiates agreements with universities in other countries which involve its sending selected faculty for varying lengths of time to provide technical assistance and training.

Wherever international education advocates find themselves on the status quo-change continuum, they may benefit from analyses offered by organizational theorists. The change process in open, complex organizations such as colleges and universities share certain commonalties. Difficulty is the major one. Structured roles have proven their viability over time, therefore the burden of proof rests with the change agent. This suggests that international educators should not feel necessarily that the rejection of their ideas is unique to them. Nor should they think that it means a rejection of international education as a whole. It is best to assume the least pejorative of the reasons for inaction or rejection. Take the decision-maker at her word, assume the best of intentions, and continue presenting a reasonable case. As several of the case studies show, patience can pay off over time. A martyrdom mentality can mask ineffectiveness as well as inhibit action when conditions do change allowing a program to take hold.

Discussions of change in organizational texts advise change agents to not see themselves as taking on a whole institution. It may be enough to revise the mindset and behavior of some of its members, which can be a monumental task in itself. One means of accomplishing this, according to the texts, is to change the premises for actions by manipulating the system of rewards and incentives. In several case studies, administrators did just this; for example, Eastern Michigan University's dean announced the policy of considering successful grant writing and administration as the equivalent of other faculty development and university service activities.

Organizations also can change the kind of personnel hired as one of most effective ways of influencing long-term development. Some deviance from conventional career qualifications can produce people willing to consider new directions. This points to a need for internationalizing colleges and universities to revise the hiring process. International expertise and experience should be included in recruiting both faculty and, where relevant, administrators. Kalamazoo and Saint Olaf Colleges have adopted this change strategy.

However international educators think of their role, as boundary spanning, change agent, or some other conceptualization, a reality check always proves useful. Sociologist James March, mentioned previously, has developed an explanation for the fact that effective administration depends on pragmatism as well as planning. His "garbage can" model of organizations provides a healthy corrective for those who view good administration as an exercise in direct cause and effect. According to the "garbage can" concept, problems and proposed solutions are tossed together into an administrative unit. They mix, interact with each other and with other problems and solutions in a context of precedents, vested interests, and differing personalities. The whole takes on a life of its own. What comes out often are decisions, actions, programs which do not conform exactly to original intentions or even expectations.

This perspective is contrary to the view of organizations as mechanisms for rational planning and implementation. An assumption of rationality produces administrators in colleges and universities who have difficulty with faculty committees. March's analysis, to the contrary, provides a different measure for administrative success. Good administration is not meticulously following a plan but producing decisions and programs that work. This depends on consensus, cooperation, and flexibility in open, decentralized organizations. International educators must be prepared to take advantage of serendipity, of unforeseen contingencies. Such a readiness to act based on random encounters was important in the initiation of several of the twenty-five case studies, notably at Eastern Michigan University and the University of Rhode Island.

An Endnote
Judging by the case studies in this book, international education shows more health and vigor than even some of its practitioners realize. While this observation may seem tautological, based as it is on twenty-five successful programs, many other such examples exist. Together they comprise the leading edge of many more to come. The programs described in the previous chapters indicate a promising future solidly built on a proven past. The field is moving forward. Its practitioners and proponents have retained their enthusiasm. Far from lethargic and self-satisfied, interviewees on most of the twenty-five campuses evidenced a dynamic dedication to continuing program development.

Notes

1 Boyer, Ernest L., *The Undergraduate Experience in America*, New York: Harper & Row, 1987, 281.

2 Lambert, Richard, *International Studies and the Undergraduate*, Washington D.C.: American Council on Education, 1989, 162.

3 Ibid., 41.

4 Ibid., 127.

5 Groennings, Sven and David S. Wiley, *Group Portrait: Internationalizing the Disciplines*, New York: The American Forum, 1990, 29.

Worcester Polytechnic Institute
Studies in Science, Technology, and Culture

Worcester Polytechnic Institute Studies in Science, Technology, and Culture aims to publish monographs, tightly edited collections of essays, and research tools in interdisciplinary topics that investigate the relationships of science and technology to social and cultural issues and impacts. The series is edited by Lance Schachterle (Chair, Division of Interdisciplinary Affairs and Professor of English, WPI) and Francis C. Lutz (Associate Dean for Projects and Professor of Civil Engineering, WPI). The editors invite proposals in English from beginning and established scholars throughout the world whose research interests focus on how science or technology affects the structure, values, quality, or management of our society. The series complements WPI's commitment to interdisciplinary education by providing opportunities to publish on the widest possible diversity of themes at the intersection of science, technology, and culture.